THE RACEGOERS'
ENCYCLOPEDIA

JOHN WHITE

THE RACEGOERS' ENCYCLOPEDIA

The complete A to Z
of flat and National Hunt racing

FOREWORD BY LORD OAKSEY

CollinsWillow
An Imprint of HarperCollinsPublishers

I have lived
To see inherited my very wishes,
And the buildings of my fancy.
Coriolanus, Act 2, Scene 1

My endeavours
Have ever come too short of my desires,
Yet filled with my abilities.
King Henry VIII, Act III

*For all my family
and in loving memory of
Bill and Ron Cliffe*

First published in 1992 by
Collins Willow
an imprint of
HarperCollins Publishers
London

© John White 1992
The Author asserts the moral right to be identified as the author of the work.
A CIP catalogue record for this book is available from the British Library
ISBN 0 00 218404 4

Designed and produced by Toucan Books Limited

Printed and bound in Great Britain by HarperCollins Manufacturing, Glasgow

At the time of going to press, Racecourse Technical Services were
completing re-measurements of race distances on
British flat racecourse, and some reductions and changes to
the fixture list were finally agreed.
As far as possible, account has been taken of these changes.

Contents

Acknowledgements 6

Foreword by Lord Oaksey 7

A-Z 8

Maps 250

Index 255

Acknowledgements

My debts to my wife as my typist and to my long-suffering and
supportive children are vast.
Mr Tim Neligan of United Racecourses has kindly given assistance,
as have several Clerks of English and Irish racecourses,
of whom Mr Tony Mulloy of Ballinrobe Race Committee
went to great lengths to be helpful.
Like most turf writers I have gleaned a good deal of valuable information from
several issues of *The Sporting Life* and the *Racing Post*,
as well as of *The Weekender* and *Raceform Update*.
My thanks also to Timeform Organization for the racecourse maps.
Mr George Ennor, the President of the Horserace Writers' and
Reporters' Association, kindly undertook to check the
entries and to ensure their comprehensiveness.
Special thanks are also due to my editor, Mr Michael Doggart,
to his assistant Ms Kirsty MacDougall Stott and to Mr Robert Sackville West.
Finally, I am grateful to my grandfather for taking me to Ascot as a child and
for kindling my interest in the turf, and to the late Alfred Cope,
a gentleman among bookmakers,
whose much slimmer annual racegoer's encyclopaedia
did much to inspire this present work.

Foreword

by Lord Oaksey

Newcomers to horseracing are apt to feel like visitors to
a not particularly friendly foreign country. There is a grave shortage of
signposts and the inhabitants speak a strange, mostly unintelligible language.
To this extraordinary world, John White has compiled a comprehensive
and invaluable guidebook. If you can take on board all the advice,
information and history which his encyclopedia contains you will be a great
deal better informed than a large majority of the 'experts' you meet on
a racecourse or in a betting shop. What's more you will be able to
understand a lot of what they say.
I don't think John claims to guarantee your backing winners or
making money. He is too old a hand for that. But quite apart from
the pleasure you will get from just thumbing through the anecdotes with
which this book is crammed, it is, as McCririck would say,
Double Carpet ON (see page 71!) to make racing far more fun
than you could have hoped for without it.

ACCEPTORS

Term used to denote horses that stand their ground in races after various forfeit stages have been reached. In allowing this to happen their owners, in effect, signal their acceptance of the weights allocated to them by the official Jockey Club handicapper. Some shrewd judges argue that if what seems a punishingly high weight is accepted by a horse's connections, this may well suggest it has yet to reveal its full potential in public and has enough in hand to spring a surprise at good odds!

ACCUMULATOR (OR ROLL-UP)

One stake bet on four or more horses which brings a return only if all of them are successful. Since such multiple occurrences are extremely difficult to predict, this particular wager (which when it involves a large number of selections is often referred to as a roll-up) is understandably beloved of the bookmaking fraternity.

If winners are found, one's bookmaker obligingly invests both the profit and the original stake on each successive selection as stipulated on the betting slip. However, there are considerable advantages to be gained in organizing one's own accumulator. Firstly, one can select horses racing, not just on one day, but at any time and over any period. Moreover, one can

defer one's decision on when precisely to make one's final selection of the series.

Some punters who apply these 'do-it-yourself' principles may prefer, once two, three or four winners have impressively materialized, to bank a sum equivalent to twice their original stake to ensure that, should the roll-up sequence be subsequently broken, an overall profit is nonetheless finally made.

The roll-up is one wager whose popular appeal has increased considerably in recent years through the televising of a set number of races each Saturday (the one day on which betting shop proprietors handle as much as 30 per cent of their weekly business). Both the broadcasting authorities themselves and leading bookmakers have publicized such television coverage and both have challenged the punter to name the winners of all the races involved on special coupons, so as to facilitate the making of what is essentially an accumulator confined to specific races.

ACROSS THE CARD

This fairly exotic wager involves multiple bets – doubles, trebles and accumulators – that concern races run at the same time but which are staged at different race meetings on any one racing day. Backers should note that because it is difficult for bookmakers to calculate their liabilities on such concurrent wagers some impose limits on what can be won if these prove spectacularly successful.

It should be noted that some trainers make particularly determined bids to land across-the-card doubles and even trebles.

ACTION

The way a racehorse moves. Jack Leach, one of the most entertaining of racing writers, once revealed that this was what had interested him more than anything else to do with horses and that Nothing Venture (winner in the 1920s of the Wokingham Handicap and the Ayr Gold Cup) with his effortless action was the best mover he ever saw. As Leach wisely reasons in his *Sods I Have Cut on the Turf*, one cannot 'lay down a law and say that because a horse is a good mover it will be a good horse, but it does help'.

This particular belief prompts several shrewd paddock judges to give serious consideration to runners whose walk around the tarmac oval of the parade ring is so fluent as to be hardly audible. Indeed, if such a runner is what Leach has described as a 'perfectly balanced horse with a natural flow of rhythm that looks like poetry in motion' then this may well be one to side with if the form book also offers some encouragement. Indeed, many a champion has prevailed on account of the economic, non-wasteful nature of his action.

As for daisy cutters – horses with low actions – and others which, in contrast, have high knee actions, that peerless judge the late Phil Bull (the founder of *Timeform*, the one publication that so comprehensively documents the actions of all previous runners) declared that the former find it harder to pull their feet out of heavy ground than the latter. Indeed, horses with a really 'round', high knee action are often excellent movers on mud.

ADELPHI HOTEL

Now thoroughly refurbished by the Britannia Group, this famous and elegant hotel has been the scene of many a spectacular Grand National celebration dinner, so splendid that dining tables were decorated with the colours of the first three finishers and proceedings were rounded off by a gala ball for as many as 1850 guests.

Sadly, all too often the connections of more recent National winners – such as trainer Jenny Pitman whose 1983 win with Corbiere was toasted at a motorway service station – are more likely to return home in triumph than to move on from Aintree to the nearby Adelphi for some sumptuous junketing. However, the hotel's post-race ball, now that it has recently been revived, thanks largely to generous sponsorship by the Variety Club of Great Britain, seems likely to gain in popularity.

Thanks to a £6 million refurbishment programme, the Adelphi is an enticing blend of modern-day convenience and old-world grandeur. A health club complete with gymnasium, saunas, a jacuzzi, steamroom, solarium, squash courts and a magnificent swimming pool can be found in the basement, while above this the accommodation, dining and entertaining areas feature the beautifully restored oak panelling, marble-pillared corridors and decorative wrought ironwork that for years have made the Adelphi the first choice of well-heeled members of the racing fraternity.

ADVANCE (IN THE BETTING, THE MARKET)

Term applied to a horse whose odds contract sufficiently to allow it to improve its position in the betting market.

AESCULUS PRESS

Appropriately distinguished by its horse chestnut motif, this publishing house, responsible in the main for annual guides to flat and jump racing, is based at Oswestry in Shropshire and is run by the dynamic David Ikerrin who has also produced publicity material linked to major races for Ladbrokes the bookmakers. Rigorous computer-derived analyses, together with informed articles by acknowledged experts on racing are what Aesculus Press mainly makes available through such annual compilations as the *Ladbroke Pocket Companion* (a general guide to each flat and jumping season), *Course Form* (a digest of statistics relating to past achievements at racecourses), *Trainerform* (an in-depth analysis of handlers' strategies), *Form Horses* (an expert evaluation of the top performers of the previous season) and the innovative *Directory of Horses* which ingeniously rearranges the official form book horse by horse, rather than by race.

AGED

A blanket expression used to denote racehorses that are more than six years old. Not all such runners are spent geriatrics, and some National Hunt runners have won races when almost three times the age of the youngest of 'aged' racehorses.

AIDS

A term used to describe the various means adopted by jockeys to increase the rate at which they are propelled along on horseback. These include using their legs, hands, heels, voices and bottoms, to help their mounts act in such a way as to avoid danger or disturbance, or to pull out something extra in a tight finish. A whip is the only material aid a jockey is permitted to use.

AINTREE

Aintree Racecourse Co Ltd
Ormskirk Road
Liverpool L9 5AS
Tel. 051 523 2600

How to get there:
From North: M6
From South: M6
From East: M62

From West: M57
By Rail: Aintree Sefton Arms; Liverpool Lime Street
By Air: Liverpool Speke; Helicopter facilities

As the home of the Grand National, the world's most famous and widely watched horse race staged on Merseyside as one of the rites of spring, Aintree (originally 'one tree') is a suitably singular racecourse that is formidably reflective of its Viking ancestry. As enigmatic and paradoxical as it is unparalleled, this is a course that offers its visitors even more surprises, delights and occasional disappointments than vastly dissimilar Epsom where the Derby is staged just two months after the National.

Still accessible by rail (as it was when the first 'Grand Liverpool' steeplechase there was won by the appropriately named Lottery in 1839), the course can no longer be reached by paddleboat via a nearby canal. Instead, the vast majority of the thousands of modern-day racegoers who flock to the again

AINTREE: The 1935 Grand National was won by Reynoldstown. This was something of a family affair; Mrs Furlong (back to the camera) is greeting her owner husband, Major Furlong, who leads in the winner, ridden by their son, Mr F.Furlong.

AINTREE: Red Rum (left) snatches victory from the gallant Crisp in the 1973 Grand National.

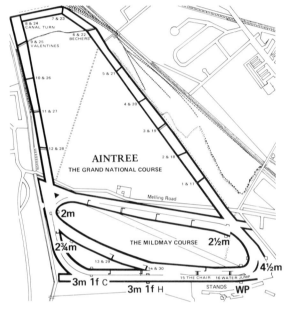

AINTREE: Plan of the course, which includes the Grand National course.

flourishing three-day April festival arrive by car. Perhaps mindful of the fact that Aintree was used for flying displays as early as 1909, a minority of racegoers (among them that small number of National Hunt jockeys who are sufficiently affluent to do so) arrive at the course by air, disembarking from helicopters that land on part of a 6-acre enclosure. Small fixed-wing aircraft can land 7 miles away at Speke, while arrivals at Manchester airport can avoid a 40-mile road journey by making prior arrangements with Helicare (Tel. (051) 427 1571).

One of the biggest surprises to Aintree's first time visitor is that there are, in fact, three courses, all left-handed but otherwise very dissimilar. The Grand National is run over 4 1/2 miles – the longest race distance to be found in Britain. It involves the separate National course whose distinctive, formidable and famous fences (among them the Chair, Valentine's

and Becher's Brook) are not negotiated by the steeplechasers that run on the separate Mildmay course (named after perhaps the unluckiest jockey not to have won the National). This course, a 1 1/2 mile fairly rectangular affair that features sharper turns and much less taxing fences of the type found on many park courses elsewhere, tends to favour fast, front-running chasers since these are seldom overhauled on the final, short 260-yard run-in.

It is, of course, a far different story over the National course, as was spectacularly demonstrated in 1973 when perhaps the unluckiest equine loser of Aintree's big race – the gallant runaway top-weight Crisp – was finally caught at the death by Red Rum who prevailed narrowly in a then record winning time.

Like many a tiring National leader before him, Crisp found the gruellingly long 494-yard Aintree run-in all against him. Indeed, this particularly taxing final demand on a horse's stamina and courage does much still to ensure that, even though radical alterations were made to many fences featured in the National prior to its 1990 running, this race will present steeplechasers with an extremely searching test.

Aintree's hurdle course – a far from tight affair that extends for approximately 10 furlongs – is as flat as both the Mildmay and National steeplechasing courses and, like the latter, features a testingly long run-in.

Aintree's topography, it must be said, tends to interfere with the view of many of its patrons which is one reason why giant Star Vision screens have been erected in some public enclosures. Indeed, those sufficiently fortunate, affluent and foresighted to find themselves in one of the many tents, boxes, chalets and hospitality suites beloved of Aintree's many corporate entertainers are far less likely to get an interrupted or indistinct view of the racing but may well forgo the less sophisticated and cheaper pleasure of picnicking point-to-point style close to a formidable fence and then watching the rest of the big race in thrilling close-up on a portable television.

The fact that bear-baiting and cock-fighting took place at Aintree perhaps explains why the sport that has superseded them there is enjoyed in such a hedonistic and informal manner. Other than the avoidance of nudity, as occasionally favoured by the odd drunken streaker, no restrictions are placed on the dress of racegoers. Children are admitted free at all meetings, save on Grand National day itself and disabled racegoers are well catered for. Most appropriately, too, given the National's recent 150th running, Aintree also has its own racing museum.

From 1972 until 1992, the Spring Festival was the only meeting staged at Liverpool all season. Justly billed as offering 'three days of top-class competitive racing', its thrilling last-day finale is, of course, the National. However, on each of the two days prior to this, a taste of the real thing to follow is provided by a race run over some of the National fences. Becher's, Valentine's and the Chair are all jumped during the John Hughes Memorial Chase (formerly the Topham Chase) on the Thursday and also on the following day in the amateurs' Grand National, the Foxhunters' Chase.

Three top-class pattern races run on the first day and the inclusion of a prestigious hurdle race and a championship event for horses that have run in National Hunt flat races on the Friday card, do much to ensure that the two-day prelude to Grand National day is suitably exciting. As for the rest of the Saturday card, the Aintree Chase for top-class 2-mile 'chasers and the Captain Morgan Aintree Hurdle for high-class 2 1/2-mile hurdlers do much to make the meeting even more memorable.

AIR TRAVEL TO RACECOURSES

Those wishing to fly to racecourses, but who want to avoid the difficulties that can be involved in such a proceeding should ring the numbers listed against the racecourses and await instructions on how to make a happy landing!

Aintree (051) 523 2600
Ascot (0279) 814632
Ayr (0292) 264179
Bangor on Dee (0981) 250436
    (for light aircraft (051) 339 4141)
Beverley (0482) 867488
Carlisle (06973) 42634
Cartmel (09312) 392
Cheltenham (0242) 513014

Devon and Exeter (0803) 812289
Doncaster (0302) 320066
Edinburgh (0292) 264179
Epsom (0279) 814632 (Derby meeting only)
Fakenham (0328) 862388
Folkestone (0303) 66407/68449
Goodwood (0243) 779222
    (fixed-wing aircraft (0243) 774261)
Haydock Park (0942) 728017
Hereford (0432) 273560
Huntingdon (0480) 53373/54610
Kelso (0573) 24767
Kempton Park (0932) 782292
    (fixed-wing aircraft 09905 7700)
Leicester (0533) 716515
Lingfield Park (0342) 834800
Ludlow (058) 477221
Market Rasen (0673) 843434
Newbury (0635) 40015
Newcastle (J091) 236 2020
Newmarket (0638) 662524
Nottingham (0602) 30757
Perth (0738) 52311 (none on-course, but facilities
    at Perth aerodrome three miles away)
Pontefract (0977) 703224
Redcar (0642) 484340 (2 miles from racecourse)
Ripon (0765) 603696
Sandown (0372) 463072
Stratford on Avon (0789) 267949
Taunton (0823) 337172
Thirsk (0845) 522276 (on hockey pitch)
Wetherby (0937) 582035
Wincanton (0963) 32344
Windsor (0753) 865234
Wolverhampton (0902) 24481
Worcester (0905) 25364
Yarmouth (0493) 851500
York (0904) 704922 (4 miles to the west)

ALLEN, J.A. & CO. LTD.

1 Lower Grosvenor Street
Buckingham Palace Road
London SW1 0EL
Tel. (071) 834 5606

For the racing fan no trip to London should be undertaken without a visit to one particular concern that specializes in books about horses. This is J.A. Allen, which retains some of the old-world charm that once characterized the bookshop at 84 Charing Cross Road. Vast stocks of books on racing, bloodstock breeding, as well as equestrian art and history can be inspected on the premises or ordered by mail-order customers from a catalogue. Browsing is always a delight during a visit to J.A. Allen's impressively situated bookshop.

Old-fashioned courtesy and personal service are the keynotes here and the range of works available by American and Commonwealth authors, as well as home-based ones, is remarkably wide.

ALLOWANCES

Horses ridden by inexperienced jockeys – conditional apprentice or amateur – are obviously at rather a disadvantage and so have set deductions made from the weights they would have carried if a fully-fledged jockey had ridden them. These deductions depend on the past riding record of their riders.

Those with no or few past successes are entitled to have a 7 lbs allowance deducted from their mount's originally allocated weight, a fact which is signalled by the horse's racecard number appearing in red letters against a white background on the runner's and rider's board. Rather more successful jockeys are entitled to a 5 lbs allowance, shown in black figures against an orange background, while those close to graduation to fully-fledged jockey status can claim a 3lbs allowancs, shown by white figures against a blue background. Alternatively, a rider's entitlement to one of these allowances may be announced separately under the display of runners and riders.

Some shrewd judges are convinced that, in the case of a particularly promising claimer, the allowance granted may generously belie his or her considerable ability. For this reason, very talented apprentice jockeys, especially those claiming 3 lbs allowances, are often booked by trainers to whom they are not indentured since their skills in the saddle seem to suggest they are not really 'entitled' to this concession.

Another type of allowance – a rather controversial and sexist one – concerns the 3 lbs or 5 lbs that colts concede to fillies in certain races. On occasion this has allowed a mare or filly really to demonstrate her 'superiority'!

ALL RIGHT, THE (OR 'WEIGHED IN' SIGNAL)

Announcement made by hoisting a blue flag on the number board that the jockeys of all the horses concerned in a finish have weighed in and that no objection to these placings has been lodged. This is the signal a prudent bookmaker waits for, unless he has previously agreed to settle winning bets on a 'first past the post' basis (a practice which is apparently more common north of the border).

Most course bookmakers may decide to pay out small amounts on such a basis before the 'all right' is actually signalled. However, as many members of their profession have had their fingers burnt by placing them prematurely into their satchels to pay out supporters of both the actual, but subsequently disqualified, winner and the horse to which it eventually has to concede victory, most bookmakers defer payment until the blue flag is clearly visible.

ALL-WEATHER RACING

Though hardly popular with the racing public, this innovation has precluded the cancellation and hence loss of racing fixtures and much consequent revenue.

From the start at Southwell, all-weather racing allowed lady jockey Alex Greaves to steal some limelight in the initial absence of many top-flight male rivals. During December 1989 and January 1990 Alex became Southwell's unofficial all-weather 'queen' and the darling of its racegoers by achieving a staggering near 66 per cent strike rate on all her mounts!

The all-weather surface in use at Southwell is Fibresand, while at Lingfield reliance is placed on Equitrack, an artificial surface pioneered in the USA.

ALSO RAN

A blanket expression used to describe the performance of runners that failed to 'trouble the judges' by being placed in their respective races. In previous years surprise runners would be seen to have 'also ran' at race meetings, much to the disgust of stay-at-home backers who were denied all knowledge of this fact.

AMATEUR RIDERS

Once popularly known as 'hand pumpers', these performers add a welcome Corinthian flavour to racing, especially that conducted under National Hunt rules. The Princess Royal is just one among a select band of modern-day amateurs whose presence in races has made these even more sporting affairs. Interestingly, the fastest and third fastest Grand National winning times were set by amateurs: by Marcus Armytage on Mr Frisk in 1990 and by Dick Saunders on Grittar in 1982.

AMATEUR RIDERS ASSOCIATION OF GREAT BRITAIN

This exists to encourage amateur riders' races under both codes. A member of FEGENTRI (the International Federation of Gentlemen Riders), it organizes British teams of amateur jockeys to represent their country against foreign rivals in specially staged races. One, the splendidly named Moët et Chandon Silver Magnum, is run over the Derby course at Epsom, over which the Princess Royal partnered Against the Grain in 1985.

ANNUAL MEMBERSHIP

This entitles subscribing racegoers to metal badges which guarantee admission to all of a racecourse's annual fixtures, so enabling considerable savings to be made. Clearly then, annual membership can make an ideal Christmas gift for the keen racegoer.

ANTE-POST BETTING

The making and taking of wagers before betting actually takes place on the racecourse. Originally 'pencillers' or 'legs', as embryo bookmakers were known, would congregate at a wooden post (quite separate and distinct from that used to mark the end of contests elsewhere on the course) around which they would conduct their business on the move, pencilling in the details of their transactions in their betting books as they 'legged' their way through the throng.

Today ante-post markets are formed on many major races each season and, because these generally feature far more generous odds overall than will be available on the day of the race, they induce many punters to make their wagers well in advance. However, there is one proviso to this proceeding which makes it especially propitious to the bookmaker rather than the backer. Should any horse that has been supported ante-post fail to start because of a training setback, a change of plan on the part of its connections or through being incapacitated at the hands of dopers, the stake involved is lost to the bookmaker. Again, if one has supported a runner ante-post in a race like the Lincolnshire Handicap in which the draw plays a decisive part, one can find that just prior to the race it is allotted a stalls position that is so unfavourable as effectively to put paid to its chances.

However, the ante-post method of betting does offer the serious backer a rare chance of profiting from the success or even the failure of a horse he has supported months before its race! This is because, if he has had the foresight to take the long odds originally available well in advance of the race on a horse whose price subsequently shortens in the betting, he can 'play bookmaker' and 'lay off' his bet. What he must do here, in fact, is to become a 'better round' – that is to say behave like a bookmaker whose prices are 'over round' and whose book is balanced so as to produce a profit whatever transpires. In other words, having originally placed an ante-post bet of say £50 at 8-1 and then seen this price subsequently plummet to 2-1, he seeks out a fellow punter and offers to lay him a value bet of 5-2 to £100. This accomplished, he stands to make a profit should the horse either win or lose. The following detailed explanation should make this clear:

Original ante-post wager = £50 at 8-1

a. If the horse involved wins

(i) A return of £450 will be produced i.e. £400 profit plus the £50 originally staked.

(ii) From this £400 profit the backer has to pay out his winning 'client's' profit of £250 (he, of course, also returns the £100 stake he has held); thus a clear profit of £50 is made.

b. If the horse involved loses

(i) The backer's own bet produces a loss of £50 (wagered ante-post at 8-1).

(ii) The backer pockets the losing £100 of his client; thus a clear profit of £50 is made.

The fact that, of the fifteen horses quoted at less than 40-1 in the first ante-post show of odds for a recent running of the Derby nine were eventually 'scratched', serves as a reminder of the risk inherent in the 'laying off' procedure. However, this risk can be reduced if the ante-post backer defers supporting his fancy until a few weeks, rather than months, before a race since this is a time when stable aspirations start to become firm intentions which will be reported in the racing press.

Finally, it is always instructive to compare the final ante-post show with the first one to appear on the boards of bookmakers actually trading on the racecourse. If a runner is 'pushed out' to an opening price that is far more generous than its last ante-post quotation, the backer should be suitably suspicious. Conversely, if a horse drops steadily in price in the ante-post market and then receives support on the course that reduces its price yet further, this will usually indicate that the horse carries strong stable confidence.

'ANY TO COME' BET

This involves the backer's instruction (given in writing or by telephone) that if his first wager in a series produces a return, his bookmaker is to extract a stipulated sum from this to finance one or more further bets. This instruction often features the words 'any to come' but can be expressed in any one of the following rather more cryptic ways: 'any back', 'draw', 'if cash', 'play', 'roll' or 'shift'.

❗ APPLE CORE

Rhyming slang for a score or 20-1.

APPRENTICES

When looking back at the leading apprentices of the past one realizes that very few became successful jockeys of long standing. Until they have ridden ten winners, apprentices can claim 7 lbs if riding against fully fledged jockeys, 5 lbs until they've ridden fifty winners and 3 lbs until their winning tally exceeds seventy-five.

APPROXIMATE ODDS BOARD

Before the recent advent of closed-circuit television screens which now give tote patrons an instantaneous, if still rather approximate, indication of the possible size of particular dividends, the Approximate Odds Board fulfilled this function more graphically, if rather more crudely. This greatly missed device translated its predictions of possible winning tote dividends into odds and displayed these rather dramatically in the form of readings on vertical scales.

ARAB INFLUENCE

Few perhaps realize that in many respects modern-day Middle Eastern patrons of British racing have thoroughly deserved their recent spectacular successes. Indeed, the Classic victories of Arab owners have helped to repay the vast 300-year-old debt British horseracing has long owed to a handful of Arabian steeds imported into this country during the seventeenth century. Indeed, of the three stallions from which thoroughbred racehorses all over the world are descended, two undoubtedly hailed from the desert kingdom of Arabia.

The first, the Darley Arabian, a colt with a distinctive white blaze and three white feet, was acquired in 1704 by a Yorkshire squire, James Darley, as a result of his family's diplomatic and commercial connections with the ancient Syrian city of Aleppo.

Some measure of the contribution to the breeding of thoroughbreds made by this particular stallion can

ARAB INFLUENCE: The Byerley Turk, the third Eastern founding father of thoroughbred racehorses was caught by Captain Robert Byerley while fighting the Turks.

be gained from the realization that within sixty years he had started the line of Eclipse, a great-great-grandson who not only became a racing legend by winning all the twenty-six races and matches he contested, but also achieved spectacular success at stud by siring no fewer than 344 winners and producing 100 descendants that were capable of winning the Epsom Derby!

The second Arab stallion whose contribution to the breeding of thoroughbred racehorses has proved crucial was the Godolphin Arabian. A brown horse with a white spot on his off-hind, he had become something of a 'dark horse' by the time he arrived in England around 1730. Subsequently purchased by a Mr Edward Coke of Derbyshire, he was eventually sold to Lord Godolphin, by whose name he was to become well known in Britain.

Foaled in 1724, the Godolphin was a pure-bred Jilean of 15 hands that in his own time produced Matchem, the colt responsible for a crucial sire line that in recent times has produced four Derby winners in Captain Cuttle, Coronach, Call Boy and Santa Claus and which has survived in the United States through no less a champion than Man O' War, the most famous of all American racehorses.

The so-called Byerley Turk, the third Eastern founding father of thoroughbred racehorses, was also very probably of Arabian descent. He certainly arrived in England before the Darley or the Godolphin Arabian – as early as 1689, in fact, after Captain Robert Byerley had apparently captured him when fighting against the Turks at Buda some two years earlier.

At stud the Byerley enjoyed even more success than he had on the field of battle. Indeed, during the early part of the eighteenth century, the descendants of his great-great-grandson Herod – horses like Thormanby, Bay Middleton and the Flying Dutchman – became sufficiently illustrious to make his blood as prized as that of the Darley Arabian.

In modern times the injection, not so much of Eastern blood, but of Arab capital into British horse-racing has revitalized the sport and assured its future. That this is so was due partly to the foresight and initiative displayed by Major Derek Wigan and Colonel Peter Hamer who in 1977 masterminded a Jockey Club mission to the Gulf states to induce wealthy and prestigious Arab owners to support the racing and breeding industries of Britain, rather than those of France or the United States. Among such owners, who since 1977 have placed hundreds of top-class thoroughbreds in training in England and

who began in the 1980s to purchase some key British studs, the most influential have been the Saudi Arabian Prince Khalid Bin Abdullah (a close relative of King Fahd) and four sons of the Ruler of Dubai.

ARTISTS, EQUESTRIAN

Many of these no longer depict horses in the 'rocking horse' style once beloved of painters of earlier centuries. Not surprisingly, racing provides artists with a vast range of attractive subjects and many a coffee table book is devoted to some wonderful renditions of the colourful racing scene.

Those wishing to commission studies of their equine heroes should contact the Society of Equestrian Artists, whose annual exhibition is some consolation for the rather dreary racing fare on offer in the run-up to Christmas. The Society can be contacted through its Honorary Secretary at 33 Pealsham Gardens, Fordingbridge, Hants SP6 1RD.

ASCOT

Royal Enclosure
Ascot
SL5 7JN
Tel. (0344) 22211

How to get there:
From North: M1
From South: A3
From East: M3
From West: M4
By Rail: Ascot
By Air: Helicopter facilities

Ascot is located some 26 miles from London and affords access by road, rail and air (through its helicopter pad). It offers excellent facilities and viewing and provides arguably the best racing in Europe.

Races on this Group One, rather triangular looking track of 1 mile 6 furlongs 34 yards are run either on the straight mile course or on sections of the round course. A spur provides the former section which is known as the Royal Hunt Cup course after a prestigious handicap staged at the royal meeting. This straight presents a stiff test to those running on it since they have to cope with some rising ground. The round course, which is used for races of 1, 1 1/4. 1 1/2, 2 miles 24 yards , 2 1/2 miles and 2 miles 6 furlongs and 34 yards, is also undulating.

As can be readily appreciated, Ascot places a high premium on jockeyship. Horses running on the round course must be kept clear of converging rivals as they round the final bend and should not be asked to make up too much leeway in the mere 2 1/2 furlongs that remain. On the straight course, the sheer width of the track means that horses tend to race in two distinct groups and an inexperienced jockey may, in moving his mount from one side of the track to another, inadvertently extend the distance over which it has to race by a quite alarming proportion.

To some extent Ascot represents a test of adaptability because of its short run-in, its undulations and its right-hand character. Above all perhaps, it puts the stamina of horses on trial since it is essentially stiff, even severe, if the going is heavy. In general it tends to suit strong, resolute and long-striding gallopers rather than animals which appreciate tighter and less turns sweeping bends.

As for the draw, this is generally believed to confer no major advantage. However, if there is some give in the ground and the stalls are in a central position, low numbers may enjoy an advantage in the relatively short races that are staged on the straight course. Since Ascot is a right-hand track, it is also conceivable that high-drawn horses may be marginally favoured in longer races over the round course.

Some backers consider that the fiercely competitive nature of racing at Ascot and the fact that the conformation of the course is so tricky and demanding conspire to cause rather too many upsets in form – a large number of which have come to be associated with many races, particularly big handicaps, that are staged at the royal meeting. Indeed, statistics relating to the fate of Ascot favourites do seem to lend some substance to such misgivings.

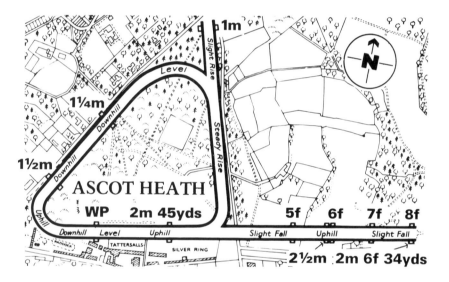

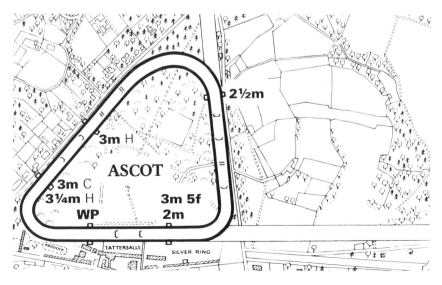

ASCOT: Plans of the Flat course (top), and the National Hunt course (bottom).

The luck of the Irish seems to hold good on the Berkshire course, where their runners often manage to improve by several pounds on their past running, so specially prepared are they to put up superlative performances. At few other racecourses in the world are so many valuable and prestigious races run in such a short space of time as is the case during the four-day royal fixture that forms such a colourful and fashionable highlight of the social season. Despite the formality that is *de rigeur* in the royal enclosure, the mid-June meeting is a far from stuffy affair. Although pomp and circumstance do put in an appearance on the Heath, they do so in the acceptably picturesque shape of the Windsor greys that on each of the four days of the royal meeting pull the open landaus in which the Queen, the Duke of Edinburgh and other members of the royal family travel past the stands on their way to their private box.

Run on the opening day is the Coventry Stakes, a Group Three 6-furlong race for two-year-olds in which colts have to concede 5 lbs to fillies. Other important sprints for first-season performers at the royal meeting are the Group Three Queen Mary Stakes for two-year-old fillies which is run over the minimum distance, as is the Norfolk Stakes (known as the New Stakes until 1972) in which both colts and fillies can compete on the third day of the festival and which is also a Group Three event.

Two-year-olds are not permitted to take part in another prestigious race that is staged over the minimum distance at Royal Ascot – the Group Two King's Stand Stakes – widely regarded as one of the 5-furlong sprint championships of Europe and open to both colts and fillies.

Another sprint for horses of at least three years of age is the Cork and Orrery Stakes, a Group Three race that by tradition is run on the third day of the royal fixture. This highly competitive race can prove something of a lottery and is often won by an outsider.

Although as a handicap it neither forms part of the pattern system nor is listed as important, another 6-furlong race, the Wokingham Stakes, is perhaps the royal meeting's best known sprint. Like the Cork and Orrery, it is often captured by a horse that fails to figure at the head of the market and has thrice been won by members of the Sutcliffe training family.

Only one pattern race over 7 furlongs is staged at Royal Ascot, the Group Three Jersey Stakes for three-year-olds which at starting have not won a Group One or Two pattern race.

As for mile events, the best known is the Royal Hunt Cup, first run in 1843 and which now qualifies for listed status. Like the Wokingham this is a highly competitive race in which over the years some major coups have been engineered.

The most prestigious mile race at the royal meeting is the Group One St James's Palace Stakes for which three-year-olds compete on the opening day. Understandably this is often won by the colt that has captured the 2000 Guineas some six weeks earlier. Since the war this particular double has been achieved by Tudor Minstrel (1947), Palestine (1950), Nearula (1953), Darius (1954), Right Tack (1969), Brigadier Gerard (1971), Bolkonski (1975) and To-Agori-Mo (1981).

Another mile event, the Coronation Stakes, is a slightly less valuable Group One affair and is confined to three-year-old fillies. Understandably, too, this race is often won by a horse that has already captured the 1000 Guineas. On no less than four successive occasions from 1952 to 1955, and again in 1967, 1970 and 1979, this proved to be the case.

If they hold engagements at the royal meeting, many horses that have run in the Epsom Classics less than two and a half weeks earlier may well decline them, while those that do go to post often fail to perform impressively, not so much on account of exhaustion but because of the very different terrain they encounter on the Berkshire course. Indeed, it is seldom that the owner of a Derby or an Oaks winner risks letting it take its chance against fresher horses that might defeat it and so seriously diminish its value at stud.

The record shows that in modern times no Derby winner has moved on to Royal Ascot to win the King Edward VII Stakes which is the colts' equivalent of the Ribblesdale Stakes. Despite this, this Group Two contest has in its time been won by horses of Classic standard – for example by Light Cavalry before this impressive three-year-old captured the 1980 St Leger.

A valuable race over the Derby distance that is staged at the royal meeting is the Hardwicke Stakes which is one of the major attractions of the final day. This is restricted to four-year-olds and upwards and frequently attracts top class Irish and French thoroughbreds, many of which have triumphed in recent seasons.

Several famous stayers' races are staged during the June festival. By far the best known and the most prestigious is the Group One Ascot Gold Cup over 2 1/2 miles which is run on ladies' day, traditionally the most fashionable of all. This race dates from 1807 and in its long history has produced thrillingly close

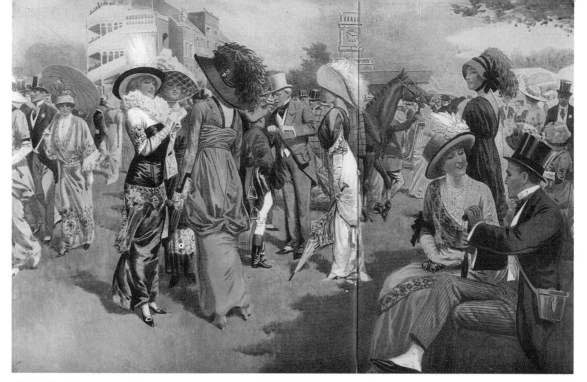

ASCOT: The Ascot Gold Cup is a race over two and a half miles and is traditionally run on ladies' day. This print from 1914 shows the splendour of the occasion which continues to the present day.

finishes and even controversy, as was the case when Rock Roi was disqualified after winning on two separate occasions in 1971 and 1972.

In modern times no longer do Classic winners remain in training for a third season with the express aim of capturing this famous prize. However, that a Gold Cup was formerly regarded as furnishing conclusive proof of pre-eminence on the part of a thoroughbred is suggested by a glance at the record books. This will show that Persimmon (1897), Gay Crusader (1917), Gainsborough (1918), Owen Tudor (1942) and Ocean Swell (1945) all achieved the Derby-Gold Cup double.

Since the vast majority of pattern races that attract the best modern British thoroughbreds involve contests of less than 2 miles – and sadly there is even pressure to make this the maximum race distance – it is unlikely that another Classic winner will ever add its name to this select group of staying champions.

Two other Royal Ascot marathons also deserve a mention – the Queen's Vase over 2 miles 45 yards, which was first run in 1838 and which is now confined to three-year-olds, and the well-known if less prestigious, Ascot Handicap Stakes, a now unlisted event over 2 1/2 miles.

The longest race staged at Royal Ascot and also in Britain, brings the four-day festival to a close. Known to generations of backers as the 'Getting Out Stakes', this is the now unlisted but well-known

Queen Alexandra Stakes of 2 miles 6 furlongs 34 yards. First staged in 1865 and formerly rather more prestigious than at present, it is best known for having been 'farmed' by the legendary Brown Jack on no less than six occasions, the last in 1934.

If the majority of Royal Ascot patrons see fit to bid farewell to the Berkshire track on the concluding Friday of the festival, those whose interest is primarily in the horses, rather than the people who watch them, tend to return on the following day for what is now known as the Ascot Heath meeting. While this does not feature a pattern or a listed event, it attracts high-class fields and forms a fitting end to a fine week's racing. Indeed, top-class racing is guaranteed at any Ascot fixture. The first of the season, for example, which takes place at the end of April, features the Group Three Sagaro Stakes over 2 miles 45 yards which commemorates the French horse that captured the Ascot Gold Cup on three successive occasions in 1975, 1976 and 1977.

Another listed event at this spring meeting, which was once important enough for its results to be recorded in racing annals, is the Victoria Cup, originally run at Hurst Park and a competitive 7-furlong handicap. A further event staged at the first Ascot meeting is the 10-furlong White Rose Stakes for three-year-olds that have not won a pattern race.

After the royal meeting in June, the most prestigious is the Diamond fixture in late July, the centrepiece of which is Britain's richest race, the Group One King George VI and Queen Elizabeth Diamond Stakes in which top-class thoroughbreds of three years and upwards from many parts of Europe compete over the Derby distance. Most appropriately, this race was won by Her Majesty the Queen's Aureole a year after the Coronation. So important is the King George VI and Queen Elizabeth Diamond Stakes, that it is as highly regarded by top breeders in Kentucky's blue grass country as the Epsom Derby and Longchamp's Prix de l'Arc de Triomphe. Indeed, since its inception in 1951, the 'King George' has been won by no fewer than twelve Derby winners from Tulyar (1952) to Generous nearly forty years later. Another important event to be staged at the De Beers sponsored Diamond meeting in late July is the unlisted Brown Jack Handicap over a distance of 2 miles 45 yards. This contest commemorates perhaps the best-loved stayer that has ever graced the royal meeting and whose six Queen Alexandra Stakes wins at that meeting will never be forgotten by those old enough to have seen them.

The so-called Festival of British Racing provides some top class autumn racing on a Saturday in late September. Its highlights are three races run over a mile – the Royal Lodge Stakes (a Group Two event), the Group One Queen Elizabeth II Stakes (conceivably Europe's premier race over this distance) and the Group One Fillies' Mile. Finally, the Group Three Diadem Stakes helps to provide what is probably the best value to be found anywhere in Britain at a top-class race meeting.

Ascot is also a top-flight jumping course and one of the principal races, staged over stiff fences on what is in essence a galloping course that finds out inexperienced novices and represents a true test of stamina, is the H. & T. Walker Gold Cup. A handicap 'chase over 2 1/2 miles and run in mid-November, this race is often won by seven-year-old 'chasers that were placed last time out.

The listed 3-mile SGB Handicap Chase is a pre-Christmas 'cracker' and for some runners sometimes serves as a lead-in to the King George VI Chase run at Kempton on Boxing Day. Previously won by horses of the calibre of Arkle and Midnight Court, this 'chase often falls to an eight-year-old.

Dress requirements at Ascot are understandably stringent for the formal royal meeting: ladies are not allowed to sport shorts or wear trousers in the members' enclosure in which men must wear a jacket, collar and tie or a jacket and polo neck during the winter.

AT THE FLIP (TIP): Offering 'inside information' or 'stable secrets' regarding a possible winner.

❗ AT THE FLIP (TIP)

Involved in the business of giving tips in exchange for money. Some tipsters make a personal approach to the unwary tyro on the racecourse and attempt to sell him a racecard inscribed with what they allege is 'inside information'. Others may advertise in sporting publications in which they commonly offer to pass on 'stable secrets' or what they allege is 'genuine' information. In as much as some of these particular operators pass on information that is genuine, in that it relates to actual runners, their conduct cannot be challenged in a court of law. This is not to suggest, however, that the business of giving an 'egg-flip', or tip, attracts only undesirables. Not all tipsters are charlatans. Indeed, some are sincere or even shrewd.

Sadly, modern race crowds are far less likely to be harangued and cajoled by exponents of the art of 'egg flipping' as was formerly the case. Personalities such as the late Ras Prince Monolulu, who claimed descent from the same Abyssinian royal blood as Emperor Haile Selassie and did much to enliven the atmosphere on racecourses until the early 1970s, have not been replaced in any significant numbers.

The truth is, of course, that the financial rewards of this curious profession are irregular. Writing over thirty years ago, Anthony Reed was able to observe that, despite the fact that few tipsters survived the vicissitudes of their bizarre lifestyle, there was 'no apparent shortage of recruits to replace them'. Today, however, this is no longer the case. Tipsters are missing from fourth-grade provincial racecourses and are currently found only on big race days at top-class courses that are well patronized.

AUCTIONS

These follow selling races and observing and listening to them is guaranteed to increase the enjoyment of the racegoer. Auctioneers are often amusing and entertaining, as are some of the ploys trainers have adopted in order not to have to spend much to buy in their winners. On one occasion the former Newmarket trainer Walter Griggs even put a muzzle on one of his successful platers once it reached the winner's enclosure, and this ruse did 'muzzle' a few would-be bidders!

AUTHORITY TO ACT

If, as is often the case, an owner needs to delegate responsibility for such tasks as entering, withdrawing or declaring a horse, he can fill in an official form consigning his 'authority to act' to his nominee – usually the trainer of the animal concerned.

AUTUMN DOUBLE

A bet involving an attempt to nominate the winners of two handicaps, the 9-furlong Cambridgeshire run at Newmarket in October and the 2 miles 2 furlong Cesarewitch at the same meeting a few weeks later.

Since both these races are highly competitive, commonly contested by large fields and run at the back end of the season when upsets in form are fairly frequent, horses that manage to win them generally start at odds which when coupled together produce a handsome return.

The two events always provide a strong ante-post betting market and an incentive to gamble heavily. Indeed, many punters bravely, if perhaps rather foolishly, attempt to land what is perhaps the most difficult multiple bet of the season, save for the so-called 'Spring Double' which involves the Grand National and the Lincoln Handicap.

Understandably, only a very few have trained, nominated or backed the winners of the Cambridgeshire and the Cesarewitch in the same year. The trainer Sam Darling was able to build what is now Henry Cecil's base at Warren Place, Newmarket on the proceeds of a winning double on Masked Marvel (at 100-8) to win the Cambridgeshire and Forseti (at 25-1) to win the Cesarewitch in 1925, while thirty years later the tipster Keystone of the *Sunday Despatch* selected Retrial, successful in the former race at 18-1 and Curry in the latter at 100-6.

Some, such as James McLean and Barry Hills, have managed to land one leg of the Autumn Double in spectacular style. Then there was Charles Beattie who on behalf of the trainer W. Waugh placed such a sizeable stable commission on Verdict, the winner of the 1923 Cambridgeshire, that he was able to pocket the sum of £30,000 for himself.

Even more impressively, one of the greatest sums ever to have been won on the English turf was paid out as a result of a Cambridgeshire victory – that of Winkfield's Pride at 5-1 in 1896. Backed down ante-post on the eve of the race to single figure odds by Charlie Mills (like Beattie, another stable commissioner), this colt eventually won in a common canter and so enriched his connections by a sum reputed to be a quarter of a million pounds!

Such a sum was unquestionably won when the legendary 'Hermits' of Salisbury Plain – the reclusive racing syndicate masterminded by Captain William Purefoy and A. P. Cunliffe – managed to win the 1903 Cambridgeshire with Hackler's Pride which started at 6-1 and was ridden by Jack Jarvis who later achieved so much distinction as a trainer. Amazingly the 'Hermits', operating from their base at Druid's Lodge, repeated this feat the following year when the same horse triumphed at odds of 7-2!

AYR

Whitletts Road
Ayr
KA8 QJE
Tel. (0292) 264179

How to get there:
From North: A78
From South: M6
From East: A70
From West: A70
By Rail: Ayr
By Air: Glasgow Airport; Helicopter facilities

Scotland's premier track, some 417 miles from London, can be reached by rail from Euston via Ayr station. It lies north-east of the town close to the A70, A77 and A719. The course is an hour's drive from Glasgow and its landing strip can accommodate helicopters. It is a wide left-hand oval of 1 mile 4 $\frac{1}{2}$ furlongs. The only undulations it features are rather gentle – indeed, its generally flat nature makes it a very fair track. Upsets in form cannot therefore justifiably be blamed on its conformation. Above all, the course is admirably suited to strong galloping types since its long run-in of 4 $\frac{1}{2}$ furlongs gives a jockey sufficient time in which to make his or her run

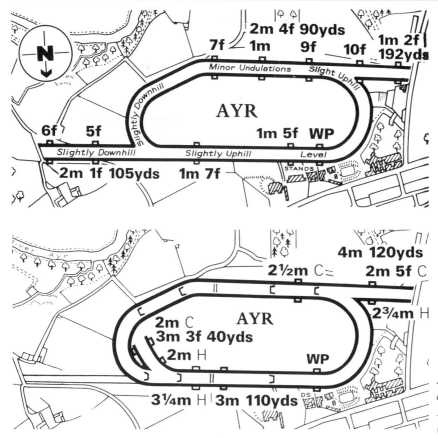

AYR: Plans of the Flat course (top), and the National Hunt course (bottom).

or the opportunity to ride a finely judged waiting race. To the backer's advantage is the fact that the track dries out extremely quickly and thus the going is rarely heavy.

Various spurs provide straight stretches; on one that is especially wide 5 and 6 furlong events take place, while another gives opportunities to stage 10 and 11 furlong races which involve parts of the round course.

It is generally agreed that the draw does not greatly influence the results of races on this course. However, since places in the draw extend outwards from the left, low-drawn horses racing on the round sections on this left-handed course (over distances of 7 furlongs, 1 mile, 1 mile 2 furlongs, 1 mile 2 furlongs 192 yards, 1 mile 5 furlongs 13 yards, 1 mile 7 furlongs and 2 miles 1 furlong 105 yards) may enjoy an understandable, if none too pronounced advantage. As for races over 5 and 6 furlongs on the straight course, the draw presents no appreciable advantage except perhaps when large fields face the

starter. In such circumstances low numbers are preferable, especially if the stalls are positioned on the far side of the course.

Ayr benefits from enlightened management by Mark Kershaw who does so much to stage attractive programmes that some trainers are fond of going north of the border and a few even nominate Ayr as their favourite racecourse.

The National Hunt highlight of Ayr's season is the Scottish Grand National which is often run in the sun of late April on going that is frequently firmer than that found at Aintree two weeks earlier. Past winners often go in again in this 4 mile 120 yard marathon that now-retired trainer Neville Crump won five times and in which seven- and nine-year-olds seem to do best.

The most prestigious race staged at Ayr on the flat is part of its four-day Western Meeting in late September. This, the Ayr Gold Cup, a 6-furlong cavalry charge of a sprint first run in 1804, frequently falls to an improving three-year-old.

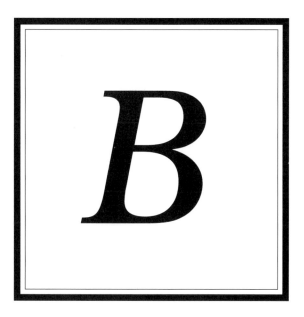

BACKER'S GRAVEYARD

Term used to describe a race meeting, a particular type of race or an actual event that seldom brings success to favourites or well-fancied horses. Royal Ascot has been so described since many of the horses it attracts each June are top-class and thus difficult to distinguish between. Indeed, a horse that heads the Ascot market does not always have an outstanding right to do so.

Those events on the calendar to which this morbid description is sometimes applied are those which customarily feature upsets in form. All four legs of the Spring and Autumn Doubles can be so regarded, as can other open handicaps like Ascot's Royal Hunt Cup and sprints which generally attract large fields such as the Stewards' Cup at Goodwood.

Finally, there are many who regard investment in all large handicaps, sellers, apprentice events and races run for minimum amounts of prize money as a fatal proceeding.

BALANCING A BOOK

An ideal to which a businesslike bookmaker aspires but does not always attain. Such an operator will try to ensure that his total take will exceed the sum that the victory of any horse in the race will oblige him to extract from his satchel.

By making the totality of the odds he quotes 'over-round', the bookmaker is set fair for the making of a profit but will, in fact, do so only if the liabilities he incurs on each of the runners remain roughly in line. Of course, in practice bookmakers do not always receive sums of money for each of the supported runners that are of exactly the right size to allow them to equalize the liabilities they have incurred on them. However, by laying off any liabilities that create an imbalance in his books the bookmaker can restore the 'over-round' state and so free himself from serious risk.

Some bookmakers despise such subtle forms of liability control and leave their books unbalanced in the belief that it is necessary to protect themselves only against horses they adjudge capable of winning the race, rather than against the victory of any runner. Irish course bookmaker Francis Hyland is a prominent exponent of that practice.

BALLING

Term used to describe what happens when snow is compressed to an ice-like slippery consistency within the confines of a horse's shoes. Understandably, this makes negotiation of snow-covered racecourses difficult. Some shrewd connections seek to minimize this problem by greasing the feet of their runner before it leaves its racecourse stable. Indeed, Grudon's Grand National victory in a blizzard in 1901 was in large measure due to two pounds of butter being smeared in its hooves. The 9-1 third favourite literally skated in.

BALLINROBE

Ballinrobe
Co. Mayo
Southern Ireland
Tel. (092) 41476

How to get there:
From North: N84
From South: N84
From East: R331
From West: R331
Approximately 15 miles from Castlebar

This tight right-handed track of only a mile in extent can be found close to Joyce country on the Plains of Ellertrin, 13 miles from the railway town of Claremorris from which it can be reached on the R331. It is used for both jump and flat racing over distances of 6 furlongs, 1 1/2 miles, 2 miles, 2 1/2 miles and 3 1/2 miles. Given the tightness of its bends, those drawn high on the outside enjoy an understandable advantage.

The fact that this extremely scenic Irish course has stabling for eighty-three horses means that the five meetings that are staged on it often attract sizeable fields. Racing takes place on one day in April, on another in mid-June, for two consecutive ones in late July, and there is an autumn fixture in mid-September. Adaptable types with a definite turn of foot often prevail at these meetings if their jockeys have them handy as they round the final bend.

BANGOR ON DEE: Plan of the course. This popular course, hardly a testing affair for the horses and riders, is where the author Dick Francis had his first racecourse ride.

BANGOR ON DEE

Bangor on Dee
Nr. Wrexham
Clwyd
N. Wales
Tel. (0978) 780323

How to get there:
From North: M6
From South: M6
From East: A525
From West: A5
By Rail: Wrexham
By Air: Helicopter facilities

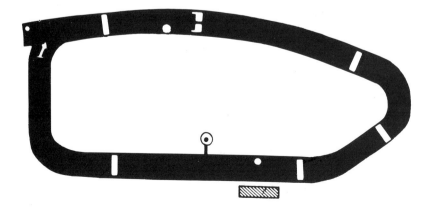

*BALLINROBE:
Plan of the course.*

This track, where author Dick Francis had his first racecourse ride, is an unspoilt rustic gaff savoured by sporting racegoers who go there not to be seen but for the sake of meeting together and watching contests made the more sporting by their often fairly humble nature.

This Deeside course, which forms part of the pretty Bryn y Prys estate, is 5 miles from Wrexham. Bangor can be reached by rail via Wrexham station, while those arriving in fixed-wing aircraft, if previously phoning (051) 339 4141 to contact Alfred McAlpine plc, may be given permission by this most generous sponsor to use its private landing strip which is 6 miles from the course.

Those arriving by helicopter can land on course at Bangor where the absence of a grandstand is something of a downer when the heavens open but does mean that there is even more space for the delights of picnicking in point-to-point style on the side of one of the many old riverbanks that provide such an excellent view of the racing.

Straight sections of track are conspicuously absent at Bangor whose 1 1/2-mile, mainly flat, track possesses a turn or two that approaches the tightness of the circuit at nearby Chester. The bends here are left-handed and the tightest is the Paddock bend.

As on many a sharpish track, front runners are often favoured here despite the fact that some can be finally pegged back on the longish 325 yard run-in. Its minor undulations and relatively easy fences – apart from an open ditch which finds out some suspect jumpers – means that this track is hardly a testing affair.

Restaurant facilities, which are fully utilized on McAlpine day in late April or early May, are available in the paddock enclosure. It is also most appropriate that, given its old-world charm, Sotheby & Co. also sponsor some races run on this beautiful racecourse. Such is their love of Bangor that some locals eschew the cover that cars provide in the wet.

BAR

An expression that accompanies reference to a particular rate of odds, e.g. 3-1 bar. It announces that all bar the favourite in a race are quoted at the rate of 3-1 (in the case of the second favourite) or at longer odds.

BATH

Bath Racecourse
Lansdown
Bath
Tel. (0225) 424609

How to get there:
From North: M5
From South: M5, A36
From East: M4, A4
From West: A38
By Rail: Bath
By Air: Light Aircraft and Helicopter facilities

The racecourse at Bath is situated to the north-west of the town which can be conveniently reached by train from Paddington, a mere 107 miles away. Special bus services from Bath and Bristol run to the track which is to be found at Lansdown on terrain that can usually be relied upon to produce good going. It is a left-handed oval of 1 mile 4 furlongs 25 yards in length.

The mile course – over 7 furlongs – on which low-drawn horses enjoy an edge starts from a spur which extends inside the main circuit, while yet another allows races of 1 1/4 miles 46 yards, and 1 mile 3 furlongs and 144 yards to be staged. Horses running over these two particular distances encounter some fairly extensive straight sections which are far from common on this sharp circuit.

Indeed, horses have to be able to negotiate its tight turns in order to stand a real chance in the

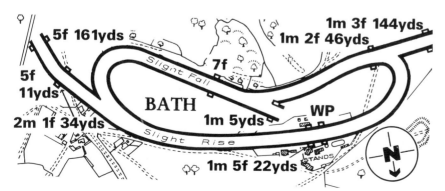

BATH: Plan of the course.

longer races that are held at Bath. Even in sprint races, which are held over 5 furlongs 11 yards and 6 furlongs 161 yards, contestants encounter only a furlong or so of straight level ground. Thereafter they have to descend and negotiate an elbow which, because it bends quite sharply to the left, gives an advantage to low-drawn horses.

In view of the fact that all runners at Bath have to face this bend and encounter an uphill run-in that extends testingly for nearly half a mile, the Lansdown track, especially since its round sections are fairly undulating, can be regarded as tricky. Not only does it put a horse's speed, stamina, resolution and adaptability on trial, it also makes heavy demands on the skill of its rider. Horses need to be handily placed round its bends and if possible shot out of the elbow on the straight course. Thus, both adaptable galloping types and jockeys who have been conspicuously successful on this fairly lowly course should receive close scrutiny.

However, in view of the demanding, even bizarre, conformation of Bath racecourse, and the fact that the generally rather poor horses it attracts have to race at the unusually high altitude of 800 feet (which some believe accounts for so many freak results), the backer should perhaps avoid heavy investment at Lansdown.

BEATEN FAVOURITES

Paradoxes are always intriguing and truth in racing terms is often surprising. For example, the tag 'beaten favourite' can provide a profitable pointer rather than, as one might well expect, an indication of a runner to avoid.

There is even a plan whose basic principle involves supporting a favourite that has previously been beaten in a far less prestigious and valuable race than that in which it is due to compete – a seemingly illogical proceeding but one that over the years has produced several long-priced winners.

The trick, of course, is to determine when such previously disappointing runners should be forgiven for their lapses from grace. This is naturally a difficult proceeding, but amongst the comments of their disappointed connections there will often be found excuses relating to unsuitable going, distances or courses, ill luck or injury in running, injudicious riding, receiving an unfortunate draw, being left well behind in the early stages of a race, or being given too much to do in the final stages.

Then there is the belief of Bob Butchers, formerly Newsboy of the *Daily Mirror*, that horses are just like people in having their off days. Like humans too, as well as occasionally feeling and performing under par, horses can become tired and jaded through too much racing. Indeed, some supporters of beaten favourites support those whose lapses last time out (as the sequels to strings of far more impressive runs) have caused their trainers to rest them for longish spells so that they can return to the racecourse thoroughly refreshed. If such publications as *Superform* are consulted, any beaten favourites that 'go well when fresh' can be identified.

Often, after losing as unfit favourites but having become fitter in the process, some runners quickly take their chances in more prestigious races. If these happen to be staged on tracks on which such runners have previously scored, or over ideal distances and optimum going, they may well succeed at long odds that belie their actual chances.

The blinkers of hope and optimism necessarily worn by many owners and trainers may well blind them to the possibility that other connections may have done as much, if not more, to win races and thus the confidence that installs some runners as market leaders can be naive and so misplaced.

Publications such as *Trainerform* (published by Aesculus Press) will indicate the types of races in which particular trainers' favourites do well, and if any of these were previously unsuccessful, there may be grounds for giving them a chance to atone.

❗ BEES/BEESWAX
Rhyming-slang reference to betting tax.

BELLEWSTOWN

Drogheda
Co. Louth
Southern Ireland
Tel. (041) 38368,

How to get there:
From North: N1
From South: N1
From East: N51
By Air: Dublin Airport
Approximately 25 miles from Dublin

This truly rural racecourse claims the distinction of being the oldest in the British Isles, but is not even marked on a map of Ireland published by the Readers' Digest Association! However, racegoers will easily find this track if they turn off the N1 at

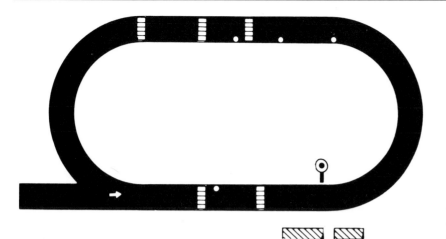

BELLEWSTOWN:
Plan of the course, the
oldest in the British Isles.

Julianstown which lies a mere 25 miles north of Dublin.

A surprising number of Irish racecourses are right-handed and interestingly Bellewstown was numbered among these until just over 100 years ago when a change in the location of the grandstand made left-handed running a more logical proceeding.

During its long history Bellewstown has enjoyed a good deal of royal patronage, initially when a former mayor of Drogheda persuaded King George III to sponsor a valuable race called His Majesty's Plate in 1780. Subsequent monarchs sponsored races until, sadly, in 1980 a 200-year-old tradition of royal sponsorship was allowed to lapse.

Used until 1977 for steeplechasing, Bellewstown now stages flat and hurdle races and one of these once featured Seamus McGrath's Allangrange which, despite finishing unplaced here, subsequently landed a five-timer that included the Irish St Leger run not far away at the Curragh.

Some ultra-tight turns once made Bellewstown a dangerous course to ride after a shower of rain, but now its bends are well cambered. Understandably, on what remains a fairly sharp track, low-drawn horses are at an advantage. Bellewstown is proving increasingly popular as an evening venue and now stages three successive twilight cards in July.

BEST TURNED OUT AWARD

This accolade goes to the runner in a race that a designated paddock judge declares is best prepared for its race by its stable lad or girl to whom a prize – usually a cash reward or a gift – is then presented. Some racegoers set a good deal of store by runners on whom care has been lavished in the belief that such attention reflects great expectations.

BEST WATCHED

Term applied to a runner that, through lack of race fitness, recent lacklustre form or unsuitable race conditions, seems unlikely to prevail in an impending race. This term need not be a permanently dismissive one, since the horse to which it is applied might in future more propitious circumstances be one in which to take a financial rather than a merely watching interest.

BET BAR ONE/BETTING 'WITHOUT'

A practice adopted by certain bookmakers who announce that the odds they quote against horses named on their boards are based on their prospects of winning the 'race' to finish second to a runner that these bookmakers nominate as the likely winner.

This practice (which arose out of the need to induce punters to take an interest in races involving runners with outstanding claims and so starting at prohibitively short odds) has in recent seasons been extended by some bookmakers to involve every race on the card. If a horse supported on this basis manages to win its race or runs second to the unquoted contestant (so vindicating the bookmaker's judgement) the backer is paid the rate of odds displayed against its name at the time the bet was struck. However, if it runs second to any other contestant no return will be forthcoming.

A most useful racing publication by Malcolm Howard, entitled *How to Find Value when Betting* (Raceform Publications), even includes a table that indicates which 'betting without' odds should be taken.

The odds quoted by bookmakers 'betting without' should be carefully compared with those offered by bookmakers offering odds against all the runners elsewhere in the ring. Sometimes exceptionally good value can be obtained if one supports a runner that one strongly fancies will defeat a 'false' favourite.

BET OFF THE BOARD

Expression used to describe the activity of bookmakers who, in contrast to their colleagues on the rails, lay bets (provided these involve an acceptable liability) according to the prices on display on their boards.

BET OFF THE CARD

Practice adopted by rails bookmakers who, rather than demean themselves by publically displaying their prices, inscribe these on their 'twist' cards and reveal them on request to their clients, many of whom have credit accounts and pass their instructions over the rails that divide the members' enclosure from Tattersalls.

Incidentally, rails operators can, in confiding details of their prices, quote rates that may be lower than those generally available on the boards of other bookmakers trading in the ring.

BETTER OFF

If two runners that have already taken each other on are again in contention and one of these re-opposes with a weight advantage it did not previously enjoy, it is said to be 'better off'.

However, experience has often shown that horses adjudged to have sound prospects (on the basis of altered weights) of turning the tables on rivals that have beaten them often fail to capitalize on this advantage. This may be because many runners-up are fully extended while winners often win 'cleverly' with something in hand.

BETTING AGAINST HORSES

This represents the aspiration of many a businesslike racecourse bookmaker who sets out to lay a large number of the horses against whose chances he has quoted odds that, in totality, amount to an acceptable percentage of 'over-round' (i.e. percentage profit). Obviously, the more horses he can lay the greater the likelihood that he will make his profit.

Indeed, it is only when the bookmaker's chances of receiving the return he seeks, like those of a backer, depend upon the fate of one or a few animals that it is odds against his success. Naturally, the making of a one-horse book (like the making of a one-horse selection) does involve some risk since it reduces the layer to making a guess, however intelligent this may be, that a

horse will lose. Many bookmakers have made fortunes by standing just one horse to lose a fortune but, understandably, this practice has put many others out of business.

A far more prudent bookmaking practice is to take bets against as many horses as possible. Obviously, business involving a large number of horses will be brought to a bookmaker only if there is not much to choose between them. This will be the case if they have been well matched by the handicapper or are facing stiff competition from horses of high class, each one of which is doing its utmost to capture a considerable prize at a prestigious meeting. In such circumstances, which are produced by many major handicaps during the season, outsiders have as fair a chance of winning as shorter-priced contenders.

In such races, as Charles Sidney has revealed in his instructive book *The Art of Legging* (Maxline International), bookmakers may bet 'evens to the field money' – that is stand one or two runners to lose as much as they have taken, stand some others to lose smaller sums and hope that another runner on which they have incurred only a small liability will in fact run away with the race.

BETTING BOOK

Complete record of one's wagers, the compilation of which is *de rigeur* for the serious backer. 'Leviathan' gamblers of the past, many of them aristocrats of their day, recorded their wagers in suitably impressive leather-backed volumes.

Such a book (the backer's equivalent of the bookmaker's field book) should ideally resemble a ledger in which the entries are tabulated, as in the following example:

Horse			
Date		Opening price	
Race		Starting price	
Time		Price taken	
Meeting		Result	
Win		Lose	
Running Total			

BETTING BOOTS

The expression to 'put on one's betting boots' owes its origin to the fact that some members of the book-making fraternity once wore especially built-up boots so they could reach up to their lists of runners that were held aloft by their board boys. Betting boots are put on by backers who mean business and so dress for it!

predictions this involves relate to starting prices rather than opening rates. It can often prove illuminating if the closing rates in the racecourse market are rapidly compared with averages of various pundits' estimates of starting prices produced on the day before the race.

At such a time, many hours before the race is due to be run, the starting price compiler may be far more impressed by the prospects of a particular horse than are its connections on the following day. If there has been any belated evaporation of confidence, this may well be indicated by a disturbing disparity between the odds actually quoted against the horse involved and the shorter ones appearing in the 'morning line' (as the starting price forecast is called in North America). Conversely, if confidence has increased, the reverse is true.

Sometimes, such comparisons of actual with forecast rates can reveal the presence in the market of 'corner' horses – runners quoted as rank outsiders or unmentioned in newspaper predictions of probable starting prices which then unexpectedly, but for a reason that is worth trying to assess, play a prominent part in the market.

BETTING SHOPS

Modern-day *habitués* of licensed betting offices, as betting shops are officially known, enjoy an audio-visual coverage of racing that is highly sophisticated and extensive. It was not always thus, since only recently have betting shops rid themselves of the rather disreputable associations they acquired in the bad old days.

Indeed, before 1960 betting slips and accompanying sums of money would be furtively passed over the counters of public bars for later collection by the 'runner' of the local off-course cash bookmaker who would sometimes ply his trade from what often resembled an innocuous garden shed. From the early 1960s, however, such a ludicrous situation no longer obtained and bookmakers could apply to committees set up under the Betting and Gaming Act for permits to ply their trade and for licences to run betting offices.

BETTING SLANG

Much of the appeal of horse racing involves its special language, a large proportion of which is made up of slang. Thus, that extremely rare racecourse denizen, the regularly winning backer, is known as a 'wide sham', betting tax is painfully described as the

BETTING FORECAST: The popular television betting-guru John McCririck at the racecourse.

BETTING FORECAST

Basically, two attempts are made to predict the prices at which the runners in a race will be quoted in the betting market. One, sometimes known as a 'tissue' or 'tishy', is designed to assist bookmakers in the difficult task of determining the prices to display in their opening 'show'. It commonly consists of a twist card which indicates, by means of a cross, a dot and a capital C, the likely first and second favourites and a third runner about which it will be wise for the layers to be careful. If a bookmaker's tissue also suggests which particular prices should be featured in the opening 'show', it is probable these will represent poor value as far as the backer is concerned. It is worth remembering that the expert who advises bookmakers will appreciate their initial vulnerability and thus will recommend that they quote opening rates that are distinctly ungenerous, and which usually prove 'over-round' by well over 20 per cent.

The second type of betting forecast is, of course, that supplied by an acknowledged expert to a sporting daily or a national newspaper. The

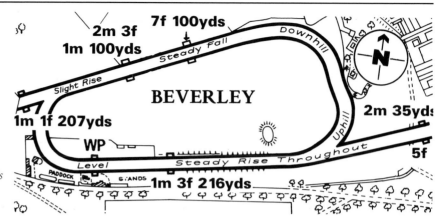

BEVERLEY: Plan of the course. The Kiplingcotes Derby, said to be the world's oldest horserace, was run in the region as early as 1519.

'battle' by bookmakers, and odds are referred to in such colourful rhyming slang terms as 'scruffy and dirty' (100-30).

The cypher-like way in which numbers are reversed (e.g. enin for nine and rouf for four) is one particularly interesting feature of the language of bookmakers that, since it is intended to be secret, necessarily includes much slang.

BETTING UP TO

By 'hedging' or 'bluffing' – that is, refusing bets – a bookmaker can control his liabilities. His overall aim may well be to bet up to a certain amount. This means that, should any one of the horses on which he has taken bets win the race, it will cause the same sum, or very nearly this, to be paid out of his satchel. If, for example, a bookmaker has laid £400 to £200 against a well-fancied contestant at 2-1, he may well decide to bet up to a £600 stake-out and so would do his level best to lay £450 to £150 against a 3-1 chance and £500 to £100 against a 5-1 shot. Then, should any of these market leaders win its race, the bookmaker will take the same sum of £600 from his satchel.

BET WELL

Expression used to describe the behaviour of a bookmaker who, in 'betting against' a large number of horses in a very open race like the Lincoln Handicap or Wokingham Stakes, works to a sizeable margin of 'over-round'. In order to 'bet well', a bookmaker must take business from a large number of clients who support many different horses. Open handicaps at prestigious meetings give rise to heavy wagering and are often won by outsiders on which bookmakers have such small liabilities that they are able to retain most of the 'field money' – the total sum that backers have staked with them.

BEVERLEY

Beverley Racecourse Co Ltd
19 North Bar
Within
Beverley HU17 8DB
Tel. (0482) 867488

How to get there:
From North: A1(M)
From South: M1
From East: A1035
From West: M62, A1079
By Rail: Beverley
By Air: Helicopter facilities

Beverley racecourse lies on common land known locally as the Westwood, a mile to the north west of the town on the A1079 from York, and can be conveniently reached via the M62. Special buses provide a connection between Beverley station, accessible from King's Cross, and the track itself which extends for around 1 mile and 3 furlongs and is stiff, egg-shaped and right-handed.

The 5-furlong course, which starts on a spur, features continuously rising ground. It also bends slightly to the right to join the round course after approximately 1 1/2 furlongs. This confers an appreciable advantage on high-drawn sprinters, especially if the stalls are positioned on the far side. Since horses racing over the minimum trip at Beverley face a straight yet very testing uphill run-in of around 2 1/2 furlongs, their claims should be considered only if no doubt whatsoever can be entertained about their stamina. Indeed, any first season performer that is successful over Beverley's minimum distance, is likely to stay 6 furlongs on far easier courses.

Some moderately undulating ground is to be found on the round course. For example, horses run downhill round the penultimate bend and then travel uphill before entering the finishing straight. Significantly, it is on entering this that jockeys with sufficient experience of this demanding track can poach a lead which they have then to sustain over the punishing 3 furlongs and more that remain. Understandably then, Beverley is not really a suitable course for the adoption of waiting tactics. It would seem to suit long-striding gallopers that are sufficiently adaptable to race against the collar around its well-banked but fairly sharp right-handed turns and have sufficient resolution and courage. Since such a large proportion of the 7 furlong 100 yard course, of the 1 mile 1 furlong and 207 yard race distance, of the 1 mile 3 furlong 216 yard course, and the stayers' distances of 2 miles 35 yards and 2 miles 3 furlongs involve right-hand bends, horses running on them which are highly drawn are distinctly favoured. Form students should give the claims of course and distance winners particular consideration.

An efficient watering system ensures that hard ground is seldom encountered; on the other hand, when the going at Beverley is soft it may pay to take a second look at any dour stayer that is known to be a confirmed 'mudlark'.

Those attending Beverley should be aware that such casual attire as jeans, T-shirts and shorts are not encouraged in the members' enclosure. An excellent view is afforded from here of Beverley Minster which, along with the racing, is clearly visible from well-positioned grandstands.

Not all racegoers realize that the Kiplingcotes Derby – held by some to be the world's oldest horse race – was run in the Beverley region as early as 1519.

❢ BICES
Slang for twos (2-1).

❢ BINS
Slang for binoculars. Most racegoers favour a pair that allows the colourful racecourse scene to appear seven times more prominently. One enterprising manufacturer has now produced a sophisticated pair that allows the punter to scan bookmakers' boards and then observe the race itself at long range.

BIZARRE MOMENTS
The frozen action of a past horse race that forms the subject matter for the question 'what happened next'

that is often posed to quiz game contestants testifies to the fact that racing can produce many bizarre moments. Indeed, an Irish runner once ran in and won a race at Cheltenham with a small hole in its leg filled with polyfilla, while Moifaa won the 1904 Grand National after being shipwrecked off the Irish coast.

Many readers are likely to remember that Devon Loch pancaked, after looking as if he had jumped an imagined obstacle on the run-in of the 1956 Grand National, and may recall that Caughoo, uncharitably, was believed by some to have hidden in the fog and thus completed only one circuit at Liverpool before winning the 1947 running of this often extraordinary race.

As for racing on the flat, on one bizarre occasion, Todd Sloane lay down in the paddock and refused to ride a particular runner, while a lady jockey once lost her breeches during a race. Then there was the time at Royal Ascot (of all places) when an inebriated and incontinent stable lad urinated into a flower bed in the parade ring.

An even more freakish moment in racing occurred when the horse the notorious swindler Horatio Bottomley had arranged to win a three-horse seller dropped dead in running, leaving the two other jockeys he had bribed at a complete loss as to what they should do! As for Bottomley, he was warned off!

Perhaps the most bizarre race so far contested was a three-horse affair for four-year-olds and upwards run at the Curragh. As was recalled in *Racing Review* in 1954, hot favourite St Dunstan was waiting at the start for the off when a racegoer studying the conditions of the race noted that he was a three-year-old and thus not qualified to run. Bell H, the only other runner worth serious consideration, was made a lightning favourite just before the off but the jockeys knew nothing of all this. The race started and Bell H when disputing the lead with St Dunstan, with Marble Hall a long way behind them, swerved, crashed into a stone bollard and broke his neck.

St Dunstan had been disqualified before the start, but when it came to awarding the race to the outsider of the party, Marble Hall, the same racegoer made another discovery – that the jockey was not qualified to ride. There being nobody left to whom to award the race, it was declared void!

BLEW UP
Explosive-sounding term used to denote that a horse was so out of condition when running in a race that it suddenly faded from serious contention.

BLINKERS: This shows the effect of blinkers on racehorses. This aid causes them to focus directly on the scene in front of them.

BLINKERS

Device that reduces the field of view available to a horse and which causes it to concentrate on its task of racing. Misleadingly regarded as the unmistakable badge of the rogue, the 'blinds', as they are sometimes known, can cause an animal that first wears them to improve on his previous form by as much as 2 stone! Blinkers can cause some horses to run rather too freely, but, in general, their use is beneficial in saving the wearer a number of unnecessary hidings or in helping it improve so much that it pleases its connections.

BLOWER/BLOWER ACTIVITY

Telephone arrangement whose principal purpose is to allow bookmakers in licensed betting offices who have become over-committed on certain runners to reduce their liabilities by 'sending down' sums of 'hedging' money to the course. In practice, a direct telephone line connects the racecourse to bookmakers. Leading layers like Ladbrokes make their own arrangements through which, on occasion, large sums from betting offices are channelled back to the course, not just for hedging purposes but to bolster up what in recent years has become an ailing 'live' racecourse market. Such is the size of sums that can be sent down to the course on the 'blower' that course trading can be disproportionately influenced by public activity in the many betting shops of a bookmaking multiple.

Blower activity or 'office support' (the term used to describe sums sent down to the course by heavy layers who make their own arrangements) can radically change some of the prices that make up the course market.

BLUE BET

The striking of a large, yet actually 'bogus' bet all too noisily and flamboyantly on a particular runner. Gullible members of the public, on witnessing this, may imagine that the investor involved is a confident professional, inspired stable commissioner or a particularly shrewd operator and may thus rush forward to follow his example, only to find that by the time they have placed their bets the odds in question have been trimmed to levels that are lower than those available elsewhere in the ring.

BLUE RIBAND OF THE TURF

It was apparently Disraeli who first so described the Derby, which to a greater extent in his time than in more modern times was responsible for the absence from Parliament of its more sporting Members.

BLUFF

Verb used to describe the action of a bookmaker who refuses a bet because he is over-committed on a runner it involves, or because he has already levelled his liabilities on all the contestants in a race and thus is unwilling to revise his calculations.

Interestingly, such was the support for the ill-fated Shergar, the eventual odds-on winner of the 1981 Epsom Derby that, just prior to his triumph, he apparently became impossible to back with some 'bluffing' bookmakers who, in common with many other shrewd judges, considered that this colt richly deserved to be the shortest-priced Derby favourite in recent years.

BOARDSLAYER/BOARDSMAN

Racecourse bookmaker who, in common with most of his colleagues, trades according to prices displayed on his betting boards. The most prominent and senior of such operators will be found in Tattersalls nearest the pitches of the rails bookmakers. The cries of boardsmen do much to give the betting ring its racy flavour.

BOARD PRICES

These refer to currently available odds that are displayed on the board of a racecourse bookmaker or on one wall of a licensed betting office. Those found in the latter location are the only odds available off-course that allow the backer to predict the precise outcome of the wager he contemplates. They are supposed to reflect on-course rates, but the delay that is inevitably involved in their compilation and transmission means that in practice they often prove a rather pale reflection. For example, the first show of odds to reach a licensed betting office seldom features the rates that shrewd 'early birds' amongst course backers will have snapped up and so 'killed off' by the time those who make a rapid, but hardly instantaneous, initial assessment of the state of the market for transmission off-course actually make their initial observations.

There is one further way in which the board prices displayed in betting shops can work against the best interests of the backer. On occasion they prevent him from calculating the precise and possibly significant extent to which an outsider's odds have contracted since the commencement of betting. This is because reports of early 'shows' that are heard in a betting shop are seldom so comprehensive as to include a price for each outsider. Instead they contain statements such as 10-1 bar that follow details of the prices currently available on-course about the more fancied contestants. This can mean that several horses whose names appear on betting-shop lists are left for fairly long periods without precise quotations. What is worse, the individual prices these animals belatedly do receive in quite late shows may not refer to the prices initially quoted, but may in fact reflect rates to which some of them may have quite significantly 'advanced' in the betting.

Finally, board prices in betting shops can obscure the disquieting fact that certain horses have failed to find support at the prices initially 'floated' by racecourse bookmakers. Sometimes the first off-course prices that are quoted on favourites and fancied horses may not in fact be the opening prices quoted by bookmakers brave enough to 'go up early' and open up the on-course market, but rather those rates to which book-makers have advanced in order to bring in business.

BOGEY

The one horse whose victory will oblige bookmakers to pay out the greatest sum from their satchels and so make the smallest conceivable profit on the race in question.

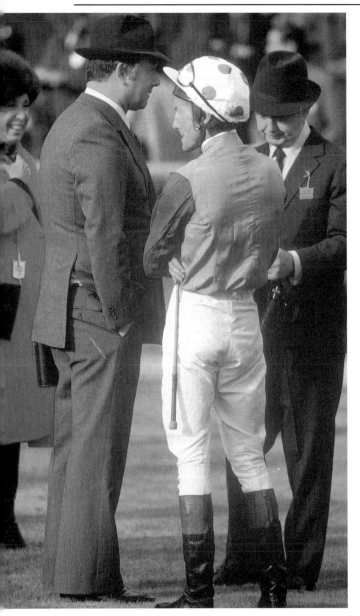

JOCKEY BOOKINGS: Racing's living legend, Lester Piggott, with Robert Sangster and the Irish master trainer Vincent O'Brien.

BOOKINGS, JOCKEY

The victory of the Irish runner Royal Academy in a million-dollar Breeders' Cup race in America in 1990 owed a good deal to the inspired riding of Lester Piggott whose performance reminded many of the day at Epsom in 1972 when only this peerless jockey's expertise was responsible for Roberto's narrow Derby victory over Rheingold.

On both these occasions – even though twenty-eight years separated them – Piggott had been specially booked by Irish master trainer Vincent O'Brien, a point which would not have escaped those wise enough to set store by the fact that when trainers expect to send out winners they often make phone calls to jockeys whose services they do not retain.

Fortunately, the *Racing Post* provides up-to-date information on which particular jockey/trainer combinations have proved propitious at particular meetings in the past in the form of wins to booking statistics. Since the financial consequences of supporting these combinations are also revealed, backers subscribing to the 'jockeys for trainers' approach are thoroughly catered for in this most useful feature.

BOOKMAKING

As Charles Sidney once succinctly explained, bookmaking involves a layer accepting bets from backers on his own terms or, in some cases, on negotiated ones. The layer who has accepted a number of bets on the runners in a race is said to have 'made a book' on this event.

Originally owners of horses bet against each other on the outcomes of match races and it was not until the end of the eighteenth century, when these particular contests had largely given way to others with more than two runners, that a man called Ogden first made a book in a manner that has been endlessly emulated in the past 200 years.

Ogden's many successors – course bookmakers, off-course operators and proprietors of licensed betting offices – have made their involvement in racing pay by:
(i) framing prices and balancing their liabilities so as to produce a degree of 'over-round' or percentage profit whichever horse wins
(ii) attracting heavy betting on big races (especially those which are handicaps and attract large fields)
(iii) offering short prices on favourites and long-looking ones on rank outsiders
(iv) accepting multiple bets
(v) limiting their liabilities on races in which form tends to work out well
(vi) hedging the bets of well-known 'sharps'
(vii) treating all trade betting i.e. that done by other bookmakers, with due respect.

Modern-day bookmaking chains such as Ladbrokes or William Hill know that any one of their individual licensed betting offices can have a losing day but also realize that any losses so occasioned are as nothing compared with the profits the majority of their outlets produce on any racing day. In fact, by not depending on

BOOKMAKING: An 1864 view of bookmakers going about their trade taking bets on the St Leger in Fleet Street.

one hen for their eggs, by framing odds designed to give them 'an edge' and by operating according to as many of the above principles as they can, such 'major players' in the world of bookmaking assure themselves of a profit whatever the results of the races on which they offer odds.

BOOKMAKERS' PROTECTION ASSOCIATION (BPA)

Sabian House
26-27 Cowcross Street
London EC1 6DQ
Tel: 071-253 0044

After the First World War protection rackets organized by racetrack gangs gave horseracing a very bad press. Violent scenes involving bids to establish a monopoly on the supply of lists of runners to racecourse book-makers were witnessed at Brighton's Kemptown course and later at Lewes. In 1921, since racecourse executives were unable to keep the razor gangs at bay,

bookmakers took it upon themselves to establish the Bookmakers' Protection Association, the members of which were quite prepared to pay for the services of personal bodyguards. The eventual arrest of the race gangs and the development of better racecourse security under the auspices of the Jockey Club meant that the BPA could concern itself with protecting the trading interests rather than the physical health of its members!

Today, a bookmaker's membership of the BPA can be regarded as a guarantee that, should he be involved in a dispute with a backer, the organization will act as a scrupulously fair arbitrator. Thus, what began as a necessary protection against strong-arm tactics has become an organization that demands high standards of professional practice from its members.

BOOKS ON RACING

The literature of the turf presents a rich chronicle of what John Welcome has tellingly described as 'racing's triumphs and tragedies, its fun and failures, its lasting allure and never-ending fascination'.

It is possible to savour these away from the racecourse if one immerses oneself in compilations of anecdotes, reminiscences, memoirs, autobiographies, and the plethora of other available literature on racing. In addition, however, racegoers anxious to sample such reading matter, as well as study prints, cartoons, cigarette cards and paintings, should make a beeline for one of the specialist racing book dealers whose stalls are now frequently found on racecourses.

! BOTTLE (OF GLUE)
Rhyming slang for two (2-1).

! BOTTLE AND A HALF
Rhyming slang for two and a half to one (5-2).

BOUGHT IN
Said of a runner retained by its connections after winning a selling or auction race. When these individuals pay large sums so as not to have to part with a winner, they may be thereby indicating that they have even 'greater expectations' regarding its future on the racecourse.

BRAVERY ON THE RACECOURSE
Whether it be in the form of a St John's Ambulance attendant shielding an injured jockey with her body (as happened on the landing side of a fence at Stratford races in 1987), the negotiation of the final two fences of the Grand National without being able to see them (this happened to Lord Mildmay on Cromwell in 1947) or the triumph over the near tragedy of his cancer that in 1981 led Bob Champion to Liverpool glory on Aldaniti, bravery is, in fact, a prerequisite for the daily participation in the sport of its equine and human performers.

There have been brave horses like Humorist who, despite a tubercular lung condition, lasted out most gamely to win the 1921 Derby and courageous jockeys like Jessica Charles-Jones and Jimmy Harris whose successful fight against injury and disablement from racing accidents has permitted them to train racehorses from their wheelchairs.

BREEDER
Person or entity that owns the dam when its foal is dropped.

BREEDING
The fact that an English or Irish Classic is seldom won by an animal without a Classic pedigree shows that in racing (despite the odd turn-up) breeding usually tells.

Even though, as Jack Leach once put it, 'an unfashionably bred horse occasionally flashes across the racing firmament' – Bachelor's Double, the winner of the 1909 Irish Derby, had a host of non-winning ancestors, and the pedigree of Irish Elegance, the 1918 July Cup winner, was not even registered in the General Stud Book – it is seldom that the progeny of such plebeian champions make good on the racecourse. Indeed, 'breed the best to the best and hope for the best' is a maxim that is as true today as when it was first coined. It certainly represented the approach of those who arranged for thirty-seven mares to be serviced by the Darley Arabian, the Byerley Turk and the Godolphin Arabian – three notable Arab stallions imported into England and Ireland between 1687 and 1729, so the racing stock indigenous to these countries could be 'beefed up' by their hardiness and stamina.

So much carefully controlled in-breeding has taken place in the 250 years since the importation of these founding fathers of the thoroughbred, that the many volumed Stud Book is thicker than Debretts and the modern-day thoroughbred breeding industry is so complex and extensive that both the *Sporting Life* and the *Racing Post* give it regular coverage and a weekly publication, *Pacemaker Update*, points to frequent correlations between blue equine blood and racecourse successes. However, the often disappointing performance of so many high-priced yearlings should serve as a constant reminder that, even with their computer-aided technology, breeders still don't really know how to make sure the characteristics they desire are transmitted to a foal. This is perhaps why pedigrees should not form the starting point in any process of winner finding.

BRIEFS
Term used by bookmakers to refer to the betting tickets they issue as receipts to their clients.

BRIGHTON

Brighton Racecourse
Brighton
Sussex BN2 2XZ
Tel. (0273) 682912

How to get there:
From North: A23
From East: A27
From West: A27
By Rail: Brighton
By Air: Shoreham Airport

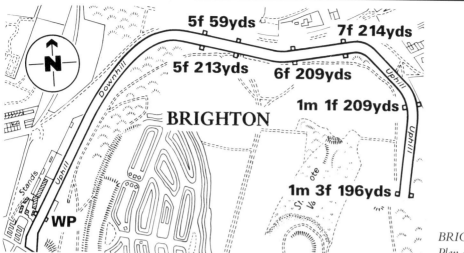

BRIGHTON:
Plan of the course.

The Brighton track is to be found some 400 feet above sea level at Kemptown, 2 miles due east of this famous coastal town which benefits greatly from its excellent rail link with London some 53 miles away. It seems appropriate that so cosmopolitan a town has such a distinctive, pleasantly informal and quite spectacularly sited racecourse which is an essentially three-sided affair running round a downland shoulder which reminds many of its patrons of a rather singular horseshoe. This broad course is so undulating it is often likened to a switchback. It extends for 1 1/2 miles and is rather reminiscent of the distinctive Epsom Derby course, since it bends quite sharply to the left and includes many severe gradients.

For these reasons, Brighton is a specialists' track. In fact, it tends to favour compact, well-made contestants that are sufficiently speedy to get quickly into their strides and make the running, and which are adaptable enough to remain sure-footed on its severely undulating terrain and fairly tight turns.

The 1 1/2-mile course actually extends for 1 mile 3 furlongs and 196 yards and soon features ground that ascends to a sharp left-hand bend. A further uphill stretch is followed by a second, sharper left-hand turn that leads into the track's V-shaped top section, along which races are staged over 1 mile, 7 furlongs and 214 yards, a slightly 'short' 6 furlongs and 5 furlongs and 59 yards.

Sprinters need to be 'shot' from the stalls so as not to run wide as thy plummet pell-mell round the course's final turn (whose negotiation can unbalance long-striding galloping types). This bend curves to the left, which gives jockeys who have previously mastered Brighton's topographical vicissitudes a valuable opportunity to poach an advantage of a length or two

which they then have to try to maintain throughout the subsequent straight, yet undulating, 3 1/2-furlong run-in. This continues to descend until the two-furlong marker and then rises in a manner that is sufficiently steep to find out any 'short' runners. The ground then levels out over the final 100 yards to the finish.

Naturally, it is widely believed that on such a sharp left-hand course, horses with a low draw are greatly favoured. This is the case, but only if they have the speed to 'fly' from the stalls and the resolution to maintain a relentless gallop to the finish. If the latter condition is not met, and those on the inside start to tire and 'roll' towards the rails, horses in the centre of the course are at an advantage. Lowly drawn runners enjoy an edge in sprints and races run over 1 mile 1 furlong 209 yards and 1 mile 3 furlongs 196 yards.

BRITISH RACING SCHOOL, THE

Snailwell Road
Newmarket
Suffolk
Tel: (0638) 665103

The training of stable staff to an appropriately high standard is the remit of this organization whose nine-week basic courses are taken by suitable sixteen- and seventeen-year-old school leavers whose weight is no more than 7 stone in the case of boys, 8 stone in the case of girls.

Thirty such pupils – either direct entrants or those sent on the recommendation of trainers – can be accommodated on the courses, five of which are offered each year. Some 85 per cent of the 150 or so trainees who take these basic courses pass them and go on to find employment in the racing industry, and around a quarter of such graduates eventually achieve the satisfaction of riding as apprentice jockeys. In 1990, for example, eighty had ridden in public with twenty-eight of them riding 114 winners. The needs of apprentices are also catered for at the school via an advanced course held once a year on which they are taught to improve their race and work riding.

All running costs are met by the school which is funded jointly by owners, trainers and the Levy Board. The current establishment, which replaced a similar operation at Goodwood, was officially opened by the Prince and Princess of Wales on 25 November 1988, and in its first seven years at Newmarket it trained 700 stable staff.

Under its director, Major M.F.T. Griffiths, its chairman, Mr Tim Holland-Martin, and such trustees as Her Majesty's Representative at Ascot, Sir Piers Bengough KCVO, OBE, trainer John Dunlop and former trainer Michael Pope MC, it seems odds-on that the school will continue to play a major part in the training of some of the most important personnel in racing.

BROOD MARE
Mare kept at stud for breeding purposes. Occasionally one has taken a break from this activity and won a race, despite carrying a foal!

BUMPER
National Hunt flat race for amateur riders and conditional jockeys, some of whom, in bumping round racecourses and sometimes into each other, no doubt first gave rise to this rather unfairly dismissive general term. A bumpers' contest is designed to give purpose-bred steeplechasers and hurdlers an introduction to racing.

BUMPING AND BORING
This occurs when, in failing to keep a straight line, a runner bumps into a rival or interferes with it by leaning on it, sometimes so seriously as to ruin its chances of winning.

BUST
Term used for a horse that has nothing left to give at the business end of its race.

BUSY
Said of a horse with which connections are rumoured to be trying to win.

BUY MONEY
To wager at odds-on.

BUZZER
Horse that is involved in a buzz of excited conversation; on the racecourse such a horse is likely to be well fancied or may be a springer in the market.

BUZZING
Said of a runner that is apparently raring to run for its life.

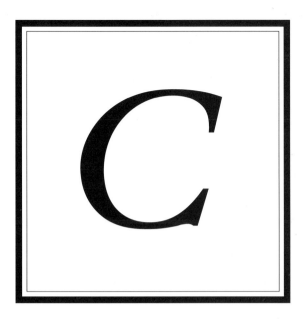

CAMERA PATROL

Even the most cursory study of the history of horseracing will reveal the extent of malpractice of which a number of horses and their riders have been guilty in their time. In the 'good old days', the latter would seek such unfair advantage at the starts of races that these were frequently delayed and repeated, while during running they might seek to disadvantage rival horses or gain an edge over them by knocking them out of contention, boxing them in or even, rumour has it, by hiding in fog so as to reduce the number of times a circuit had to be negotiated!

The modern-day movie camera that (from both head-on and the side) films the way races are run does much to preclude cheating, sharp practice or rule infringement on the part of either horses or jockeys that once may have made racing more colourful, but did so much to dim its reputation.

Nowadays it is not just ecstatic owners, proud trainers and delighted jockeys who decide to purchase camera patrol or other films of particular races, but also punters. Camera patrol films can be obtained from Racecourse Technical Services of 88 Bushey Road, Raynes Park, London SW20 0JH, whilst other video films of races can be supplied by Pics on Day Video of 52A South Street, Worthing, Sussex, who can provide a recording of any race run in Britain.

CANADIAN (Coronation, American, Australian or Super Yankee)

Wager of five selections that involves twenty-six bets – a 10p Canadian on horses ABCDE (costing £2.60) produces ten doubles: AB, AC, AD, AE, BC, BD, BE, CE and DE; ten trebles: ABC, ABD, ABE, ACD, ACE, ADE, BCD, BCE and CDE; and finally a five-timer, ABCDE!

CAPTAIN

Term used by a bookmaker to refer to his field book. The captain is designed to facilitate the complex task of clerking. It is divided into a number of main columns headed with the names of runners, each of which is divided into five subcolumns. Such a format is shown below:

Racing certainty				
900	700	200	200	1
1350	350	100	300	2
2150	600	200	500	3
2950	600	200	700	4
3150	150	50	750	5
3750	450	150	900	6
Z	V	W	X	Y

In column V the clerk enters the amount his 'Guv'nor' has laid to lose as the result of a particular wager, and in column W he shows the amount of the stake involved; thus these two adjacent columns are used to record individual bets, hypothetical examples of which, struck at 7-2 and 3-1, appear in the above example. In column X the clerk keeps a running total of all the stakes (or the field money) so far taken on the runner in question. The name or *nom de course,* (the racecourse pseudonym) of the backer involved (if he is known to the layer), as well as the number of the 'brief' or betting ticket issued as a receipt, are entered in column Y. Finally, a running total of the liabilities the layer has incurred on the runner in question is kept in column Z – which is the first entry in the field book so that the presence of any dangerously over-large liabilities can be immediately detected.

CAREER PRIZE MONEY

A useful statistic given in both the *Sporting Life* and the *Racing Post* that indicates the total sum won by a horse in its career. If the figure is divided by the number of victories a runner has previously registered, an approximate indication of its class will be provided.

CARLISLE

Carlisle Racecourse
Blackwell House
Blackwell
Carlisle CA2 4TS
Tel. (0228) 22504

How to get there:
From North: A74(M)
From South: M6
From East: A69
From West: A75
By Rail: Carlisle
By Air: Helicopter facilities

Carlisle racecourse, situated some 300 miles from London, can be reached after leaving junction 42 of the M6 or after a rather spectacular run from Euston to Carlisle station, a mile away from the course. It is a pear-shaped, quite severely undulating affair which on the flat runs right-handed for just over a mile and

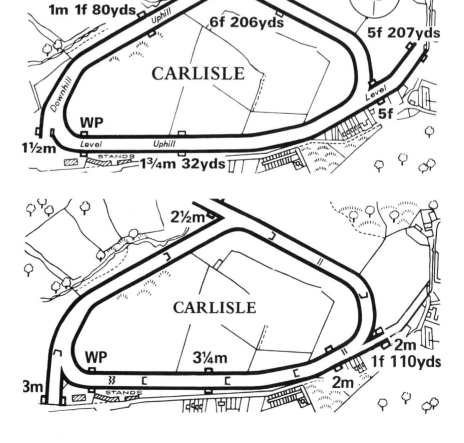

CARLISLE: Plans of the Flat course (top), and the National Hunt course (bottom).

a half. Runners over this particular distance start from a spur and first race right-handed and downhill for around 3 furlongs. Beyond the 1 mile 1 furlong 80 yard start they ascend as they approach the turn into the back straight which starts about a mile from home. Races over this distance are started from a second spur at the top of the track.

After racing on the level back straight, runners in non-sprint races swing fairly sharply to the right before encountering a finishing stretch that features a testing 3 1/2-furlong run-in whose steeply rising ground flattens out only 50 yards or so from the finish.

A third spur that is perhaps more of a turning chute allows races to be run over 5 furlongs 207 yards and 6 furlongs 206 yards. Horses tackling the latter trip find that it features two very different, if almost equal sections of track. The first of these is a bend that for around 1 1/2 furlongs turns to the right and then sweeps more gradually in this direction as it eventually joins the round course and enters the finishing straight; the second is the run-in itself which is fairly punishing, especially for two-year-olds whose claims should be seriously considered only if no doubts can be entertained about their stamina.

As for the draw, it is of little consequence in races run on the round course, but horses allotted high numbers in sprint races are understandably favoured on this right-hand track when the stalls are positioned on the far side. However, the Carlisle course has a clay subsoil so soft ground conditions sometimes prevail, and in such a case low-drawn sprinters may for once enjoy an advantage, especially if they happen to be long-striding gallopers.

Horses tend to run well on this rather lowly but demanding course if they are ridden by jockeys who can bring them with well-timed runs, if they can adapt to the fairly easy right-hand bends and longish stretches of undulating ground that are found on the round course and if they have the finishing speed to sprint to the line over the last 50 yards of level ground.

Carlisle's picturesque setting in some of Cumbria's delightful lakeland also appeals to the jumping fraternity. The National Hunt track extends for 13 furlongs and is on the stiff side, not because of its nine birch fences faced with gorse but because of the fact that severe undulations and an uphill finish of more than 250 yards mean that it takes some getting, especially when the going is heavy. This can often be the case in a wet winter in this never too dry part of the world.

❗ CARPET

Three to one (3-1). (NB: Double carpet is not 6-1 but 33-1.)

❗ CARPET AND A HALF

Seven to two (7-2).

CARTMEL

Cartmel Racecourse
Cartmel
Nr. Grange-over-Sands
Cumbria
Tel. (05395) 36340 (race days)

How to get there:
From North: M6
From South: M6
From East: A65
From West: A590
By Rail: Cark & Cartmel
By Air: Cark Airport; Helicopter facilities

CARTMEL: Plan of the course.

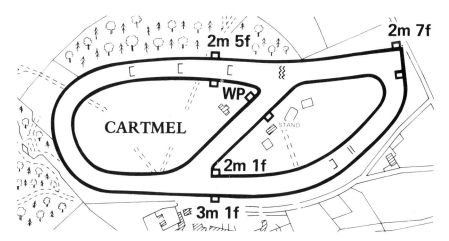

(Overleaf) An 1871 poster showing a mixed card at Cartmel races.

CARTMEL
RACES

WILL TAKE PLACE

ON WHIT-MONDAY, MAY 29TH, 1871,

AT 1 O'CLOCK IN THE AFTERNOON.

STEWARDS :—MAJOR AINSWORTH, H. H. PALAIRET, ESQ., AND CAPTAIN WESTROPP.

Judge.—MR. HOGGARTH.   Starter.—MR. RAWSTHORNE.   Clerk of the Scales.—MR. T. ORR.

HURDLE RACE.

A Sweepstakes of £1 10s. each, with £15 added. Heats about a mile and a quarter, over four flights of hurdles ; second horse to save his stake. Three-year-olds to carry 9 stone 8 lbs ; four, 10 stone 12 lbs ; five, 11 stones 7 lbs ; six, and aged, 11 stones 10 lbs. Mares and geldings allowed 3 lbs ; Thorough-breds 7 lbs extra. Three horses to start or the public money will not be given. The Winner to pay £1 to the race fund. This race is restricted to horses, the *bona fide* property, for six months, of gentlemen residing within a circuit of 30 miles.

THE HARTINGTON STAKE.

A Sweepstakes of £2 10s. each, with £20 added. Heats about a mile and a quarter, over four flights of hurdles ; second horse to save his stake. Weights, penalties, and allowances as in the Hurdle Race. Three horses to start or the public money will not be added. The Winner to pay £2 to the race fund.

THE INNKEEPERS' STAKE.

A Sweepstakes of £1 each, with £10 added. Heats about a mile and a quarter ; second horse to save his stake. Weights, penalties, and allowances as in the Hurdle Race, except the winner of the Hartington Stake, which will carry 7 lbs extra. Three to start or the public money will not be added. The winner to pay £1 to the race fund.

THE CONSOLATION STAKE,

FOR BEATEN HORSES. Entrance 10s., with £5 added. About a mile and a half. Weights, penalties, and allowances as in the Hurdle Race. Three to start or no race.

TROTTING MATCH.

Entrance 2s. 6d. Heats about a mile and a quarter. Three to start. Saddle for the winner, and bridle for the second horse.

Conditions.

To CLOSE and NAME on or before WEDNESDAY, MAY 24TH, 1871, to MR. JOHN BARBER, Cartmel, Grange, Lancashire. Entrance money to be paid at the time of entry. Colours of riders to be declared at the time of entry, under a penalty of 10s. All disputes to be settled by the Stewards, or whom they may appoint, and their decision to be final. ALL THESE RACES ARE CONFINED TO REGULAR AND BONA FIDE HUNTERS NOT IN ANY TRAINING STABLE.

A Hound Dog Trail in the morning, dogs to start at ten o'clock sharp. A Foot Race on the ground as usual.

The victory at Cartmel on August Bank Holiday Monday in 1974 of Gay Future, the horse that featured in an attempt by its Irish connections to sting British bookmakers to the tune of £300,000, really placed this delightful Lake District jumping track on the racing map and was the main reason it now enjoys sophisticated links with the outside world and its betting shops, such as telex and fax facilities as well as racecourse telephones, whose absence in 1974 was the reason Cartmel was chosen for the Gay Future Coup.

Travellers to Cartmel can take the M6 and should leave it when they see Barrow-in-Furness signposted on the A590. Once Lindale has been reached on the B5272 they will find the scenic last leg of the journey to the racecourse well signposted by the AA. Rail passengers should alight at Cark and Cartmel, which is 2 1/2 miles from the course, before taking a taxi, whilst any air travellers can use the Ponderosa landing strip at nearby Flookburgh that forms part of Morecambe Bay.

As befits a track that stages many holiday meetings, the accent is on enjoyment. Indeed, so pleasant are Cartmel's sadly rather infrequent race days that if the weather is sufficiently enticing crowds of 10-20,000 flock to this picturesque playground where all the fun of the fair can be savoured.

Perhaps the sheer popularity of the track is the reason why no daily members' badges can be obtained. The dry stone walls, the sight of a nearby priory and the trees and hills so beloved of the Lakeland poets remind some racegoers of many an Irish racecourse and give ballast to minds intent on winner finding – a process facilitated by the fact that pre-race parades are a popular course feature.

Six surprisingly stiff fences have to be negotiated at Cartmel, whose sharp circuit features slight undulations on the run-in which involves a chute in the middle of the track and can claim the distinction of being the longest in the country since it extends for around 800 yards. Before reaching the winning post the runners also have to cope with some slightly rising ground.

Cartmel's tight configuration and generally flat nature mean that it tends to suit nippy and handy types rather than dour long-striding stayers. Steeplechasers that have tackled 3 miles 1 furlong here have been spectacularly involved in three negotiations of a water jump on the back straight, while long-distance hurdlers are faced with the rather rare race distance of 2 miles 7 furlongs. All in all, Cartmel is a singular racecourse of considerable charm.

CATERING, RACECOURSE

This, the traditional butt of a good deal of sarcastic, humorous and rarely appreciative comment, has of late undergone a long overdue improvement. While olfactory distress is still occasioned by the presence, even in pricey enclosures, of hot dog and beefburger vendors, some of the sustenance on offer to racegoers is most enticing, whether this be the hot Irish whiskey on sale at Cheltenham or the truly *haute cuisine* available at Goodwood.

The truth is that warm beer, chipped cups and stale food as once dispensed in course bars and tea rooms by surly casual workers, is now something that only older racegoers will remember. Their younger counterparts, especially those with members' badges or who happen to be the guests of corporate entertainers (who often employ specialist caterers to provide refreshments at the races), now, even if at quite a price, expect and receive high standards of catering.

CATTERICK

Catterick Racecourse
Catterick Bridge
Richmond
North Yorkshire
Tel. (0748) 811478

How to get there:
From North: A1(M)
From South: A1(M)
From East: A66
From West: A66
By Rail: Darlington
By Air: Helicopter facilities

Seasoned racegoers are unlikely to cite Catterick Bridge as their favourite course, but it might well be so nominated by stable staff who appreciate the accommodation it offers them. Although some 244 miles from the capital and 5 miles south-east of picturesque Richmond, Catterick can be reached fairly conveniently by southern racegoers if they board Darlington-bound expresses at King's Cross. Many of those arriving by road take the A1 as the course lies to the east of this famous trunk road. The track itself, which is close to the major training centre of Middleham, is a sharp, cramped, oval circuit of 1 mile 198 yards. It favours front runners and short-striding contestants whose strong suit is speed rather than stamina. Indeed, horses can be 'kidded' into staying particular distances at Catterick

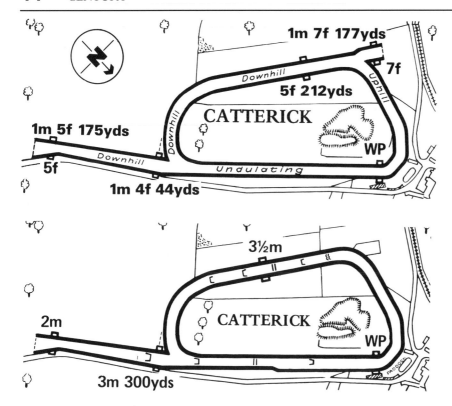

CATTERICK:
Plans of the Flat course
(top), and the National
Hunt course (bottom).

that they would not be capable of getting on more testing tracks, especially if their jockeys are experienced enough to give them a flying start and keep them in handy positions throughout their races. Understandably, many previous winners over this rather singular course relish being back on its tight turns and thus acquit themselves well.

On the round course races are run over 7 furlongs, 1 mile 4 furlongs 44 yards, 1 mile 5 furlongs 175 yards, and 1 mile 7 furlongs 177 yards over ground that in the finishing straight undulates mildly and includes an uphill section beyond the winning post. There are two spurs; one helps to provide a 7-furlong course on which runners initially race downhill, while the other allows 5-furlong sprints to be staged as well as contests over 1 mile 5 furlongs 175 yards. Runners in sprints run downhill for much of their journey.

Fast times are often set on the sprint course, the first 2 furlongs of which involve a fairly steep descent into a left-handed bend. The final 3 furlongs of the Catterick track make up a straight run-in which features slight undulations as it falls to the post and so increases the sprint course's suitability to short-running 'pigeon catchers'!

Fortunately, soft or heavy ground is rare because the Catterick course has a fast-draining gravel subsoil that guarantees good natural drainage.

Racegoers are guaranteed an excellent view of the action at Catterick – a point not lost on National Hunt enthusiasts who congregate here in fair numbers during the winter months. The jumping track takes little getting, as its eight fences are hardly formidable affairs. It tends to suit small, handy, front-running speedsters that can poach leads around its tight turns that are long enough to prevent their being pegged back on the short 240-yard run-in. Dour gallopers tend hardly to get going or to be able to stretch out and settle down on this rather workaday, although true spectator's track. Previous course and distance winners should receive the close attention of form students.

CENTURY

£100.

CHALK JOCKEY

Not until jockeys take rides on racecourses on a regular basis are boards, properly painted with their names, hoisted on the runners' and riders' board. Those not accorded this distinction may have to have their names 'chalked up' for display – a practice which has given rise to the rather disparaging description of 'chalk jockey'. In time a rider so designated may become a champion.

CHANGE OF STABLE

A change of environment is often as therapeutic and revitalizing for racehorses as it is for humans. For this reason, the *Racing Post* prints a daily list of horses that are about to race for new trainers for the first time. If study of the form book suggests such animals are in with a chance they may well be worthy of support, especially if contractions in their opening prices suggest their new connections may have some confidence in their chances.

CHAMPIONSHIP, APPRENTICES'

A glance back though the records of those apprentices adjudged to be champions in past racing seasons, through having ridden more winners than any of their rivals, will reveal that while some move on to become competent or top-flight jockeys, others fail to fulfil their early promise. Thus, the post-war list of champion apprentices contains names like Lester Piggott, successful in 1950 and 1951, and Pat Eddery, who triumphed some twenty years later, as well as those of young riders like D. Coates and R. Dicey (joint champions in 1968) who failed to make significant headway against fully fledged rivals.

CHAMPIONSHIP, BREEDERS'

This is won each season by the individual or stud that has bred horses that together have captured the most prize money. Post-war winners of this annual tussle have included the Aga Khan in 1947, 1948, 1949 and 1952, and his grandson, the present Aga, in 1981, while many individuals such as Marcel Boussac, Major L.B. Holliday and E.P. Taylor have become leading breeders for a particular flat racing season. This accolade is now increasingly bestowed on studs – latterly those like the Dalham Stud – that are associated with prominent Arab owners.

CHAMPIONSHIP, JOCKEYS'

Winning the annual Jockeys' Championship (that is awarded to the rider achieving the greatest number of winners in either a flat or National Hunt racing season) is such a spur to top riders that they sometimes make frantic efforts to win it.

In the 1981-82 season John Francome, after drawing level with the winning score of his injured rival, Peter Scudamore, magnanimously hung up his boots for the season so that the two of them could share the accolade of 'champion jockey'. Incredibly, this distinction was earned (with record scores achieved before rapid travel to racecourses was possible and when racing fixtures were far less frequent) by Sir Gordon Richards on no less than twenty-six occasions of which twelve were consecutive.

In fact, Sir Gordon (who is often credited with never having lost a race he should have won) would have been successful for twenty-three successive seasons had not a kick he received in May 1941 kept him on the sidelines for the rest of that season and so allowed 'head waiter' Harry Wragg to win his first and only Jockeys' Championship.

Fred Archer holds the record for the greatest number of successive Championship wins – thirteen from 1874 to 1886 – achieved before he so tragically shot himself at an early age. In modern times only Lester Piggott, with eight consecutive Championships from 1964 to 1971 and a total of eleven such victories, has come anywhere near the incredible achievements of Archer and Richards. The only contemporary jockey who looks likely to eclipse the achievements of the 'long fellow' is Pat Eddery, whose five consecutive victories from 1974 to 1977, further success in 1986 and four successive wins from 1988 to 1991 seem certain to be augmented given his considerable talent and the weight problems of his main rival, the stylish Steve Cauthen, champion jockey of 1984,1985 and 1987.

Some have contended that it would be fairer to award the Jockeys' Championship on a wins to (many) runs basis and interestingly, such a yardstick reveals that in a career curtailed at twenty-nine, Fred Archer won on 33.99 per cent of all his mounts, a figure well in excess of the 22.29 per cent achieved during his much longer career by Sir Gordon Richards and a slightly less impressive percentage so far recorded by the recently 'revitalized' Lester Piggott. Nevertheless, Piggott's record of having ridden more Classic winners than any other jockey seems destined to stand for many a season.

As for post-war champion jump jockeys, Peter Scudamore seems certain to establish a definite lead over John Francome, whose seven victories are rivalled only by the five of Tim Molony, four of them successive until the win of Fred Winter in the 1952-53 season gave this ex-paratrooper the first of his four National Hunt Jockeys' Championships.

CHAMPIONSHIP, OWNERS'

The annual tussle between the major payers of racing's bills is settled according to prize money won during a flat or National Hunt season. By the first half of this century, royal winners such as Edward VII (when Prince of Wales) in 1900 and George VI

OWNERS' CHAMPIONSHIP: Sheikh Mohammed, one of the most sucessful racehorse owners, flanked by his brothers.

in 1942 and aristocratic ones like Lord Derby in 1911, 1923, 1927, 1928, 1933, 1938 and 1945 had been displaced by affluent foreign ones such as H.H. Aga Khan and the French textile magnate, Marcel Boussac. While Her Majesty the Queen won the Championship twice in the 1950s (in 1954 and 1957), the 1960s saw many victories going to American millionaires such as Mr J. McShain (the constructor of the Pentagon) and Mrs H. Jackson. This trend continued in the 1970s when championships were won by Nijinsky's owner Mr Charles Englehard, by art connoisseur Mr Paul Mellon and by Mr Nelson Bunker Hunt (in 1973 and 1974).

By the 1980s the winning run of millionaire Robert Sangster (in 1982, 1983 and 1984) was brought to a halt by the victory of Sheikh Mohammed, the most successful of four members of Dubai's racehorse-owning royal family. The Sheikh's subsequent achievement in winning four more successive Owners' Championships (1986-89) brought him a record 'five timer'. Indeed, only the victory of his brother Hamdam al Maktoum in 1990 denied Sheikh Mohammed a sixth successive victory.

CHAMPIONSHIP, TRAINERS'

In its time the Trainers' Championship – awarded to the handler who wins more prize money than any other in a racing season – has been won by true masters of a craft that many who have graduated to it

from the saddle have seen as far more demanding and stressful than jockeyship.

In the twentieth century Alec Taylor (1862-1943) won his profession's highest annual accolade on twelve occasions, seven of them consecutive from 1917 to 1923. Taylor trained winners of 1003 British races that included twenty-one Classics. He was particularly successful in the Oaks in which his policy of bringing along his horses patently bore fruit in the form of eight victories.

Taylor won his last Championship in 1925 and for much of the following quarter of this century victory in this went either to Fred Darling, first successful in 1926 or to Frank Butters who initially achieved this distinction in 1927. The former, a ruthless but widely respected martinet who ran his stable with military precision and perfectionism, landed six Championships in all, three in succession (1940-42), and sent out nineteen Classic winners including seven in the Derby – Captain Cuttle (1922), Manna (1925), Coronach (1926), Cameronian (1931), Bois Roussel (1938), Pont l'Evêque (1940) and Owen Tudor (1941).

Frank Butters (1877-1957), was a remarkable trainer who in his very first season landed the Trainers' Championship as private handler to the 17th Earl of Derby at Stanley House in Newmarket. A truly charming, generous and imperturbable individual, Butters will always be associated with the Aga Khan for whom he trained nine Classic winners including the unbeaten Triple Crown winner Bahram, and Mahmoud, the record (hand-timed) winner of the 1936 Derby. In his career Butters won 1019 British races worth over £930,000.

For much of the third quarter of this century Noel Murless was the dominant flat-race trainer with nine victories, three of them successive from 1959 to 1961. Murless masterminded many major successes that included the Derby victories of Crepello (1957), St Paddy (1960) and Royal Palace (1967), as well as sixteen other Classic victories. He was knighted in June 1977.

The tender loving care that characterized Murless' training methods has also been a feature of the approach to racehorse handling of his daughter's former husband Henry Cecil who, since 1976, has himself carried off nine Trainers' Championships. Like his father-in-law Cecil has achieved particular success with fillies, notably with the 1985 Triple Crown winner Oh So Sharp. To date this mercurial Newmarket-based master trainer has managed to win the Derby twice with Slip Anchor (1985) and

Reference Point (1987), but during the 1980s he achieved even greater success in the St Leger by winning this Classic four times with Light Cavalry (1980), Oh So Sharp (1985), Reference Point (1987) and Michelozzo (1989).

In recent seasons the only trainers to offer any threat to Henry Cecil as champion trainer have been Michael Stoute, with three victories in 1981, 1986 and 1989, and Dick Hern who supplemented an early victory in 1972 by again prevailing as champion in 1980 and 1983. For the Aga Khan, Stoute sent out Shergar (1981) and Shahrastani (1986) to win the Derby and Aliysa to win the Oaks (and so supplement his success with Unite in 1987). However, Stoute suffered a serious blow when the detection of camphor in Aliysa's system led to her disqualification and so caused her disgruntled owner to transfer all his English-trained horses to France and Ireland.

Some consolation for Dick Hern's displacement as principal royal trainer came his way when Nashwan won the 1989 Derby, so supplementing his previous victories in the race with Troy ten years earlier and the gallant Henbit the following year.

As for the National Hunt Trainers' Championship since the war, former champion jump jockey and now retired handler Fred Winter won this on no fewer than eight occasions. His run of successive victories was ended by Peter Easterby.

Mention must be made of thrice-successful Michael Dickinson whose successive victories in the 1981-82, 1982-83 and 1983-84 Championships, and the fact that he trained the first five home in the 1983 Cheltenham Gold Cup, mean that he too will be forever remembered as another 'champion' National Hunt trainer.

In the late 1980s and early 1990s, the jumping Trainers' Championship has been farmed by Martin Pipe, a most professional and meticulous strategist who many feel will soon prove to be the most successful National Hunt trainer of all time.

Of course, winning the annual Championship is by no means the only yardstick of training excellence. One interesting measure of the versatility of racehorse handlers is success in sending out winners of both the Grand National and the Derby and in the twentieth century only two trainers, Willie Stephenson (who rode Niantic to dead heat with Medal in the 1927 Cambridgeshire) and Vincent O'Brien, have achieved this particularly demanding feat, the former with Oxo and Arctic Prince and the latter even more impressively via

three successive National winners (from 1953 to 1955) and seven Derby winners.

Another Irish trainer, the veterinary surgeon Dermot Weld, almost achieved another most difficult training feat – sending out the winners of the Spring Double of the Lincoln Handicap and the Grand National in the same year. This would have been the case had not Greasepaint been beaten into second place in the 1984 National, since only days earlier Weld's Saving Mercy, a 14-1 chance, had won the Lincoln.

CHEAP RING
Enclosure often found in the centre of a racecourse far away from the main ring in Tattersalls. Here are to be found the 'fiddlers' – bookmakers who accept small bets and hedge those that involve them in over-large liabilities. Their pitches are located in an area rather patronizingly regarded as 'outside' by Tattersalls' operators.

CHELTENHAM

Cheltenham Racecourse
Prestbury Park
Cheltenham
Glos GL50 4SH
Tel. (0242) 513014

How to get there:
From North: M5
From South: M5
From East: A40
From West: A40
By Rail: Cheltenham Lansdown
By Air: Helicopter facilities

If asked to name their particular version of paradise, many racegoers would place Cheltenham's spectacularly amphitheatrical racecourse that nestles under Cleeve Hill high on their shortlist. Indeed, many superlatives have been lavished on this track which in the minds of many is quite simply the best steeplechase course this side of creation and which is unquestionably Britain's leading National Hunt racecourse. As the Irish would say, there is 'crack' aplenty to savour here, especially at the three-day festival in March whose telling description as one of the 'rites of spring' testifies to its unparalleled splendour and firmly established place on the social calendar.

The course can be reached by rail from Paddington via Cheltenham Spa whence special buses provide a shuttle service to Prestbury Park.

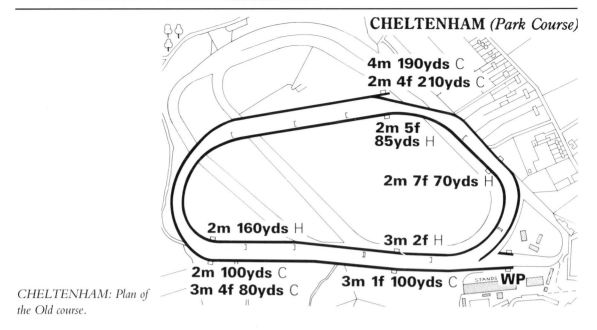

CHELTENHAM *(Park Course)*

4m 190yds C
2m 4f 210yds C

2m 5f 85yds H

2m 7f 70yds H

2m 160yds H

3m 2f H

2m 100yds C
3m 4f 80yds C

3m 1f 100yds C

WP

CHELTENHAM: Plan of the Old course.

Motorists travelling from the east on the A40 should approach via Winchcombe while those arriving by way of the M4 and M5 should leave at exits 15 and 4 respectively.

One measure of Cheltenham's excellence is that the majority of the jumping season's grade one contests are staged upon it on one or other of two left-handed, oval-shaped and very undulating courses. The first of these, the so-called 'Old' course on which the Cheltenham Gold Cup was staged until 1958, extends for 1 1/2 miles and involves nine formidable fences of which only one is found in the finishing straight. The Old course's final feature is a most testing uphill run-in of 350 yards that often proves the undoing of non-stayers lacking the courage and resolution that enabled the peerless Golden Miller to win five Gold Cups and so be commemorated by a splendid racecourse statue.

The slightly longer new circuit of ten fences follows the same route as its predecessor but leaves it after the seventh fence before again rejoining it after the tenth. On the new course the run-in is 237 yards long and a chute in the middle of the track allows hurdle races of 2 1/2 miles and chases of this distance as well as of 4 miles to be staged.

In the words of John Welcome, to act on this racecourse (since it provides a severe test of both its courage and conformation) 'a horse must be able to gallop, both up and downhill'. Cheltenham certainly takes some knowing and thus past course winners, partnered by jockeys with high 'wins to mounts' ratios, should receive special attention. Countless

races have been lost at Cheltenham at the third last fence, often by jockeys on heavily backed contenders driving their mounts too hard as they race downhill to this obstacle so that these crash out of contention or slip up on its landing side.

As was rather worryingly proved when a complete stranger to her, on two separate Gold Cup days, either shook the hand or kissed the cheek of the Queen Mother, Cheltenham is an open racecourse on which the movement of racegoers is hardly impeded by barriers based on segregations of class or status.

For many racing enthusiasts, the best way to begin the New Year is to attend Cheltenham's two-day fixture that always takes placeover that Bank Holiday. Another January fixture, staged at the end of the month, features three classy steeplechases that act as a curtain raiser to the festival meeting itself. The latter is so famous and popular that, as the course brochure puts it, the 'whole world of steeplechasing descends on the elegant Spa town of Cheltenham'. The nineteen races staged during the festival offer prize money well in excess of £1 million.

By tradition the meeting opens with the 2-mile Supreme Novices Hurdle, a highly competitive affair that always attracts a huge field. Six-year-olds and classy speedsters should receive serious consideration here. Also staged on the opening day is the Arkle Challenge Trophy, a 16-furlong 'chase for future champions run to commemorate the best post-war 'chaser to have won the Cheltenham Gold Cup and so deserve the tribute of a racecourse statue. Seven-year-olds are worth consideration in the Arkle, as understandably

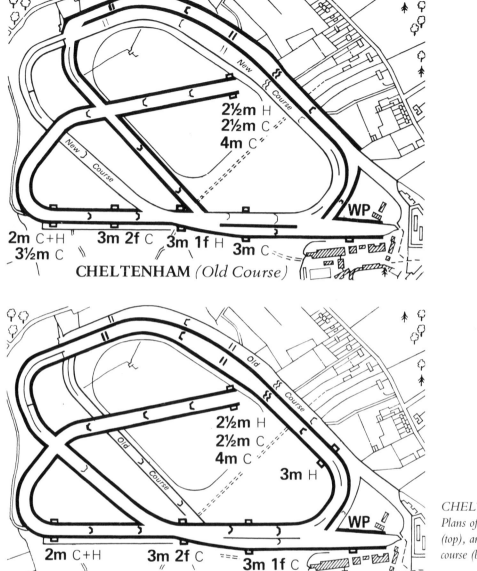

CHELTENHAM *(Old Course)*

2½m H
2½m C
4m C

WP

2m C+H   3m 2f C   3m 1f H   3m C
3½m C

CHELTENHAM *(New Course)*

2½m H
2½m C
4m C

3m H

WP

2m C+H   3m 2f C   3m 1f C

CHELTENHAM:
Plans of the New course
(top), and the Park
course (bottom).

---

are Irish contenders and, rather unexpectedly, horses that have previously fallen or unseated their riders.

The highlight of the festival's opening card is, of course, the Champion Hurdle and here it may pay backers to be mindful of the multiple successes of several horses that the past results of this matchless contest so prominently feature. Interestingly, Dawn Run was not one of these but, of course, achieved fame, and is commemorated in bronze, as the first horse to win both the Champion Hurdle (in 1984) and the Gold Cup two years later. Six-year-olds often acquit themselves well in the Champion Hurdle as do well-fancied horses, probably because

all the runners are well-exposed and experienced, take each other on at level weights and usually go round at a cracking pace.

The Stayers' Hurdle is also on occasion won by a past winner. Six-year-olds are again well worth considering in this, if little doubt can be entertained about their ability to last out this race's 25 furlongs. The Fulke Walwyn Kim Muir Challenge Cup Handicap Chase is an important 'prep' race for the Grand National. A 3-mile 'chase for amateur riders, this often falls to a nine-year-old, but seldom to an outright favourite.

The finale to the first day, the 2-mile Grand

Annual Challenge Cup is a 'chase in which eight-year-olds have previously run well and favourites again proved rather disappointing.

The second day starts with the 2 1/2-mile Sun Alliance Novices' Hurdle and here the possession of previous winning form – especially on the part of six-year-olds – is often a propitious pointer. Next comes Wednesday's centrepiece, the 2-mile Queen Mother Champion Chase, which commemorates steeplechasing's most sporting and popular owner. This is often won by a past winner and is not usually a race for outsiders. Eight-year-olds have an excellent record in this race which is one of the few run at the festival in which form tends to work out well. Gamblers often find the Coral Golden Final, a handicap hurdle of 3 miles 1 furlong, a far more attractive prospect. In this, proven stayers and course winners often go well. Recent winning form is almost a prerequisite and the records suggest that six-year-olds have often prevailed. The Sun Alliance Chase – the 'Novices' Gold Cup' – is a real test of stamina in which seven-year-olds should be respected. The 4-mile National Hunt Challenge Cup is an even more gruelling test of stamina and of the jockeyship of the amateur riders to which it is restricted. The possession of past winning form (particularly in Ireland) is often a recommendation in this marathon in which seven-year-olds have performed very creditably. The final race on the second day of the festival commemorates Lord Mildmay, undoubtedly the unluckiest jockey in Grand National history, and one of steeplechasing's most sporting owners prior to his tragic death by drowning. The Mildmay of Flete Challenge Cup is a handicap 'chase of 2 1/2 miles, in which favourites are frequently turned over. Eight-year-olds have a good record in this race and a previous course winner often goes in again.

The Triumph Hurdle, the curtain raiser to the festival's final day, is a race that is now attracting and has recently been won by runners from top flat racing stables. The Christies' Foxhunters' Chase – won in history-making style by Caroline Beasley on Eliogarty at the 1983 festival – always provides a splendid spectacle as, of course, does the highlight of the entire festival, the Gold Cup. This, the blue riband and championship of steeplechasing, is a race in which, despite the odd upset (like Norton's Coin at 100-1 in 1990) form tends to work out well. Past winners sometimes register repeat victories in this race in which seven-and eight-year-olds have previously run particularly well.

Also staged on the festival's final day is the Ritz Club National Hunt Handicap Chase. This 3-mile 1-furlong affair is often captured by an eight-year-old and sometimes by a previous winner. The festival's next race is the Cathcart Challenge Cup, a 2 1/2-mile 'chase in which course and distance winners should be respected and older runners not discounted.

The last race run on the final day in which 'getting out' is often a difficult undertaking, is the 2-mile County Handicap Hurdle; five-year-olds often figure prominently, especially if carrying less than 11 stones.

While on three magical days in March championship races are staged for each type of horse involved in National Hunt racing – there is now even a festival bumper – on thirteen other racing days, many other fine races are also staged at Prestbury. The most prestigious, the Mackeson Gold Cup, is a handicap steeplechase of 2 1/2 miles that takes place early in November. This is often landed by a seven- or an eight-year-old.

On one of two other so-called 'premier days' – a Saturday in early December – the A.F. Budge Gold Cup Handicap Chase is run over the Mackeson distance. In its time this has been won by such classy 'chasers as Pendil and Flyingbolt and is a race in which eight-year-olds should be respected.

The Cheltenham season always closes with an idyllic fixture that to steeplechasing's *cognoscenti* is pure magic – the hunters' meeting that always takes place on the first Wednesday evening in May and attracts a most colourful cross-section of English sporting society from the shires. One race on this card, the 4-mile Hunt Steeplechase, often provides a thrilling finish.

In the autumn of 1991 Cheltenham's far-sighted management opened a new Park course by linking the 2 1/2-mile chute with the round course. Thus horses can now race at Cheltenham on a less undulating and testing track.

CHEPSTOW

Chepstow Racecourse
Chepstow NP6 5YH
Tel. (0291) 622260

How to get there:
From North: M5
From South: M5
From East: M4
From West: M4
By Rail: Chepstow
By Air: Helicopter facilities

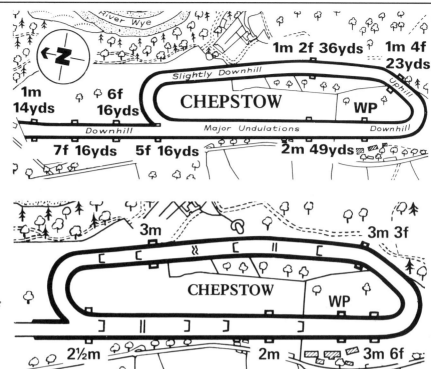

CHEPSTOW: Plans of the Flat course (top), and the National Hunt course (bottom). Chepstow is the most recently constructed racecourse in Britain.

Located 135 miles from London, Chepstow racecourse, since it was established in 1926, is the most recently constructed of British racecourses and offers a large number of fixtures. It forms part of Piercefield Park, a most picturesque stretch of undulating and wooded parkland that can be reached after a two- to three-minute drive northwards from the Welsh side of the Severn Bridge. Its position two miles away from the M4 makes it particularly suitable for racegoers who leave the motorway at junction 22. Chepstow can also be reached by train from Paddington.

The track used for flat racing is a left-handed oval which, although it has an extensive circumference of almost two miles, does not suit every strong, long-striding galloper, since its pronounced undulations include some quite severe and tricky gradients. However, a horse that has courage and sufficient stamina should not be unduly inconvenienced, especially if it is sufficiently adaptable to avoid becoming unbalanced as it negotiates the switchbacks and the sharp left-hand turns on the round course.

The straight 1-mile 14-yard course (along which starting stalls are also placed at 7, 6 and 5 furlongs) initially runs downhill, joins the round course just after 3 furlongs and then begins to undulate. It rises sharply for two furlongs or so and then further major undulations are encountered before the finishing line is reached.

Most judges maintain that on the straight course, high-drawn horses have the edge especially when the stalls are positioned on the stands side and the going is anything but soft or heavy, while on the round course (as is to be expected on a left-hand track) those drawn low nearest the inside rail are favoured in races over 10 furlongs 36 yards, 12 furlongs 23 yards and 2 miles 49 yards.

Since the subsoil of the straight course consists of clay, heavy going can sometimes chop the speed of sprinters and milers and put their stamina fully on trial.

Chepstow's near five-furlong run-in gives patient jockeys riding in the longer races the opportunity to come gradually from behind and wear down the opposition.

The flat course, initially dubbed the 'Goodwood of the West', has not enjoyed sufficient popularity to deserve this description. This has perhaps been because its inaccessibility prior to the building of the Severn Bridge meant that it tended only to attract moderate flat race performers. In many minds, Chepstow is chiefly remembered as the track on which Sir Gordon Richards went through the card on 4 October 1933 and then on the following day won the first five races. This remarkable achievement is commemorated by the staging of the Sir Gordon Richards Handicap at an evening meeting in late July.

The former Welsh Derby, now open to horses aged more than three and named the Welsh Brewers' Premier Stakes, is the most prestigious race run on the flat at Piercefield Park, but this seldom attracts a top-class or sizeable field when it is staged each July.

As it happens, Chepstow is far more popular as a National Hunt course (of, in essence, two long straights, two tight turns and 11 fences) than as a venue for flat racing. Indeed, the sight of steeplechasers (especially those contesting the 3-mile 6-furlong Welsh Grand National in late December) against the course's sylvan backcloth, is both stirring and picturesque. The Welsh National frequently falls to a far from over-burdened, but improving, seven-year-old staying 'chaser and in its time has often been farmed by one or two particular trainers. In the not so prestigious Welsh Champion Hurdle, run over 2 miles in early April, attention should be paid to well-fancied five-year-olds.

CHESTER

Chester Racecourse
Chester CH1 2LY
Tel. (0244) 323170

How to get there:
From North: M6
From South: M6
From East: A51
From West: A51
By Rail: Chester General
By Air: Helicopter facilities

The ancient racecourse of Chester, on which racing took place for a silver bell as early as 1541, is situated close to the River Dee and is bounded by part of a Roman city wall; it is three-quarters of a mile from Chester's mainline station which can be conveniently

CHESTER: This old engraving of Chester races clearly shows the course bordered on one side by the River Dee, and on the other by the Roman walls of the town of Chester; it is partly due to these features that it is the smallest and tightest racecourse in Britain.

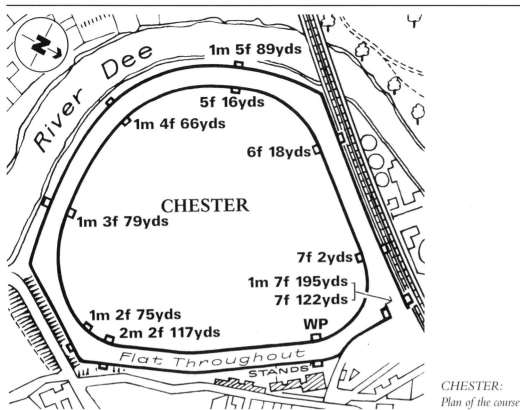

CHESTER:
Plan of the course.

reached from Euston some 180 miles or so away. It is the smallest and tightest track in Britain. Indeed, in constituting what is almost a continuous and extremely sharp left-handed turn, it reminds many racegoers of a saucer or a site for chariot racing.

The track itself, which is flat throughout, extends for a mere mile and around 60 yards and thus does not give large, galloping types a chance to get into their long strides. Indeed, such animals often become unbalanced or run wide round Chester's sharp left-handed bends. These naturally tend to be appreciated by small or medium-sized horses that are sharp-actioned and sufficiently speedy to fly from the stalls. Front runners and horses that like to lie up with the leaders often do well on this singular track as, understandably, do previous course winners or 'Chester specialists'.

The longest races on the 'Roodeye', and the only ones in which it is really possible to ride a waiting race, are staged over what can amount to a rather gruelling 2 miles 2 furlongs 117 yards in the course of which the runners pass the stands on three separate occasions! A famous event run over this marathon distance is the Chester Cup, first staged in 1824, which, while not a Group race, invariably provides a thrilling spectacle and, since it is run at such a

blistering pace throughout, makes considerable demands on stamina. The Cup is always a major betting race at the prestigious three-day May meeting and in the nineteenth century ranked second only to the Derby in the ante-post wagering it attracted.

Another prestigious race is the Group Three Chester Vase run over 1 mile 4 furlongs 66 yards. First run in 1907, this event, since it tests the adaptability of Epsom hopefuls, is rightly regarded as a Derby trial. Indeed, in 1981 Shergar, like Papyrus (1923), Hyperion (1933), Windsor Lad (1934) and Henbit (1980), went on to win the turf's premier classic after victory in 'The Vase'. Chester's other Group race, the Ormonde Stakes, is named after the unbeaten Triple Crown winner of 1886. A weight-for-age contest of 1 mile 5 furlongs 89 yards, it frequently falls to a four-year-old – sometimes to one as illustrious as Derby winner Teenoso, who captured it in 1984.

It has been estimated that the services of a jockey who can get his mount to put its near fore forward and go the 'shortest way round' are equivalent to a 7 lbs pull in the weights. Above all, jockeys must be in contention as they round the final bend at Chester if their mounts are to stand any chance of reaching the frame, since the run-in of only 230 yards – the shortest of any British track – is insufficient for the making of any really significant late headway.

A low draw in sprint events, especially when the stalls are placed near the inside rail, is worth several pounds, and can sometimes prove the decisive factor.

The going is often good on this delightful Cheshire course where races are usually truly run. Chester, above all, provides spectacular viewing since its tightness and walled-in nature gives the impression that racehorses run faster here than anywhere else in Britain. That minority of runners known to appreciate its configuration may again do so!

CHILDREN AND HORSE RACING

Whilst no one would advocate the admission of minors into Britain's now far more reputable betting shops, under certain conditions horse racing is a sport that children can thoroughly enjoy.

The pleasures of the sport can be most fully savoured by the under-sixteens if their parents (at no cost incidentally) take them into enclosures in the middle of racecourses. Topographically, many tracks are distinguished by central mounds from which all the running can be seen. Being in the centre of a racecourse has a further advantage, in that both parents and children feel they are actually in the country.

If racing is, as Phil Bull once described it, a 'great triviality', then it should appeal to children as an activity in which they can participate with their parents. Fortunately, racecourse executives are now doing a great deal to make racing appeal to families by admitting children at no charge and providing enticing facilities. On offer at Ascot, for example, is a playground in the Silver Ring supervised by trained nurses which contains swings, roundabouts, a sandpit and other attractions and, during winter, there is an indoor playroom.

❢ CHING AND A HALF

Slang for eleven to two (11-2).

C OF E

A reverential reference, replete with irony, to the Customs and Excise Authorities – the recipients of the betting duties that bookmakers are obliged to pay.

CIGARETTE CARDS

In the half century or so between 1888 and 1939 more than thirty manufacturers of cigarette cards on four continents produced in excess of seventy different sets, each of which dealt with a particular aspect of horse racing. Thus the sport's pictorial possibilites were plumbed and opportunities given for the assembly of some attractive collections.

An early set to appear in Britain was put out in 1890 by the American firm of Kinney Brothers while the first UK-produced 48-card set was issued nine years later by Kinnear Limited.

In time, Ogdens became the best-known producer of racing-theme cards and in the 1900s one of their most popular sets was entitled 'Owners' Racing Colours and Jockeys'.

Understandably, famous jockeys and horses have often featured as subjects, and many such cards are now eminently collectable and, in some cases, quite valuable. For example, an owners and jockeys set put out by Salmon and Gluckstein at the turn of the century has changed hands for in excess of £500.

Several sets present information that would benefit modern-day racegoers. For example, one issued in 1926 by W. Sandorides entitled 'Famous Racecourses' was specifically designed to allow the backer to assess the suitability of these to future runners upon them, while yet another series explained the function of key personnel and terminology in racing.

CLAIMED

Expression used of a runner acquired on payment of a certain sum stipulated in the conditions of a race following its running, or, alternatively, of a jockey held to the obligations of his or her retainer by the trainer or owner who has first claim on his or her services.

CLAIMER

Description of any apprentice, amateur or conditional jockey whose lack of past success brings with it an entitlement to ride at 3, 5 or 7 lbs below the weight allotted to his or her mount.

CLAIMING RACE

Contest in which any runner may be claimed for a certain sum as stipulated in the conditions governing its running.

CLASSICS, THE

So influential as tests of the three-year-old thorough-bred are the 2000 and 1000 Guineas (both run over 1 mile at Newmarket in the Spring), the Derby and Oaks, run over 12 furlongs 10 yards at Epsom in early June and the Doncaster St Leger, run over 1 mile 6 furlongs 132 yards at Doncaster in September,

THE CLASSICS: *This print from 1837 by James Pollard, shows racing in one of the seasons five Classics – the St Leger – which is run at Doncaster in September.*

that they have many prestigious equivalents worldwide. For example, in Italy both the Oaks d'Italia and Derby Italiano are staged in midsummer.

Such is the prestige of racing in England and Ireland that the winners of these two countries' five Classics vastly enrich their owners and become immensely valuable stallions and brood mares when retired from racing.

CLASS IN RACEHORSES

Over the years several attempts have been made to assess class in the racehorse. Significantly, most watch holders concede that because standard times for a racecourse are obviously dependent upon the ability levels of the horses that typically run on it, a speedy performer will find it far easier to run a race in a time below par on a low-grade course such as Hamilton Park, than on a top-class course such as Ascot, Newmarket or York.

One worthy attempt to define class is that by Kenneth Robertson (author of *A Background to Horse Racing)*: 'class above all pre-supposes the ability to quicken the pace at any stage in a race.'

Other attempts to evaluate and express class involve the sums of prize money contestants have previously netted, or the averages of those provided by the executives at particular racecourses. For the former approach, one simply divides a horse's total earnings or, perhaps rather more relevantly, those achieved in the current season, by the number of victories it has registered during the relevant period. Fortunately, precise data on prize money are given daily in the *Sporting Life* and the *Racing Post*.

Such a calculation also enables comparisons to be made with other monetary evaluations of class in relation to racecourses which involve calculating the average value of races staged on them. In this connection the most thorough compiler of turf statistics, John Whitley, the proprietor of Racing Research and Computer Racing Form of Halifax, has applied data to the *Ladbroke Companion to Flat Racing*. His figures provide assessments of the average ability of horses running on Britain's many racecourses, and also show the averages of the various sums of prize money the executives of these courses make available to contestants. Correlations between these two sets of figures suggest that prize money does seem to offer a useful general guide to class. As is to be expected, highly-rated horses compete for decent prize money, while lacklustre performers race for poor purses.

The figures featured in Whitley's two sets of data seem to confirm much of the thinking behind the thoroughly businesslike approach to making money from racing of former owner Sir David Robinson who would grade both horses and racecourses into three colours: red for outstanding, blue for good and green for fair. Horses and tracks would be matched accordingly, the strategy only being modified if a 'red' horse, say, was aimed at a big race at a 'green' meeting.

Such flexibility is important and should prevent too many inappropriate general judgements being made about the class of racecourses according to the prize money their executives make available. For example, Epsom's average prize money is obviously inflated by the inclusion in calculations of the vast sums on offer in its two Classics. Another anomaly that threatens the correlation between the ability of racehorses and the grades of tracks they race on is the fact that during their first season several potentially high-class horses race at rather lowly tracks such as Yarmouth and Salisbury, and thus compete for sums that hardly reflect their probable ability, or compare with purses they will seek to capture later in their careers.

CLERK OF THE COURSE

This course official has one of the most demanding jobs in racing. He or she is appointed by a racecourse's executive (or by several of these as in Ireland) and is paid by this body, but also needs a Jockey Club licence.

The clerk has to devise an annual programme of meetings and then determine its constituent races well in advance of their staging. To this busy official is also entrusted responsibility for the general arrangements involved in staging a race meeting in a proper manner. These include assuring the track is in a condition fit for racing, checking that distances are accurate and courses properly marked, making sure the runners are paraded and saddled, providing each of them with a clearly numbered cloth and preventing any disqualified person from being associated with any runner.

Naturally, the clerk's responsibilities extend to include the provision of a humane killer for the putting down of seriously injured racehorses, as well as such matters as the printing of racecards.

One of the main tasks of the modern-day clerk is to act as public relations officer and to attract as much sponsorship of races as is possible.

On racedays the clerk co-ordinates the work of other racecourse officials – the stewards, starter, clerk of the scales and groundsmen.

Perhaps the most difficult task that may face a clerk is whether to allow racing to take place in inclement weather.

CLERK OF THE SCALES

One of the most important announcements on the racecourse and certainly among the most eagerly awaited (as, before it is made, unless they are incautious, bookmakers decline to pay out on the result of a race) is the news that the runners have 'weighed-in'. It is made via the clerk of the scales who is licensed by the Jockey Club and paid by them.

This particular official who has to provide the starter with a list of the riders, runners and (if appropriate) the latters' position in the draw, and have this information displayed on boards hoisted high on the course, is kept so busy weighing jockeys in and out that he is seldom able to see a race.

CLONMEL

Powerstown Park
CIonmel
Co. Tipperary
Southern Ireland
Tel. (052) 22611

How to get there:
From North: N8, R689
From South: N8, R671
From East: N24
From West: N24
By Rail: Clonmel
By Air: Light Aircraft facilities

Clonmel is a tight course extending for only 10 furlongs and is used for both flat and jump racing. The most prominent configurational feature of the circuit is its hill whose descent can unsettle some ungainly performers. The draw would appear to have little bearing on results of races run at Clonmel, the most important of which are the Captain Christy Novices Chase, the Seamus Mulvaney Chase and the Tipperary Cup.

Writing of Clonmel, which is Tipperary's chief town, Benedict Kiely once commented that ideally he would approach it by having himself 'delivered by helicopter at four hours before noon on a sunny morning'. Racegoers who wish to follow this excellent advice should make for the 400-yard

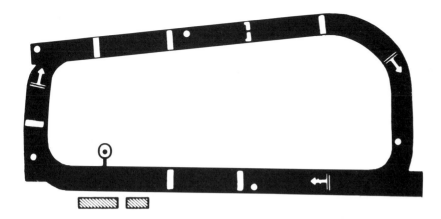

CLONMEL:
Plan of the course.

airstrip, after first obtaining permission by phoning (052) 22611. The course is set in some beautiful parkland that befits Clonmel's original meaning 'the meadow of honey'. The course can be reached on the R672 and R671 by those travelling north from Dungarvan. Racegoers travelling from Waterford should take the N24, those coming from Kilkenny the N76, and travellers from Cork should take the N8 and join the N24.

Clonmel's local paper has been described as the voice of a land that takes its horses (and dogs and hunting) seriously. The fact that this town has a racecourse is in part due to its close association with the Tipperary foxhounds.

CLOTHING, RACING

Racing has long been associated with dressing up, or in, particular clothes. Interestingly,the racecourse is one of the few places where the hat-wearing habit of pre-motoring days persists. Ideally dress should be both functional and stylish. With regard to Cheltenham, Mr Edward Gillespie, its managing director, recommends that those attending the March festival sport seasonal headgear, footwear and warm clothing, while at Ascot Sir Piers Bengough, Her Majesty's representative, is ultimately responsible via his gatemen for ensuring that the strict dress code of the royal enclosure remains unbreached. Barbours and Burberrys as well as *haute couture* and the magnificent creations of milliners all make up the sartorial side of the racecourse scene.

At a surprising number of courses no particular form of dress is stipulated. However, at Pontefract, Beverley, Sandown and Cheltenham shorts and T-shirts are discouraged in the members' enclosure. At Chepstow, Stratford and York, jackets and ties are *de rigueur* in the members', whilst at Epsom on Derby day, morning dress becomes obligatory in the club enclosure where celebrities rub rather stylish shoulders with regular racegoers.

The Haydock management insists that trousers and shirts be worn in the members', but does not insist on ties, while Newbury's administrators stipulate that men must wear a shirt and tie. Polo necks can be worn as an alternative to collars and ties at Ascot's winter jumping fixtures. Bare chests are expressly banned in Newmarket's Tattersalls and in the Members at Windsor. Jeans and T-shirts are not to be worn in Tattersalls at Worcester. Without being very specific, Towcester's management disallow anything 'too informal' in its most expensive enclosure.

CLUB MEMBERSHIP

This way of attending a course's fixtures throughout the year and of gaining admission to its best enclosures and facilities is available on annual subscription. Membership often brings such further benefits as free racecards, car parking privileges and participation in social events.

Joint memberships for married couples are available and sometimes members are entitled to take in a day or two's racing at other tracks.

CLUBS, RACING

Racing clubs, the majority of which are regional, organize visits to racecourses, stables and studs, hold a variety of social functions and offer opportunities to listen to and meet the sport's celebrities. Some even sponsor races, allow members to participate in racehorse-owning syndicates and have their own private facilities on a racecourse.

The Federation of British Racing Clubs of 4 Bosley Crescent, Wallingford, Oxon. (Tel. (0491) 32399) represents:

The North-West Racing Club (0200) 22428
The Yorkshire Racing Club (0709) 524871
The Scottish Racing Club (041) 3570331
The West Midlands Racing Club (021) 4261877
The East Midlands Racing Club (0602) 281624
The Cheltenham and Three Counties Racing Club
    (0242) 527762
The West Berkshire Racing Club (0491) 32399
The London Racing Club (071) 393 2312

❗ COCK A DEAF 'UN

Slang for 'refuse to listen'.

❗ COCK (LE)

Slang for ten (10-1).

CO-FAVOURITE

Horse which shares its position at the head of the market with at least one other horse.

COLOURS OF RACEHORSES

The differentiations between racehorses by colour is crucial and is indicated on racecards. Such information is essential for identification and description.

Racehorses are designated (according to the colour of the hair that thickly covers their outer skins) as brown (br), bay (b), chestnut (ch), black (bl), grey (gr) or roan (ro). There are several different shades of bay, chestnut and grey.

Bays have a brown coat, black mane and black tail and distinctions are sometimes made between a bright bay (which often has a black dorsal stripe), a mahogany bay, a red bay and a brown one. Bays may have white markings and usually have black legs; brown horses are black with brown muzzles and brown rims to their nostrils. Chestnuts have golden yellow to dark reddish-brown coats and their manes and tails are of a similar hue or are lighter.

Horses that are completely black, save for white markings, are simply described as black, while bays, chestnuts and blacks are called roans when odd white hairs are distributed throughout their coats.

Greys only gradually become so and, like the celebrated steeplechaser Desert Orchid, they usually take on a whitish hue over the age of ten. If dark patches are found throughout the coat, its owner can be described as a 'dapple grey'.

COLOURS, RACING

A vast number of racing colours are registered with Weatherbys. In the eighteenth century, racing colours were rarely sported and, if worn at all, involved plain colours — red, yellow, green and blue. Indeed, at times the difficulty of judging finishes was compounded by the fact that in the same race there could be three or four riders in red jackets. If two of these fought out a finish surrounded by their mounted supporters, the judge's nightmare can only be imagined.

It was not until 1811 that a section of the Racing Calendar was given over to colours worn by riders. Racing silks, or more accurately jerseys when worn by National Hunt jockeys, represent one of the brighter and more colourful parts of the racing scene. Some date from the sport's early days at Newmarket in 1762.

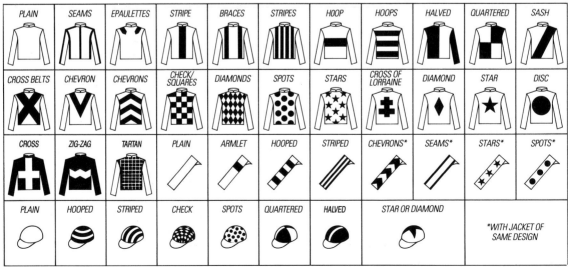

COLOURS OF RACING: This table shows the permitted designs some of which date from the early days at Newmarket in 1762.

Many colours in the spectrum are permissible as long as the chosen combination and patterns – hoops, stripes, polka dots, crosses and zig-zags being the most common – are not already registered under the name of a rival owner.

The diagram (below left) is a pictorial indication of permissible designs for jockeys' jackets, sleeves and caps.

COLOURS, WELL-KNOWN CONTEMPORARY

The best known of these for both flat and National Hunt racing are depicted in some annual guides and on occasion in racing dailies.

COLT

Ungelded male horse of four years or under.

COME ON (FOR RACE)

Said of a contestant whose most recent performance on the racecourse has been such as to suggest that it will strip fitter and run even more impressively next time out.

COME ON MY SON!

This traditional Cockney exhortation to a runner to give of its best and win its race is often heard in grandstands, especially in the South of England.

COMING RIGHT

Said of a runner whose condition and recent gallops or racecourse form suggest it is about to do itself full justice. If speed figures relating to its recent runs reveal an improvement or the horse shows distinct signs of physical well-being in the paddock, it may well be 'coming right'.

COMMENTARIES AND COMMENTATORS

Whether heard at racecourses, or on radios, betting shop loudspeakers, telephones or televisions, live commentaries on races add a great deal to the excitement inherent in the running of races to a finish. Whatever the manner of delivery, commentaries are such a vital ingredient in racing's cocktail of excitement that their absence or distortion is immensely irritating.

COMMISSION AGENT

Individual who passes on business to large firms of bookmakers and is paid as a commission a percentage of its total value or, alternatively, the aggregate of several individual 'rewards' which will vary

according to the acceptability of the wagers involved. Obviously these will differ greatly.

The fact that commonly no commission is paid to an agent who passes on wagers on odds-on chances and runners in very small fields unless, rather expectedly, they are beaten, and that twice as much commission is often paid for business involving accumulators than for wagers on non-handicap runners, would seem to suggest these wagers usually enrich bookmakers.

Interestingly, the term 'commission agent' and the somewhat synonymous title of 'turf accountant' give sensitive modern layers two ways in which they can avoid having to style, announce and advertise themselves as mere 'bookmakers'.

COMPANY OWNERSHIP

This is an increasingly popular method of racehorse ownership. Sometimes horses are named after the companies that own them or after the products or services which these provide. Thus the intriguingly named Cronks Garages Limited have owned Cronks Courage, the Edinburgh Woollen Mill, the appropriately named Tartan Tailor, while Food Brokers Limited have had considerable success with Maryland Cookie.

COMPUTERS AND RACING

Interestingly, Charles Babbage's pioneering work on the development of a computer was encouraged by a patron with an interest in horse racing. Doubtless he would be envious of modern-day followers of the sport who can acquire 'minders' of various types to ensure that their assessments of the prospects of racehorses do not feature irrational betrayals of logic or of lessons they have previously learnt the hard way. The simple pocket calculator can be used to make a rapid check on the prices that make up a betting show so as to determine whether a book, i.e. a complete set of prices for a race, is not excessively or unfairly 'over-round'. The calculations concerned here involve dividing the right-hand side of each runner's odds by the sum of both sides and adding the resultant figures together. The amount by which the total of such calculations exceeds 100 is the bookmaker's profit margin.

Since horse racing form is assessed in so many quantitive ways (many involving form and time ratings), since form lines and betting shows are presented numerically and since a horse's fitness is commonly gauged by the number of days since it last ran, any imaginative backer can use his pocket calculator to make processes of racehorse selection more precise.

Racegoers can even purchase a special racing-orientated pocket calculator, the Startrack Racetrack Computer, billed as an 'electronic rating system', which features five pre-programmed mathematical procedures. This device can accommodate an alternative method of racehorse selection to that stipulated in the instructions.

Lap-top computers and truly pocket-sized computers (like the Psion Organiser) can be used actually at the racetrack! Artronic Systems Limited of Deeming, Little Thorpe, Ripon, Yorkshire can supply its impressive Formaster horserace predictor system for operation on the Psion. Backers with IBM systems or those compatible with them can now purchase perhaps the ultimate in computer-aided winner finding – a form book database updated by weekly discs. Form can be read electronically and selections made on that basis.

COMPUTER STRAIGHT FORECAST

The nomination, in correct order, of the horses finishing first and second. The fact that dividends are calculated by computer according to a complex formula accounts for the rather impressive title of this wager. Stakes are included in any returns and dividends declared to a £1 unit. It is instructive to compare these dividends with those offered by the tote.

CONDITIONAL JOCKEYS

Inexperienced riders over fences and hurdles under National Hunt rules. They are the equivalent of apprentice jockeys on the flat and ride at weights lower, according to lack of experience, than those stipulated in the conditions of races or by the handicapper. When conditionals ride in races restricted to them rather than against fully-fledged jockeys they do not always claim such allowances.

CONDITIONS RACE

One in which the weights of the runners are allocated, not by the official handicapper, but according to generalized judgements involving such variables as age, sex, past prizes won, penalties and even horses' purchase prices in the sales ring.

So-called Group races staged at set points in the flat racing season so as to provide appropriate searching tests of top-class performers, be these first-season types, three-year-olds or older horses, are the most prestigious of all conditions races.

CONFORMATION

Round-hoof'd, short-jointed, fetlocks shag and long,
Broad breast, full eye, small head, and nostril wide,
High crest, short ears, straight legs, and passing strong,
Thin mane, thick tail, broad buttock, tender hide:
Look, what a horse should have he did not lack...
Shakespeare, *Venus and Adonis*

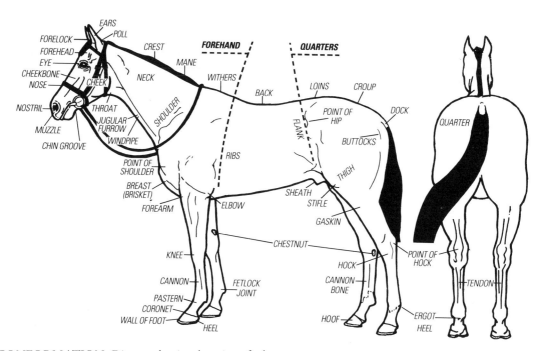

CONFORMATION: Diagram showing the points of a horse.

Conformation must at least have some value and that this is the general view is apparent at every sale ring where there is no doubt whatever make and shape command a price.
Dennis Craig.

Conformation is a great thing to look for - a good head, of course, but most important is an oblique shoulder, a deep girth (plenty of room for heart and lungs) and a wide behind.
Jack Leach.

The virtual impossibility of writing anything authoritative on the subject of conformation was once highlighted by the trainer Peter Walwyn: 'It's rather like being asked to describe a pretty girl. One man can look at a horse and like it very much, but another may not be able to stand the sight of it.'

Despite the differences in expert opinion which make the study of conformation both fascinating and frustrating, it is possible to make some general observations on this subject that it should pay the backer to heed. Indeed, if a selection based on form and time is also a 'winner on looks' then so much the better!

Obviously, if a horse is correctly built and balanced and its parts are in proportion to each other then one is entitled to suppose that its training and previous racecourse performances will not have imposed undue strain on its 'framework' and that it will not labour or become unbalanced during racing.

While, of course, perfect or excellent conformation is no guarantee of success on the track, its possession by a racehorse does increase its chances of victory.

Bahram, the unbeaten Triple Crown winner of 1935, was a horse which that noted judge, John Hislop, once credited with 'faultless' conformation ideally suited to Epsom's Derby course and, by studying the illustrations opposite, particularly that showing the points, it should be possible to draw some general conclusions about conformation that most observers might accept.

As Dennis Craig puts it so succinctly in his *Penguin Guide to Horse Racing* one of the most important factors in conformation is the perpendicularity of the slope from the point of the shoulder to the point of the elbow. Also desirable are an intelligent and handsome head, a long, strong, light and muscular neck (bringing the centre of gravity well forward), low, free, well-placed elbows, sloping shoulders, high withers running well back,

good depth at the brisket, body well-ribbed up, a short back, good fetlocks and pasterns and plenty of bone in the leg below the knee. The last named attribute (in a list that in many respects describes Bahram) is certainly something to look out for in jumpers. There is such a thing as the 'stamp of a 'chaser' and a horse's capacity to soar over fences depends on possession of certain features as much as fitness. It is impossible to over-estimate the importance of a jumper's hind legs, particularly the hocks, which some feel make up the 'engine' that provides it with the propulsion it needs to take off.

Horses are not jumping animals by nature and to cushion the shock their suspension systems receive they need to be strong, sound and supple, not only in their hind and forelegs, but also in their thighs, forearms, sloping shoulders, high withers and backs.

The important point that a jumper's hocks, as well as being straight and wide (and certainly not 'sickle-hocked' or 'cow-hocked') should be under its centre of gravity so as to give it good balance, provides a useful reminder that the best negotiators of obstacles are often rather balletic performers.

Even more about conformation can be learnt by checking comments on particular attributes against photographs of horses that display these, such as appear in the highly collectable *Timeform Annual Guides to Racehorses*.

CONTRACT, TO
Said of odds which shorten in the market. The proportion by which prices contract can be highly revealing.

CONVERSION TABLES *(see over page)*

COOKED
Said of a horse seen to have no chance of winning, having given its all to no avail.

❗ COP
Slang for to win.

CORNER HORSES
One of the many approaches to winner finding which involve possibly significant movement in the betting market concerns 'corner' horses – those which start at shorter odds than in the forecasts.

If a runner that is forecast at long odds in a national newspaper or, better still, a specialist racing daily, opens and remains at *(continued following page)*

WEIGHT CONVERSION

st	lb	kilo	st	lb	kilo
7	0	44	9	12	62
7	1	45	9	13	63
7	2	45	10	0	63
7	3	46	10	1	64
7	5	46	10	2	64
7	6	47	10	3	65
7	7	47	10	4	65
7	8	48	10	5	66
7	9	48	10	7	66
7	10	49	10	8	67
7	11	49	10	9	67
7	12	50	10	10	68
7	13	50	10	11	68
8	0	51	10	12	69
8	2	51	10	13	69
8	3	52	11	0	70
8	4	52	11	1	70
8	5	53	11	2	71
8	6	53	11	4	71
8	7	54	11	5	72
8	8	54	11	6	72
8	9	55	11	7	7
8	10	55	11	8	73
8	11	56	11	9	74
8	13	56	11	10	74
9	0	57	11	11	75
9	1	57	11	12	75
9	2	58	11	13	76
9	3	58	12	1	76
9	4	59	12	2	77
9	5	59	12	3	77
9	6	60	12	4	78
9	7	60	12	5	78
9	8	61	12	6	79
9	10	61	12	7	79
9	11	62			

DISTANCE CONVERSION

1 furlong is taken as equal to 200 metres

(continued) a much shorter price on the bookmakers' boards, this may well be because a sizeable stable commission has already been placed on it.

Another plan which is based on morning lines (as betting forecasts are known in America) involves the purchase of a late morning daily such as the *Morning Advertiser* or the mid-day edition of a suitable evening newspaper and then noting disparities between its prices and those compiled earlier by experts who have been unable to take account of raceday factors. Many professionals feel the compiler of the *Morning Advertiser's* forecasts has an uncanny knack of veering away from a horse that the national dailies have predicted will be favourite, but which in the event proves easy to back in the course market.

The 'sharp' responsible for the *Advertiser's* tishy often identifies as likely favourites horses which have been comparitively neglected by those who have had to work to far tighter press deadlines.

Conversely, of course, there are occasions when rival stable confidence in another horse (rather than anything being untoward) is all that causes a forecast favourite to fail to become the market leader.

If this confidence proves misplaced then the horse favoured by the off-course forecasters may well win at excellent odds.

CORPORATE ENTERTAINING

The entertainment of business associates and clients in some style amidst the luxurious settings of hospitality suites, boxes or marquees (some in attractive tented villages) has become a feature of the modern-day racecourse scene.Specialist firms can make all the arrangements for the increasing number of concerns which rightly believe that goodwill is likely to be generated among guests they invite to the races.

As Cliff Wood has put it, 'racing's combination of frenetic activity followed by periods of relative calm make it the ideal lubricant for business negotiation'.

CORRUPTION

Malpractice and fraud within the racing industry.

A whole spate of works published in the late 1970s and early 1980s have focused closely on the many different and often ingenious ways in which cunning and deception have been practised on the turf. Scandals from the past and modern-day methods of cheating have been so closely analysed that it has become all too easy to conclude that racing is a thoroughly rotten sport.

This, in fact, is far from the case. The really bad crooks don't last long in racing – the game wouldn't last if they did. Indeed, the following fairly full list of ways in which fraud has been practised on the turf could be counter-balanced by another detailing existing deterrents against them.

Corruption has naturally involved jockeys and it has even been alleged that riders' rings have existed to fix the results of races. Some jockeys have been ordered, persuaded or bribed by employers or by bookmakers to cause their mounts either to whip round or lose ground at the start, to go the 'long way round', to become hopelessly boxed in, to run out, suffer interference in running or even to fall.

The simplest method by which jockeys can 'pull' their mounts is to restrain them so that they fail to fulfil their potential in a way that escapes the notice of the stewards. This contrasts sharply with the rather more risky ploy of riding at a lower weight than that recorded by the clerk of the scales. In former days some riders weighed-in and out with whips containing lead and contrived to exchange these for far lighter conventional ones.

Saddles that are lighter or heavier than those taken to the scales also affect a mount's performance. It would also seem that one or two of the tales of jockeys in foggy conditions making fewer circuits of courses than officially required are not in fact apocryphal!

Many varied instances of fraudulent practice on the part of trainers have been recorded including ringing in or 'ringing the changes' with horses. This practice involves running horses that are physically reminiscent of other animals, but so superior to them that they win easily or so inferior that they are accorded a long price when next they run.

A good many sordid tales of punters attempting to defraud bookmakers could be related. One recently concerned a sonic gun that was alleged to have stunned Ile de Chypre and prevented it from winning a race at Royal Ascot. Similarly, there are many well-documented instances of odds being 'pinched' by bookmakers – especially those offered by on-course operators on runners at other 'away' meetings. There has even been an imaginary race meeting at a place called 'Trodmore' – a stranger than fiction factual story.

COUP

A serviceable definition of what a coup is might be: a wager – often on a horse starting at, or backed down from, a generous price – that proves spectacularly successful and greatly enriches those involved.

Over the years some of the bold attempts that have been made to 'beat the book' in a really big way have featured both chicanery and the inevitable reluctance of bookmakers to settle the extra 'sharp' bets involved. Both ringers (smart performers masquerading as 'no hopers'), and horses ingeniously and surreptitiously backed to win small fortunes have featured in major plots that have sometimes sent their perpetrators to prison.

In modern times, two attempted coups have become colourful parts of racing's folklore.

The Francasal affair, staged at Bath in the 1950s, was a particularly audacious, but bungled, bid to deprive bookmakers of £60,000. More recently, in a masterly plan of Tony Murphy's, Gay Future was coupled in hundreds of trebles with two non-runners for camouflage purposes. The coup inspired a book and a film and has been further commemorated by the opening of a 'Gay Future' cocktail bar in Cork City!

COUPLED BET

On occasion, a backer, confident that a race is going to be won by one of two or three runners, may wish to avoid reproaching himself if he makes the wrong choice between them. In such circumstances, it may be appropriate to attempt the ambitious strategy of betting 'coupled' – a ploy often adopted by professionals, the stakes for which are indicated on page 86.

COURSES CLOSED

Since racecourses by their very nature take up large tracts of often valuable land, and some can find the going tough financially, it is inevitable that a few are forced, or tempted by developers, to close down. This sadly has been the fate of, amongst others, Alexandra Park in London (whose distinctive 'frying pan' track was last raced over on 8 September 1970) and Phoenix Park which closed its turnstiles twenty years later.

A glance at old racing annuals reveals how many and varied are Britain's 'lost' racecourses: from humble country jumping circuits like Wye in Kent to urban tracks like Bromford Bridge in Birmingham at which a meeting was last held on 21 June 1965. Two much mourned examples are Lincoln and Manchester, the respective homes of handicaps that by tradition have heralded and closed the flat racing season. Other fairly recent casualties have included Hurst Park and Lanark, whose ancient Silver Bell used to be Britain's oldest race. Not even the appealing configuration of some courses has saved them from extinction. Thus, horseshoe-shaped Lewes was allowed to lapse on 14 September 1964. Racegoers with long memories may recall the even earlier demise of right-handed Derby whose flat, oval course of 10 furlongs had easy turns, and of Gatwick where the high-drawn often flew in on its 'landing strip' of a straight mile course!

Fortunately, some tracks have not been altogether lost to racing. One such is Bogside, former home of the Scottish Grand National and of flat racing, which closed on 10 April 1965. Now humble, but often exciting, point-to-point meetings are held on its fine old racing surface.

COVERED UP

Said of a horse that is not allowed to take a leading part in a race until its closing stages. Some animals need to be ridden along in the ruck and only exposed to 'daylight' at the end of the race. Such a requirement makes considerable demands on jockeyship.

COVERING ONE'S SELECTIONS

Backing horses in more than one way, for example, as singles and also in accumulative bets.

CREDIT ACCOUNT

It is the backer's responsibility to monitor his liabilities and not exceed any agreed limit. Bookmakers do not always inform their credit account customers when their limits have been reached, but render accounts at regular, often fortnightly, intervals instead. If debts that these feature are not settled promptly, any wagers that are subsequently made may well become void.

Whilst in modern times, bookmakers, principally through the BPA and the National Sporting League, have weeded out the undesirables and the 'welshers' from their profession, sadly some of their credit account customers have run up debts totalling vast sums.

Such contemptible behaviour has always been observable on the turf and in former times irresponsible young bloods thought no more of bilking their bookmaker than their tailor!

The bugbear of being owed as much as an eighth of the total sums wagered with them on credit has naturally caused bookmakers to close ranks and though their trade associations to 'post' known defaulters and to keep extensive records that enable the credit-worthiness of prospective clients to be rapidly checked. However, the precautions of the BPA and the National Sporting League can provide no panacea for the plague of bad debts that so many of their members contract. Indeed, not even recourse to the courts can remedy this situation since gambling debts are not enforceable at law.

In fact, no gambling debt is recoverable outside the courts unless 'consideration' has been given. This could take the form of settlement being rewarded by a promise not to report the client to Tattersalls Committee which has the authority to settle all questions relating to bets, to adjudicate on all cases of default and to report defaulters to the Jockey Club.

CROOKED

Expression used to denote a horse that is allegedly not trying.

CURRAGH, THE

Curragh Racecourse
Co. Kildare
Southern Ireland
Tel. (045) 41205

How to get there:
From North: N80
From South: N9
From East: N7
From West: N7
By Rail: Curragh Mainline
By Air: Helicopter facilities

Cross-country horseracing originally formed a part of many a fair or 'oenach' (one of whose meanings is the 'contention of horses') and one well-known such event was held at the Curragh (racecourse) of Kildare where contests, some of them chariot races, took place involving horses (many imported from Wales) that were ridden by noblemen's sons and the red branch knights of pre-Christian Ireland.

Races have thus been staged for centuries on the vast grassy limestone plain that, appropriately, is the

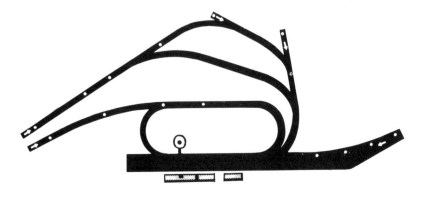

THE CURRAGH: Plan of the course.

home of all five Irish Classic races and the headquarters of both the Irish Turf Club and National Hunt Committee in Ireland's equivalent to Newmarket.

As is the case with the Suffolk town, the Curragh has attracted a nearby National Stud as well as a sizeable cluster of prominent stud farms and racing stables run by trainers who take advantage of the local turf, a unique combination of red fescue and brown bent grass, ideally suited to the galloping of racehorses.

The course itself is a horseshoe-shaped, right-handed affair whose lack of severe undulations, sharp bends and any marked topographic eccentricity makes it a very fair test of the thoroughbred.

This track extends for around two miles and on its straight course races are staged over 5 furlongs and, thanks to a dog leg of a spur, also over 6, 7 and 8 furlongs. Alternatively, races can be run over 2 miles, 14 furlongs, 1 1/2 miles and 10 furlongs. The Irish Derby course is regarded by many as a demanding test, far superior to, and fairer than the Epsom Derby course.

As for the draw, it is generally held that it has no marked effect, except in sprints in which high-drawn horses may be at a slight advantage.

The track can be reached directly by helicopter and (on race days only) in trains that make a 40-minute non-stop run from Dublin's Heuston station to Curragh Mainline which conveniently is a mere 500 yards from the stands.

Those travelling by road can approach the course on some extremely scenic routes and will find it is some 29 miles south-west of Dublin. The course enclosures, most commendably, are combined into one area, save on Group One days and Irish Derby day which is now a Sunday in late June or early July.

As is appropriate for Ireland's showpiece track, the Curragh has excellent amenities including a completely covered tote area, and seats reservable on a daily basis (for which tickets can be obtained at the racecourse office by the parade ring). Fruit is even on sale and hot *table d'hôte* luncheons are available in the first floor restaurant area above the tote hall in the grandstand, which also includes an enticing panoramic bar and a novel fish and tea bar. There is even a pub under the grandstand.

Children are extremely well-catered for at the Curragh, in a tiny tots centre at the western end of the grandstand.

The richest pickings on offer at the Curragh are naturally the Irish Derby, the Irish Oaks, 2000 Guineas, 1000 Guineas and the St Leger, while the 7-furlong National Stakes staged in early September is also a most prestigious race for first-season performers (as Roberto showed as long ago as 1971). The very first two runnings of the Irish Derby, in 1867 and 1868, went to English raiders thereby establishing a trend that modern-day handlers like Michael Stoute have sometimes followed. Another top-class Curragh race is the Moyglare Stud Stakes for two-year-olds that is the highlight of a Sunday card in early September. The Irish Lincoln run in the Spring and the Irish Cesarewitch are always exciting races on which fortunes can be wagered.

As befits a course so steeped in tradition, the Curragh stages several races that commemorate past champions. Thus, the Gladness Stakes, run in mid-April, recalls the horse that won the Ascot Gold Cup, the Goodwood Cup and the Ebor Handicap at York.

The Tetrarch Stakes, run at the end of April, is named after the horse one noted judge has described as 'unquestionably one of the most remarkable ever seen on the turf and possibly the fastest', while Pretty Polly and Meld – fillies that captured the English Triple Crown in 1904 and 1955 respectively – are commemorated in Group races run in midsummer and late August.

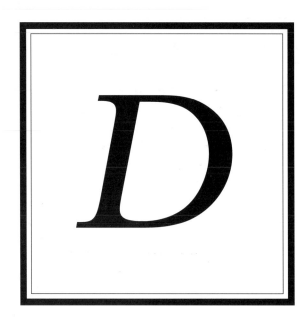

DAM

Female parent of a horse.

DARK HORSES

Unexposed runners whose prospects may be better than is suggested by the lack of obvious pointers to their chances. One well-known judge, Marten Julian, sets such store by these performers that he publishes annuals and bulletins in which they are brought to light.

DEAD HEAT

None too frequent, but highly exciting outcome to a horse race. Before the advent of photo finish equipment, this was probably an appelation that did less than full justice to many an outright winner. Infamous examples of a dead heat include the 1961 Cambridgeshire in which the spoils were shared by Violetta III and Henry the Seventh. Another race run over a similar distance, the 1984 Lockinge Stakes, involved a photographically recorded dead heat between Cormorant Wood and Wassl. Double Shuffle and Turkoman were also inseparable in a thrilling finish to the 1982 November Handicap.

Two of the most exciting dead heats must have been those that proved the final outcomes of two long distance races: the 1953 Doncaster Cup run on Town Moor over a gruelling 2 1/4 miles and the 1967 Park Hill Stakes run on the same course over 14 furlongs 132 yards.

Bookmakers' rules stipulate that, in the event of a dead heat, what has been staked on either runner is halved and payment is made at the rate of odds originally accepted.

Both dead heaters each have to carry a penalty if the conditions of their next races require this.

DEAD WEIGHT

If a jockey is due to ride at a weight considerably in excess of his natural one, his mount has to carry the 'deficit' via a heavier saddle. This additional weight is 'dead' and cannot be shifted so as to make its presence less onerous. Some backers are disinclined to risk their 'brass' on runners whose jockeys' natural riding weights will be augmented by lots of lead.

DEBUTANT

Horse having its first outing.

DENTIST

Disparaging reference to a racecourse bookmaker who, probably because he is not paying for the services of a tic-tac, is one price or more adrift of his colleagues, and thus offers the backer better value.

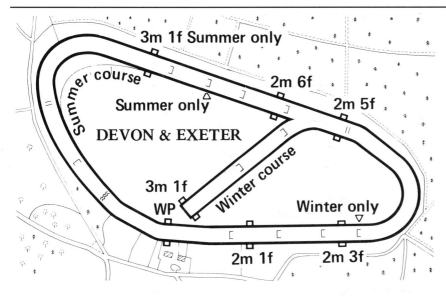

*DEVON & EXETER:
Plan of the course.*

DEVON & EXETER

Haldon Racecourse
Nr. Exeter
Devon
Tel. (0392) 832599

How to get there:
From North: M5
From South: A380
From East: A30
From West: A30
By Rail: Exeter St Davids
By Air: Exeter Airport, Helicopter facilities

Devon and Exeter's friendly fixtures are actually staged at Haldon in a truly rural and picturesque setting on the fringes of Dartmoor's forestland. The extensive right-handed, oval-shaped track that runs through gorse and heather is close to the A38 Plymouth to Exeter road and is six miles west of the latter town, whose airport can accommodate airborne racegoers arriving in fixed-wing aircraft. Helicopters can land (by prior arrangement) at Haldon itself. Rail travellers should alight at Exeter St Davids which can be reached after a fairly fast journey of less than 200 miles from Paddington.

The A30 is the route west to Haldon, while those coming from Plymouth should take the A38. The Exeter-Plymouth bus service will drop you at the racecourse.

Most appropriately, the Plymouth Gin Haldon Gold Cup is the most prestigious (since listed) race that takes place on Devon and Exeter's rather hilly track, whose often quite severe gradients mean that past course and distance runners should be respected. Such runners are unlikely to be long-striding gallopers who often find this course's gradients and undulations rather unsettling. The uphill run-in is 300 yards long.

Devon and Exeter, which has a slightly more upmarket ambience about it than nearby Newton Abbot, is a country course patronized by county types and the many holidaymakers who flock to the late summer fixtures that are staged right at the start of National Hunt racing's 'little season'.

DISASTERS, RACING

These, so numerous as to spawn a work devoted exclusively to them by John Welcome, range from the ill-fated Derby of 1913 in which Emily Davison died (see page over) and a disgraceful disqualification robbed an owner who had survived the Titanic's sinking, to the mêlée at Becher's in the 1967 National that allowed Foinavon to register a 100-1 victory.

Golden Miller's fall when the 2-1 favourite in the 1935 National, the heartbreaking failure of Lord Mildmay to win this race in 1936 when Davy Jones ran out before the last fence, the tragic death of the Irish mare Dawn Run in France and of Golden Cygnet at Ayr, the leaping of an imaginary obstacle by Devon Loch in the 1956 National, and the suicide of Fred Archer in 1886 at the age of only 29, constitute some of the best-known disasters that have occurred in a sport characterized by so many daily triumphs over difficulty and in which risk taking is a prerequisite.

DISASTERS: (see preceding page) In one of the most notorious of racing disasters, also captured on film, the Suffragette Emily Davison died when she ran out of the crowd in front of Amner – King George V's horse – as it came round the final turn in the 1913 Derby.

DISPUTES (See Rules of Betting, Tattersalls). Those between backers and bookmakers are often settled by on-course ring inspectors – respected individuals who are remarkably successful in arbitrating between disputants. Away from the racecourse, the *Sporting Life* operates a 'Green Seal Service' in which arbitrational judgement is delivered on disputes whose details are submitted in writing.

The official body to which betting disputes can be referred for settlement is the Tattersalls Committee. Its secretary is Mr Peter Guard, who can be contacted at PO BOX 13,19 Wilwyne Close, Caversham, Reading RG4 OEP.

DISQUALIFICATION

This fate is indicated by the appearance of the letter 'D' in a horse's form line. It is a judgement imposed by the stewards if the horse has been the subject of

one or more of a vast array of unacceptable situations or practices, which range from the presence in its tissue of 'prohibited substances' to the fact that it has, 14 days prior to a race, visited an unregistered equine swimming pool. Many disqualifications (such as that of Royal Gait in a recent Ascot Gold Cup) are for riding practices.

DISTANCE

Term signifying either the length of a horse race or a winning margin in excess of 240 yards (see below).

DISTANCE, THE

The final 240-yard (219-metre) stretch of a horse race. At some courses this is marked by a post so jockeys do not mistime their finishing efforts. If the furlong plus by which a horse wins makes notions of lengths redundant, it is said to have won by a distance.

DISTANCE TRAVELLED TO RACE

Much store is set by the belief that horses sent on expensive journeys to race on courses remote from their stables will be bidding to do more than recoup the cost of transporting them there. The *Racing Post* includes a regular Traveller's Check column in its daily racing coverage.

DOG

Ungenerous horse that perversely promises much, yet fails to do its best and thus disappoints. Most unfairly, this dismissive term is often applied to several perfectly genuine, if temperamental, types who may 'turn it up' in the closing stages of a race merely because they are in physical distress or some respiratory discomfort.

DOMINO

Complex wager on four selections producing 28 bets.

DONCASTER

Doncaster Racecourse
Leger Way
Doncaster DN2 6BB
Tel. (0302) 320066

How to get there:
From North: A1(M)
From South: M1
From East: A180(M)
From West: M62
By Rail: Doncaster
By Air: Helicopter facilities

Doncaster's Group One racecourse, some 160 miles from London, can be reached by rail from King's Cross (arrive Doncaster Central) or via the A1 and the M18 and M180.

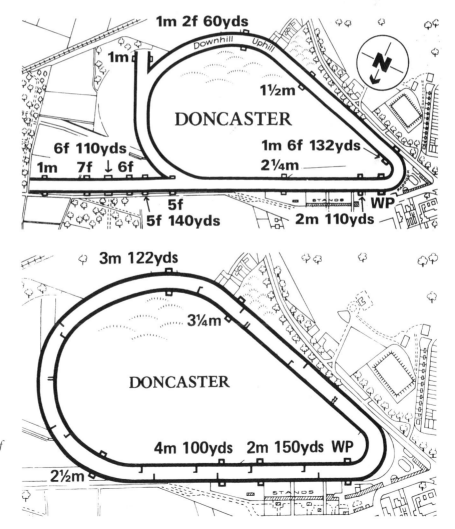

DONCASTER: Plans of the Flat course (top) over which the St Leger is run, and the National Hunt course (bottom).

It is perhaps appropriate that its postal address is Leger Way since Town Moor is the home of Britain's oldest Classic, run over a distance of 1 mile 6 furlongs 132 yards, that almost constitutes a complete circuit of this largely flat, 15 1/2-furlong left-handed course which seems to favour long-striding galloping types with a turn of foot, the performers to which the 4 1/2-furlong run-in is particularly suited. The round course is shaped like a cone or pear and the only undulations it features are provided by a small hill some ten furlongs from the finish. It is used for some races over 1 mile, for events over 1 mile 2 furlongs 60 yards, 1 1/2 miles and 2 1/2 miles, as well as for contests over the St Leger distance. The course only turns to the left in a most accommodating, gently sweeping fashion. Lowly drawn contestants enjoy an advantage only in races from 8 to 12 furlongs run on the round course which in modern times has been used to stage the Lincoln Handicap on only one occasion (in 1978).

Horses tackling the round mile start from a short spur and then sweep left-handed before joining the finishing straight which forms the final section of the very wide straight mile course that is partly provided by a second spur.

Since the draw on Doncaster's straight course can prove crucial to high-drawn runners, it is imperative that a jockey is sufficiently experienced either to profit greatly from a favoured stalls position or to overcome a poor draw.

The turf on Town Moor provides some of the best racing ground in the country and sticky conditions are usually precluded by its sandy subsoil.

The Group One St Leger is contested early in September. This, the oldest of the Classics, was first run four years before the Derby in 1776 to commemorate Lt.-Gen. Anthony St Leger (originally pronounced 'Sellinger'), a resident of Park Hill, which gives its name to another race for three year-old fillies that is also run over the same distance each September.

One of the biggest nineteenth century St Leger coups concerned Elis, whose owner Lord George Bentinck hit upon the ingenious idea of running this 1835 Molecomb Stakes winner so frequently in the south during the summer of the following year that few would feel he was likely to line up for the St Leger after walking all the way to Doncaster from his Goodwood stable. However, Elis was spirited northwards in a horse van drawn by four other horses – a virtually unprecedented ploy – and he duly landed the Leger at 7-2.

Gladiateur in 1866 was an even more widely travelled French winner while Ormonde, Persimmon and Nijinsky are just three other Derby winners to have prevailed at Doncaster to perhaps prove the adage that 'while the fittest horse wins the 2000 Guineas and the luckiest horse wins the Derby, the best horse wins the St Leger'.

This race is the highlight of Doncaster's most prestigious four-day September fixture, a major attraction of which is the May Hill Stakes, a mile race for first-season fillies, first run in 1981. Also staged at this meeting are the prestigious Park Hill Stakes and the Doncaster Cup, an often thrilling marathon which has most frequently fallen to a four-year-old.

As for the Laurent Perrier Champagne Stakes, this is a top-class 7-furlong contest for two-year-old colts and geldings.

Yet another feature of the three-day September fixture is the Flying Childers Stakes, a 5-furlong race for two-year-olds that commemorates the so-called 'first great racehorse', which was foaled in 1715.

Late in the autumn, a most prestigious Group One mile race for two-year-olds, the Racing Post Trophy, is staged. Infrequently won by a horse destined for Classic success, it nevertheless attracts first-season performers of the highest calibre.

By tradition, Doncaster fixtures in March and November have opened and closed the turf flat racing season, most spectacularly via the Lincoln and November Handicaps. These are major lotteries, as the victory in the latter of Tearaway at 40-1 in 1955 aptly confirmed. In recent runnings of the Lincoln Handicap, four-year-olds have fared slightly better than five-years-olds, while the 'November' is often lifted by a late improving three-year-old.

Doncaster's jumping track has fairly easy fences and like the flat course tends to suit long-striding gallopers. Its best known jump race is the Golden Spurs Handicap, a 3 1/4 mile 'chase staged late in January. The Freebooter Novices Chase run in early December commemorates the 1950 Yorkshire-trained winner of the Grand National.

Doncaster has benefited greatly from a multi-million pound redevelopment which includes a splendidly appointed exhibition and conference centre, complete with a Triple Crown bar and a luxurious grandstand built by Cheltenham sponsor, A.F. Budge Limited. Moreover, the St Leger meeting in September now includes a ladies' day, recently revived after a lapse of twenty years. These innovations have kept this historic racecourse in racing's first division.

After 1904 horses were no longer openly doped and racing was thus largely freed from a practice that had brought it serious discredit. However, in modern times several doping scandals have come to light. In the 1950s and the 1960s , there was a disturbing resurgence of the doping menace.

One particularly infamous and sensational instance of nobbling which made national headlines concerned Pinturischio, the ante-post favourite for the 1961 Derby, trained by no less than Noel Murless of Warren Place. This colt was 'got at' in such a callous fashion that his connections were forced to scratch him from the Derby.

Even more recently, some startling revelations about the administration of anabolic steroids (now banned by Jockey Club Regulations) to racehorses have been made.

However, in general, British racing has over the years been largely free of such an evil influence most notably in recent years when the detection of drugs has become a very sophisticated science.

DOUBLE
Win or each way wager in which a backer couples two horses to win their separate races.

❗ DOUBLE CARPET
Slang for 33-1.

❗ DOUBLE NET
Slang for 20-1. A tic-tac signals this price by repeating the sign for 'net' or ten.

DOWNPATRICK

Downpatrick Race Club
Ballydugan Road
Downpatrick
Co. Down
Northern Ireland
Tel. (0396) 612054

How to get there:
From North: A22
From South: A25, B176
From East: A25
From West: A2, A25

Although the attractive Georgian town of Downpatrick is famous for St Patrick's gravestone, a large piece of granite which lies in the grounds of Down cathedral, its racecourse is by no means a backer's graveyard.

DOPING: Enoch Wishard, who became the leading trainer in 1899 despite the fact that some of his horses had been injected with stimulants.

DOPING
Administering a substance to a horse that is designed to impair or dramatically improve its race performance.

Chemically sophisticated examples of this practice became more widespread with the arrival on the British racing scene of American turf personalities in the mid-1890s.

In 1899, one particular American, Enoch Wishard, became the season's leading trainer with 54 winners. A good deal of his success apparently stemmed from the fact that some of his runners were injected with stimulants which, it should be stressed, were not prohibited by the rules of racing in force at the time. This practice had been perfected by American trainers in order to revitalize horses exhausted by running round dirt tracks in the course of race meetings that commonly extended for ten or more days. Wishard made £2 million on the British turf before a Jockey Club decision to clamp down on doping and ban its perpetrators forced his stable to decamp to France.

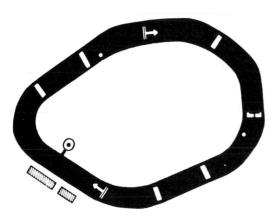

DOWNPATRICK: Plan of the course, which is home to the Ulster Harp National.

The Ulster Harp National (formerly run at the Maze racecourse) it is a tight, slightly undulating right-hander on which the draw is insignificant and some classy performers can sometimes be seen tackling its circuit of six obstacles and its uphill finish.

The course is a forty-minute bus ride from Belfast. Motorists can journey to the course on the A7. Racegoers travelling east from Newry should take the A25. Racecourse manager, retired Squadron Leader Ian Duff, has made recent improvements to this pleasant course whose sharpness however precludes the accommodation of helicopters.

DOWN ROYAL

Down Royal Corporation of Horse Breeders
Maze
Lisburn
Co. Antrim BT7 5RW
Northern Ireland
Tel. (0396) 621256

How to get there:
From North: M1, M2
From South: A1
From East: M1
From West: M1
Approximately 15 miles from Belfast

A right-handed affair, Down Royal extends for approximately 1 mile and 7 furlongs. This angular track's slight undulations give little trouble to the many novices who receive a very fair introduction to racing round its five turns. The top bend is in fact the tightest of these, if not exactly a ninety-degree

affair. There is a climb to the last bend and a downhill run to the home straight rising gradually to the post. Down Royal's 5-furlong sprint course is reputed to be one of the fastest in Ireland.

The Down Royal Corporation of Horse Breeders was established by a royal charter of James II in 1685 for the improvement of horse breeding in the County of Down. Given this prestigious connection, it is appropriate that at Down Royal are staged each year the Ulster Derby, the Ulster Champion Hurdle, a champion hunters' chase, and the Ulster Oaks.

Lisburn is the nearest railway station and motorists leaving Belfast, should head for Lisburn by taking the M1 (A1) motorway. The track is known as the Maze because of its proximity to the prison of that name. There are no tote facilities on course.

DREAM WINNERS OF RACES
The outcome of horse races have sometimes actually been dreamt. In 1871, Lord Poulett, a leading owner and supporter of steeplechasing, confided to the jockey he had engaged to ride his diminutive grey The Lamb that in a dream he had seen 'The Liverpool' run and that The Lamb had prevailed by four lengths! He swore the jockey to secrecy and doubtless reduced his life expectancy when later cheering his frisky nine-year-old to a two length victory at 5-1.

During the Edwardian era Lord Randolph Churchill won a considerable amount of money on the Oaks as a result of a dream. He had a large bet, as the number of the horse he had seen romp home in his dream was the only high one on the card and an outsider.

DRESS REQUIREMENTS (See Clothing, Racing)

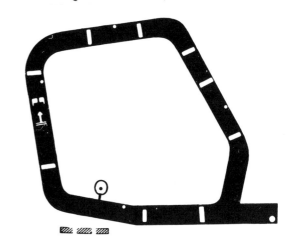

DOWN ROYAL: Plan of the course, which was established by a royal charter of James II in 1685.

DROP FENCE

Fence whose landing side is lower than the point from which steeplechasers leave the ground on its take-off side.

Until 1990 extremely formidable examples of such fences at Aintree troubled many a Grand National runner. Drop fences are also a feature of Haydock's attractive racecourse.

DROPPED IN CLASS

Designation used to denote horses that are racing in far from exalted company for the first time. The 'longest' drop is probably from the heights of non-selling races to the depths of sellers. Time after time, such events are won by horses used to racing in more prestigious races and whose indifferent form is often better than that registered by seasoned 'platers'.

DUNDALK

Dundalk Racecourse
Dowdallshill
Dundalk
Co. Louth
Southern Ireland
Tel. (042) 34419

How to get there:
From North: A1, N1
From South: N1
From West: N53
By Rail: Dundalk
By Air: Dublin Airport
Approximately 50 miles from Dublin

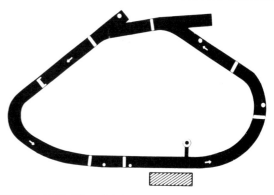

DUNDALK: Plan of the course

Dundalk is seldom listed in the index of tourist guides to Ireland, which is an unpardonable omission since its racecourse, sheltered by the Carlingford mountains, is most distinctive both in terms of its character and its scenic location against the mountains of Mourne.

Situated close to Dundalk station and on the main Dublin-Belfast road this is a left-handed affair that extends for some 10 furlongs.

Rather pear-shaped and subject to extremes of going, it tends to ride rather soft in the winter and to firm up in the summer.

It presents jumpers with seven obstacles, two of which are near the stands in the finishing straight and rather close together, which can present problems to tiring finishers.

Over the years the principal races staged at this very fair course have been the Mickey McArdle Novice Chase, the Caroll Handicap Hurdle and the Rossbracken Handicap Chase.

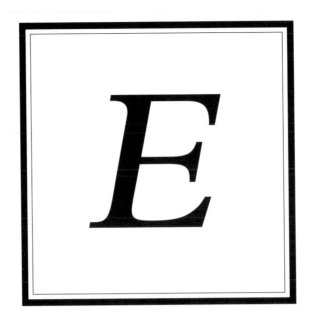

EACH WAY

Wager in which half the stake is to win only and half for the horse in question to be placed e.g. a £5 each way on a selection involves £5 to win and £5 for a place, giving a total stake of £10.

Advocates of win-only betting often argue that the vast majority of heavy business that is booked with the major rails bookmaking firms (much of it 'on the bough' or on credit) involves win only wagers. That this has increasingly been so in modern times is partly due to restrictions recently imposed on each-way betting. In the 'good old days' when place odds were generally one quarter of quite generous starting prices, it was often possible to bank on the belief that one, two or even three carefully selected horses (say two-year-olds unsoured by their short experience of racing) were very likely to be placed in races with eight runners – the optimum number for each way wagering.

Today, despite the paltry one-fifth of its starting price that is paid on a horse placed in a sizeable field and the punitive burden of off-course taxes, there are still circumstances in which this particular form of betting is advisable.

Firstly, it is important to appreciate when not to bet each way. It is folly to do so even at 'over-round' odds in any race (particularly a handicap) with a large field – one of more than nine runners. Such an open contest is designed to equalize the winning chances of all its runners and in practice often features a close finish.

An examination of probability ratios will refute the common view that an each-way bet is only worthwhile on a horse with a starting price of at least 5-1.

Each-way betting is more advantageous than win-only on handicappers starting at fairly short odds, and is far more so on similarly priced horses running in non-handicaps. If, moreover, exhaustive calculations show such contestants to be greatly favoured by the non-handicap situation, their each-way claims should be seriously considered.

It is prudent to wager each way for one further reason: the generous treatment one receives if one's selection – say a 2-1 chance in a non-handicap of eight runners – manages only to be placed. The bookmaker will conveniently, but quite arbitrarily, divide the price quoted against a win by a fifth. This fixed fraction makes life easier for his settler but may substantially underestimate the actual chances a horse has of being placed and so give something away to the backer. After all, an each way bet made on-course on a 2-1 chance finishing second or third will bring in a return that will enable the backer to recoup 40 per cent of what he has lost. This is no mean saving and the return involved is likely to be greater than the paltry place dividend the Tote would pay to a patron choosing to make a win and place wager on such a short-priced selection.

EACH-WAY CHANCE

A rather confusing term to describe a runner that is considered to have genuine place prospects. However, connections may use it euphemistically to intimate that their contender, in fact, has no such prospects.

EACH WAY, EQUALLY DIVIDED MULTIPLE BETS

A popular wager in the North. All winnings plus stakes from win or place bets are re-invested, half the returns being staked to win and half to place.

EACH WAY, MULTIPLE BETS

In these, half the stipulated stake of a win-only wager plus any winnings are re-invested to win. The other half of the original stake concerns a place-only wager and any winnings plus this stake are re-invested to place.

EARLY BIRDS

Backers who take generous-looking ante-post odds or those quoted in early betting shows in advance of most backers, in the belief that the value inherent in these prices is unlikely to last for long.

EARLY BIRD BONUS

Inducement that one well-known major bookmaker offers backers who are prepared to be 'early birds'.

EARLY MORNING PRICES

Ante-post odds, usually featuring well-known races that several bookmakers advertise in the *Sporting Life* or *Racing Post* on days when racing cards are particularly attractive, televised or involve feature races.

On application by telephone, one particular bookmaker even offers early morning ante-post prices on each of the day's forthcoming races.

EAR 'OLE

Tic-tac signal for 6-4; so-called because it involves touching the left ear with the fingertips of the right hand.

EARWIGGING

Listening into the confidential and possibly highly revealing conversation that passes between connections.

EASE

Said of a horse whose price eases i.e. is extended in the market because it fails to find significant support.

EASE UP

Necessary behaviour on the part of a bookmaker who is approaching, or has reached, his 'bet up to' or maximum liability figure. The first 'take-out' column in his 'captain' will tell him whether to 'bluff' bets or to 'hedge' them – the two ways in which easing up can be effected.

EASY TO BACK

Description applied to a horse whose support in the market presents the backer with little practical difficulty.

Obviously, if very few people actually take a price that bookmakers are quite happy to lay, such a situation will arise, especially if this price has 'eased'.

EDINBURGH

Musselburgh Racecourse
East Lothian
Scotland
Tel: (0292) 264179

How to get there:
From North: M90, A9
From South: M6, A74, A702
From East: A1
From West: M8
By Rail: Waverley
By Air: Edinburgh Airport, Helicopter facilities

This racecourse is actually situated at Musselburgh, five miles or so from the Scottish capital in a maritime location on the Firth of Forth.

It can be reached by rail by taking an express from King's Cross to Edinburgh's impressive Waverley station whence a 'super sprinter' service can be taken to Musselburgh itself. Motorists travelling from the South should take the Great North Road (A1).

The track, with its naturally sandy subsoil and sometimes windy situation close to Muirfield golf course, is one on which sticky conditions are seldom found. It is an oval right-hander of only 10 furlongs that features occasional, very minor undulations and has a straight run-in of 4 furlongs. However, it does not really suit long-striding, galloping types, since its turns, despite being cambered, are tight, especially into the finishing straight. Handy, adaptable types,

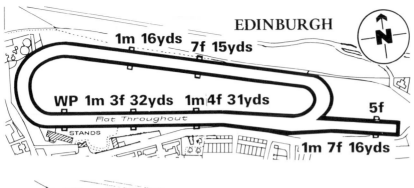

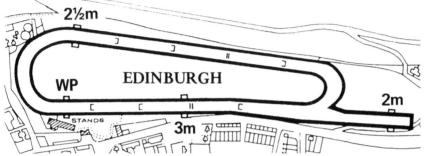

EDINBURGH: Plans of the Flat course (top), and the National Hunt course (bottom).

preferably high-drawn ones that have shown a liking for racing the 'wrong way', often go well in races of 7 furlongs 15 yards, 1 mile 16 yards, 11 furlongs 32 yards, 12 furlongs 31 yards and 15 furlongs 16 yards; all of these being race distances that take in much of Edinburgh's round course. Indeed, if jockeys do not take their mounts the shortest way round this, they can lose many lengths, a sound reason for following jockeys with impressive wins to rides ratios.

The straight course, on which 5-furlong sprints are staged, features gently rising ground in its final furlong. When the stalls are placed on the stands side, low-drawn contenders enjoy an appreciable edge, but if these are positioned on the far side, high-drawn runners are at a slight advantage. All in all, the sprint course is not so idiosyncratic as to impose anything but an easy test. A horse that can break quickly from the stalls is often favoured.

Although not a purpose-built, all-weather jumping track, Musselburgh is Britain's nearest natural equivalent to this. Its eight fences present few problems except of a 'show jumping' nature in that they are so close together down the far stretch. Victory often goes to fleet-footed types who are adaptable and can readily negotiate the many tight turns that have to be encountered in National Hunt contests run round the 11-furlong track.

The racecourse has led a charmed life, having twice been saved – first by Lord Roseberry as senior steward and then by the building of the Forth Road Bridge.

ELECTRONIC AIDS (See also Computers and Racing)

The ultimate electronic aid to the racing fan, apart from perhaps a lap-top computer with form book database, is probably the electronic message service, a pager about the size of a pack of cards on which messages can be received just about anywhere from Racepager's HQ in Esher. These feature daily going reports, information on non-runners, selections, summaries of newspaper tips, results transmitted within seconds of horses passing the line, classified results, files transmitted at the end of racing, and BAGS greyhound results. In addition, important news items, such as late abandonments of meetings are flashed to subscribers to this modestly-priced service.

❗ ELEF
Slang for eleven (11-1).

❗ ELEF A VIER
Bookmakers' exotic term for 11-4.

ENCLOSURES
Whether the exclusive royal enclosure at Ascot or areas inside courses that for centuries have been common land, as at Epsom, racecourse enclosures are a fairly recent provision.

It was in the last century that fences were introduced in a pioneering way at Sandown and other park courses so that the worst elements of Victorian sporting society might not offend the sensibilities of lady racegoers and more genteel patrons.

Today, different priced enclosures, some complete with uniformed attendants or 'jobsworths' to keep out those failing to dress appropriately or display the appropriate badges, make racecourses thoroughly 'chequered' affairs. On most tracks, the cheaper course enclosures offer inferior facilities, but some provide splendid views of the action.

Tattersalls, something of a half-way house socially and financially, is separated from the members' by iron railings.

Some racecourse enclosures are reserved for functions put on by corporate entertainers.

ENEMY
Suitably belligerent way in which some backers refer to bookmakers.

❗ ENIN
'Reversed' term for nine or 9-1.

❗ ENIN TO ROUF
'Reversed' term for 9-4.

ENQUIRIES
Requests for prices received by rails bookmakers, many of which come from their clients in the members' enclosure.

ENTERTAINING AT THE RACES (See Corporate Entertainment)

ENTRIES
These have to be made well in advance of the running of races and a vital part of any trainer's task is to study the Racing Calendar published by Messrs Weatherby in which these are officially listed. Thus the possible plans of rivals can be revealed. A useful feature entitled 'Treats in Store' in the weekly *Sporting Life Weekender* shows horses entered for coming major races and study of these can be most illuminating.

ENTRIES, ANALYSIS OF
Backers who wisely believe that scrutiny of the races in which a trainer has entered his horses speaks volumes for his or her estimation of their ability and potential, may want to subscribe to *Future Form*, a weekly publication in which entries are regularly and rigorously scrutinized. Alan Lury and his staff at *Future Form* (82 Girton Road, Cambridge), argue

that much can be learnt about a trainer's estimations of truly 'dark horses', untried or inexperienced charges, by studying the value and importance of the races in which they have been (often expensively) entered to run in future.

EPSOM

Racecourse Paddock
Epsom
Surrey KT18 5NJ
Tel. (03727) 26311

How to get there:
From North: A24
From South: M23
From East: M25
From West: M25
By Rail: Epsom, Epsom Downs, Tattenham Corner
By Air: Helicopter facilities

Epsom racecourse, a mere 17 miles from central London, is readily accessible by road or rail, there being no fewer than three nearby stations. It is the home of the Derby, arguably the most famous horse race in the world and, in the view of Hugh McIlvanney, 'one of the last genuine folk festivals left to us', which came into being in a rather bizarre fashion in 1779 when Sir Charles Bunbury lost the toss of a sovereign to the 12th Earl of Derby and so forfeited his right to name a new mile race for three-year-old colts.

The two aristocrats felt that such an event would provide a fitting companion for the Oaks – a 12-furlong race for three-year-old fillies, named after the hunting lodge of Lord Derby – and won for this true child of fortune by his filly Bridget on its inaugural running in 1779. As for the Derby, justice was finally dispensed when Sir Charles Bunbury's Diomed ran out its first winner in 1780 at 6-4. Lord Derby himself had to wait until 1787 when another 'aristocrat' Sir Peter Teazle, a horse he had named to honour his second wife, triumphed at 2-1.

There were, perhaps, two main reasons why the Derby and the Oaks caused such an initial stir and were beginning to alert far-seeing entrepreneurs to their commercial potential by the time the latter event had been run for the first time as a 12-furlong affair in 1784. Firstly, they featured no preliminary heats which, until Lt.-Gen. Anthony St Leger's innovation at Doncaster in 1776, had represented the standard way in which races were decided on the English turf. The Derby and the Oaks thus

EPSOM: Home of the world's two most famous 12 furlong races – the Oaks and the Derby. Racing to the finish on one of his many Derby successes, champion jockey Lester Piggott brings home Nijinsky to a famous victory in the 1970 Epsom Derby.

accelerated the change towards the modern practice of deciding races at one running. Secondly, the colts' Classic was given the ultimate accolade when Disraeli called to mind a part of the insignia of the Order of the Garter, when he described the Derby as the 'blue ribbon (riband) of the turf.

The occasional criticisms that have over the years been made of the Epsom Derby have mainly stemmed from disquiet that the world's best known race is run over such a singular 12-furlong course. That this, in fact, poses a threat to the valuable thoroughbreds that race upon it, is a belief that the full catalogue of recent Derby catastrophies would seem to justify. For example, despite storming home in the 1980 Derby, Henbit was found to have cracked a cannon bone in his off fore. Tragically, this injury prevented him from ever again distinguishing himself on the racecourse. Such accidents should, however,

be placed in perspective and be seen as the penalty that some horses with less than perfect conformation occasionally have to pay if they fail Epsom's searching test or meet with ill-luck in running. The risk that their charges may sustain injury in a race in which some jockeys abandon their customary caution and ride at a dangerously wild pace on constantly changing gradients, may deter a few owners from letting their horses take their chances. However, the Derby still deserves Disraeli's eulogy.

A Derby winner can bring a fortune in stud fees to its owner. Shergar, for example, the ill-fated 1981 winner, was syndicated for £10 million.

The present Derby course was first used in 1872, after complaints were finally heeded that the steep 1-in-18 gradient in the first 500 yards of the new 1848 course influenced results to a disproportionate extent.

Contestants tackling a mile and a half and (as

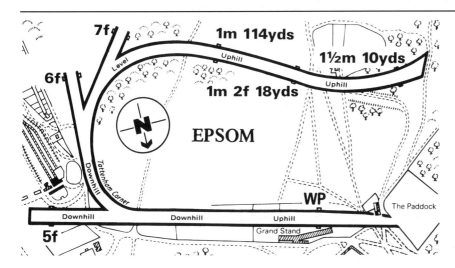

EPSOM: *Plan of the course.*

discovered in 1991) 10 yards at Epsom initially encounter ground that rises quite steeply and then turns appreciably to the right. By the time it enters the section that runs past the mile post, the Derby field has raced round something of a dog leg. With just under a mile to run, at a point where again a road traverses the course, the track starts to swing quite sharply to the left. It also continues to rise, but in a more gradual, if uneven, manner. At the top of the hill, some 166 yards short of the half-way mark at the 6-furlong pole, the Derby runners meet ground that is 134 feet higher than that at the start and then race on a level stretch of almost 300 yards, that includes quite a large part of this first left-hand bend which is longer and rather more gradual than its sharp successor at Tattenham Corner. This famous feature of the Derby course used to be far sharper prior to its alteration earlier this century and is preceded by a steep descent of 40 feet in 300 yards which has proved the undoing of so many ungainly Derby runners. After Tattenham Corner comes the run-in of just under four furlongs, the ground continuing to fall, but at a gradually decreasing rate until a mere 100 yards remain.

It is from this position well inside the crucial final furlong that the ground appears to rise steadily to the winning post. This is, in fact, an optical illusion under which tiring Epsom finishers, quite as much as a whole host of turf writers, have plainly laboured. As the Ordnance Survey map confirms, the ground is practically flat. A thorough survey carried out in 1980 shows a rise of barely three feet over 100 yards.

Even more surprising is the fact, pointed out by Mr T.P. Neligan, the Managing Director of United Racecourses Limited, that at the winning post the ground slopes away from the stand very sharply – by

five feet in fact across the course – so a horse rounding Tattenham Corner crossing over to the stands side and then gradually back towards the winning post on the far side could probably maintain a downhill momentum all the way!

All in all, although Epsom is not really a testing track, its 12-furlong 10-yard course does impose a true test of stamina. The initial uphill section is taken at a taxing pace which saps the strength of non-stayers and leaves them with little in reserve by the time they face the long run-in. As well as making demands on the stamina, courage and resolution of its contestants, the brisk pace of the Derby puts their speed on trial.

Perhaps the heaviest demands the Derby makes are on the adaptability of those taking part. As John Hislop has stated so succinctly, 'the perfect Derby horse must be able to race smoothly and effectively under a number of distinctive and different circumstances'. So an almost flawless conformation is required. Indeed, it is rare that a Derby winner's physical make-up can be seriously faulted.

Despite its difficulties and the significant fact that only the very best of jockeys like Steve Donoghue and Lester Piggott have been described as 'Derby specialists', the course should not present accomplished jockeys with any serious difficulty. Apart from ensuring that their mounts are not asked to tackle the initial uphill stretch at too taxing an early pace, jockeys should take them the shortest way over its first 4 furlongs. For low-drawn horses, this entails tacking over from the inside rails towards the far rails at the 1 mile 2 furlong gate, and then moving smartly back again to regain an inside berth in time to save ground around the first long left-hand bend. As for Tattenham Corner, most jockeys like to be lying 'handy' as it is negotiated, although many a Derby has been won by a horse that has appeared hopelessly boxed-in or too far behind at this particular point. On the run-in itself, it is vital that horses are kept balanced as they descend ground that slopes from left to right towards the inside running rail. The centre of the course is the ideal position, since it gives the jockey clear ground from which he can deliver his final challenge, as Lester Piggott demonstrated to such good effect on his very first Derby winner, Never Say Die, in 1954.

Epsom is also associated with other well-known races which sadly in recent seasons have lost much of the kudos they enjoyed long before many major flat races were 'listed' or given 'pattern' status. One such event was the Great Metropolitan Handicap, first run in 1846 over Epsom's now defunct, perhaps even eccentric, 2 mile 2 furlong 'Great Metropolitan' course, which started just beyond the winning post in front of the stands. This race, once popularly known as the Publicans' Derby, today is not even accorded 'listed' status, but figures as a lowly handicap run over a mere 12 furlongs 10 yards in late April.

The Great Metropolitan is, however, one of the two highlights of the first Spring meeting when interestingly both the Derby and the Oaks were originally contested. The other is another well-known Epsom race, the 1 mile 2 furlong 18 yard City and Suburban Handicap first run in 1851.

Events run over 7 and 6 furlongs at Epsom are started from short spurs which soon lead into the round course, while races over 5 furlongs are staged on the 'Egmont' course which for Epsom is unusually straight. The belief that this is the world's fastest sprint course is strengthened by the fact that the fastest time ever recorded over 5 furlongs was clocked by Indigenous, a four-year-old who humped no less than 9 st 5 lbs to victory on firm going at the 1960 Derby meeting at an average speed of 41.98 mph.

All events run over the minimum distance at Epsom start from a third spur after which comes a 4-furlong run-in. Not surprisingly, sprinters that can fly from the stalls and continue to make the running at a relentless gallop are at an advantage as the track they race on is almost all downhill, although it is possible for a horse to win if it is brought from behind by an experienced jockey who is a good judge of pace.

At Epsom, with the stalls in any position, high-drawn horses, if they have the speed to fly from the gate and maintain a fast pace, are favoured in sprints and even more so in races up to 10 furlongs if the going remains good or firm (as it often is, since the track has a chalky subsoil). In such events, the acquisition

and retention by jockeys of ideal places from which to deliver effective challenges is far more crucial than the allocation of any particular position in the draw.

As for other prestigious races staged at Epsom, the Group One Coronation Cup run over the full Derby distance, is often captured by a (sometimes French) four-year-old middle distance performer in peak form, while two other notable events are staged at the June meeting, the Diomed Stakes (run to commemorate the winner of the first Derby) over 1 mile and 114 yards and the Northern Dancer Stakes, a 12 furlong 10 yard handicap run in memory of the sire of such Derby winners as Nijinsky, The Minstrel and Secreto.

EQUINE RESEARCH STATION
Animal Health Trust
PO Box 5
Balaton Lodge
Snailwell Road
Newmarket CB8 7DW
Tel. (0638) 66111

The remit of this organization, which is solely dependent on voluntary contributions, is to investigate problems of health and disease, not just on racecourses, but in horses and ponies of all types. It also records horses' blood types, which is important in establishing the parentage of foals.

EQUINE SWIMMING POOL
Most useful means (as with human beings) of establishing and maintaining fitness. One of its main functions is to enable a lame horse to keep on exercising and to stay fit. Many racehorses can be brought on by several lengths through swimming. Indeed, many trainers make it a prelude to actual training on the gallops. It should be noted that if horses are found to have been trained in inappropriate pools, they can be disqualified.

EVERY CHANCE
A horse is said to have had this only when it has failed to make much of it.

❢ EXES
Slang for six to one (6-1).

❢ EXES AND A HALF
Slang for six and a half to one (13-2).

❢ EXES TO ROUF
Since 'rouf' is a scrambled version of four, this term signifies 6-4.

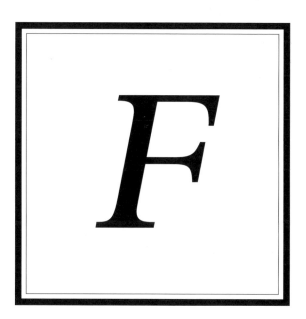

❢ FACE

Slang for five to two (5-2).

❢ FACES

Slang for backers who are greatly feared in the ring because their past wagers have proved so successful. If such individuals, who are generally professional backers, stable commissioners or very astute owners or trainers, are recognized by the bookmakers who take their money, these particular traders will, probably after they have hedged some of the 'smart money' involved, alert their colleagues.

Some bookmakers can increase their profits by what is known as 'betting to faces' – hedging bets taken on certain runners that are thought to come from an inspired source and attracting good business for their rivals by extending the odds they quote against them.

FADED

Fairly self-explanatory adjective for runner once in serious contention that does not remain so in a race's latter stages.

If the form book or one's specialist racing newspaper reveals that a runner, especially a jumper, faded first time out – perhaps through lack of race-fitness – it should not be ruled out of calculations.

FAIRYHOUSE

Fairyhouse Club Limited
Ratoath
Co. Meath
Ireland
Tel. (01) 256167

How to get there:
From North: N2, N3
From south: N2, N3
From East: R125
From West: R125
By Air: Dublin Airport
Approximately 15 miles from Dublin

The Irish Grand National is the traditional highlight of this course's three-day Easter fixture. This also features the Gold Cup Hurdle, the Huzzar Handicap Hurdle, the Power Gold Cup and the Dan Moore Handicap Chase.

The 'National' is run over 3 1/2 miles and was first contested in 1870. It has been won by Gold Cup and Grand National winners alike, as Desert Orchid (in 1990) and Rhyme 'n' Reason (in 1985) both confirmed. Seven-year-olds have easily the best record in this often gruelling marathon in which

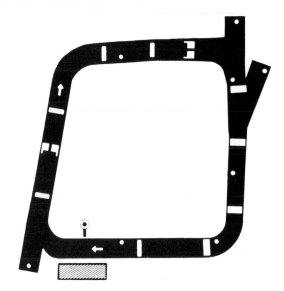

FAIRYHOUSE: Plan of the course, which is the home of the Irish Grand National.

Brown Lad thrice prevailed.

As a racecourse, Fairyhouse came into being when the now defunct Ward Union Hunt transferred from Ashbourne in County Meath in the middle of the last century. It is a right-handed, good galloping circuit on which both National Hunt

and flat racing are staged. The flat and hurdle tracks are both undulating in places and extend for some 15 furlongs, while the steeplechase course is a furlong longer.

One race run over the latter is the highlight of an early March fixture. This is the Dawn Run Chase which commemorates the only jumper to have captured both Cheltenham's Champion Hurdle and Gold Cup.

The track, which presents jumpers with eleven obstacles, is a decidedly square-shaped affair whose wide straights, very fair fences and invariably good going (thanks to its sandy subsoil) are much appreciated by trainers, jockeys and spectators.

Fairyhouse has always enjoyed progressive management and a large proportion of its takings is ploughed back into providing more and better accommodation.

Dublin airport is only 10 miles away.

FAKENHAM

Fakenham Racecourse
The Racecourse
Fakenham
Norfolk NR21 7NY
Tel. (0328) 862388

How to get there:
From North: B1105
From South: B1065
From East: A1067
From West: A148
By Rail: King's Lynn
By Air: Helicopter facilities

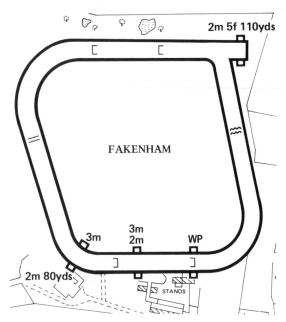

FAKENHAM: Plan of the course. Its proximity to the royal residence of Sandringham is one of the reasons why this small East Anglian course plays host to the Queen's Cup and the Prince of Wales' Cup.

The fixtures staged on this East Anglian country course, although fairly minor, are friendly sporting affairs especially if the weather is fine enough to have a picnic in the course enclosure.

As is appropriate on a course on which so many hunters' races are staged, and which is owned by the West Norfolk Hunt, something of a point-to-point atmosphere prevails at Fakenham whose proximity to Sandringham is the reason why the Prince of Wales' Cup and the Queen's Cup are two prestigious races that are contested each season.

The track is left-handed and square looking and, since it is only one mile in extent, is a tight affair that is less well suited to long-striding gallopers than to handy front running types that can cope well with its none too severe undulations.

FALLS: Probably the most serious danger facing jockeys or indeed their mounts is the fall. This picture shows riders tackling one of the fearsome fences in the Grand National at Aintree.

The 200-yard uphill run-in is the only course feature that is in any way testing, since Fakenham's six fences are far from formidable and good ground is much more common than firm, soft or heavy going, such is the excellent drainage provided by the course's sandy subsoil.

Rail travellers will find, rather irritatingly, that after travelling from King's Cross or Liverpool Street to King's Lynn or Norwich, they still have a journey of more than 20 miles to complete to reach the course which is more conveniently accessible from the former town on the A148 than from the latter on the A1067. Air travellers in fixed-winged aircraft may land at Little Snoring airstrip which is five miles from the course.

❢ FALL

To lay a horse at a longer rate of odds than that at which it eventually starts. In bookmaking this is an occupational hazard to which a 'dentist' is particularly exposed.

FALLS

These, the bugbear of National Hunt (and occasionally) flat race jockeys, can cause them injury, disablement and even death. In recent seasons, though such measures as the replacement of concrete posts and wooden running rails with plastic alternatives and new regulations regarding the avoidance of jockeys too injured to be moved out of the way of horses, a good deal has been done to ensure that the consequences of falls do not become even more distressingly dire.

For racehorses, too, many measures have been taken to try to prevent their falling and to minimize their suffering following this fate. For example, the Grand National course was so radically altered for its 1990 running that a record time on the fast ground that then prevailed was almost inevitable.

Only at Aintree, Ascot, Cheltenham, Haydock Park, Newbury, Newcastle, Sandown Park and Wetherby would most judges agree that the fences are formidable.

'FALSE' FAVOURITE

A horse heading the market whose right to do so can be questioned because it figures in the opening show at a rate of odds that suspiciously is far more generous than its last ante-post quotation, or because its opening odds are trimmed by a far smaller proportion than that by which the price of its principal market rival contracts, or, because the odds against its winning (computed from form and time ratings) may not correlate with either its opening quote or starting price. Sometimes when a horse on which they are initially unwilling to trade fails to receive a market quotation in the first betting show, bookmakers make a great show of laying another runner against the field, thereby suggesting it is the undisputed favourite.

FASHION AND RACING

These have gone hand in hand ever since, in the nineteenth century, racecourses were fenced off into separate enclosures to protect the sensibilities of ladies from undesirables. Articles with such titles as 'Seen at Goodwood' have long appeared in society magazines, fashion journals and even racing publications, while *The Times* still devotes a page or two to the season's sartorial highlight, Ascot's royal meeting. This is so fashionable that television commentary teams include fashion experts whose comments have nothing to do with horses. English race meetings which some attend so as to be seen as well as to watch the racing are: Ascot, Ayr (for the Western meeting in September), Chester (in May), Epsom (for the Derby meeting), Goodwood, Newmarket (July meeting), Sandown (on Sloane Ranger night) and York (in August). Cheltenham attracts the county set who have their own night out at this track on the first Wednesday evening in May.

FAVOURITE (AND FAVOURITES' RECORDS)

Term applied to a horse which either solely or jointly heads the betting market through being quoted at the shortest price.

FAVOURITE (AND FAVOURITES' RECORDS): Favourites are treated with the upmost respect, for they carry with them the hopes, and possibly fortunes, of many. This print from 1861 shows one such horse as the centre of the crowds' attention.

Many thousands of backers make predictions of the outcomes of particular examples of certain types of races which are based on either the impressive general record of well-fancied horses in such events, or the good record of the market leader in past runnings. Such thinking is unfortunately based on the questionable assumption that the result of a specific race is in some way influenced by one apparently significant aspect of its history. As R. W. Griffiths stated so succinctly, 'It doesn't take a logician to realize that current rather than historic factors wield the greater influence on a contest, or that competing horses rather than non-competitors should be considered ...'

The title 'favourite' is necessarily artificial and ephemeral and designed to operate within the context of one race only. It is a short-term status which is initially allocated in betting forecasts, perhaps established by layers and confirmed or transferred by the distribution of punters' money.

To base any selection method on the shortest-priced horse is, to say the least, dabbling with an imprecise science. To back a favourite just because it has a good record in a particular race is futile.

Many followers of market leaders subscribe to another fallacious view that such animals are strongly fancied; in fact, many 'false favourites' go to post in the course of a season. What is more it should be realized that, understandably, connections are as fond of long-priced winners as the ordinary punter!

However, it should not be imagined from the above comments that carrying out research into the fate of favourites and other horses that have played a prominent part in the betting market is an entirely futile proceeding. If the results of such work are interpreted in a restrained and relevant manner this will provide a few useful general pointers.

The most exhaustive survey into the fate of horses figuring prominently in the betting market was that conducted by Paul Major in his book *Horse Sense* which covers 5000 British races and most illuminatingly indicates that in some 72.2 per cent of these the winner came from the first three positions in the betting market. Another respected authority, Methodmaker of the *Raceform Handicap Book*, once maintained that in 83 per cent of races, victory goes to a horse which occupies one of the first five places in the betting.

Statistics show that lower-priced contestants fare best in non-handicaps open to horses of all ages, which is one further reason for betting in top-class pattern races since their race conditions are expressly designed to attract such animals. Favourites have such a good overall record in these events because so many of them have a genuine entitlement to head the market. They are frequently fairly obvious form horses, whose advantage in taking on their rivals on a weight for age, rather than ability, basis in a non-handicap is readily appreciated by both bookmakers and backers alike.

Some punters believe in following beaten favourites, through presuming they are frequently placed to retrieve the cash their connections have lost through their defeat. A few backers even support a beaten favourite which runs in a more prestigious and valuable race next time out, because it will be carrying a lot less weight.

Any indiscriminate following of beaten favourites is not recommended. On the other hand there are sometimes valid explanations for the defeat of a market leader last time out, and if such an animal appears genuine and seems to be better suited to the conditions of a race it is about to contest, it should not be disregarded.

FEEL THE GROUND

A horse which experiences discomfort as its feet encounter firm ground is said to 'feel the ground'. Only a minority of racehorses relish running on such terrain and identifying these can be worthwhile.

FIDDLER

Bookmaker operating 'outside' in a minor ring who only 'bets up to' a small amount. His limited capital means he may have to 'bluff' some bets or reduce his liabilities on certain runners if these become dangerously large by 'hedging' with other bookmakers in the main ring.

FIDO

Bet on five selections producing ten doubles and ten trebles.

FIELD BOOK (See Captain)

The book in which his clerk records each of the many individual bets a bookmaker lays to his clients.

FIELD MONEY

The sum of the many separate amounts of money that have been staked on the outcome of a certain race with a particular bookmaker. The bookmaker's clerk enters this figure in the fourth column of his captain (see under this entry). At major meetings a vast sum can constitute a bookmaker's field money.

FIELD MONEY TABLE (To the nearest stake unit)

Odds	Stake	Odds	Stake	Odds	Stake	Odds	Stake
50-1	2	7-2	22	Evens	50	2-7	78
33-1	3	10-3	23	20-21	51	1-4	80
25-1	4	3-1	25	10-11	52	2-9	81
20-1	5	11-4	27	5-6	54	1-5	83
16-1	6	5-2	29	45	56	2-11	85
14-1	7	95-40	30	8-11	58	1-6	86
12-1	8	9-4	31	4-6	60	1-7	87
10-1	9	2-1	33	8-13	62	1-8	8
9-1	10	15-8	35	4-7	64	1-10	91
8-1	11	7-4	36	8-15	65	1-12	92
15-2	12	13-8	38	1-2	67	1-14	93
7-1	13	6-4	40	49	69	1-16	94
6-1	14	11-8	42	40-95	70	1-20	95
11-2	15	5-4	44	2-5	71	1-25	96
5-1	17	6-5	46	4-11	73	1-33	97
9-2	19	11-10	48	1-3	75	1-50	98
4-1	20	21-20	49	3-10	77		

FIELD MONEY TABLE

Useful collection of figures which indicates various market prices and the stakes that have to be invested at these rates to bring about a return of 100 points. Such figures for 'coupled' betting appear above. If a field money table takes a more precise form and expresses individual odds in terms of exact percentages, the backer can, from complete betting shows, calculate the degree of 'over-round' to which a bookmaker is working, i.e. the margin of profit he is planning to make.

FIELD, THE

Reference to all of the runners in a race. If mention of a particular rate of odds precedes this expression, e.g. '3-1 the field', this means that these odds are those currently quoted against the favourite's prospects of defeating all of its opponents, i.e. the whole 'field'.

FILLY

Female horse that is under the age of four.

FILMS, RACING

Whether involving chariot races, mythical Aintree wins (as in National Velvet), or based closely on actual horses – such as Phar Lap, Gay Future (the coup horse), or Aldaniti – racing films vividly demonstrate how racing's heady mix of action, suspense and excitement makes for splendid screen entertainment.

FIND LITTLE

Said of a horse that, when asked by its jockey to make a greater effort, only marginally manages to do so.

FINISHING POSITIONS

Some backers believe that if the number that indicates the most recent of these in a horse's formline produce certain permutations, e.g. 014, this is a particularly propitious pointer. Since a finisher shown as third last time out may have been beaten by a furlong in a three-horse race it is folly to regard any particular combination as somehow magical!

FIRM

Said of a horse, other than a rank outsider, whose price in the market neither contracts nor lengthens but holds steady.

FITNESS, RACE

Although some trainers are adept at producing horses that can win first time out, even after layoffs as long as several years in some impressive cases, there is no doubt that horses fit from having had a recent run often enjoy a distinct advantage. The problem, however, is how to gauge the likely extent of the advantage conferred by a recent 'pipe opening' placed or winning run.

There may well be sound physiological reasons why recent participation in a short rather than a long race is likely to confer a greater advantage.

Obviously a sprint should not take as much out of a horse as would a long-distance slog.

Given that steeplechasers and long-distance performers on the flat need time to recover from their exertions, the backer might do well to concentrate on mature sprinters that turn out after a recent run. Like human athletes, equine sprinters often 'peak' for a short period in a season, but within this can register victory after victory!

If mature sprinters not only have the benefit of a recent promising run, but are also well drawn and top-rated by a time expert, they may well turn out to be true 'pigeon catchers'. Statistics also show that in 2-mile hurdle races, rather than in much more exhausting steeplechases, runners with recent promising form are frequently successful.

FIVESPOT

Special bet offered by Ladbrokes on five selections that produces a total of 15 bets: five singles, four doubles, three trebles, two four-timers, and one five-fold accumulator.

FLAG

Four selections combined in 23 bets. It consists of a Yankee plus four selections covered in single stakes about bets.

FLAG, THE WHITE

When the runners have arrived at the start, the roll has been called by the starter and he is ready to send them on their way, a white flag is hoisted and the field is then under 'starter's orders'. From that moment any horse backed becomes a liability to bookmaker or backer.

FLIMPING

Attempting to persuade a backer to accept a price which is about to be extended or can be bettered elsewhere. Sometimes a bookmaker's floorman can do this effectively by recommending to all and sundry in a loud and hardly confidential manner that his employer reduce, as a matter of some urgency, a particular rate of odds that is showing on his board. Such behaviour is a well-known 'come on'.

FLOORMAN

Apart from ham-acting in the above manner, this particular bookmaker's functionary spends his time ensuring that the prices his 'guv'nor' quotes are in line with those available elsewhere in the ring and in carrying out any 'laying off' or 'hedging' that may be necessary. Thus floormen are seldom seen carrying much overweight. Many have exotic nicknames and are colourful members of racing's varied cast.

FOLKESTONE

Folkestone Racecourse
Westenhanger
Hythe
Kent
Tel. (0303) 266407

How to get there:
From North: B2068
Fom South: A259
From East: M20
From West: M20
By Rail: Westenhanger
By Air: Helicopter facilities

Just to the north of Hythe, seven miles north-east of Folkestone, is the only track now left in the 'Garden of England'. It occupies a suitably pretty site at Westenhanger adjoining a country station of that name which lies on the mainlines to the Kent coast from Charing Cross or Waterloo which are approximately seventy miles away. Londoners travelling here by road should take the A20 and then leave the M20 at junction 11.

The track itself is a pear-shaped affair that runs right-handed for 1 mile and 3 furlongs over ground that although frequently undulating, does so in none too pronounced a fashion.

Horses contesting races over 2 miles 93 yards, 1 mile 7 furlongs 92 yards and 1 $1/2$ miles start from various points along the 6-furlong course, pass the stands, and then make a complete circuit of the round course, before finally negotiating the run-in of approximately three furlongs.

The 6-furlong course, which is straight throughout, largely features a gently undulating terrain. The round course tends to level out as the post is approached.

When the stalls are positioned on the stands side, high-drawn runners are slightly favoured at Folkestone in 5-and 6- furlong sprints. By contrast, in races run on the fairly tight right-handed turns of the round course, the advantage lies with those allotted high positions in the stalls, especially in races over 1 mile 1 furlong 149 yards and 12 furlongs since these particular distances involve so much turning track.

'Handy' horses which are adaptable and sure-

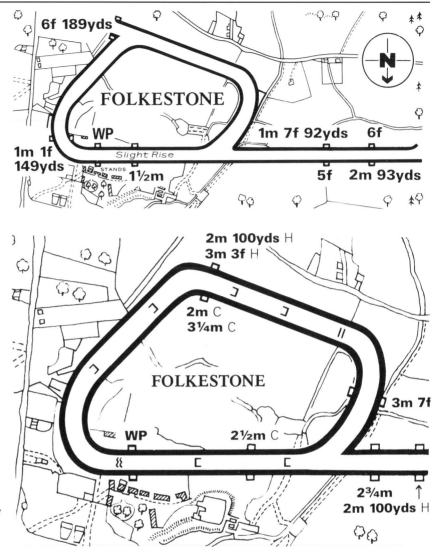

FOLKESTONE: Plan of the Flat course (top), and the National Hunt course (bottom).

footed, tend to appreciate Folkestone's fairly sharp and awkwardly right-handed bends and its frequent undulations that make it resemble a rather gentle switchback. Runners on both the straight and the round courses need to be ridden by experienced jockeys who can keep them balanced if the ground becomes slippery.

Folkestone is generally considered to be an easy course that does not really favour the long-striding, resolute galloper whose strong suit is stamina. Indeed, short runners, if handled by tactically astute jockeys, can win over distances on this rather lowly track over which they would not triumph elsewhere.

The 1962 2000 Guineas winner Privy Councillor is commemorated by the most prestigious flat race (a 6-furlong sprint for three-year-olds) run at Folkestone in mid-April. The 5-furlong Metropole Challenge Cup for first-season performers is staged at the end of May.

National Hunt racing is also staged at Westenhanger over eight very easy obstacles and the fact that the run-in for steeplechasers only extends for a furlong (and that for hurdlers for only an additional 30 yards) means that nippy front-running jumpers often enjoy an advantage.

One particular evening meeting in early May is confined to hunter 'chasers and attracts both followers of hounds and point-to-point. Its light-hearted atmosphere seems appropriate, as one race staged is the Cuckoo Maiden Hunters' Chase.

Folkestone's French connection, recently made much stronger by the building of the Channel Tunnel, has been recalled by such races as the Le Touquet Novices Hurdle.

FOLLOW THE MONEY

A betting ploy that, if it is to be successful, should be practised with some discrimination. A better tactic is to determine which horse is causing bookmakers to revise their original estimate of its chance by the greatest proportion.

FONTWELL PARK

Fontwell Park
Near Arundel
West Sussex BN18 0SX
Tel. (0243) 543335

How to get there:
From North: A29
From South: A29
From East: A27
From West: A27
By Rail: Barnham
By Air: Chichester Aerodrome

Figure-of-eight courses leave some horses at sixes and sevens and that is why those that have repeatedly shown that they relish running on its left-and right-handed 'chase course are often worth yet another interest at Fontwell Park. The situation and picturesque setting of this singular Sussex course that lies between Goodwood and Chichester less than sixty miles from London explain its popularity. Most Londoners arrive at the track initially via the M23 and then take the A29 until it meets the A27. Thereafter, the course is well-signposted.

Rail travellers should head for Barnham station, which is readily accessible from Victoria, and then take a 3-mile bus ride to the course, which offers no facilities for air travellers.

A good view is available from the three grandstands of the somewhat disorientating sight of steeplechasers negotiating the seven fences on Fontwell's tight circuit of just over a mile. It ends with a short run-in of only 230 yards which rather distinctively runs uphill and slightly to the left and so makes a last further demand on the adaptability of the 'chasers that have finally to tackle it.

Nickel Coin, the 1951 Grand National winner, is recalled by a 'chase run at Fontwell over 2 $^1/_2$ miles. This race is staged at an early October meeting.

As for hurdlers, the well-known 1966 Champion Hurdler Salmon Spray has been commemorated by a Fontwell contest staged in late October. This, like all races run over the minor obstacles on this track, only involves tight left-handed turns and four flights on each circuit.

FOOD ON RACECOURSES (See Catering, Racecourse)

Whether featuring whelks, distinctive doughnuts (as at Cheltenham), sausage rolls or the lavish culinary delights served up by specialist racecourse caterers in well-appointed restaurants, racecourse food is something that defies generalization. Much of it no longer deserves to be the butt of dismissive humour.

FORECASTS

The computer forecast is a bet offered by bookmakers. Clients have to name the first two finishers in correct order. It is possible in fields of five or more to make a reverse or dual forecast bet on the tote, in which case one's named pair can finish in either order.

FORFEIT, DECLARATION OF

If an owner of a horse or his credited agent declines at a stipulated stage before a race is run to pay a further sum so as to keep this animal in a race, forfeit of the initial entry fees will be declared.

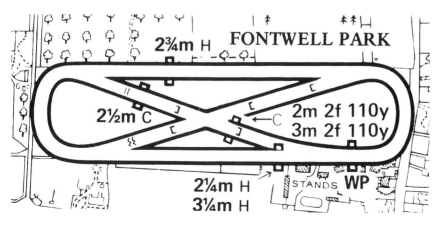

FONTWELL PARK:
Plan of the course.

FORFEIT LIST

A list (published regularly in the *Racing Calendar*) of all persons who have defaulted on payments due for entering a horse and failed to meet other financial obligations and who are thus debarred from running their horses or taking part in other racing activities. It is not concerned with betting debts.

FORM AND TIME RATINGS

These, as Alex Bird, Britain's most successful post-war punter once pointed out, form the foundation of successful betting. When assessing the ratings of private handicappers and specialists in race times, one should remember that they relate to past performances and thus make no allowance for factors on the day which are likely to prove crucial. The going, jockeyship, the course and the distance of the race in question, need to be taken into account and the 'raw' ratings provided by form and time experts in the national and sporting press amended accordingly.

Of the various private handicaps that are published in national dailies only a few – the W factor ratings of the *Daily Express* and the Spotform feature in the *Daily Mirror* for example-make any allowance for such race-day variables.

Three further factors, each of which is evident from study of a horse's past form and which may entitle it to have its rating increased are, consistency, evidence of recent improvement and the possession of courage. Consideration of these factors constitutes a useful way of refining racehorse ratings.

FOUR FURLONG RACES

The last of these was a selling race staged at Hurst Park on 27 May 1912. The Jockey Club, alarmed that such events and other sprints over 5 and 6 furlongs might become too frequent and so have an adverse effect on the thoroughbred, finally abolished all half-mile sprints at the start of the 1913 season.

FREE HANDICAP

A race staged over 7 furlongs at Newmarket each spring, for which every two-year-old with good enough form is given a weight during the previous winter. Some of the few top-class horses to have won the Free Handicap are Mid-Day Sun, Wilwyn, Quorum, Petite Etoile and Moorestyle.

FRESH, GOES WELL WHEN

Description applied to a racehorse whose form suggests that it performs well after a longish break from racing.

FRONT LINE LAYER

Bookmaker who occupies a premier pitch in the front line of the main ring in Tattersalls.

FRONT RUNNERS

Horses that bowl along and lead their fields. Courses with short run-ins tend to suit such performers. The most spectacular and unluckiest front runner of recent times was Crisp, who was heartbreakingly beaten after leading for almost every yard of the fast-run 1973 National, that Red Rum, receiving 23 lbs, snatched from him virtually on the line.

G

GALLOPING TRACK

One that is far from tight, is sufficiently lengthy and free of any configurations likely to unbalance long-striding racehorses, so giving these a chance to stretch out and to get fully into their strides.

GALWAY

Galway Racecourse
Ballybrit
Galway
Ireland
Tel: (091) 53870

How to get there:

From North: N17, N84
From South: N18
From East: N6
From West: N59, R336
By Rail: Galway
By Air: Galway Carnmore Airport

Fairly riotous celebration has always been something of a feature at Galway ever since a band of hard riding sportsmen from the local hunt acquired their rather apt name of the Blazers by burning down a nearby hotel. Indeed, the hospitality at Galway's

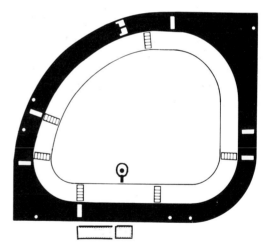

GALWAY: *Plan of the course, over which the Waterford Crystal Handicap, the Northern Telecom Handicap Steeplechase and the Galway Plate are run.*

legendary week-long festival meeting in late July and early August is so overpowering that one needs stamina of one's own to last the course.

In quieter moments one can appreciate the view of Galway castle and the beautiful backdrop provided by the far-off Clare coastline.

Galway's right-handed track might appear to be a

fairly easy affair but is anything but that, as an uphill run to the last jump is cunningly contrived to find out the non-stayer. The course, a distinct switchback only about seven furlongs round, is a tight, sharp affair over which past winners naturally have a good record; some judges believe high-drawn horses have a slight advantage in races run over 7 furlongs and 1 mile.

The popular Galway Plate regularly attracts the attention of English trainers and jockeys. Other well-known festival races that have proved popular have been the GPT Amateur Handicap, the McDonogh Handicap, the Galway Hurdle, the O'Malley Construction Handicap and the Oranmore Dairies Handicap Hurdle.

The autumn meeting is generally a three-day event in early September. Here the most prestigious races contested are the Old Vic Series Handicap, the Waterford Crystal Handicap Hurdle and the Northern Telecom Handicap Steeplechase, while at a recent innovation – an October Bank holiday meeting – the Bank of Ireland has sponsored an enticingly billed 'family race day'.

Some racegoers travel to the track daily on the N59 from accommodation taken on the Connemara coast. The many 'Dubs' who drive in from their country's capital do so along the N4 and N6, while Limerick-based racegoers can travel north on the N18. Galway station is well served.

To top jockey Tommy Carmody, Galway *is* the Irish National Hunt season. It certainly is a meeting at which the volume of money wagered is prodigious and the 'crack' unrivalled.

Galway races, it seems, date back to the eighteenth century and in the words of Arthur Macgahon 'still live up to those exciting days when a horseman in a hunt or a race who did not choose the highest stone wall or jump the most dangerous course to follow, was a man who would never do for Galway'!

GAME, THE

A reference that can have both a general and a particular meaning; the former to the horse racing industry, the latter to the contest between bookmaker and backer.

GARAGE

To retain some of one's winnings, rather than add them to one's next stake.

GELDINGS

Emasculated male racehorses. Such animals, for fairly obvious reasons, find the negotiation of fences and hurdles far more comfortable.

GENERAL STUD BOOK

The Debrett of racehorses. First compiled as a register by James Weatherby of the family that still act as racing's 'office manager', this work lists all genuinely thoroughbred racehorses and their progeny that have been foaled in the British Isles. In the case of the latter, their eligibility for entry now has to be supported by the results of blood tests.

New volumes of this breeder's directory appear every four years and annual supplements provide updates of eligible foalings.

GETTING OUT STAKES

Backer's optimistic reference to the last race on a racecard. The County Handicap Hurdle at Cheltenham's March festival and the Queen Alexandra Stakes at Royal Ascot in June have been well-known examples.

❗ GIMMEL

Slang for three to one (3-1).

GO FOR A WALK (IN THE MARKET)

Said of a horse whose odds move outwards in the betting as it fails to find support.

GO FOR THE GLOVES

To make a confident, substantial bet.

GOING, THE

A vital race-day factor. Its range includes heavy, soft, good to soft or yielding (the more descriptive term that is preferred in Ireland), good, good to firm, firm or hard.

Only a few horses are truly at home in mud or really relish soft going, so it is a considerable advantage to know their names.

Phil Bull, the founder of Timeform, is credited with the theory that a light horse (particularly one carrying a light weight) may do well in heavy conditions as it will skim over the top of the mud, since requiring less effort than a heavier horse to pull its feet out.

In addition, a horse with a high-knee, round action is able to pull its feet out of heavy ground far more easily than one with a low 'daisy cutting' action. Other experts argue that horses with little 'donkey' feet tend to be 'stick in the muds', while those with large 'policeman's feet' can happily splash along on top of it.

Correspondingly, it is only a minority of horses that really relish hearing their feet rattle on really firm or hard ground, and for this reason trainer Jenny

Pitman is loath to run her charges during National Hunt's little season in September.

Raceform and *Chaseform* notebooks, via their invaluable 'Index to (past) Winners' feature and, of course, specialist racing dailies most usefully detail the ground conditions on which past winners have scored and on which racecourses.

In France, a penetrometer be used to guage the going.

GOING REPORTS

Advance information on the likely going provided in newspapers, radio bulletins or on Ceefax. The longest range going reports appear in the *Sporting Life* and the *Racing Post*.

'GOOD' MONEY

Money staked on a particular runner. Bookmakers may regard this favourably merely because it amounts to a considerable sum. Alternatively, they may do so because it comes from known 'sharps' – backers whose judgement is respected in the ring.

GOOD THING, A

Horse that seems invincible.

GOODWOOD

Goodwood Racecourse Limited
Goodwood
Chichester
West Sussex P018 0XP
Tel. (0243) 774107

How to get there:
From North: A286
From South: A286
From East: A27
From West: A27
By Rail: Chichester
By Air: Chichester Aerodrome; Helicopter facilities

Goodwood, like Epsom and Royal Ascot, is not just a racecourse but also the setting for a social occasion of some significance. The track is one of the most peculiarly shaped and picturesque in the world.

That the course should be so distinctive was the deliberate intention of the two men responsible for its creation and development, the Duke of Richmond and Lord George Bentinck. As a typical Victorian patrician, the former was anxious that racing be 'divested of its coarse and disgusting accessories'. Since his extensive private estate took in a crest of the Sussex Downs, he had an ideal opportunity both to create a distinctive racecourse and to deny entrance to undesirables.

Thus, almost from its inception, Goodwood became part of the social season. Still today, many of those who go racing to be seen will be found at Goodwood's main midsummer festival.

It seems appropriate that currently the most expensive enclosure from which in Victorian times even the divorced were excluded, is now known as the 'Richmond', after the fastidious aristocrat.

The Duke would doubtless have been disconcerted had he lived until 1875 to witness the Bohemian behaviour then seen on Trundle Hill,

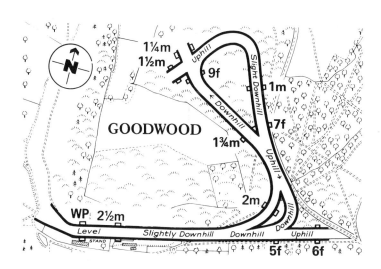

GOODWOOD: Plan of the course.

GOODWOOD: *Lord Bentinck, one of the two men responsible for the creation and development of the course.*

now a cheap rather than a free enclosure well beyond the pale, whose patrons pay a modest sum for a rather distant view of the racing.

It seems unfair that, while the Duke is commemorated through the 6-furlong Richmond Stakes run at the main midsummer festival meeting, Lord George Bentinck, who may have hastened his early death by so energetically designing and laying out the present track, is recalled only by a race that is named after Surplice, the horse he sold two years before its Derby triumph in 1848.

The singular course, which has hardly changed since Bentinck's day, is a complex affair whose peculiarities conspire to produce one of the most breathtaking sights in British racing.

Basically it resembles an equilateral triangle that has lost one of its sides. The far side is very unusual in that it features a tight loop and two turns for home. Horses racing over 5 furlongs encounter one of the fastest sprint courses in Britain and start from stalls that are positioned only a few yards beyond the point at which horses taking part in 7- and 8-furlong events round the lower of the home turns. The best known 5-furlong sprints staged at Goodwood are the King George V Stakes, in which three-year-olds often go well, and the Molecomb Stakes for first-season performers.

A spur which extends beyond the 5-furlong gate allows exciting 6-furlong events to be staged on a straight course known as the 'Stewards' Cup' course, after an historic and highly competitive handicap and heavy betting medium that is quite often won by a three-year-old that can fly along this far from level course. Right from the start, the horses face a taxing climb for a furlong or so and then encounter ground that falls sharply. Thereafter, they have less of a switchback to negotiate.

Horses taking part in Goodwood sprints enjoy an advantage if they can fly from the gate or are habitual front runners. So much descending ground will further suit types ridden by experienced jockeys who can both keep them balanced and help them conserve something for the closing stages of their 'cavalry charge'.

Several important races over the less common distance of 7 furlongs are contested at Goodwood: two such are the Lanson Champagne Vintage Stakes for two-year-olds, and the Prestige Stakes for three-year-old fillies that takes place in late summer.

Horses that run over 7 or 8 furlongs on this track run round the lower and the sharper of the two bends into the straight and then face what is an unusually long run-in of almost five furlongs. Success in these races often goes to horses well-rated by stop-watch holders that can take undulating ground in their stride and handle what must be one of the sharpest, if well-banked, right-handed bends in the country.

Of pattern races run over a mile, the Sussex Stakes staged in midsummer is regarded by many as the 'Mile Championship of Europe'. Three-year-olds often run well in both this and the 1-mile Celebration Mile that is contested a month or so later. The Golden Mile Handicap, an extremely valuable and highly competitive affair in which three-year-olds have performed creditably, was first run in 1987 and is now a major midsummer attraction.

Ten-furlong events are staged over what has been called the 'Craven' course, which starts on the near side of the loop. From here, the runners make their way home by the shortest route which takes them round the higher and more gradual of the bends into the finishing straight. This track is used to stage the Predominate Stakes and the well-known Lupe Stakes in May, the even more prestigious Nassau Stakes for fillies and mares and also the highly competitive Leslie and Godwin Spitfire Handicap (which is often farmed by previously successful handlers).

Another mile-and-a-quarter race, the recently established Select Stakes, is a weight for age contest staged in September, in which it often pays to side with a four-year-old.

Races over a full 12 furlongs are run over what was once known at the 'Gratwicke' course. This severe test of stamina starts from a short spur which extends from the top of the loop on its near side. Its first furlong is straight, but after running uphill it swings to the right, quite gradually at first and then very sharply as it rounds the north-eastern side of the clump, a raised section of the course that lies within the loop.

From this point, the runners enter the straight on the far side of the loop and drop down into an appreciable dip that makes them temporarily invisible to grandstand patrons. A downhill run into the finishing straight via the lower of the two home turns completes the course. The most important 12-furlong race staged each year is the Gordon Stakes for three-year-olds whose running often provides a St Leger pointer.

Events over 1 3/4 miles are run over what is known as the 'Bentinck' course, which appropriately takes in almost all of the track designed by Lord George.

Long-distance races provide Goodwood racegoers

with much prolonged pleasure and some are run over 2 miles and 3 furlongs in front of the grandstands some way down the finishing straight. After negotiating this part of the track over which they race in reverse, the runners negotiate a left-hand bend that turns quite sharply into a straight section of less than a furlong. After this, the track describes something of a dog leg as it diverges slightly to the left on its way to the 1 3/4-mile start and the loop at the top of the course.

The 2 mile 5 furlong course which presents an even more demanding test of stamina and adaptability – only at Ascot is a longer distance raced over on the flat in Britain – is known as the 'Cup' course after the time-honoured Goodwood Cup, first staged as long ago as 1812, the year of Napoleon's retreat from Moscow! Interestingly, this particular race provided the French with a victory of a very different type when Beggarman triumphed in its 1840 running and thus recorded one of the earliest Gallic triumphs on the British turf.

By tradition, horses taking part in this particular marathon line up for a flag start and jump off from a point well under a furlong beyond the winning post. After they have raced the 'wrong' way along the home straight to the two mile three furlong start, they face exactly the same taxing experience as horses that run over this particular marathon distance. Understandably, many previous winners of the slightly shorter Ascot Gold Cup have often triumphed in the Goodwood Cup.

Many races run on this course make considerable demands on a horse's stamina if they are run at speed over its severely undulating sections. However, it is sometimes possible for an experienced jockey to win on a doubtful stayer. This is because the many turns and banks on this track make it possible for such a rider to position his horse so that it is prevented from perceiving clearly what lies ahead of it. Such a tactic can be tantamount to removing as much as 7 lbs from its back. Gordon Richards was apparently most adept in covering up many of his Goodwood mounts in this way so that they could neither become bored nor daunted. In fact, many a long-striding dour stayer finds it difficult to cope with the sharp turns and steep descents of the round course and thus can be beaten by a horse covered up in the Richards style.

The going at Goodwood is seldom heavy since a porous chalky subsoil lies beneath its lush downland turf. In the rather rare event of soft going, some jockeys tend to move their mounts over to the stands side where the ground is supposed to be easier to negotiate.

As for the draw on this delightfully picturesque course, those allotted high stalls positions in races from 7 to 12 furlongs seem to be favoured.

Firm going is a distinct possibility at Goodwood, since four of its meetings take place in late summer or the autumn, yet the turf is sufficiently springy to take the jar out of the ground.

The view at Goodwood, especially from the main grandstand, is regarded by many as the finest on a

From Start to Finish

Above: Racegoers on the road to the Derby, from a painting by George Cruickshank, circa 1850.

Right: The 'race of the century': Grundy neck and neck with Bustino in the King George VI and Queen Elizabeth Diamond Stakes at Ascot in 1975.

Lords of the Ring

Above: The betting ring

Left: A pitch

Centre: Chalking up prices

Bottom left: Market moves

Bottom right: Paying out

*Who looks best in the paddock? Students of conformation
search for final clues before placing their bets on a novice hurdle
at the Cheltenham Festival.*

From Parade to Presentation

Right: Trooping the colours: horses parading before the Gold Cup at Royal Ascot.

Below: Fair and square at the start: a clean break from the stalls at Kempton Park.

Right: Powering home: it's Generous, ridden by Alan Munro, winning the 1991 Irish Derby, held at the Curragh.

Below: Collecting the spoils: Sheikh Hamdam al Maktoum, owner of Nashwan, receiving the trophy for the 2000 Guineas at Newmarket in 1989.

Champion Jockeys

Above: Lester Piggott rides Teenoso to victory in the 1983 Epsom Derby.

Above: A Spy cartoon of the legendary jockey, Fred Archer.

Top right: Peter Scudamore with champion National Hunt trainer Martin Pipe.

Bottom right: Pat Eddery in the weighing room at Newbury.

On the Cards

In the half century or so between 1888 and 1939, more than thirty manufacturers of cigarette cards on four continents produced over 70 different sets - many of which are now collector's items.

GOODWOOD: Coming in for the Gold Cup, a print from 1838 which also shows the splendid grandstand.

British racecourse and thus it is perhaps appropriate that a race is staged annually in memory of the BBC racing commentator, Clive Graham. The course is 706 feet above sea level, providing an excellent vantage point from which to view the Sussex Downs and the distant English Channel. For these, and several other reasons 'glorious' Goodwood marks, for many racegoers, the highlight of the flat racing season.

It can be reached rapidly from London, which is a mere 70 miles away, on trains from Victoria, London Bridge and Waterloo to Chichester station, some five miles from the course. Goodwood lies just off the A286 Chichester to Midhurst Road; those arriving in fixed-wing aircraft can land at Goodwood's airfield, a mere 2-mile taxi ride away from the course.

GO ON
Course of action resorted to by a bookmaker who feels he can quite safely continue to stand bets on a particular runner.

GO ON MY SON (See Come On My Son)
This is also the traditional way in which, during the closing stages of a race, some backers give vocal support to their fancies.

GOT AT
Doped. Usually this involves 'nobbling' – administering a substance to a horse to impair its performance in a race which in normal circumstances it would probably win.

GO UP EARLY
To offer odds well in advance of one's fellow bookmakers. In his earlier days, the late William Hill had sufficient faith in his own judgement as a rails bookmaker to quote odds on runners in the first race almost half an hour before it was due to be run, and on subsequent contests as soon as their predecessors had been decided.

Intrepid traders such as Hill were on occasion almost 'knocked off their joints', i.e. besieged by clamouring 'early birds', backers desperately anxious to take advantage of what they considered generous opening prices about certain runners. It is seldom, however, that opening prices feature any real generosity; the opposite, in fact, occurs since bookmakers recognize their initial vulnerability.

If, surprisingly, an opening price proves far longer than the forecast rate, the backer should infer that the layer has good, up-to-date reasons for taking a pessimistic view of the animal's chances and is thus offering what may not be a good rate of odds at all.

GOWRAN PARK

Gowran Park
Gowran
Co. Kilkenny
Southern Ireland
Tel. (056) 26110

How to get there:
From North: N9
From South: N9
From East: R202
From West: N10
By Rail: Kilkenny
By Air: Kilkenny Airport

Haydock has a beautifully sylvan parade ring but some feel Gowran Park's is more attractive. This track is undeniably large and well able to put both the speed and stamina of National Hunt performers on trial. It is yet another Irish right-hander, whose last two fences are clearly visible from its stands. Often when racing is impossible 'over the water', Gowran Park's most important race, the Thyestes Handicap Chase, won in the past by such champions as Arkle, Flyingbolt, and Brown Lad, duly goes ahead and thus ensures that its quality field attracts the attention of both English and Irish jumping enthusiasts. This 3-mile race often provides a pointer to the prospects of Irish contenders for top-class honours at Cheltenham and Aintree. Other well-known races run on this dual-purpose track have been the Red Mills Trial Hurdle, the Avonmore Classic Trial, the McEnery Perpetual Handicap, the Tetratema Hunters' Chase, and the Duggan Memorial Hurdle.

The course can be reached by rail via Killkenny station and from Naas or Waterford on the N9.

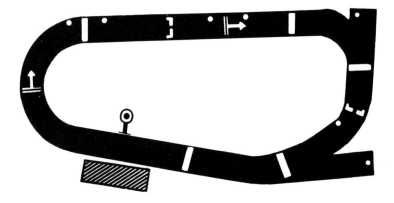

GOWRAN PARK: Plan of the course.

GRADUATION RACE

Race designed not for maidens, but for horses that have not won more than one race or a specified number of races.

GRAND

£1000.

GREEN SEAL SERVICE (see Disputes, Betting)

A most useful arbitrational service provided by the *Sporting Life* in which judgements are offered on disputes involving backers and bookmakers. The rulings on rule interpretations it provides are invariably the result of sober thought and just deliberations.

GROUP RACES

In collaboration with the administrators of racing in other European countries, the Jockey Club has ensured that top-class British flat races not only make suitably taxing demands on thoroughbred racehorses but also fit into a well thought out 'pattern' of highly competitive top-class racing. In Britain there are well over 100 such flat race events involving distances ranging from 5 to 21 furlongs (as in the Goodwood Cup, the longest pattern race staged in Britain).

Pattern races are further subdivided (according to prize money and importance) into three Groups numbered from One through to Three.

Many backers concentrate their attention on these contests in the wise belief that the stronger competition they feature increases the chances of form working out, a belief often supported by the good record of the past favourites that have contested them.

Over the sticks there are 24 Grade One races (10 of them staged at Cheltenham), and 60 or so other races (a few of them limited handicaps) have been designated as Grade Two contests. Group Three status is enjoyed by just over a dozen open handicaps.

! GUV'NOR

One's employer: a bookmaker in the case of a clerk or floorman, a trainer in the case of a jockey or a stable employee.

HAMILTON PARK

Hamilton Park Racecourse
Bothwell Road
Hamilton
Lanarkshire ML3 ODZ
Tel. (0698) 283806

How to get there:
From North: M73, M74, M180, A9(M), A80
From South: M74
From East: M8
From West: M8
By Rail: Hamilton West
By Air: Glasgow Airport

The Hamilton Park track, which is pleasantly situated 10 miles south-east of Glasgow, was first used in July 1888 when a group of whisky distillers' dream of bringing horse racing nearer to Glasgow finally came to fruition in a fenced-off section of a park belonging to Lord Hamilton.

Glasgow airport should figure in the flight plan of air travellers while those arriving by rail, perhaps from Euston, should travel on from Glasgow Central to Hamilton West station.

Motorists making the short trip from Glasgow should leave the M74 at junction 5 (those coming from England should leave at junction 4). Then, like those driving in from Edinburgh (who should leave the M8 at junction 6), they should look for signs indicating the B7071 along which the course will be

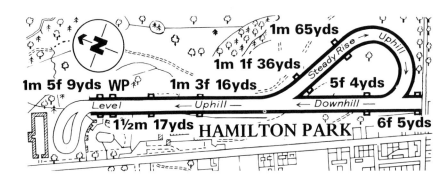

HAMILTON PARK:
Plan of the course.

found between Hamilton and Bothwell. The proximity of a local mausoleum should not deter racegoers!

The Hamilton Park course is a compact, peculiarly shaped 13-furlong affair, rather reminiscent of a badminton racquet complete with a carrying strap at the end of its handle! Its straight course consists of a 6-furlong stretch.

Horses in the sprints face a fairly stiff task since the surface they race over is far from level, the undulations on the 5 furlong 4 yard and 6 furlong 5 yard courses being reminiscent of a switchback. Horses racing on the latter track start from a short spur and initially race over fairly level ground. Subsequently, this descends (quite gently at first, then steeply) into a dip near the 3-furlong pole. This infamous feature has effectively 'found out' many well-fancied and handily-placed contestants. Its negotiation can prove very taxing in heavy going, which can be fairly common at Hamilton because its clay subsoil retains water so well.

In the closing stages of Hamilton sprints, the contestants face another rather punishing test of their strength. After emerging from the dip, they have to negotiate ground that rises gradually at first and then much more steeply in the penultimate furlong. Indeed, respite only comes in the closing stages when level ground is finally encountered.

Highly drawn sprinters seem to be favoured at Hamilton (when especially on soft or heavy ground, the stalls are placed on the stands side) as are horses which contest races over 1 mile 65 yards and 9 furlongs 36 yards since they have to run round a semi-circular section of track that bends appreciably to the right before it joins the straight course shortly before the 5-furlong gate.

Horses taking part in races over 11 furlongs 16 yards and 12 furlongs 17 yards actually jump off from points along the straight that are even nearer the winning post, and they are then ridden the 'wrong' way down the course.

Long-distance events over 1 mile 5 furlongs 9 yards are also run 'in reverse' and are started from a point just beyond the winning post which means that those involved have a rather rare initial opportunity to race over a level stretch of ground!

The sweeping right-handed turns at Hamilton are fairly gentle and thus make no great demands on jockeyship which, however, is tested to the full by several other features of this track. If horses perform best when 'held up' they may well appreciate the long 5-furlong run-in on which it is possible for an experienced jockey to ride a late finish to good effect.

In recent seasons the Hamilton executive have devised several schemes and improved facilities to attract Glaswegians. Unfortunately, only one evening meeting is currently staged on a Saturday, the one night when, by tradition, Glaswegians tend to spend freely.

Other measures include regular 50 per cent reductions on admission prices for the unemployed, concessions for the disabled and special terms for family groups attending certain evening meetings.

A recent colourful and most popular move has been to hold a Saints and Sinners Club of Scotland charity evening in early June. This, coupled with improved facilities for stable staff, seems to augur well for Hamilton's future.

❢ HAND
Slang for 5–1.

❢ HAND AND A HALF
Slang for 11–2.

HANDICAP
Race in which a Jockey Club official has done his level best (through form book study, past experience, the weight-for-age scale, computer-aided information processing and personal judgement) to equalize the chances of horses due to contest a race by allotting them unequal weights reflective of their varying abilities.

HANDICAPPER
Jockey Club (or Irish Turf Board) official to whom the compilation of handicaps is entrusted. Less than ten such officials compile handicaps staged in Britain, while five carry out this demanding and vital task in Ireland.

HANDICAPPING
The task of the handicapper.

HANDICAP MARKS
Official Jockey Club ratings expressed as weights that are allotted to horses in the comprehensive official handicap that covers all horses contesting either flat or jump races.

These handicap marks are subject to ongoing amendments. Both current as well as past marks are documented by the *Sporting Life* and *Racing Post*, the former in a most useful feature that is entitled 'Ahead of the Handicapper'. This shows the official handicap ratings a declared runner raced off in its last three handicap outings, and, even more usefully to reveal if a handicapper is improving, shows the current mark off which it is due to race, as well as that from which it will do so in a future handicap.

Both publications feature 'Today's Ratings' which very usefully show the official handicap marks a handicapper ran off in its last four handicaps, together with the mark it is about to race off. These figures include penalties and overweights and will allow the backer to judge consistency, recent form, and evidence of improvement.

By charting horses' many movements up and down the official Jockey Club handicap ratings, and also by identifying one or two which have had the advantage of a promising run after the date on which their most recent (i.e. impending) handicap ratings were compiled, the backer can row in with improving types and those whose full measure may not yet have been taken by the handicapper.

HAND PUMPER

Somewhat patronizing reference to an apprentice jockey. Its ecclesiastical connotations are intriguing.

❗ HAND TO ROUF

Slang for 5–4.

HANG

To veer off a straight course. Such behaviour, sometimes caused by tiredness in the closing stages, may cause a runner to lean on, or collide with, a rival.

HAVE THE STRINGS ON

Said of a horse reputedly not 'off', i.e. about to be allowed to win its race. Sometimes the 'strings' are in fact pulled to prevent such a runner playing a prominent part in proceedings.

HAYDOCK PARK

Haydock Park Racecourse Co Ltd
Newton-le-Willows
Merseyside WA12 0HQ
Tel. (0942) 727345

How to get there:
From North: M6
From South: M6
From East: A580
From West: A580
By Rail: Newton-Le-Willows
By Air: Helicopter facilities

Haydock Park racecourse came into being at the close of the nineteenth century. Its recent development and support by the Levy Board, its status as the north-west's premier racecourse, its proximity to the M6 and M61 motorways and the vast population centres of Manchester and Liverpool as well as its excellent facilities all account for its present popularity.

Some London-based racegoers start their 200-mile journey to the track by taking a train from Euston to Wigan or Warrington Bank Quay (mainline) and thereafter find that a taxi-ride is necessary. The alternative is to motor to junction 23 of the M6 and then follow the signs directing patrons a further half a mile or so to the course that lies on the A49 near Ashton.

Haydock offers its patrons such facilities as a £2.5 million Members/Tattersalls stand, a giant 100-inch TV screen and a clear view of its high-class racing. The 13-furlong circuit itself is oval and virtually flat.

Haydock's left-hand bends are fairly easy to negotiate and its many extensive straight sections – two of which form a kink or elbow in its back stretch – allow long-striding, galloping types to come into their own.

Negotiation of the long 4-furlong or so straight run-in, which rises slightly but almost continuously for much of its length, makes a final demand on the stamina of all those that run on this important top-class track. It is also an experience that is appreciated by horses that have to be 'held up' and prevented from making a premature finishing effort.

Those tackling sprint distances at Haydock enjoy a double advantage if they are fast starters and, if the stalls are positioned on the stands side, they are highly drawn on what is a straight section of track. When the going is soft this particular advantage is increased, particularly over 6 furlongs, over which in early September the top-class Sprint Cup is staged, a race that is frequently captured by a four-year-old.

When the ground is dry, horses allocated low numbers in the draw are favoured in races over 7 furlongs 30 yards, since for a fair proportion of this particular distance, they negotiate a semi-circular, if fairly gentle, left-hand bend. The best-known race run over this unusual race distance is the listed John of Gaunt Stakes that is contested in Derby week.

'Mile' races at Haydock, such as the important Silver Bowl Handicap staged in late May, actually involve a distance of 1 mile 30 yards and start from a point towards the end of one of the two straight sections of track on the back straight.

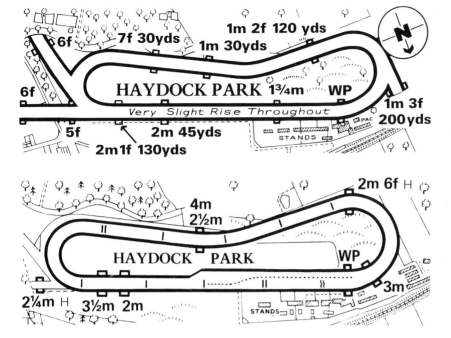

HAYDOCK PARK: Plans of the Flat course (top), and the National Hunt course (bottom).

Runners in races over 10 furlongs 120 yards have to negotiate the kink in the course about nine furlongs out, while those that tackle a further furlong and 80 yards, initially along a second spur, run over a course on which the prestigious Lancashire Oaks for three-year-old fillies is run in early July – on the same main card as the Old Newton Handicap which is named after a local hunt and former Lancashire racing venue.

Long-distance races over 2 miles 45 yards are also staged at Haydock and are started from a point in the finishing straight that lies between the 4- and the 3-furlong poles.

Interestingly, one particular Haydock meeting held in midsummer has commemorated the contributions made to English racing by such jockeys as Fred Archer, Steve Donoghue, Frank Wootton and Freddy Fox.

With its ten testingly stiff obstacles, many of them drop fences, Haydock is a jumping track on which a victory for a chaser augurs well for a run over the Grand National obstacles at Liverpool.

The course holds two important main jumping meetings in January. Firstly, the top-class Newton Champion Chase of 2 1/2 miles is staged, while a fortnight later comes a first-class fixture that includes three prestigious races: a Champion Hurdle trial, a Long Distance Hurdle of 3 miles and the Peter Marsh Chase over the same distance. An important Grand National prep race, the well-established

Greenalls Gold Cup in which seven- and nine-year-olds seem to go well, is also staged ten days before the Cheltenham festival at another early March Haydock fixture. This 3 1/2-mile 'chase is staged on the same day as the Timeform Chase which itself is often won by a horse well-rated on time, and frequently by a seven-year-old.

All steeplechasers at Haydock have to negotiate a water jump positioned in front of the stands. This obstacle and the open ditch are not jumped on the final circuit which ends in a run-in of around two furlongs.

Hurdle races at Haydock are staged on a rather tight track that runs inside the 'chasing circuit.

HEAD LAD

Trainer's vital right-hand person who carries out duties some have likened to those of an RSM or ringmaster. In the good old days some head lads held a licence for ladies who trained in all but name.

A few head lads graduate to the ranks of top-class trainers. A recent example is Barry Hills who, thanks largely to a golden win on Frankincense in the 1968 Lincoln Handicap and other gambles landed by a head lads' syndicate of which he was a leading member, was ultimately able to set up as a most successful trainer.

Such can be the skill of a head lad that his (or her) departure can cause a decline in the fortunes of a racing stable.

HEAD LADS' ASSOCIATION, THE NATIONAL

Not a gamblers' syndicate, but rather the official body that represents the interests of these vital members of the racing industry. Its headquarters are to be found at 196 New Cheveley Road, Newmarket, Suffolk CB8 8BZ.

HEINZ

Well-named 57-bet wager that involves six selections so fully permed as to produce 1 sixfold, 6 five timers, 15 fourfolds, 20 trebles and 15 doubles.

HELD

Expression used of a horse that seems likely to be re-defeated so disadvantageous to it is the difference in the weights now allotted to it and those allotted to a previous rival.

HEREFORD

Hereford Racecourse
Roman Road
Holmer
Hereford
Tel. (0432) 273560

How to get there:
From North: A49
From South: A49
From East: A438
From West: A438
By Rail: Hereford
By Air: Helicopter facilities

This right-hand track of 12 furlongs is a mile away from the railway station of the county town (itself 123 miles from Paddington) whose name it bears. It can be reached by heading north out of Hereford on the A49, a route which should be used by racegoers travelling from Leominster. The A49 and then the A495 are recommended to southern-based visitors, while those from the Midlands arrive from Worcester on the A4103.

The course (now into its third century) lies in a pleasantly rural location that also contains a golf course.

Hereford provides a searching test of the jumpers it attracts in fairly large numbers since they have to race the 'wrong' (right-hand) way round it, cope with nine fairly stiff obstacles and tackle a sharp downhill home turn. These particular course features make it worthwhile to consider past course and distance winners, especially those sent out by handlers whose runners have achieved excellent wins to runs ratios.

Hereford's appeal perhaps explains why Sir Piers Bengough, Her Majesty the Queen's representative at Ascot, officiates as a steward at its fixtures, at one of which a hurdle race is staged in memory of Fred Rimell, the famous jockey and trainer from the neighbouring county of Worcestershire.

HEXHAM

Hexham Racecourse
High Yarridge
Hexham
Northumberland NE46 2JP
Tel. (0434) 603738

How to get there:
From North: A68
From South: A68
From East: A69
From West: A69
By Rail: Hexham
By Air: Helicopter facilities

Hexham can rival some scenically impressive Irish country courses such is the splendour of its rural location. A hillside 800 feet above sea level provides the ideal site for its grandstand from which a

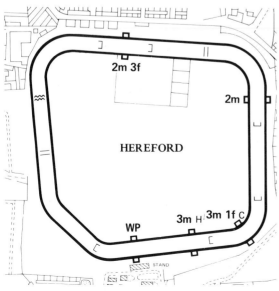

HEREFORD: Plan of the course. Racing here is staged in a clockwise direction.

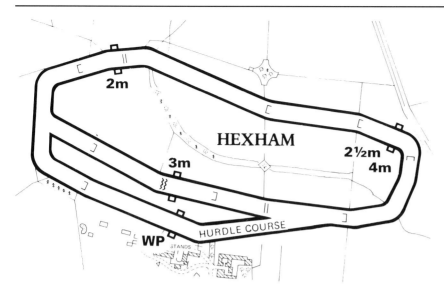

HEXHAM: Plan of the course.

magnificent view can be gained of steeplechasers taking its ten fences. These, despite being easy, are positioned on a 12-furlong, left-handed track that is testing in nature as its later stages feature a steep climb, respite from which is only offered by a short 250-yard run-in that eventually features flat ground.

Another configurational peculiarity is a downhill stretch that extends (from the point where races over 20 furlongs are started) for almost half a mile to a pronounced dip. Not surprisingly, on this taxing track one should side with runners with proven stamina and which are adaptable enough to cope with its quite severe gradients.

Since Hexham is 280 miles from London, some southerners are deterred from attending its fixtures although these are savoured by many of racing's *cognoscenti*. The point-to-point, rather Corinthian flavour of this Northumberland gaff is only to be expected since the principal race it stages is the fine-sounding Heart of All England Hunters' Steeplechase.

Air travellers will need to leave their (fixed-wing) aircraft at Newcastle-upon-Tyne's airport, while those travelling from London King's Cross will find Hexham station is a one-and-a-half-mile taxi-ride from the course. Motorists should head for the A69 which links Carlisle with Newcastle, and will find the course lying 38 miles east of the former town and 20 miles west of the latter city.

Racegoers should note that Hexham's exposed situation is such that no fixtures are held in January or Feburary.

Ridley Lamb used to be a top course jockey here and it is appropriate that this trainer is now a local steward.

HOD

Container, rather reminiscent of a Gladstone bag, in which a bookmaker deposits the banknotes and cash he takes from racecourse backers.

HOLIDAYS, RACING

Package deals often arranged to take in a particular prestigious race meeting that is staged abroad or in a particularly attractive part of the British Isles or Ireland.

Some racing holidays involve extensive travelling, for example, to see the series of top-class Breeders' Cup races that are held in America each autumn.

HOOD

This is a fairly formidable aid to concentration that connections fit to some runners in the hope that it will improve their prospects. As it covers the ears, its main purpose is to reduce the degree to which a racehorse may be distracted by noise.

Other types of hoods are used to protect horses either from inclement weather prior to their races, or to allow handlers to blindfold them if they are upset by the sight of starting stalls or the prospect of entering these.

HORSERACE BETTING LEVY BOARD

Horserace Betting Levy Board
52 Grosvenor Gardens
London SW1W 0AU
Tel. (071) 730 4540

Now over thirty years old, this organization imposes a levy on the profits of bookmakers and the tote so as to contribute to the costs of improving the breeds of racehorses, the advancement of veterinary science and education, all of which bring about the general improvement of the sport. These improvements include on-track technical and security services, prize money, farriery, racecourse improvements, support of point-to-points and apprentice training.

Criticism voiced at the beginning of the current decade regarding the financing of racing may mean that the Levy Board will have to take a tougher stance.

The Board has subsidiaries in Racecourse Technical Services, whose vans are a familiar sight to racegoers, and United Racecourses, the administrators of Epsom, Kempton and Sandown Park.

HORSERACING TOTALIZATOR BOARD
(See Tote Betting)
> Tote House
> 74 Richmond Road
> Putney
> London SWI5 2SU
> Tel. (081) 874 6411

Commonly known as the 'tote', this organization provides backers with an alternative to betting with bookmakers and uses its profits to support the racing industry.

The modern-day tote is a three-fold operation. It still serves its original function (as from 1928) of providing pool betting on the racecourse, where computerized win/place and dual forecast bets are organized. Betting on credit represents a second branch of the tote's business. There is a tote credit office on every racecourse where clients can also bet at bookmakers' starting prices.

Tote bookmakers represent the tote's third line of business and operate both off-course and on-course betting shops in which only placements of cash are accepted.

HORSERACE WRITERS' ASSOCIATION
Lively newsletters penned by its president, George Ennor, are just one feature of this, the craftsman's guild-cum-'trade union' of racing scribes. Membership is drawn from all those who hold an annual press badge from the Joint Turf Authority or whose business entitles them to enter press rooms and utilize press facilities provided on racecourses. Each November, the Association makes awards to those jockeys, owners and trainers adjudged to have done most during the preceding 12 months to promote the image of the sport. Lord Derby makes his own personal award to a member of the press at this organization's annual awards ceremony.

HORSERACE ADVISORY COUNCIL
> 52 Grosvenor Gardens
> London SW1W 0AU
> Tel. (071) 730 4540

Established after the recommendation of a royal commission on gambling, this organization was set up to provide a forum for debate of matters affecting the racing industry by those invited to give it broad representation. The HAC advises the Horserace Betting Levy Board, consults with the stewards of the Jockey Club, formulates views, exchanges these with other bodies and makes recommendations to various government departments. The Jockey Club, the Horserace Betting Levy Board, the Betting Office Licensees' Association, the National Association of Bookmakers and the Horserace Totalizator Board all send observers to HAC meetings.

HUMOUR IN RACING: Jockey Lavinia, Duchess of Norfolk sports Mickey Mouse colours.

HUMOUR IN RACING

Whether featuring the wry comments of television commentator John Francome, selected gems from the vast array of works that make up the literature of the turf, or the spontaneous quips the making of which constitutes the daily round and common task of many employed in racing, this represents one of the sport's most enticing constituents. Among many, Susan Gallier, Mackenzie and Selby, Jack Leach, John Francome, John Welcome, William Saroyan and, amongst racing journalists, John Oaksey, AIastair Down and James Lambie have brought many a smile to their readers, while among American writers, Damon Runyon and William Murray, author of *Horse Fever* (published by Dodd Mead), are definite front runners.

HUMOUR IN RACING: This horse certainly sees the funny side of its action, having sucessfully thrown its rider over the very fence that it should have jumped itself!

HUNTER 'CHASERS: Dick Saunders winning the 1982 Grand National at Aintree on Frank Gilman's hunter-chaser Grittar.

HUNTER 'CHASERS

Hunters that race on National Hunt racecourses (from February onwards) in what is the 'second half' of the steeplechasing season. Such horses have to be certified by masters of foxhounds as having been genuinely and fairly ridden to hounds prior to competing in hunter 'chases.

In many such events there are 'stand out' bets as frequently large numbers of 'no hopers' take on a mere handful of horses which have genuine chance;

the latter can be identified by using specialist hunter form services that are available on subscription.

Race distance, jumping ability and jockeyship particularly influence the outcomes of hunter 'chases, which provide gilt-edged, money-making opportunities as well as truly sporting spectacles.

Advance guidance on which hunter 'chasers to follow in an impending season has been given in *Ladbrokes' Annual Pocket Companion to the National Hunt Season* (published by Aesculus Press), while Brian Beel gives hunter 'chasers fairly detailed coverage in *The Times*.

HUNTINGDON

Huntingdon Racecourse
Brampton
Huntingdon
Cambridgeshire PE18 8NN
Tel. (0480) 454610

How to get there:
From North: A1(M)
From South: A1(M)
From East: A604
From West: A604
By Rail: Huntingdon
By Air: Helicopter facilities

Despite being far from scenically splendid, Huntingdon has a convenient location just off the A1 and the excellent drainage provided by its gravel subsoil means its fixtures are seldom rained off.

Like much of East Anglia, this track is flat and fairly featureless; a right-handed oval that extends for 12 furlongs. There are nine fences on its circuit which ends in a shortish run-in of only 200 yards.

Horses well-rated by stop-watch holders go well on this track which can be taken at speed by runners able to handle the track's right-handed configuration. For this reason, past course and distance winners that are top-rated on time are worth consideration. A few horses, particularly novices, are troubled by the track's penultimate fence, but this, and another in the finishing straight, are the only two difficult obstacles.

The course lies 21 miles north-east of Bedford, just outside Brampton, itself two and a half miles from Huntingdon, so Londoners have only 60 miles to motor to the track. The A604 is the route motorists should look out for and the course lies one mile south-east of its intersection with the A1. Rail travellers when alighting at Huntingdon (a stop on the express route from Edinburgh to King's Cross) will find they have a further 2 1/2 miles to travel to the course by taxi. There is a fixed-wing aircraft landing strip a mile from the course and helicopters can land in its centre by prior arrangement.

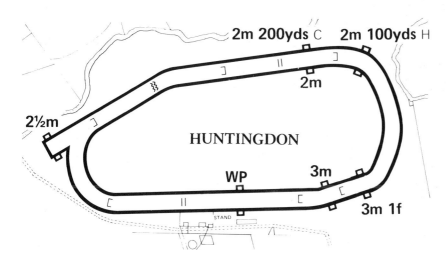

HUNTINGDON: Plan of the course.

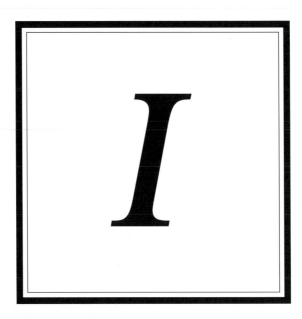

IDENTIFICATION OF RACEHORSES

Vital proceeding designed to preclude the practice of 'ringing in' by running a racehorse that bears a striking resemblance to a 'no-hoper' but which is vastly superior to it. One such ringer masqueraded as the significantly named In The Money at Newton Abbot on August Bank Holiday Monday, 1978. Rather than the American practice of tattooing registration numbers inside horses' mouths, racehorse identification in Britain and Ireland hinges on passports which diagrammatically document their colouring and distinctive markings. No horse can enter a racecourse if its passport is not presented and this document has to be available should the course vet wish to compare it with the animal it purports to identify.

IN-BREEDING

The mating of a brother and sister, sire and daughter, or son and dam. Far from being disapproved of, this practice has been a feature of thoroughbred breeding for centuries.

INDEX TO WINNERS

Most useful feature in both *Raceform* and *Chaseform* notebooks. It shows the courses, distances and the states of the going that were involved in racehorses' previous victories.

INJURED JOCKEYS' FUND

> The Injured Jockeys' Fund
> PO Box 9
> Newmarket
> Suffolk CB8 8JG
> Tel. (0638) 662246

This, one of racing's most deserving of charities, has benefited greatly from the patronage of steeplechasing's best-known supporter, the Queen Mother. The IJF is a trust that gives assistance to those many National Hunt (and flat) jockeys whose severe injuries have forced them to hang up their riding boots.

The fund derives a large part of its income from the sale of its most attractive Christmas cards and calendar. Special events and functions such as dances provide further funds, as do many often generous donations which, whatever their size, are always much needed and gratefully received by the fund's secretary.

INNS, RACING

These may either be so designated by their names (for example, the Grand St Leger in Doncaster) or on account of their locations near racecourses or racing centres. The best racing inns are described in the annual publication *Travelling the Turf*.

INSIDE INFORMATION: Any scrap of information on a horse's form might help determine the outcome of the race, and possibly help someone to win a fortune.

INSIDE INFORMATION

Many true stories could be related about fortunes won on the strength of crucial information; some backers, though, have been grateful for smaller but much-needed sums which have occasionally been wrested from bookmakers. Such was certainly the case when trainer Ron Thompson made a fraternal gesture to striking local miners at Stainforth by tipping them Kindred, the winner of The Grey Horse Selling Hurdle at nearby Sedgefield a few seasons ago!

Betting expert Ron Pollard has declared that the best way to lose money is to back all the horses that are backed by owners and trainers! However, the telephone tips of some jockeys have disproved the centuries old adage about their being the world's worst tipsters.

Some backers analyse the 'stable hints' carried by the popular racing dailies or monitor the fate of each horse recommended by newspaper correspondents based in training centres in a bid to determine which information is 'wheat' rather than 'chaff'. Another approach is to note whether any of the 'stable hints' is associated with a trainer who has sent out a recent winner. Often a fancied runner from a recently successful stable will follow its companion into the winners' enclosure.

The main thing is to be neither too gullible nor too cynical and to adopt methods such as the above to ensure that what one learns is methodically and profitably sifted. In the nineteenth century a certain Mrs Merryweather achieved enormous fame and notoriety on account of her 'knowledgeable advices' and even married one particularly rich purchaser of her information.

This she sold in a circular in which she presented herself as a 'jockey's wife, with a husband unable to work in consequence of having sustained a paralytic shock to his lower limbs'.

In return for her information, Mrs Merryweather did not ask for charity, but being anxious for the sake of her small children declared herself 'glad to hear from gentlemen who take an interest in racing'.

INSPECTOR OF COURSES

Vital Jockey Club employee whose duties involve reporting on racecourses, making periodic inspections of these and reviewing the 'fixed equipment' they feature. Ex-jockeys are sometimes appointed as inspectors in the wise belief that their past experience will have sensitized them to the need for racecourses to be maintained in a way that is conducive to the safety and welfare of horses, jockeys and spectators and to the fit and proper running of races.

INTELLECTUAL APPEAL OF HORSE RACING

To racegoers who have grown used to being told it is a 'mug's game' it must have been refreshing to hear that two distinguished American academics recently concluded that no one, not even brain surgeons, makes decisions that are more intellectually demanding than those arrived at by successful backers, and to learn that a British lecturer is advising managers to take the types of carefully calculated risks these canny individuals are used to facing.

Appreciation of the intellectual demands made by systematic racehorse selection comes from two of America's most prestigious universities, Cornell and Michigan where Steven Ceci and Jeffery Liker interviewed fifty regular racegoers whose winners to selections ratios over the past 16 years had been no greater than one in two. These individuals, one of whom had a winning bets percentage of 93, were asked to make their selections for fifty imaginary races and these were then analysed in terms of the variables that had influenced them to determine which were considered most important.

The researchers found that the key attribute of the successful gambler was the 'ability to think in a complex interactive manner using novel and complicated sets of data'. Ceci and Liker's conclusions complement the preliminary findings of Johnnie Johnson, a lecturer in the Industrial Economics Department of Nottingham University, whose similar study concluded that gamblers could teach British managers a 'good deal about decision-

making in the face of uncertainties'. Johnson's pragmatic conclusion is that managers must learn to gamble more, since the aim of business is to 'make a profit and profit is often the reward of risk-taking'.

Bookmakers' standard ploy of taking bets of a certain value on as many of the runners in a race as possible involves the considerable intellectual exercise of offering prices and juggling bets so as to produce a certain percentage profit. As it happens, the fairly complex and, for most, the thoroughly mysterious procedure necessary to produce this has only twice been explained to the layman in the last half century – in Phil Bull's *How to Make a Book* (1945), and subsequently in Charles Sidney's *The Art of Legging*.

Professional handicappers also demonstrate a capacity for intense intellectual endeavour and the application of common sense.

The doyen of private handicappers was, of course, Dick Whitford erstwhile form ratings expert at the *Sporting Life*, whose readers he provided with a single universal handicap whose spread of 0 to just over 100 encompassed a seven stone weight range sufficient to embrace the very worst and best of flat race performers. He discovered that it was possible to fit horses into a mathematical pattern and to make one 'gigantic jigsaw of the whole racing scene'. To his surprise he found that what happens in racing is not 'so much a matter of chance as a matter of consistency in the thoroughbred'.

Attempts to rate the times horses take to complete their races also involves rigorous intellectual endeavour.

Finally, there is one further argument to put to those who regard racing as a triviality: the intellectual challenge of trying to breed champion racehorses. Currently some training for this activity is available as part of the stud and stable husbandry course offered by the West Oxfordshire Technical College. This would seem an ideal educational sequel for those leaving Slindon College in Sussex whose headmaster has sponsored races at nearby Fontwell Park, and recognized racing's intellectual appeal by including it on his curriculum!

INTERNATIONAL CLASSIFICATIONS

By the end of January each year, an international panel of handicappers produces handicaps for the top two-year-olds, three-year-olds and four-year-olds and above that ran in Europe during the preceding flat racing season. These handicaps range from a maximum mark of 140 (10 st) to a minimum one of 100 (7 st 2lbs).

In the case of both three- and four-year-olds (and

older horses), their classifications are broken down into separate handicaps for the race distances of 11-plus furlongs, 9.5-plus furlongs, 7-plus furlongs and 5-plus furlongs.

First-season performers are assessed in a single undifferentiated handicap extending from 125 (9 st 7lbs) to 104 (8 st), which allows interesting comparisons to be drawn with the weights given to Europe's most promising two-year-olds in the European Free Handicap that is staged at Newmarket in mid-April.

IN THE FRAME

Said of placed runners, which have small square number boards bearing their racecard numbers placed in a frame that is hoisted aloft so the result of a race is clearly visible.

IN THE HUNT

Said of a runner, not necessarily one in a hunter 'chase or point-to-point, that is in with a chance by being well in contention during its race.

IRISH NATIONAL HUNT STEEPLECHASE COMMITTEE

The Curragh
Co. Kildare
Ireland
Tel. (045) 41599

Official body controlling races staged in Ireland over fences and hurdles.

IRISH RACING WRITERS' ASSOCIATION

Like its British counterpart, this is both a 'trade union' and another means whereby horse racing in all its aspects is promoted.

IRISH TURF CLUB

The Curragh
Co. Kildare
Ireland
Tel. (045) 41599

Ireland's equivalent of the Jockey Club dates from 1790 and is the governing body of Irish racing.

Its seven stewards are served by a secretarial arm whose chief executive goes by the splendid title of 'Keeper of the Match Book'. The Irish Turf Club is quite distinct from the Irish Turf Board. Its remit is basically to oversee and organize the sport's equine and human performers.

The Turf Club has an influence on Irish racing that socially, commercially and industrially is all pervasive. Its basic functions concern administration prior to racing, the imposition of rules and regulations, the enforcement of discipline at race meetings and what has been described as 'follow-up administration' at these.

The Club appoints officials, adjudicates on disputes and publishes its own newspaper called the *Racing Calendar*.

The Turf Club also acts as Irish racing's treasurer and in this capacity gives charitable support where needed within the racing industry.

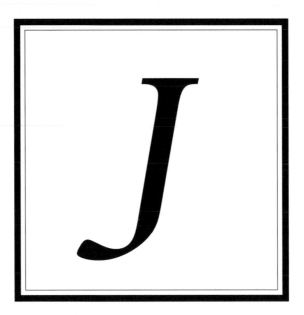

JACKPOT, TOTE

An ambitious and well-named wager on the tote whereby the backer is required to pick the winners of successive races (usually six in number). If there is no outright winner, the balance of the jackpot pool is carried forward.

JOB

Horse on which its connections intend to gamble heavily, so carefully prepared is it to run for its life. In former days, a good living could be earned by 'stable commissioners' – men especially employed to place sizeable commissions on stable 'jobs'. Some stable commissioners were shrewd enough to amass vast fortunes; 'Scotch' Johnnie Marr, for example, left a sum on his death in 1950 that today would be worth around £2,225,000. One of the largest post-war jobs engineered on the British turf was in Royal Ascot's Queen Alexandra Stakes in 1947. No less than £40,000 was placed on Monsieur l'Amiral at all rates from 12-1 to 7-2, prior to this horse's eventual triumph.

JOCKEYS' ASSOCIATION OF GREAT BRITAIN, THE

This body, a company limited by guarantee, was founded in 1967 and now officially represents jockeys riding both on the flat and over obstacles.

The first of its stated aims, to maintain the highest standards of honour, integrity and courtesy among jockeys and to support and protect the character, status and interests generally of the jockey's profession, shows that it has something of the status of a guild.

Naturally, it also seeks to further its members' interests and welfare, especially as these involve racecourse facilities and matters of safety.

Perhaps, rather appropriately, since an accident ended his impressive riding career, the former flat-race jockey Paul Cook has served as joint chairman along with National Hunt jockey Peter Scudamore.

The Association has been fortunate in having a regular column in the *Sporting Life*.

Perhaps mindful of the fact that many jockeys have died penniless, the Association has its own pension fund and savings plan and, as one would expect, a variety of insurance services.

The Association is also commercially active in making available riding equipment and clothing to its members and in contributing to the Injured Jockeys' Fund.

A subsidiary, the Jockeys' Supporters Association, allows the public to meet the men and women whose skills in the saddle they so admire and often travel long distances to watch.

JOCKEY CLUB, THE

42 Portman Square
London W1H OEN
Tel. (071) 486 4921

The authority that governs British flat racing and steeplechasing. It has strong royal connections in that its patrons are the Queen and the Queen Mother and its meetings are attended by Prince Philip, the Prince of Wales and the Princess Royal.

Originally a metropolitan social organization that met at various locations in fashionable London, the Jockey Club strengthened the links between racing and coffee houses when it built its own coffee room at Newmarket in 1752.

Such was the influence of Jockey Club members (they are still self-electing and self-perpetuating, if now not just aristocratic or British) it was perhaps inevitable that in time they would act as racing's regulators, arbiters and administrators.

In its early days, thanks largely to three members who became so-called dictators of the turf, Sir Charles Bunbury (1740-1821), Lord George Bentinck (1802-48) and Admiral Rous (1791-1877), the Club mainly addressed itself to ridding the sport of abuses and to drawing up rules to ensure its proper staging. Thus, when previously unconsidered eventualities (like doping, first in evidence early this century) arose, regulations were eventually drawn up to deal with them.

The Club has made itself more representative of a wider range of interests within racing by electing non-British owners and, since 1977, increasing the number of females to its ranks.

It organizes the day-to-day running of racing via a Wellingborough-based secretariat, that since 1770 the family firm of Weatherby has provided. The work of modern-day Jockey Club stewards has involved four main spheres of activity: licensing

THE JOCKEY CLUB: Distinguished members of the jockey club standing outside the weighing room at Newmarket with the jockey Steve Donoghue.

racecourses and rules, discipline and administration, finance and fixtures, and prize money.

Even though one or two of its recent decisions have been derided in the racing press, the Jockey Club is now far less autocratic and far more prepared to tack to the winds of change sweeping through modern-day racing than many might believe. It remains widely respected. In December 1991 it was announced that the Club would hand many of its traditional powers over to a British Horseracing Board but would still concern itself with matters involving discipline, licensing and security.

JOCKEYSHIP

Where jockeys figure in any form of racehorse selection, their claims and prospects should be subjected to the type of objectively statistical analysis formerly found in *Jockeyform* (an erstwhile *Sporting Life* publication), *Trainerform* (published by Aesculus Press), or currently John Whitley's impressive and innovative tome, *Computer Racing Form*. It may well pay to look carefully at the mounts of jockeys highly rated in the last-named publication's refreshingly objective and most revealing analysis.

It may pay to bear in mind a jockey's booking by certain trainers associated with many of his past successes, his 'strike rate' at certain tracks, the fact that a stable he often wins for has recently been on target and the possibility that he may have travelled a long way to reach an afternoon meeting from a fixture held the previous evening.

Of course, nothing succeeds like success and thus newspaper tables showing the current season's most successful jockeys should receive more than a passing glance.

JOCKEYS' MOUNTS

Trainers will often attempt to secure the services of particular jockeys to improve the chances of their fancied horses. Noting such special bookings or consulting analyses of trainers' behaviour, in the *Racing Post* for example, can prove illuminating.

JOCKEYS' RIDING WEIGHTS

Some backers argue that a horse carrying a 'live' movable burden in the form of its jockey's body is less handicapped than one whose load is partly made up of lead.

Lists of riding weights often appear in racing annuals and such publications as *Horses in Training*.

❗ JOE (ROOKS)

Rhyming slang for 'books' or 'bookmaker'. In the days when welshing was rife many a reputable bookmaker was anxious to present himself as an 'honest Joe'.

JOINT

Bookmaker's pitch on which he positions his stand with its 'silver' tray, boards, bag and umbrella. A newcomer will be given rather a remote joint and should avoid buying new tools which tend to attract undesirables.

JOINT FAVOURITE

Co-favourite, a horse which shares its shortest quotation in the betting market with at least one other runner.

JOLLY, THE

Significant term used by bookmakers to denote the favourite.

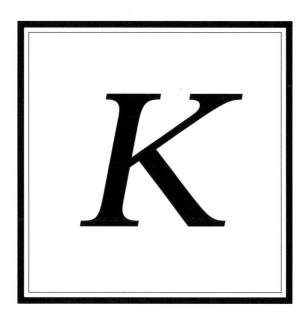

KELSO

Kelso Racecourse
Kelso
Roxburghshire
Scotland
Tel. (0573) 224767

How to get there:
From North: A68
From South: A7
From East: A698
From West: A699
By Rail: Berwick-upon-Tweed
By Air: Edinburgh Airport

Berwick-upon-Tweed is the nearest railway station to this gem of a 'gaff' which is over 300 miles from King's Cross. The journey is extended by a rather expensive 22-mile taxi-ride to the course itself.

Understandably then, most racegoers journeying from the south arrive by car via the A1 (M1) or the M6 to junction 44, before taking the A7 and A6089 to Kelso. Racegoers who travel south-east from the Scottish capital should take the A68, the A697 and finally the A6099 to Kelso; the course lies only half a mile to the north of this pleasantly situated border town. Sassenachs daunted by the thought of driving all the way to Kelso and back on a winter's day, can fly in for the races, either in helicopters that can land on the course by prior arrangement or in fixed-wing aircraft that can be accommodated at Winfield Duns, a 15-mile taxi-drive away. Alternatively, they can disembark at Edinburgh International Airport that is an hour's drive away.

Kelso consists of two sharp, left-handed courses. The circuit that 'chasers have to negotiate extends for 1 mile 600 yards and the even tighter hurdle track for only 1 mile 330 yards. Clearly then, long-striding types are at a disadvantage. So are 'chasers that lack courage and stamina since, after negotiating a downhill back stretch of track that contains tricky fences, they face a far from straight and quite punishing uphill run-in of two furlongs.

Good going, good visibility and very good cheer can almost be guaranteed at Kelso whose principal races are all 'chases. That one is called the King's Own Scottish Borders Cup seems highly appropriate since this is 'Scottish soldier' country, not far from the town of Coldstream. The fact that so many of its fixtures involve rather short winter days (that thankfully are generally free of fog) probably explains the strange rule that on-course picnics are not allowed at Kelso.

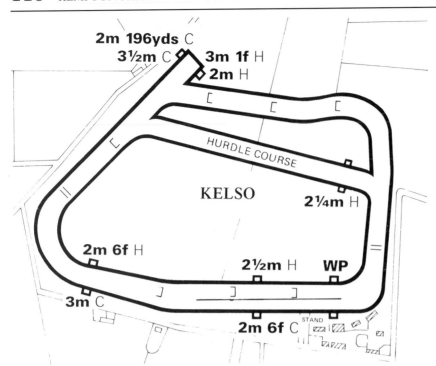

KELSO: Plan of the course.

KEMPTON PARK

Kempton Park Racecourse
Sunbury-on-Thames
Middlesex TW16 5AQ
Tel. (0932) 782292

How to get there:
From North: M1, M25
From South: A3
From East: M25
From West: M3
By Rail: Kempton Park
By Air: Helicopter facilities

It was once the custom to hold British race meetings on common land and thus to throw them open to all comers.

In 1878, those responsible for building Kempton Park did much to pioneer and popularize the novel concept of charging admission to fully-enclosed courses. The 300-acre site on which they chose to construct this suburban course near Sunbury-on-Thames, 16 miles south-west of London, had once been parkland of sufficient importance to be mentioned in the Domesday Book.

This popular course is only half a mile away from the first exit of the M3 and as London's most accessible course, has its own racecourse railway station that can be reached from Waterloo. Motorists heading for Sunbury from the capital are advised to approach on the A316 before taking the M3, while those travelling from the west should also take this particular motorway before finally driving half a mile to the track along the A308.

A glance through old racing annuals confirms the sad fact that Kempton was once a much more prestigious venue for flat racing than has been the case in recent decades. The particular race for which Kempton was long best-known – the Jubilee Handicap Stakes – was once an important spring handicap. Today it is simply a fairly important mile handicap that, although the highlight of Kempton's early May meeting, is a rather pale reflection of its former self. This race often falls to a four-year-old.

The course itself, which Fred Archer once rather intriguingly described as a 'sirloin of beef cut the wrong way', has a circumference of 1 mile 5 furlongs. It is an almost perfectly flat, right-handed triangle that is bisected diagonally by yet another separate course that cuts across its longest side. This is a dead straight sprint track on which events over 5 and 6 furlongs are staged under circumstances that favour high-drawn runners if the stalls are placed on the stands side. If, however, the ground is soft, the opposite may apply.

The spur that helps to provide the sprint course is much longer than the rather stubby affair that

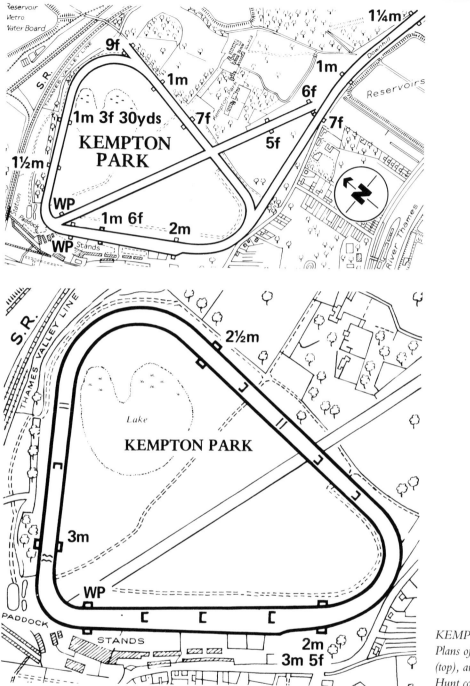

KEMPTON PARK:
Plans of the Flat course
(top), and the National
Hunt course (bottom).

projects from the penultimate bend on the round course and thus allows races to be staged over 9 furlongs.

Yet another long straight spur that projects from the final bend allows 10-, 8- and 7-furlong events to take place at Kempton Park. Since the Jubilee Handicap was (from 1887-1978) staged over its full extent, rather than over a mile as at present, this right-handed dog-leg is known as the 'Jubilee' course, on which the effect of the draw can be discounted.

Instead of running their milers over the extensive straight sections of the 'Jubilee' course, trainers can let them take their chances on the 'round' course on which events over 11 furlongs 30 yards, as well as 12, 14 and 16 furlongs are also staged.

Currently, the Queen's Prize, a handicap run over 2 miles at Kempton's important Easter meeting, once sufficiently important to be classed as a particularly prestigious spring handicap, does not even qualify for 'listed' status.

Runners tackling 2-mile races need both stamina and, above all, speed if they are to triumph on the round course which, being fairly tight, tends to favour small, neat, handy types that can adapt readily to running so much of their races the 'wrong' way round. Such stayers have to negotiate three fairly sweeping right-handed turns that make up Kempton's triangular circuit.

A premium is placed on jockeyship if, rather unusually, the Kempton going is soft. If this is the case, the best ground lies either in the centre of the track or near the stands' rails and can be best approached if jockeys swing wide as they take the final turn into the 3 1/2-furlong run-in. Kempton also stages the Easter Stakes at its two-day spring meeting, as well as the Masaka Stakes and well-known Rosebery Stakes.

The Racal-Vodafone Stakes is a valuable 10-furlong race staged in late June, but is less prestigious than Kempton's group race, the September Stakes, run over 11 furlongs 30 yards a week before the St Leger. Four-year-olds have the best record here.

In recent seasons, Kempton's rather splendid jumping fixtures have attracted far more racegoers than its flat race programmes. The best-known race – and not just for being farmed by Desert Orchid – is the King George VI Chase, the event that above all others the racing enthusiast associates with Christmas. This 3-mile Boxing Day spectacular that, in its more recent past, has twice given a French trainer a *joyeux Noel,* is notable for the amazing number of repeat victories its results have featured since 1947, as the backers of Desert Orchid, Wayward Lad, Captain Christy and Pendil know only too well. A seven-year-old is always worth some consideration in the 'King George'.

Kempton's jumping track extends for 1 mile 5 1/2 furlongs and includes ten stiff but fair fences; three plain ones in the home straight, a water jump, followed by a plain fence and an open ditch on the left-hand side of the triangle and four obstacles in the back stretch, the second of which is an open ditch. The fact that the run-in is short at only 175 yards and the circuit's turns are fairly tight for 'chasers means that speedy front runners, as Desert Orchid so often proved, are at a distinct advantage.

Apart from the 'King George', other prestigious jumping races staged at Kempton are the Racing Post Chase, also a 3-mile affair, and some prestigious hurdles – the 2-mile Christmas Hurdle, staged on the day after Boxing Day, the Lanzarote Handicap Hurdle, run if the weather permits in late January and the Tote Placepot Hurdle that provides a late February accompaniment to the Racing Post Chase.

Although a 'park' course, suburban Kempton offers racegoers an excellent view of racing. Its proximity to London makes it understandably popular.

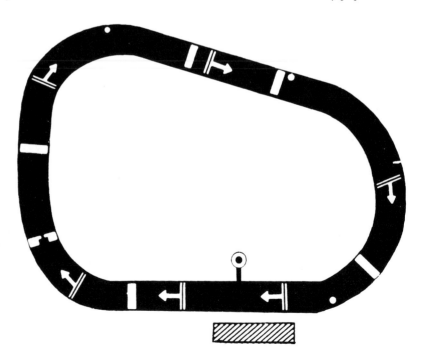

KILBEGGAN: Plan of the course.

KILBEGGAN

Kilbeggan
Loughnagore
Co. Westmeath
Southern Ireland
Tel. (0506) 32176

How to get there:
From North: N52
From South: N52
From East: N6
From West: N6
By Air: Dublin Airport
Approximately 60 miles from Dublin

This sharp racecourse only extends for nine furlongs and is also undulating, particularly in its back stretch. Only National Hunt racing is staged here, but so acceptably that the track was voted the winner of the 1990 Racing Club of Ireland Award, and the course's excellent viewing facilities and the closure of a nearby racecourse at Mullingar have ensured its popularity.

Jockeyship is vital here as large fields and tight turns conspire to produce many problems in running.

The track lies on the N6 from Galway, while Dubliners should look for this road after leaving the capital on the N4.

Two major races run at Kilbeggan have been the Michael Moore Car Sales Novices Steeplechase, run in May and invariably won by a runner whose speed rating shows it can motor round this tight track, and the Cooney Cup run in August.

KILLARNEY

Killarney Racecourse
Co. Kerry
Southern Ireland
Tel. (064) 31125

How to get there:
From North: N22
From South: N71
From East: N72
From West: R562
By Rail: Killarney
By Air: Farranfore Airport

Given its fame and its quite unparalleled scenic splendour (racegoers can watch their favourite sport taking place in front of a lake against a picturesque backcloth of heather-clad sandstone mountains) it is astonishing that very few Irish trainers or jockeys have ever nominated Killarney as their favourite racecourse.

The present-day idyllically located track is the third on which racing has taken place. The first was a point-to-point track and the second was sited on the edge of Killarney, one of the loveliest towns in Ireland in which to relax when attending the two-day fixture in May or the main July meeting. The latter starts the round of summer festival race meetings.

Rail-travellers arrive at Killarney station while motorists travelling west from Cork or south from Tralee should take the N22. The course itself is best approached via Kenmare Road or Ross Road and a large car park will be found beside the former.

KILLARNEY: Without doubt, Killarney racecourse has unparalleled scenery; racegoers can watch their favourite sport taking place in front of Lough Leane, with the heather-clad sandstone Purple Mountain of Killarney National Park providing the most splendid backcloth.

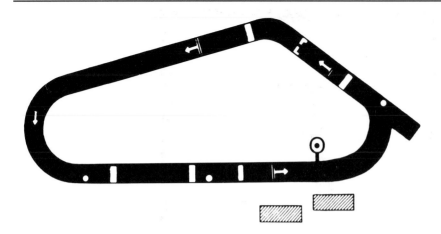

KILLARNEY: Plan of the course.

The on-course airstrip no longer being maintained, landings should be made at Farranfore airport some 10 miles or so along the N22 road from Tralee.

The Rank Cup Chase is a prestigious steeplechase as are the Doyle Brothers Chase and the Waterford Crystal Chase. Another Killarney event, the Pretty Polly race, recalls the Irish bred 1904 Triple Crown winner. Killarney offers racegoers some of the best racing fare on offer anywhere in Ireland. It can even claim the most bizarre distinction of being a racecourse on which a win was registered by a 'horned' horse, the appropriately named Something's Wong, whose 'two protuberances about an inch long placed between its eyes and ears' led one wag to observe that its dam must have attended a stag party.

The course at Killarney is an oval affair of 10 furlongs on which five obstacles have to be jumped. It was recently improved to feature a new starting chute of approximately half a furlong.

KITE
Cheque.

❢ KNOCKING JOINT
Ribald slang for a defaulting bookmaker. 'Taking the knock' is racing parlance for failing to pay.

❢ KNOCKING OUT
Artificially inflating prices available on the racecourse and so affecting official starting prices.

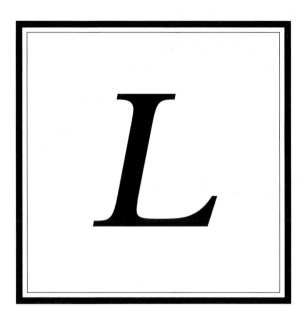

LADBROKES

Ladbrokes is the world's biggest bookmaker with more licensed betting office outlets in the UK than any of its rivals, and operates in several other countries. Thus it is rather appropriate that it gives its name to companion guides to flat and National Hunt racing that are published annually by Aesculus Press.

Towards the close of the nineteenth century, Mr Arthur Bendir, a wealthy landowner from the village of Ladbroke in Warwickshire, formed a company whose sole purpose was to 'take wagers from gentlemen wishing to pursue such sporting pleasures'.

Such a facility – a credit arrangement so as to be legal at the time – tended to be accessible to the very rich and thus from the first Ladbrokes numbered amongst its clients members of several royal households.

The modern Ladbroke Group has spread its interests well beyond bookmaking.

There is even a tic-tac signal, reverentially akin to a halo being signed above the head, which denotes that this Leviathan of bookmakers is channelling the money taken in its many High Street multiples on a particular runner into the on-course market.

Ladbrokes is a major sponsor of races staged in both Britain and Ireland.

LADIES' MOUNTS

Such is the depth of sexist prejudice against lady jockeys that their mounts often start at over-generous odds that do not accurately reflect their chances.

In some races in which lady jockeys have competed, nothing, not even the popularity of the Princess Royal, has reduced the odds of the horses they have ridden. So victories by female jockeys (even royal ones at Redcar, Towcester and Ascot on Gulfland, Cnoc Na Cuille and Ten No Trumps) have been on outsiders in the betting.

The truth is, of course (as everyone knows who has studied point-to-point performances by riders of both sexes) that a lady jockey will be doing her best to strike a blow for her sex and for equality.

In July 1988 at York the Princess Royal rode out Insular, owned by royal trainer Ian Balding, to win the Queen Mother's Cup, a race inaugurated in that year to commemorate her grandmother's passion for the turf.

LADIES' RACES

These events, generally sponsored, add a glamorous ingredient to the racing fare on offer at some tracks. The most prestigious, a truly 'diamond studded' affair, opens Ascot's King George VI meeting in late July.

Always fiercely contested, ladies' races are often

LADIES' RACES: A close finish between Mr Flint and Lady Thornton at York in 1804, shows that riding side-saddle was by no means a handicap. In this race Lady Thornton was only narrowly beaten.

'do or die' events that quite often prove to be very exciting, truly Corinthian affairs. Doubtless, they were even more so when in past decades intrepid huntswomen in full skirts and bowlers leapt side-saddle over natural obstacles such as stone walls and untended hedges.

LADS

General term for stable employees. *One of the Lads*, by Susan Gallier makes it clear that these vital racing functionaries are often female!

! LADY GODIVA

Rhyming slang for a fiver (£5).

LADY JOCKEYS' ASSOCIATION

Thornfield
Windmill
Bishops Auckland
Co. Durham DL14 0PR
Tel. (0388) 710014

The committee of this organization is made up of currently successful lady jockeys as well as pioneering riders who in the past decade or so have made spectacular headway against the headwinds of male prejudice. Thus, Maxine Juster has served alongside Elain Mellor (the four-times winner of the Lady Amateurs' Flat Riders' Championship) and Caroline Saunders, the first woman to win a champion foxhunter steeplechase event at Cheltenham.

The main aim of the LJA is to maintain 'the highest standards of honour, integrity and courtesy among lady jockeys and to support and protect their interests generally'; no mean task in an industry in which its members can still experience prejudice.

When one of its members, Jessica Charles Jones, broke her back in a fall in a hurdle race at Southwell, the LJA gave this plucky jockey much appreciated assistance in her brave bid to recover by organizing a special appeal fund and by presenting Jessica, on Boxing Day 1989, with a car that had cost £7000 to purchase and specially adapt.

LAID OUT

Said of a horse that on a long-range basis is specially and secretly prepared for victory in a particular (usually rather prestigious) race.

The top-class steeplechaser, Mill House, was 'laid out' (and backed by his owner at 200-1) for the 1963 Cheltenham Gold Cup a year before he triumphed in steeplechasing's blue riband!

LAY

To bet against. This, the business stratagem of a bookmaker, can be exploited by a backer who, having obtained a long price against a particular runner early in the pre-race betting, can then accept a bet against it from a fellow punter or a bookmaker at shorter odds!

In this way it is sometimes possible to show a profit even when the horse loses, thus making a nonsense of the belief that ante-post betting is a backer's burial ground.

LAYING FACES

Bookmakers' parlance for accepting bets from known 'sharps' – those whose betting activity has appeared 'inspired' in the past. When a bookmaker is approached by such a backer he has one of two choices: to request the 'face' to take his business elsewhere or to lay the bet required and allow it to influence his other business. He could, for example, decide to reduce his liability on the horse supported by the 'face' and 'stand' heavy bets on its rivals.

LAY OFF

Action taken by a bookmaker who has incurred such an excessive liability on a runner that he supports this himself with another bookmaker. Such 'hedging' or 'laying off' is an essential part of the risk-reduction process that is central to successful bookmaking.

LAYTOWN

Laytown
Co. Meath
Southern Ireland
Tel. (041) 23425 or 38368

How to get there:
From North: R150
From South: R150
From West: N1
By Air: Dublin Airport
Approximately 25 miles from Dublin

LAYTOWN: The only fixture on the Irish racing calendar to be held on a beach.

Given that wellingtons are *de rigeur* while it takes place, Laytown's annual race meeting, staged at a small east-coast holiday resort, is hardly Ireland's most fashionable fixture. However, it is decidedly good fun, largely because it is the only fixture on the Irish racing calendar to be held on a beach, rather than a racecourse proper.

Laytown is the only course where a winner was ever disqualified for attempted murder! One jockey complained to the stewards that his rival tried to force him into the sea knowing he couldn't swim. The consequence of this exaggerated claim (you have to go out miles for sufficiently deep water) was that this Laytown winner was disqualified for bumping and boring.

Laytown strand will be found some 27 miles north of Dublin whence it can be reached if motorists travelling on the N1 look for signposts at Julianstown. Understandably, there are no landing facilities on the strand on which the racing is naturally controlled by the tide, which when it is in puts the course under about a metre of sea water. At low tide, three hours before the first race, the clerk of the course marks out the left-handed track on the sand of the long gently sloping beach by means of poles adorned with red flags. When harrowing of the racing surface is complete, races run over distances varying from 5 to 16 furlongs can be staged.

It would be a mistake to regard Laytown as something of a toytown event since leading Irish trainers send their horse boxes to its annual meeting which became the only maritime one held in Europe when racing on the back strand at Tramore became impracticable some years ago.

Laytown's annual fixture, often staged in August, creates an atmosphere that, once savoured (as it was by the Aga Khan in 1950) is unforgettable.

LAY UNDER THE ODDS

Yet another way in which a bookmaker can do business. Backers should note that rails and 'front line' boards bookmakers are in the best position to profit from this tactic. They should also beware short prices being quoted by course bookmakers on runners at away meetings.

LEADING TRAINERS

Information on these on a course-to-course basis, complete with winners-to-runners ratios or, even more usefully, percentages is given in both the *Sporting Life* and *Racing Post* in features respectively entitled 'Leading Trainers' and 'Top Trainers'.

Sometimes trainers who have been successful at a track at a certain time of year may also be indicated, as may those who have been most successful with particular types of runners.

Course Form and *Racing and Football Outlook's* budget-priced annual guides to flat and jump racing provide useful indications of trainers who 'lead the field' at particular racecourses.

The least useful leading trainers' statistics are those that merely reveal the number of winners they have achieved on a particular course from an undisclosed number of runners over an unspecified period.

LEICESTER

Leicester Racecourse
Leicester LE2 4AL
Tel. (0533) 716515

How to get there:
From North: M1
From South: M1
From East: A47
From West: A5
By Rail: Leicester
By Air: Leicester Aerodrome

Leicester's right-handed racecourse, almost 100 miles from the capital, can be conveniently reached by train from St Pancras to Leicester (Midland) station where taxis and special buses provide transport to the track at Oadby two miles south-east of the city.

Motorists will find that the course, on which racing was first staged as a fully-enclosed affair in the early 1880s, lies on the A6 to Market Harborough. Racegoers using the M1 should leave it at junction 21, while M6 travellers should look for its second exit and then travel via the M69 to the M1 which can be used as an alternative to the A6 by those travelling southwards.

Some describe the shape of the circuit as a cross between a rectangle and an oval. In having a circumference of around fourteen furlongs it is a fairly extensive right-hander. Indeed, its long straight sections and well-banked bends tend to be appreciated by long-striding, galloping types which also relish Leicester's long four-and-a-half-furlong run-in which allows jockeys to hold up their mounts in order to unleash a late challenge.

Leicester presents trainers with a welcome (since fairly rare) chance to run their milers on a perfectly straight 8 furlong 8 yard course, which is provided by

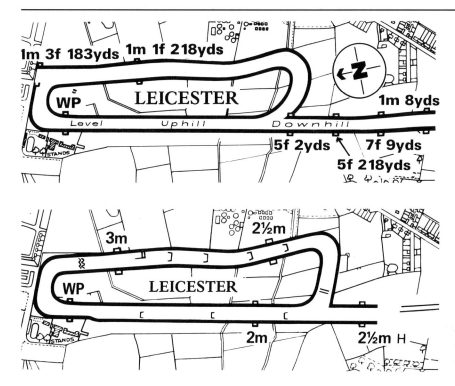

LEICESTER: Plans of the Flat course (top), and the National Hunt course (bottom).

a long, almost three-furlong spur which joins the round course just over five furlongs out. Negotiation of this particular course, which is also used for the staging of sprints and 7-furlong 9-yard events, imposes a fairly stiff test of stamina since it has stretches that at times rise quite steeply before level ground is reached as the post is approached. Backers should look to performers that seem bred to stay.

On the straight course, on which sprints of 5 furlongs 2 yards and 5 furlongs 218 yards are also run, the draw is only really significant if the going is heavy and the stalls are positioned on the stands side when low-drawn runners enjoy an edge. In races run on the round course over 9 furlongs 218 yards and 11 furlongs 183 yards, high-drawn horses enjoy a slight advantage. It is difficult to find evidence that Leicester has presented any difficulty to those who ride round its right-handed circuit. An efficient watering system prevents the going becoming too hard and, as the course drains well, its fixtures are seldom rained off.

It is also clear that the Leicester executive does its best to please those who patronize their track since a picnic park has been provided in the silver ring and parties of ten or more racegoers who book in advance are entitled to a considerable reduction on the total cost of their admission.

The course's central location means that horseboxes from all over the country can be seen in

Leicester's parking areas on racedays. Indeed, this track is renowned for staging some of the biggest cards in the country and so presenting bookmakers' clerks and chalk boys with some major headaches; at the 'back end' of the flat season, a Leicester card may attract more than 120 runners.

Leicester is also a National Hunt racecourse, yet its enviable situation in the heart of England's finest hunting country does not mean that those visiting it see steeplechasing at its finest. The 'chase track of ten fair, if fairly severe, fences (six in the back stretch, one just before the home turn and three in the home straight) forms a right-handed rectangle of 14 furlongs whose straight sections are extensive enough for galloping types to get into their long strides. If such runners have shown that they can race right-handed and have sufficient stamina to cope with the three final furlongs in which three fences have to be negotiated along with a slight elbow in the 250 yard run-in, then so much the better.

LENGTH
The measurement of a horse from head to tail.

This is the unit of distance that is used to indicate the margins by which horses defeat others. It is thus crucial in the recording of the results of races which can be won by lengths, half lengths, necks, heads and short heads.

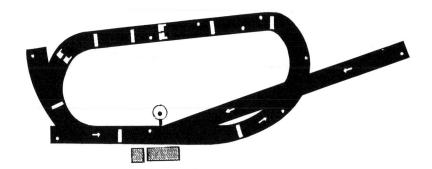

LEOPARDSTOWN:
Plan of the course.

LEOPARDSTOWN

Leopardstown Racecourse
Foxrock
Dublin 18
Ireland
Tel. (01) 893607

How to get there:
From North: N11
From South: N11
From East: R113
From West: R113
By Rail: Dun Laoghaire
By Air: Helicopter facilities

Ireland's equivalent of Sandown Park (it was once managed by a former assistant at this track and largely re-modelled on it) is a worthy challenger for the further title of the best all-purpose course in this thoroughly horse-orientated country.

Leopardstown's magnificent new multi-million pound complex provides considerable revenue on non-race days through its sports and social facilities. On the twenty-five days or so when either flat or National Hunt racing takes place, crowds of up to 20,000 get a fine view of some high-class sport in enviable comfort. Leopardstown patrons can take advantage of completely enclosed facilities made up of a betting hall, four restaurants, ten bars, and a dining room.

The track itself, which is the oldest of Ireland's now dwindling number of metropolitan tracks, is a left-handed rectangle that extends for 14 furlongs. Its long straights and sweeping bends (the last of which can cause inexperienced jockeys to lose races by coming too wide) and three-furlong run-in make it ideal for long-striding gallopers with some toe. There is a straight sprint course of 6 furlongs that ends with a fairly stiff incline. Some believe low-drawn horses are slightly favoured over 7 furlongs and 1 mile.

As for the steeplechase course, this is, in the opinion of former Irish jockey Pat Taaffe, better than any other in either England or Ireland. Of its sixteen broad fences, which have to be negotiated in 3-mile steeplechases, the three in the back stretch are quite testing, while the going, thanks to Leopardstown's excellent natural drainage and proximity to the coast, tends to be easy. This latter advantage often means that Leopardstown is the only track in the British Isles to stage a meeting during a cold snap. Firm ground is something of a rarity too, thanks to a most modern and extensive watering system.

Nowadays the nearest railway station (and port of disembarkation for the ferry from Holyhead) is Dun Laoghaire which is only three miles from the course. Motorists will find Foxrock not much more than five miles from Dublin city centre, off the Stillorgan dual carriageway that links the capital with Bray.

Leopardstown has a long association with aviation (in 1955 it became the first Irish course to accommodate helicopters) and racegoers can fly in provided they have clearance from the local garda as well as the clerk of the course.

As one would expect of a track that was the first to feature Sunday racing and *pari-mutuel* style Computote betting, Leopardstown stages some top-class flat and National Hunt racing. Its Derrinstown Stud Derby Trial, a 10-furlong race for Classic hopefuls, has previously been farmed by Vincent O'Brien, as has another rather classy race, the Leopardstown Stakes for two-year-olds.

Another race for first-season performers, the Killavullen Stakes, is a mile contest confined to fillies that has on more than one occasion been won by O'Brien's son, David, while in the all-aged Ballyogan Stakes, three-year-olds have the best record, as again does Vincent O'Brien amongst previously successful trainers.

The Harold Clarke Leopardstown Handicap Chase, which commemorates an influential

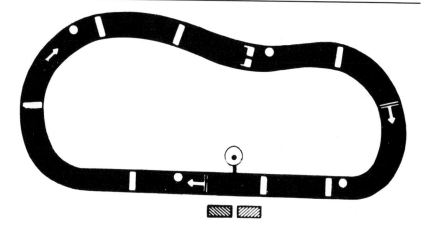

LIMERICK: Plan of the course.

administrator, often provides pointers to the Grand National, as Last Suspect proved when winning it in 1981, four years before he triumphed at Aintree at 50-1. In the 'Harold Clarke' it is often wise to side with a seven-or eight-year-old. Such runners are also worth noting in the recently inaugurated Black and White Whisky Champion Chase, while the sheer class of the 3-mile Hennessy Cognac Gold Cup steeplechase is indicated by the fact that it has often been previously captured by Cheltenham Gold Cup winners. The thrilling Findus Handicap Chase often falls to an eight-year-old, while six-year-olds should receive consideration in the Denny's Gold Medal Novices' Chase, run over 2 miles, the Ladbroke Limited Handicap Hurdle (run as the Sweeps Hurdle until 1986) and the Wessel Cable Champion Hurdle that is contested in early February.

Many feel the facilities at Leopardstown have the ambience of a tastefully equipped and luxuriously furnished airport. No wonder then that racegoers, especially lazy ones, find the going so easy at this top-class course.

Leopardstown now stages a four-day Christmas fixture and looks likely to stage more of a lion's share of the top-class racing fare on offer in the Republic.

LET DOWN

Paddock watcher's term. Despite its connotations of disappointment, it denotes a horse with a well-conditioned body!

LEVEL STAKES

Staking procedure whereby the same chosen single stake unit is wagered on each and every selection in a sequence.

LEVY BOARD (See Horserace Betting Levy Board)

LICENSED BETTING OFFICES OR L.B.O.'s
(See Betting Shops)

Such establishments were unknown before the 1960s. Before this time, off-course bookmakers were unable to trade within the law and operated from private houses or on street corners. By 1968, 15,000 betting shops were in existence. By May 1986 this figure had declined to 11,000.

Modern L.B.Os are far more welcoming and comfortable than their counterparts of more than twenty years ago and most have been liberated from their Victorian ambience though the lifting of restrictions on advertising, the serving of refreshments and the showing of televised racing by national networks or satellite.

LIMERICK

Greenpark Racecourse
South Circular Road
Limerick
Ireland
Tel. (061) 29377

How to get there:
From North: R465
From South: N20
From East: N7, R503
From West: N69
By Rail: Limerick
By Air: Coonagh Aerodrome, Helicopter facilities

Appropriately, as one of Ireland's largest cities replete with romance and history, and given its situation in the heart of some great hunting country, Limerick has its own racecourse.

This is where triple Cheltenham Gold Cup

winner Cottage Rake won his first race. It is to be found amidst the rich farming and horse breeding area that the plains of Limerick comprise.

Established in 1916 to provide southern-based enthusiasts with yet further sport, the course is a right-handed affair with a stiff, testing climb before the turn into the finishing straight. This and two closely positioned fences in the closing stages mean that Limerick is a stayers' course. Two other reasons for this are the length of the run-in from the second last and the frequency with which the going can be soft or heavy.

The most important races run at Limerick are the Munster Chase and the Munster National Chase.

The course is accessible from Limerick's railway station. Facilities for fixed-wing aircraft are available at Coonagh airstrip about three miles west of Ireland's third largest city which is some sixteen miles from Shannon airport. Racegoers arriving by helicopter should first seek permission to make an on-course landing by telephoning the racecourse.

LINE THROUGH, TAKING A
Method whereby the possible superiority or inferiority of one runner to another is assessed on evidence provided by their past performances against other racehorses. Such a consideration of what is sometimes called 'collateral form' at least gives the backer something tangible that can feature in his bid to distinguish between runners that have never previously taken each other on.

LINGFIELD

Lingfield Park Racecourse
Lingfield
Surrey RH7 6PQ
Tel. (0342) 834800

How to get there:
From North: A23(M)
From South: M23
From East: A264
From West: B2028
By Rail: Lingfield
By Air: Gatwick Airport; Helicopter facilities

Some racegoers feel that scenically Lingfield Park can rival Goodwood, although the recent redevelopment of both courses has rather reduced their aesthetic appeal. Lingfield is certainly most accessible in being only a short distance from the M23 and M25 and is well-patronized since it is less than thirty miles from the capital whence it can be reached conveniently by taking the M25 to junction 6, the A22 and then the B2028 after Blindley Heath. The commuter line from London Bridge or Victoria runs to Lingfield station which is only a 400-yard walk from the course.

Racing was first staged here in 1894 and since then, under various managers, many steps have been taken to attract spectators; for example, concessions for senior citizens and a very reasonable 'blanket'

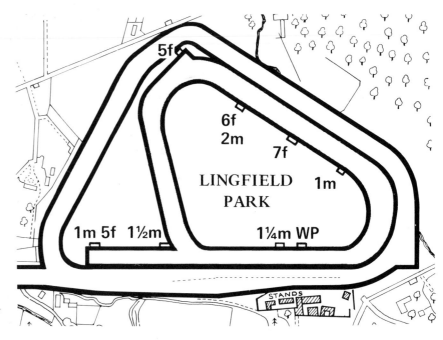

LINGFIELD: Plan of the all-weather Flat course.

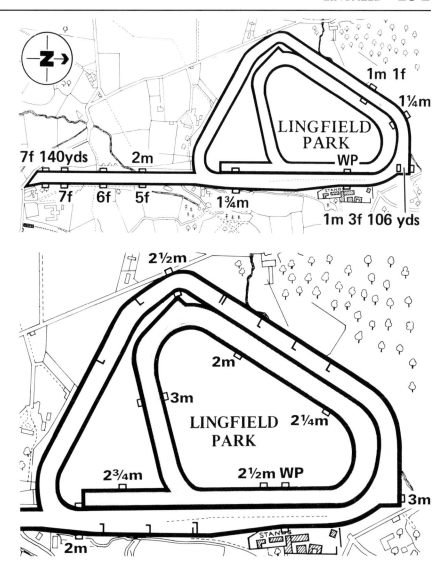

LINGFIELD: Plans of the Flat turf course (top), and the National Hunt turf and all-weather course (bottom).

sum for the occupants of vehicles entering an attractive picnic park. On top of this, a Silks restaurant has recently traded on a six-day, rather than mere race day, basis, and a brasserie and cocktail bar opens its doors every night of the week.

Such innovations have meant that, with its roof-top restaurant, its seafood bar, motel accommodation and exhibition centre, Lingfield has become a leisure complex for all-year-round use as well as a racecourse.

Lingfield's straight course allows races to be run over a 'short mile' of 7 furlongs 140 yards, as well as over exactly 7 furlongs and the shorter sprint distances of 5 and 6 furlongs. The ground involved descends for much of its length, sharply in fact over its first three furlongs or so and subsequently more gently.

Perhaps only at Epsom can a 'faster' sprint course be found.

Understandably, then, Lingfield's straight course is appreciated by fast starters, front runners and handy, sure-footed types that can keep their balance. Well-actioned animals are considered at a further advantage if allocated high numbers in the draw, especially if the stalls are positioned on the stands side. However, when it is soft or heavy underfoot, the belief is that better ground is to be found close to the far rails.

The longest races that are staged on Lingfield's straight course take place over 2 miles and are started from the 6-furlong gate. After running down the straight course for about two furlongs, the runners join the round course on which an important Epsom rehearsal takes place over 1 mile 3 furlongs 106 yards. This is the Derby trial that is contested in early May.

In that it consists of undulating, cambered terrain that involves a slight climb out of its second turn and a steeper stretch of track, that is followed by a downhill run into a tightish turn into a 3-furlong-plus home straight, Lingfield's 'Classic trial' course, though smaller than its Epsom counterpart, does quite closely resemble it in also calling for agility and balance. It is perhaps the sharp descent into the final turn, possibly sharper than that presented by Tattenham Corner, that makes Lingfield the best simulation of the Epsom Classic experience available to trainers of Derby hopefuls. Significantly, in the 1980s three Derby winners, Teenoso, Slip Anchor and Kahyasi, had previously prevailed in Lingfield's Derby trial.

The course makes considerable demands on jockeyship and one's fancy should be partnered by a rider with an impressive wins to runs record, and the nous not to run wide round Lingfield's home turn and so throw away the chance of victory.

Past course and distance winners over 10 and 11 furlongs 106 yards often go in again at several of Lingfield's afternoon and evening fixtures. In the winter, such performers should be considered on Lingfield's jumping circuit. Shaped like a cone, it runs left-handed for around ten furlongs and its many gradients, short 200-yard run-in and fairly demanding final four fences (of ten in all) can find out several contenders. This is why agile, hardy types with a turn of foot are to be fancied against long-striding rivals. As for hurdle races, these are run on Lingfield's flat course.

In the late 1980s, Lingfield was chosen as one of two pioneering all-weather courses and has thus allowed many flat race performers to race in the winter and National Hunt types to compete when racing is impossible elsewhere.

LISTED RACES

Many important events, several of them handicaps like the Chester Cup, that are no longer ranked as highly as before the present 'pattern' of carefully balanced and complementary top-class races was introduced, are 'listed' as nevertheless important. Winners of 'listed' races often have this distinction announced in bold black type when their racing records are detailed in sales' catalogues.

LISTOWEL

Listowel Racecourse
Co. Kerry
Ireland
Tel. (068) 21144

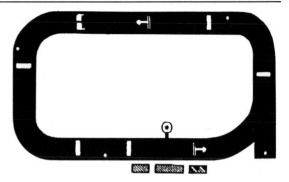

LISTOWEL: Plan of the course, which is synonymous with a marvellous atmosphere, good organization, large crowds, convivial socializing and heavy betting.

How to get there:
From North: N69
From South: N69
From East: N21, R523
From West: R553
By Air: Coonagh Aerodrome
Approximately 40 miles from Limerick

Listowel is popular among racing scribes, no doubt largely because here in late September is staged the last of Ireland's justifiably renowned summer festival meetings. This five-day affair, linked to a local harvest festival and the all-Ireland Wren Boys competition, features a great variety of races.

As for the horse boys, they make for Listowel's island course which has been the scene of racing in this Kerry town since 1858.

The historical track from which some splendid church spires are visible, is a rectangular flat left-hander that extends for over a mile and on which (if anything) high numbers are believed by some to confer an advantage. A fine view of the final two fences on the jumping circuit can be obtained from the stands.

To many, Listowel is synonymous with a marvellous atmosphere, good organization, large crowds, considerable prize money, convivial socializing, large competitive fields and heavy betting. The most important races are the Listowel Bookmakers' EBF Harp Amateur Handicap, the Guinness Kerry National, the Dawn Light Butter Hurdle, a National Hunt Flat Race Final and the long-established Smithwick's Beer Hurdle.

Listowel lies 15 miles from Tralee, from which it can be reached on the N69. Limerick-based racegoers should take the N21 to Rathkeale and then proceed along the R523. On-course car and coach parks are extensive and, unusually, free of charge – just one indication of the warm welcome extended to this popular track's many appreciative racegoers.

LITERATURE, RACING

This is by no means the monopoly of Dick Francis. Ernest Hemingway and D.H. Lawrence (in their short stories *My Old Man* and *The Rocking Horse Winner*) are just two famous writers who have contributed to what is a rich and colourful literary genre.

LIVE ORDER

Horse which finds considerable support in the market.

LONG HANDICAP

In some handicaps it will be seen that only a few runners carry more than a bottom weight that many of their rivals are also allotted. This is because adjustments have been made to the original 'long' handicap, full details of which are given in the specialist racing dailies the *Sporting Life* and the *Racing Post*. These newspapers will show that among the many runners that are set to carry the same bottom weight in the revised handicap, several had been accorded far less than this by thehandicapper. Some rapid calculations may reveal a really well-handicapped runner that has greatly benefited from being unaffected by the sometimes punitive bottom weight rule. Such a contestant is definitely one to at least consider.

❗ LONG-UN

Slang for 1000-1.

LOOKING ON

Not trying, said of a horse allegedly playing a spectator's part.

LUDLOW

The Racecourse
Bromfield
Ludlow
Shropshire
Tel. (0981) 250436

How to get there:
From North: A49
From South: A49
From East: A4117
From West: A4113
By Rail: Ludlow
By Air: Helicopter facilities

A list of the major races run on this delightful right-hand track reveals that the sport it offers is savoured by some connoisseurs of National Hunt racing.

Thus, a Prince and Princess of Wales Amateur Riders' Chase is annually contested and the course's upmarket ambience is further suggested by the fact that makers of a fine claret and Christies the auctioneers each sponsor a steeplechase.

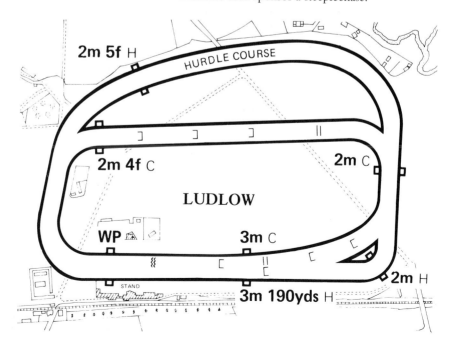

LUDLOW: Plan of the course.

The fairly tight steeplechase track, which was originally used for flat racing only until 1870, is an oval right-hander that extends for approximately twelve furlongs.

Steeplechasers running at Ludlow can stride out reasonably well if they are not inconvenienced by having to race clockwise, jump what are eight quite stiffish fences and by finally having to slog it out on the long run-in of over 400 yards to the post.

Rather unusually, the hurdle track at Ludlow runs outside the steeplechase course. It features undulating ground in its back stretch and extends for around a mile and a half.

Past course and distance winners well-rated by stop-watch holders are often supported by knowledgeable racegoers, many of them farmers.

Racegoers can journey to this very pleasant country racecourse by taking the train to Ludlow. Then they will find the course is just a mile away on the A49 (Shrewsbury) road. This particular route is also one that should be taken by northbound travellers from Leominster and Hereford.

By prior arrangement, helicopters can land on the course, but responsibility for this proceeding must be taken by their occupants.

Some enticing sport is staged at Ludlow's many exclusively mid-week fixtures, notably the Forbra Gold Cup run in memory of the 1932 Grand National winner, which, appropriately, was owned by a retired Ludlow bookmaker.

Over the years many racegoers, some of them discerning and socially well-placed, have admired the elegant ironwork on Ludlow's grandstands. In these and the course's open rooftop stand the ruddy faces of several farmers have been seen on many a Wednesday in the jumping season.

One of this select band is thrice champion National Hunt jockey Bob Davies who, as clerk of the course, does much to ensure that some enticing sport is staged on this attractively rural track.

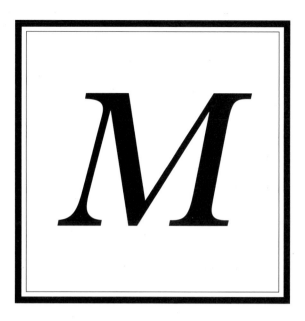

MAGAZINES, RACING

With the demise in 1989 of *Racing Monthly*, after its publishers made the mistake of also covering greyhound racing and so changing its title to *Turf and Track*, the number of magazines devoted to racing was further reduced.

However, in that year Pacemaker's weekly *Update* was launched to provide a pictorial and verbal chronicle of racing as well as many features of not merely topical concern.

As well as generally available specialist racing magazines, others are sent to the credit account clients of bookmakers (one example is William Hill's *Action Line*) or those who have such arrangements with the tote whose *Equus* magazine is lavishly produced and also available to non-tote clients.

Some racecourse owners, syndicates and racing clubs publish their own magazines. Recently a new market for racing 'magazines' has been opened up with the launch of *Racing World* , a regular video update of key races and developments in the sport.

Several defunct racing magazines are increasingly valuable as collectors' items. As a sport racing has long featured in such 'society' magazines as *Vanity Fair*. Indeed the cartoons of racing personalities that long ago featured in this particular publication are keenly sought after.

Pacemaker Update International [weekly magazine]
Haymarket Publishing Ltd
Lancaster Gate
London W2 3LP
Tel. (071) 404 4200
Racing World
Unit 1
143 Chatham Road
London SW11 5PA
Tel. (071) 924 4066

MAGNIFICENT SEVEN

From seven selections this rather exotic wager covers in rotation 7 singles, 6 doubles, 5 trebles, 4 fourfolds, 3 fivefolds, 2 sixfolds and 1, doubtless magnificent, seven-timer. Thus, all-in-all it produces 28 wagers.

MAIDENS

Non-winning racehorses of either sex. Races confined to these are usually young racehorses of two-or three-years-old. Such events attract many contenders that can be discounted and often serve to open or close race meetings. Occasionally a maiden wins a Classic: Sun Princess was one example in winning the 1983 Oaks, and Snurge, another in the 1990 St Leger. Some judges consider a maiden race can sometimes represent a sound medium for investment.

MAKING THE WEIGHT

For many jockeys over the centuries this has been a recurring problem whose severity actually varies with the time of year. Steve Cauthen is just one who has pointed out that towards the back end of the season and on the return of the cold conditions common at its commencement, it gets harder for a jockey to make his lowest riding weight. Indeed, in the autumn, jockeys stop sweating and the weight goes back on.

Some jockeys frequent the sauna but others resort to methods used by their profession for centuries.

There have, of course, always been a few methods of losing weight (like the 'pee pills' that some desperate jockeys have resorted to on occasion) which may be temporarily effective but can have possibly dangerous debilitating or dehydrating effects. One desperate tactic is to eat heartily before riding and then stick one's fingers down one's throat.

Wasting, a much more common method of losing weight, was perhaps rather more widespread for much of the nineteenth century and before, when horses went to post carrying weights as low as 5st 7lbs, a figure gradually raised to 7 stones by the 1920s as nutritional standards improved. Many jockeys desperate to win rides from the scores of young apprentices who abounded in the Victorian era literally starved themselves.

Fred Archer, the celebrated Victorian jockey, would often see his weight shoot up by a massive 35lbs in the close season from November to March.

Sweating off the pounds through gruelling road running (in the 'John Sullivans' and heavy clothes favoured by hungry boxers or marine commandos) or long sessions in Turkish baths were methods of weight reduction many jockeys favoured in the first half of this century.

Jack Leach has described how he and his colleagues wore four or five sweaters and a rubber suit! They would walk and jog about eight miles or more, then go straight into a Turkish bath for a massage.

The advantage of this method was that after racing, it could be compensated for by the good dinner its victims allowed themselves which generally consisted of 'a steak and a glass or two of champagne'. This, according to Leach, amounted to the least fattening diet it is possible to have. Modern-day dietitians might disagree with this.

Lester Piggott, whose lined face is a legacy of the fierce wasting he has endured for well over a quarter of a century, like his predecessor in the saddle,

Brownie Carslake, adopts what is perhaps the most gruelling method of weight control — that of constantly watching what is consumed. During the flat-racing season, Carslake, whose self-denial probably led to his death shortly after his retirement, survived on a piece of toast, a lightly boiled egg and a single cup of tea! Notwithstanding this he was reckoned to be one of the strongest jockeys in a finish.

MALLOW

Mallow Racecourse
Mount Ruby
Mallow
Co. Cork
Southern Ireland
Tel. (022) 22017 or 21565

How to get there:
From North: N20
From South: N20
From East: N72
From West: N72
By Air: Light Aircraft facilities
Approximately 20 miles from Cork

Mallow is situated close to Buttevant, the venue where chasing from steeple to steeple or point-to-point began in 1752 when a Mr Edmund Blake challenged his neighbour, Mr O'Callaghan, to race across country from Buttevant church to the spire of St Leger church some four and a half miles distant and so jump stone walls, ditches and hedges as these presented themselves. By keeping the steeple of the church in sight (steeplechasing) both riders could see their finishing point.

As for the course at Mallow, it is a far less drawn-out affair. A mile from the town's railway station, it is a right-handed 'galloping' track of some twelve furlongs that includes a 5-furlong sprint course.

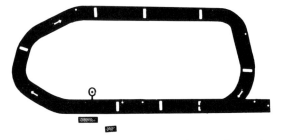

MALLOW: Plan of the course. It is close to where point-to-point racing began in 1752.

Mallow can take light aircraft thanks to its 500-metre east-west landing strip. It is also particularly accessible to Cork-and Limerick-based racegoers who should arrive via the N20. Those driving eastwards from Killarney should take the N72, as should those travelling westwards from Fermoy or Dungarran.

Mallow has been popular ever since 1924 when it was established partly to compensate for the closure of Cork Park racecourse.

MARE
A female horse of five years or more.

MARES' ALLOWANCE
Weight concession (often of 5lbs) that mares who take on colts and geldings in certain races can enjoy. Its fairly recent introduction caused some controversy and some narrow victories may be attributed to it.

MARKET MOVEMENTS
Surveys have shown that only around 15 per cent of all contractions in the betting actually involve winning horses.

Movements in the betting market that few racegoers ever consider involve disparities between rates predicted in the *Sporting Life* or the *Racing Post* and those actually quoted on course. The following 'ladder of odds' will enable the racegoer to gauge the size of this disparity. It may on occasion indicate that too great a 'bargain' is being offered in the actual betting on a particular runner.

THE 'LADDER' OF ODDS

100/1	8/1
66/1	15/2
50/1	7/1
40/1	13/2
33/1	6/1
25/1	11/2
22/1	5/1
20/1	9/2
19/1	4/1
18/1	7/2
17/1	100/30
16/1	3/1
15/1	11/4
14/1	5/2
13/1	95/40
12/1	9/4
11/1	2/1
10/1	15/8
9/1	7/4

13/8	4/9
6/4	40/95
11/8	2/5
5/4	4/11
6/5	1/3
11/10	30/100
Evens	2/7
10/11	1
5/6	2/9
4/5	1/5
8/11	2/11
4/6	1/6
8/13	2/13
4/7	1
8/15	2/15
1/2	1/8

This 'ladder' can rapidly indicate the possibly significant extents by which actually quoted rates are higher or lower than forecast ones. Many quite early market movements involve slight improvements on initially poor prices because bookmakers often recognize their initial vulnerability and so start to trade at rates that are distinctly ungenerous.

When only an outsider's odds contract to any extent and when they do so by a substantial percentage, the betting movement involved may sometimes prove very significant. Again, if it is noticed that only one of two market leaders (preferably the favourite since mere possession of this exalted status is usually sufficient to produce a great deal of imitative, as opposed to inspired, support) has its odds only marginally trimmed and an outsider has its odds cut considerably, the latter development can often provide a profitable pointer.

MARKET RASEN

Market Rasen Racecourse
Legsby Road
Market Rasen
Lincs LN8 3EA
Tel. (0673) 843434

How to get there:
From North: A41
From South: B1202
From East: A631
From West: A631
By Rail: Market Rasen
By Air: Wickenby Flying Club; Helicopter facilities

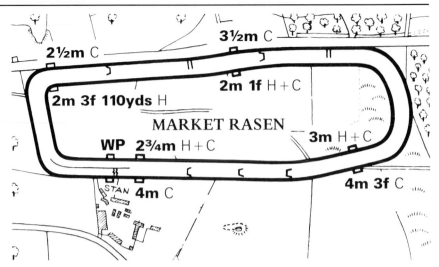

MARKET RASEN: Plan of the course.

Picturesquely situated in the Wolds and the only racecourse in Lincolnshire, Market Rasen is well-managed and has often enjoyed the distinction of closing the National Hunt season.

The track itself is a right-handed oval of 10 furlongs and features slight undulations for much of its extent. Its bends are fairly sharp and the last of these into the home straight features a slight decline; thus in the wet some runners find its negotiation difficult.

The jumping circuit contains eight fences, four in the back stretch and four in the home straight. These are far from testing and so Market Rasen usually suits handy speedsters who find no difficulty in coping with its clockwise configuration. Previous course winners are always worth consideration, while the short run-in of around a furlong tends to suit front runners.

Many meetings are held in the summer when the course's picnic area is greatly appreciated by family groups of racegoers, some of whom motor 160 miles from London.

The course is 16 miles north-east of Lincoln and a mile east of the town of Market Rasen. Those travelling north-east from Lincoln should take the A46 (Grimsby) road, as should travellers coming off the A1 from the south. The A631 will serve racegoers from Yorkshire and this, the 'racecourse road' itself (to Louth), can be joined from the M18.

Market Rasen station (which is a mile from the course) can be reached from King's Cross via Newark, while air travellers can land (without communicating with any ground staff) on a 600-metre airstrip, after gaining prior permission by phoning (0673) 843434. Alternatively, landings can be made at Wickenby Flying Club, five miles away to the south.

MATCH

The pitting of one horse against another. This form of contest went out of fashion with the commercialization of flat racing and is now rarely seen.

In former days, matches were regarded as the most sporting of contests. They not only involved rival owners competing for an even money sidestake, but often caught the imagination of whole populaces. In recent times, jockeys' matches have been special features of race meetings. John Francome has taken on Lester Piggott and Willie Shoemaker has been challenged by the latter and by Peter Scudamore.

MATCH BETTING

In yet another bid to add interest to big races, some bookmakers select two runners and quote odds against one beating the other. Such quotations, which usually appear on an ante-post basis on the morning of the race concerned, can represent remarkable value and make great appeal to backers who engage in some private handicapping of their own.

MATURITY

In racing, some backers seek to capitalize on the fact that many of the youngest racehorses of all, two-year-olds, are, in fact, well over this minimum age.

Irrespective of the actual dates on which they were foaled, all thoroughbreds are given an official birthday of 1 January. Crucially, this means that when the flat-racing season starts in March, some debutants may be as old as 2 years and 2 months through having been foaled in January, two years previously, while others with birthdays at the end of

June may not, in fact, be two-year-olds at all, but animals that have only had just over 18 months in which to mature!

Fascinatingly, a recent season-long survey of two-year-olds showed that those with January foaling dates registered almost double the number of wins achieved by first season runners born in June!

Winners to runners percentages by foaling dates for two-year-olds covering a recent season read as follows:

January foaling	12.3%
February foaling	9.4%
March foaling	9.6%
April foaling	8.3%
May foaling	7.7%
June foaling	6.9%

Clearly these figures provide an almost complete statistical vindication of the wisdom of having age and experience on your side!

MEMORABILIA, RACING

Whether featuring an actual racehorse (as is the case with former champion stayer Brown Jack that, thanks to a taxidermist, fascinates diners at the rather ominously-named stable grill in Widnes), cigarette cards or cases with turf motifs, whips, splendidly solid binoculars, horseshoes or badges that gave admission to past meetings, racing memorabilia is increasingly collectable and valuable.

MEMORY IN RACEHORSES

This is said to be remarkably well-developed, which may well be yet one further reason for supporting runners returning to racecourses on which they have previously won. Horses are also likely to remember the experience of being ridden in a way they appreciate by a particular jockey; thus a horse being ridden by the jockey it previously carried to victory may be worth backing.

MID-DAY FORECASTS

Predictions of starting prices that appear in early editions of evening papers. Many professionals pay particular attention to these since their compilers can take account of information regarding many of the coming afternoon's runners that was previously unavailable to their colleagues on the national dailies.

If a horse shown as the likely favourite in daily newspapers and the authoritative *Sporting Life* and *Racing Post* fails to figure at the head of the mid-day forecast, all may not be well with that particular animal. Conversely, the mid-day forecast may highlight a horse unquoted by earlier forecasters. Such a runner should receive serious consideration, as there may be a very sound reason for its sudden appearance in predictions of starting prices.

MINOR HONOURS

These are achieved by horses that finish in second, third and sometimes, fourth place.

❢ MONKEY

Racing parlance for £500.

MORNING GLORY

A horse that fails on a racecourse to achieve the potential it has shown during its early morning training runs.

This description has sometimes been rather prematurely employed to dismiss many a two-year-old debutant. In fairness, only a horse which has repeatedly failed to live up to its reputation on the gallops should be regarded as a 'morning glory'.

In the view of Jack Leach such an animal 'is the worst kind you can possibly get. Morning glories are the horses that break trainers, not the lazy ones.'

MOST TIPPED HORSES

The most popular selections of racing correspondents for particular races.

MOVE, A

Betting activity on a particular runner that produces a contraction in its displayed odds. As previously stated, study of market moves can be most revealing.

MULTIPLE ENGAGEMENTS

Some followers of racing argue that horses that have been expensively entered and left in several races that are due to be run on any one racing day should be given special consideration. A weekly look at the *Sporting Life Weekender* will indicate runners due to race on Fridays and Saturdays, while the *Racing Post* published before the weekend shows horses with multiple mid-week engagements.

It is often instructive to note which particular race or two or more (each of which has obliged connections to pay to stand their ground prior to the final overnight stage) a trainer has finally decided is the one in which a runner will take its chance.

MUSEUMS (See Racing Museums)

NAAS

Naas Racecourse
Kingsfurze
Tipper Road
Naas
Co. Kildare
Southern Ireland
Tel. (045) 97391

How to get there:
From North: R409
From South: N9
From East: N7
From West: N7
By Air: Dublin Airport
Approximately 20 miles from Dublin

Some twenty-one miles from Dublin can be found the chief town of Kildare, the busy industrial centre of Naas which is Gaelic for 'assembly'. This is one of the former seats of the Kings of Leinster.

Ever since 1924, Naas with its left-handed configuration, uphill finish and long run-in has been known as the 'backer's graveyard'. This is primarily because it saps the stamina of irresolute runners.

Whilst no highly prestigious races are run on this demanding track, plenty of interest has been generated by the Nas Na Ri Chase, the Slaney Hurdle, the Johnstown Hurdle, the Brown Lad Hurdle (run in honour of the three-times winner of the Irish Grand National), the November Handicap, the Carna Fillies EBF race, the Owenstown Stud FF Tuthill race and the Birdcatcher Nursery.

The last mentioned is often won by a 'pigeon catcher', while some racegoers look for a runner with a suitably eloquent name in the Racing Writers' Perpetual Trophy Hurdle.

Since Naas lies on the N7 dual-carriageway from Dublin it enjoys excellent accessibility and so draws good crowds.

NAMES, HORSES

Whilst these do much to add interest, spice and colour to the racing scene, in former days they were not even necessary. Indeed the winners of the 1797 Derby and the 1815 1000 Guineas were never distinguished by name and one 'no hoper' was given a dismissive one of He Isn't Worth A Name!

Even more bizarrely, the Earl of Abingdon registered the name Potooooooooo (Pot-8-Os) after a stable lad appealed to his sense of humour by writing this quaint version of potatoes on a feed bin.

In the long history of the turf many ingenious and

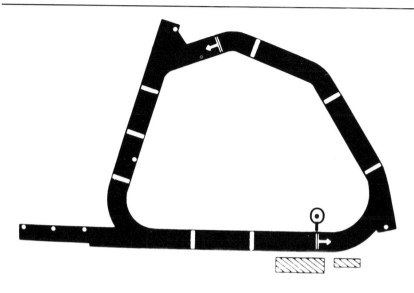

NAAS: Plan of the course.

appropriate names of racehorses have been devised. Frequently, of course, many sires and dams, although perhaps genealogically compatible, are so mismatched in terms of nomenclature that the attempts of the owners to find names for their progeny reflective of their ancestry have to be abandoned.

Individuals resident in Britain are able to be as self-indulgent as they wish when naming the horses that will carry their hopes. Those in Germany are not so fortunate, since they have to name a newcomer with the initial of its dam.

A few lucky owners find that the names of the horses from which foals are descended are so complementary that the naming of their property is straightforward. Indeed, suitable names may, on occasion, almost scream out of the stud book or at least be arrived at by ingenious associations of ideas.

Some past examples of these are Scalped, a chestnut filly by Tomahawk out of Short Shrift, Speargun by Deep Diver out of Annie Oakley, Flaming Temper, a chestnut colt out of Tyrant by Smoke Signal, Brave Talk by Derring Do out of Chatting, Dream World out of Quadrangle by Idle Thoughts, Jump for Joy (the offspring of Double Jump and Jolly June), Scarcely Blessed by So Blessed out of Parsimony and the beautifully named Busman's Holiday by Silly Season out of Clippie!

In recent years the Jockey Club has insisted that names should be limited to 18 characters; thus Itsgottabealright has been registered along with Weareagrandmother.

A university Turf Club once thought of calling a jumper Oh He's Fallen to confuse commentators.

NAMES OF RACES

The fact that the Hair of the Dog Handicap is run over the New Year period readily demonstrates that some racecourse executives show imagination and humour when naming their races.

Many races bear names that mean a good deal in the locality in which they are contested; thus the Silverstone Selling Hurdle has been staged at the nearby Northamptonshire track of Towcester; and the Madhatter Novice Chase at Haydock honours local celebrity the Rev. Charles Lutwidge Dodgson, better known as writer Lewis Carroll.

Jockeys, owners, trainers, racing administrators and equine heroes are commemorated by races that are usually run where these individuals were conspicuously successful. Thus the Steve Donoghue Apprentice Handicap at Epsom and the Brown Jack Handicap at Ascot.

Sponsorship allows those responsible to publicize their profit-making activities, many of which are totally unconnected with racing. Thus a Plumb Centre Grunfos Pump Selling Handicap has been run at Ripon.

NATIONAL HUNT RACING

This involves both steeplechasing and hurdle races as contested under Jockey Club rules or those of the Irish National Hunt Steeplechase Committee.

NATIONAL STUD, THE

The National Stud
Newmarket
Suffolk CB8 0XE
Tel. (0638) 663464

Thanks to the generosity of Lord Wavertree in making available his entire stock of thoroughbreds, the National Stud came into being in 1916.

It moved to its present premises in 1967 and now justifiably describes itself as one of the 'most prestigious' centres of the racehorse breeding industry. The stud extends to some 500 acres of paddocks.

The stud offers one-and-a quarter-hour tours which commence at its reception area at 11.15a.m.and 2.30 p.m. from Monday to Friday, from April to October. Facilities include a souvenir shop, refreshments and toilets.

NATIONAL TRAINERS' FEDERATION

42 Portman Square
London W1H 0AP
Tel. (071) 935 2055

Administered by a council and two sub-committees, one representing Flat racing trainers and the other National Hunt handlers, this organization exists to consider and promote the interests of all trainers and to encourage a close liaison with the Jockey Club and all associations connected with racing.

Legal matters, the collection of VAT, book-keeping, industrial relations, wages and veterinary affairs are all matters upon which NTF members can seek advice.

NAVAN

Proudstown
Navan
Co. Meath
Southern Ireland
Tel. (046) 21350

How to get there:
From North: R162
From South: N3
From East: N51
From West: N51
By Rail: Navan
By Air: Dublin Airport

Set in true hunting country, Navan stages many meetings in the depths of winter, on its left-handed course with its wide sweeping bends and uphill finish. Its configuration and the fact that it tends to ride heavy during wet winters means that it presents runners with a true test of stamina.

So extensive as to be used for farming, the course can be reached from Navan station. It lies north-west of Dublin off the N3. Its convenient location for city dwellers and the recent closure of Mullingar to the west means that the track is well patronized.

Whilst no major races are run here, plenty of interest has been generated by the running over the years of the Proudstown Hurdle, the Boardsmill Hurdle, the Boardsmill Stud Hurdle and the Stackallen Stud Stakes.

Troytown, the 12-length winner of the 1920 Grand National, was trained and ridden by two members of the Anthony family from the nearby Curragh and so it is perhaps appropriate that Navan's finest sounding race, the Troytown Chase, is contested annually around its tough 'chasing track of eight fences.

NEAREST AT FINISH

Said of whichever runner was making the most headway in the closing stages of a race. As a racereader's comment in the form book it may represent a propitious pointer to a horse's prospects next time out.

NEED OF THE RUN, IN

Self-explanatory term that denotes a runner not yet thought to be fully race fit or wound up. Understandably, many horses having their first runs of the season can be so described.

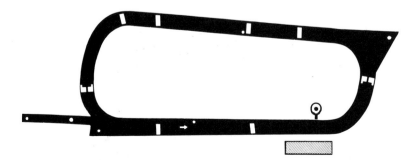

NAVAN: Plan of the course.

! **NET**

Reverse slang for ten to one (10-1).

! **NEVIS**

Reverse slang for seven to one (7-1).

NEWBURY

The Racecourse
Newbury
Berks RG14 7NZ
Tel. (0635) 40015

How to get there:
From North: A34
From South: A34
From East: A4
From West: A4
By Rail: Newbury Racecourse
By Air: Light Aircraft and Helicopter facilities

An important Group event, the John Porter Stakes, run over 1 ¹/2 miles at Newbury's first April meeting commemorates the famous nineteenth-century trainer to whom this left-handed course owes its existence thanks partly to the encouragement of King Edward VII.

Porter was in retirement when the track he had dreamed of came into being on 26 September 1905.

Its excellent conformation and proximity both to the major training centres of Berkshire and Wiltshire and to the capital just over sixty miles away have meant that, from the first, Newbury has been popular with racing's professionals.

The fact that large fields and good ground can virtually be guaranteed at Newbury is a further tribute to Porter's inspired vision. Although the track saw service in the Second World War as a railway marshalling yard and its straight course was altered in time for the 1956 season, it has largely survived in its original form.

Newbury can almost be regarded as a racecourse custom-built to put the ability of top-class thoroughbreds fully, but fairly, on trial. This is why so many two-year-olds are given their introductions to racing here, and why defeat at Newbury is so seldom blamed on the track and form from this particular course tends to work out well.

The track itself consists of a left-handed oval whose circumference extends for almost 1 mile 7 furlongs. Its long wide straights, since they feature occasional rather mild undulations, are appreciated by long-striding gallopers. If the strong suit of such animals is stamina, they find Newbury greatly to their liking since its gentle bends can be taken at a good gallop.

The longest races staged at Newbury take place over 2 miles and are started a furlong from the

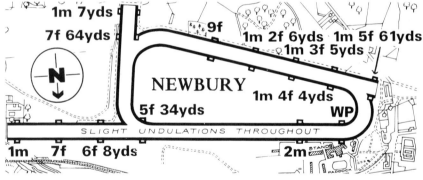

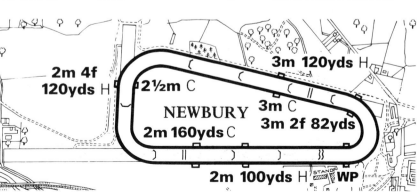

NEWBURY: Plans of the Flat course (top) over which the Juddmonte Lockinge Stakes and the Greenham Stakes (a 2000 Guineas Trial) are run, and the National Hunt course (bottom) over which the Tote Gold Trophy takes place.

winning post in front of the first grandstand horses run past as they make their finishing efforts. Since such events involve four left-hand turns, they confer an understandable advantage on lowlydrawn runners (as do, of course, shorter races of 7 furlongs 64 yards, 1 mile 7 yards, 10 furlongs 6 yards, 11 furlongs 5 yards, 12 furlongs 5 yards, and 1 mile 5 furlongs 61 yards that are also run on the round course). The first turn, like its successors a fairly gentle affair, is negotiated by those tackling 2 miles soon after they have raced across the finishing line. (Incidentally a short spur projecting from the top of the next bend allows races over 1 mile 5 furlongs 61 yards.)

The long back straight on the round course, along which starting stalls are positioned to allow races to be contested over 12 furlongs 5 yards, 11 furlongs 5 yards and 10 furlongs 6 yards is fairly level, the only significant undulations occurring just before it leads into another left-hand bend whose final stages are also encountered by those that tackle Newbury's 'round' mile (plus 7 yards) and 7 furlong 64 yard track. The latter distance is provided by a second spur projecting from the top bend of the circuit.

Every horse that races on the round course encounters gently descending ground as it approaches the easy home turn and once in the home straight finds itself on a rung that takes in most of the 5-furlong sprint course which features slight undulations throughout. This gives jockeys on horses that need to be held up a golden opportunity to poach the lead close to home from horses that have made their finishing efforts earlier.

Newbury's straight mile track, on which high-drawn runners are favoured, especially in the wet if fields are large and the stalls positioned on the stands side or in the centre of the course, is a full 90 feet wide and is partly provided by the longest of the three spurs that project from the round course. It is used to stage several important 'pattern' events. One, the Juddmonte Lockinge Stakes, in which four-year-olds often go well, takes place over its full length in mid-May. In addition a 2000 Guineas Trial (the Greenham Stakes) is started from the 7-furlong gate in April.

One important 6 furlong 8 yard race for top-class two-year-olds that takes place on the straight course in September is the Mill Reef Stakes, named after the Derby and Arc de Triomphe winner of 1971.

Several top-class races are also run on Newbury's round course. These include three prestigious races that are run over 7 furlongs 64 yards. In April three-year-old fillies contest the Fred Darling Stakes which

commemorates the famous Beckhampton trainer who sent out seven Derby winners. Others are the Horris Hill Stakes, an important test of stamina for two-year-olds in late October, and the Hungerford Stakes in August.

Some longer 'pattern' events are staged on the round course. The longest is the Geoffrey Freer Stakes run over 1 mile 5 furlongs 61 yards, also run in mid-August in memory of a Newbury clerk of the course. Another 'pattern' race, the St Simon Stakes, run over 12 furlongs 5 yards in late October, is also something of a three-year-olds' benefit and commemorates the unbeaten colt whose progeny proved so successful.

The gravel in the subsoil beneath Newbury's luxuriant and springy turf ensures that heavy ground is something of a rarity. What is more, the sting can be taken out of firm ground by Newbury's modern and highly-sophisticated watering system.

Naturally, Newbury draws a large number of its racegoers from London who should leave the M4 at junction 12 and then take the A4. Trains take around an hour from Paddington to the racecourse station that is a three minute walk away from the track itself; very attractive deals involving travel and admission are available from British Rail.

Newbury's popularity owes much to its accessibility, the first-class view from its stands and the fact that it provides such facilities as bars and refreshment rooms in every enclosure, a large club restaurant, a picnic area and a children's playground.

As a premier venue for National Hunt racing, Newbury imposes a searching, but very fair test for jumpers. The track is 80 ft wide and its considerable extent of about 15 furlongs makes it decidedly 'galloping' in nature.

The jumping circuit has easy bends, undulates in places and features eleven fences (five in each straight and one tricky cross fence before the home turn) that are on the stiff side of fair. The four in the 5-furlong finishing straight can impose quite a severe test of courage, stamina and jumping ability, especially when the going is soft or heavy.

Past winners of 'chases and hurdles are often worthy of further consideration, as are runners that have gone well previously at other 'galloping' tracks like Haydock Park, Worcester, Doncaster or Ayr.

Newbury's first big jumping race is the Hennessy Cognac Gold Cup, a handicap steeplechase run over 3 miles 2 furlongs 82 yards in late November. Previously won by stars such as Arkle and Burrough Hill Lad, this is often lifted by a seven-year-old.

The Tote (formerly Schweppes) Gold Trophy is an early February hurdle race in which some heavy betting usually takes place. Five-and six-year-olds, several from stables known to be fond of tilting at the ring, have previously scored in this open handicap. Newbury's even earlier, popular, late December fixture features the Mandarin Chase, a 26-furlong affair that commemorates the 1962 Cheltenham Gold Cup winner. Eight-year-olds have a good record here.

NEWCASTLE

Newcastle Racecourse
High Gosforth
Gosforth Park
Newcastle-upon-Tyne NE3 5HP
Tel. (091) 236 2020

How to get there:
From North: A1
From South: A6125
From East: A1056
From West: A69
By Rail: Newcastle Central, Four Lane Ends
By Air: Newcastle Airport; Helicopter facilities

An impressive racecourse is to be found in an attractive 1000-acre setting at High Gosforth Park, five miles north of Newcastle-upon-Tyne, whose associations with horse racing date back to the early 1600s.

The present course was first used in 1882 as a replacement for the Town Moor site on which racing (including the now defunct Newcastle Gold Cup) was originally staged within the city limits. Newcastle is renowned as the home of the Northumberland Plate, which was first staged on Town Moor as a relatively modest 2-mile handicap in 1833. Although it no longer attracts such high-class animals this ' Pitmen's Derby', as it is popularly known, still attracts a huge crowd when it is staged as the highlight of Newcastle's June meeting. Now run over 2 miles and 19 yards, it is often captured by a four-year-old.

The Newcastle course is a broad left-handed, rather pear-shaped oval that has a circumference of 14 furlongs. All those who race over it, be it on the straight or the round course, have to negotiate a final stretch of around four furlongs that rises slightly but relentlessly until the distance. This helps to make Newcastle a testing track that makes considerable

demands on a horse's courage, stamina and resolution, especially if it is a two-year-old having an early season run on heavy going.

Runners in the Northumberland Plate and other 2 mile 19 yard contests race entirely on the round course. They start to race about two furlongs out; then, after passing the winning post and Newcastle's well-appointed stands, they run round the first of three bends which, because they are particularly well-banked, can be taken at stamina-sapping speed and tend to reduce the advantage that following a left-handed running rail accords the lowly-drawn. After passing the 1 mile 4 furlong 93 yard gate, those on the round course encounter a second left-hand bend from which a spur projects to permit the staging of races run over 10 furlongs 32 yards. This spur is a short affair that leads into a longish stretch along which, from appropriate points, races over 9 furlongs 9 yards and 7 furlongs 214 yards are started.

The round course climbs slightly as it approaches the home turn, another well-banked affair that can be taken at speed and which runs into the straight course. Although this actually extends for 8 furlongs, in recent years no races have been staged along it over this distance. Instead, the straight course is used to stage sprints and 7-furlong 4-yard events. For the most part the ground on the straight course rises steadily until some 200 yards from the post, thus imposing a severe test of stamina that only the resolute and powerful galloper and the tough two-year-old are likely to relish.

As for the draw, in straight course races of 5 to 7 furlongs, when the stalls are on the stands side, the highly drawn are favoured. However, if there is some cut in the ground, the advantage switches to the lowly drawn. If the stalls are placed in the centre or far side, low numbers are those to look out for in draw allocations, especially if soft or heavy conditions prevail. A low draw is coveted in such conditions as the high-drawn have to waste valuable time switching to the far side of the straight where the ground rides a good deal firmer and faster.

The Newcastle course is one on which the abilities of top-class thoroughbreds can be fully tested. Not surprisingly, therefore, it is used to stage a large number of important races, some of which are also 'listed' events. The Virginia Stakes for fillies and mares is the highlight of the two-day fixture that is held at the end of August. Newcastle's only group race is the Beeswing Stakes, which commemorates a famous nineteenth-century mare, and is run over 7 furlongs 4 yards on the straight course in late July.

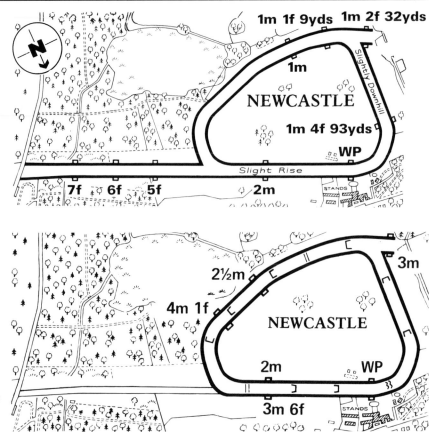

NEWCASTLE: *Plans of the Flat course (top), and the National Hunt course (bottom).*

Newcastle owes much of its popularity to the enterprise and energy of its far-sighted executive which has repeatedly demonstrated its concern for the welfare of both the racing public and those responsible for the horses that come to Gosforth. In fact, it pioneered the provision of proper accommodation for stable staff and most commendably recently spent several thousand pounds on improving facilities for female horse attendants.

With its escalators, its betting halls, attractive restaurants and modern well-heated stands, Newcastle calls to mind certain American and Australian tracks. Younger racegoers are encouraged to sample the delights of the unusual adventure playground.

Even on non-racing days, Newcastle's sporting and social facilities are in constant demand. The site is home to the permanent headquarters of the Boy Scout movement in Northumberland and also boasts a wildlife sanctuary.

The proximity of the track to major northern population centres provides a further guarantee that good crowds can pass through its turnstiles. Fortunately, as the course is readily accessible to those who live beyond Tyneside, it attracts many southern trainers. There is a helicopter landing pad near the water jump on the steeplechasing course, while fixed-wing aircraft can be accommodated at Newcastle International airport some six miles away. Newcastle is easily reached by air from Heathrow or Gatwick or by rail to Newcastle Central from King's Cross. Rail travellers should take the metro to Four Lane Ends and then make a bus journey to Gosforth.

The A1 by-passes the nearby city and runs close to the course which adjoins the B1318. There are free parking facilities.

As one of the North's top National Hunt venues, Newcastle stages some good quality racing. This takes place on a pear shaped, left-handed jumping circuit whose circumference is 14 furlongs. It is renowned for the stiffness of its eleven fences and the thoroughly testing nature of its steadily ascending home stretch of four furlongs.

Thus, proven stayers and sound jumpers should be sought at Newcastle. Those with a touch of class are often aimed at the Fighting Fifth Hurdle that is staged in late November. A win in this is often registered by a hurdler of Cheltenham championship standard: in its time the race has been won by Browne's Gazette, Gaye Brief, Bird's Nest and Sea Pigeon. The fact that the last two in this list twice won this prestigious Newcastle hurdle is a reminder of the wisdom of considering a past winner. Six-year-olds should also receive more than a passing glance.

The Eider Handicap Chase is a most enticing and thrilling marathon race of 4 miles 1 furlong that (weather permitting) is staged at Gosforth in mid-February. Often rightly regarded as providing revealing pointers to Grand National prospects, it is a favourite with local racegoers.

NEWMARKET

Westfield House
The Links
Newmarket
Suffolk CB8 0TG
Tel. (0638) 66762

How to get there:
From North: A1, A10
From South: A11(M)
From East: A45
From West: A45
By Rail: Cambridge
By Air: Cambridge Airport

As the headquarters of British flat racing, Newmarket deserves a lengthy entry. The course is as appealing as the Suffolk town of which it forms a distinct part.

Newmarket's two courses, the Rowley Mile course and the July course, form the arms of a huge Y-shaped track that imposes the best tests of thoroughbred racehorses that are available anywhere.

It is perfectly straight and extremely wide; indeed, in modern times only half of it has been used for racing, in contrast to the time when Charles II became the first (and so far the only) reigning monarch to ride a flat race winner. The Rowley Mile course (on which the only draw advantage

NEWMARKET: A print from the late eighteenth century, showing horses being exercised on Warren Hill, east of the town. In the foreground watching the training is the Prince of Wales (later King George IV).

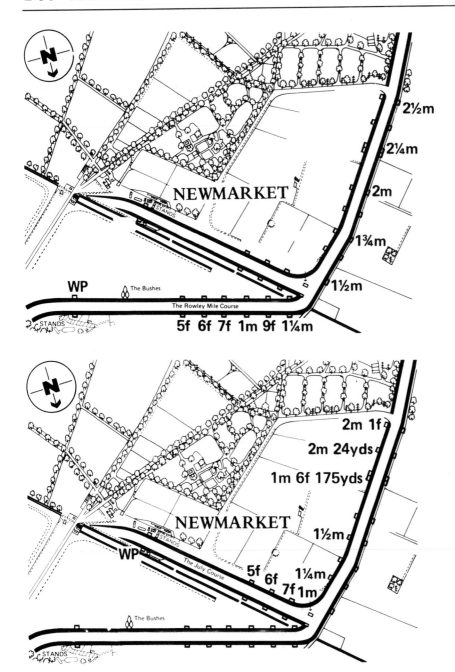

NEWMARKET: *Plans of the Rowley Mile course (top), and the July course (bottom).*

involves low-drawn horses in races from 5 to 8 furlongs when the ground is soft) is reasonably flat in its early stages but at a natural landmark around two furlongs out (which for obvious reasons is called 'the bushes') the ground dips for a furlong. Next comes a furlong or so of rising ground that continues to the line. The fact that as they emerge out of 'the dip' the runners can see rising ground extending for three furlongs well beyond the winning post (which may not be perceived and whose significance is lost on

them) is one reason why so many turn it in at this critical point in their races.

The first meeting that takes place on the 10-furlong Rowley Mile course (which also caters for longer distances by taking in the 'tail' of Newmarket's Y-shaped configuration, provided by the so-called Beacon or Cesarewitch course, and also a right-handed bend) is staged in mid-April. One of its highlights (often captured by a subsequent 1000 Guineas winner) is the 7-furlong Nell Gwyn Stakes, run in memory of Charles II's mistress whose quarters were connected by a subterranean passage with his Newmarket Palace. This interestingly, is recalled by the Palace House Stakes, yet another Group race that is staged at the second spring meeting. This is an all-aged sprint run along the shortest 5-furlong stretch of the Rowley Mile. Five-year-olds should receive serious consideration here.

As for a 2000 Guineas trial, Newmarket also stages at this early stage of the season the 1 mile Craven Stakes. In recent years this has been won by such runners as Shadeed, Dancing Brave, Doyoun and Tirol that have gone on to achieve Classic success over course and distance some two weeks later.

Both the 2000 and 1000 Guineas, the most prestigious races run on the Rowley Mile course, are contested at Newmarket's second spring meeting that takes place in late April or early May. French and Irish stables make particularly determined bids to capture the former, such is its kudos, while the latter is sometimes landed by a previously successful trainer.

Also run at the second spring meeting is an historic race with strong Jockey Club connections. This, restricted to horses owned by members of the Jockey Club or the Jockey Club rooms, is the Newmarket Challenge Whip and the trophy awarded to the winner of this 1-mile contest for three-year-old maidens is said to contain hair from the famous past champion Eclipse.

The programme for Newmarket's second three-day fixture is arranged so that between the season's first two Classics the Jockey Club Stakes is contested – most appropriately since Newmarket is where the headquarters of racing's administrators has long been located. Run over the closing stages of the Beacon course and thus soon involving a right-hand bend into the 10 furlongs of the Rowley Mile, this 12-furlong race is a top-class, early season contest for four-year-olds and upwards and in its time has been captured by some previous Derby winners (St Paddy in 1961 for example) and by horses like Ardross that have gone on to win the Ascot Gold Cup.

The July course which, like the rest of the Newmarket track, was initially laid out with horsemen and not spectators in mind, is nonetheless blessed with picturesque thatched buildings and its delightfully leafy paddock offers some welcome shade in the summer months. This particular course allows races to be run over 1 mile, 7 furlongs and sprint distances. It is straight, but after two furlongs some descending ground is encountered until the distance. The final furlong consists of rising terrain.

As it does for the Rowley Mile course, the Beacon course allows the July course to figure in the closing stages of longish races over 10 and 12 furlongs, 1 mile 6 furlongs 171 yards and 2 miles 24 yards.

Some prestigious and historic races are staged on the July course. An early example is the 12-furlong Princess of Wales's Stakes. First run in 1894, this is a race in which three-and four-year-olds understandably go well.

Also run at the first July meeting are three important 6-furlong sprints. The first to be staged is the Cherry Hinton Stakes for two-year-old fillies, while the second is the colts' equivalent, the July Stakes, first run as long ago as 1786. Then comes the third: the July Cup, an all-aged sprint of championship class, in which three-year-olds have the best record.

With the coming of autumn, the Rowley Mile course is again pressed into service and in early October the first major race involved in proceedings is another two-year-old, 6-furlong dash — the Cheveley Park Stakes, in which French and Irish raiders should always be respected.

Another top-class, 6-furlong juvenile contest that is run on the second day of the first October meeting is the Middle Park Stakes, the result of which can produce a major shake-up in long-range, ante-post betting on the following season's Classics. Seldom, however, in recent seasons has the winner of this race gone on to win the 2000 Guineas some six months or so later, Right Tack, Brigadier Gerard and Known Fact (on a disqualification) being exceptions.

A longer race run at this meeting is the Sun Chariot Stakes, named after King George VI's Triple Crown winner of 1942. This is a 10-furlong race for fillies and mares which, since it became an all-aged affair in 1974, has often fallen to a three-year-old.

At this four-day meeting an even longer race, the Jockey Club Cup, first run in 1873, is a 2-mile contest which, understandably, members of this most prestigious racing organization are very keen to win.

The best-known race run at the first October meeting is the historic Cambridgeshire, a highly competitive handicap run at a blistering pace over 9 furlongs of Newmarket's heathland. This is often won by a gutsy contender with indomitable courage that can stay ten furlongs, rather than a mile or even nine furlongs on less taxing terrain elsewhere. Runners carrying no more than 8st 7lbs often go well, and this race regularly falls to a fast-developing filly or a lightly-raced runner, rather than to the market leader.

As for the second leg of the Autumn Double, the Cesarewitch, this is the gambling highlight of the second October meeting. A race in which fillies do not have an impressive record, it takes place over twice the distance of the Cambridgeshire: 18 gruelling furlongs of featureless heathland which includes what Richard Onslow has called a 'stark staring straight' of more than a mile. The majority of past winners have been three-or four-year-olds, with the latter having the best record. Understandably, runners carrying less than 8 stone often enjoy an edge in such a long race. Rank outsiders can generally be disregarded but not lightly-raced types. Horses fresh from having been rested should be noted, as should any runner that has scored over 2 miles earlier in the season.

The Challenge Stakes is a late season Newmarket Group race that since 1976 has been run over 7, rather than 6 furlongs. Three-year-olds have the best record here.

Future 2000 Guineas prospects can advertise their claims in the Dewhurst Stakes, as did its 1969, 1975 and 1983 winners: Nijinsky, Wollow and El Gran Senor respectively. The Dewhurst often features a strong and frequently successful Irish challenge.

Also run at Newmarket in October is the Rockfel Stakes, another 7-furlong race confined to two-year-old fillies. It commemorates the 1938 winner of the 1000 Guineas, Oaks and Champion Stakes. The last-named is, in fact, the last major race of the season that is staged at racing's headquarters and an event in which some past winners of the 2000 and 1000 Guineas have understandably prevailed.

Newmarket is a connoisseur's choice of a racecourse with ample free parking available for both cars and coaches and a fine adventure playground on the July course which is currently staffed by Red Cross personnel. It is accessible by train from King's Cross, but only via a limited service to what is an unmanned halt. Indeed, such are the difficulties rail travellers can face that on race days, a coach operates from the station at Cambridge some thirteen miles away. This city is also accessible by air via Cambridge airport. Given Newmarket's vast acreage it is not surprising that this includes a 1000-metre grass airstrip.

Motorists arriving from the east and London (about sixty miles away) arrive via the A11, leaving at Junction 9 before travelling on to the course via the A1303 or A1304. Racegoers from other southern points often take the A1 followed by the A45.

However they arrive at this 'HQ', many racegoers combine their visit to Newmarket with a chance to savour what the town also has to offer by way of stables, studs, museums, bookshops and excellent training grounds.

NEWSPAPER NAPS

The once phenomenally successful tipping run of Peter O'Sullevan that led his colleagues in the press room to style him 'Peter the Great' serves as a reminder of the possibilities of profiting from the expertise of racing correspondents whose livelihoods, after all, depend on their success at winner finding.

Some tipsters, as opposed to private handicappers or stopwatch holders, who have experienced good winning runs should still heed Damon Runyon's observation that 'it is a strange thing how a tipster can go along doing everything right and then all of a sudden find himself doing everything wrong'.

This comment is certainly borne out by the fact that tipsters' performances in successive seasons seldom correlate. One reason for this is that many of them are pressurized to produce a nap in the main race of the day which is often a handicap whose compiler has done his level best to equalize the chances of all those taking part!

For this reason, and the fact that the research of David Duncan (the author of *Betting for Profit*) has demonstrated that 'only one correspondent in four shows a seasonal profit at level stakes on his naps', systematic approaches based on the personal opinions of other racing journalists (not of ratings experts), are best left alone.

NEWTON ABBOT

Newton Abbot Races Ltd
Kingsteignton Road
Newton Abbot
Devon
Tel. (0626) 53235

How to get there:
From North: A380
From South: A380
From East: A381
From West: A38, A383
By Rail: Newton Abbot
By Air: Helicopter facilities

Summer holidays would hardly be the same without the Newton Abbot fixture that, along with a Market Rasen meeting, traditionally opens the National Hunt season in August (or sometimes late July).

Given its proximity to the resort of Torquay, there is a festive atmosphere at this Devon course's 'little season' meetings which are more numerous than at any other National Hunt track.

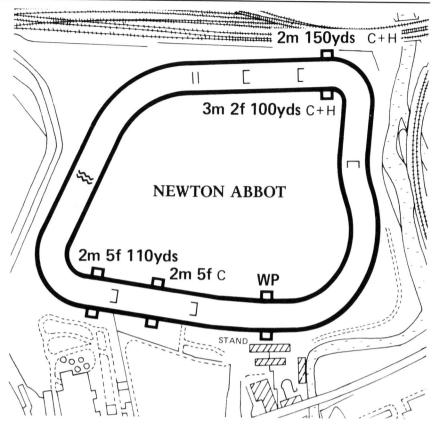

2m 150yds C+H

3m 2f 100yds C+H

NEWTON ABBOT

2m 5f 110yds

2m 5f C

WP

STAND

NEWTON ABBOT: Plan of the course.

The almost square-shaped circuit of only 9 furlongs is so tight it contains a mere seven fences which, save for the second in the far straight, cause most runners few problems., although they cannot be so easily skipped over as was once the case.

The sheer tightness of the track and its very short run-in of about 300 yards from the last obstacle means that it tends to suit nippy front-running types. Previous course winners often relish a further chance to race round its tight left-handed turns.

Those who take the train from Paddington to Newton Abbot can either take a taxi or walk a mere mile to the course itself, while motorists should leave the nearby M5 and look for signs indicating the A380 (Torquay) road. Those arriving from further west can take the A38 from Plymouth or proceed from Okehampton.

Some feel the course's proximity to an industrial estate detracts from its general location in some delightfully scenic Devon countryside. However, the view of the racing on offer is excellent.

NOBBLING

Interfering with a horse to prevent it from achieving its true running (See Corruption and Doping).

NO HOPER

Extremely dismissive term applied to a horse located 'out with the washing' at the far end of the market – one whose chance is apparently hopeless.

NON-RUNNERS

Self-explanatory term for horses which, contrary to earlier expectations, fail to line up in races.

Jokes have been made about a travelling head lad driving an empty horse box who claimed his duties involved the transportation of such contenders.

NON-TRIER

Runner that, contrary to the rules of racing, is allegedly not trying to win a race, or to achieve the best possible placing within it.

The difficulty facing course officials is that of distinguishing between real non-triers and those simply not good enough to win the races in which they have been allowed to run.

The persistence of the problem of genuine non-triers (which, in the nineteenth century, former dictator of the turf Admiral Rous used to combat by positioning himself prominently on racecourses and remonstrating with those involved) was demonstrated

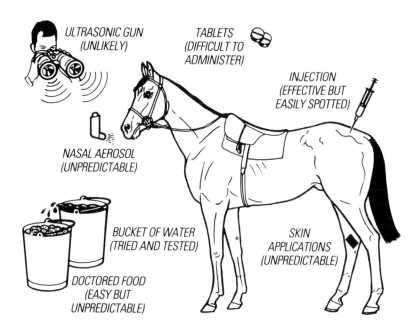

ULTRASONIC GUN
(UNLIKELY)

TABLETS
(DIFFICULT TO
ADMINISTER)

INJECTION
(EFFECTIVE BUT
EASILY SPOTTED)

NASAL AEROSOL
(UNPREDICTABLE)

BUCKET OF WATER
(TRIED AND TESTED)

SKIN
APPLICATIONS
(UNPREDICTABLE)

DOCTORED FOOD
(EASY BUT
UNPREDICTABLE)

NOBBLING (see previous page): This diagram shows just some of the ways to 'nobble' a horse.

by a report in 1991 to the effect that the Jockey Club was mounting a 'vigorous campaign' against them, including the unexpected filming of certain races.

Non-triers have figured in jockeys' conspiracies to guarantee certain forecast dividends relating to the results of races that attract very few runners. Such contenders differ greatly from those involved in another rule-breaking practice – that of 'schooling' an inexperienced novice in public or allowing a horse that has been off the course for a long time to do little more than take the air.

Jockey Club rules state that:

1. Every horse that runs in a race shall be run on its merits whether its owner runs another horse in the race or not.

2. The rider of every horse shall take all reasonable measures throughout the race to ensure that his/her horse is given a full opportunity to win or of obtaining the best possible placing.

3. It shall be the duty of a trainer to ensure that adequate instructions are given to the rider of any horse.

NO OFFERS

Some races contain a runner on which, usually for a very good reason, bookmakers are initially unwilling to take bets. This fact will then be signalled to the minor betting enclosures. This may be because they know, via their extensive intelligence service, that it will justifiably play a predominant, if not a leading, part in the market. By failing to quote a price against this 'feared' runner, bookmakers can lure money away from it in the opening exchanges, especially if they make a great show of laying another runner against the field, thereby suggesting that it is the undisputed favourite.

NOT GOING FOR THE PIECES

Said of a horse that allegedly is not bidding for the prize money awarded to those finishing in the first four in its race.

NOT OFF

Not bidding for success.

NOT SIGHTED

Term used to describe a horse that is so far behind at the end of a race that it can hardly be sighted at the tail end of its field.

NOTTINGHAM

Nottingham Racecourse
Colwick Park
Nottingham
Tel. (0602) 580620

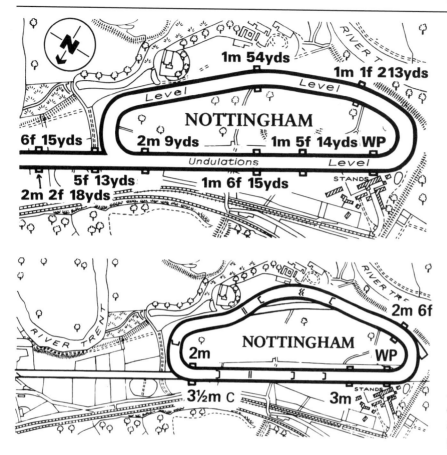

NOTTINGHAM: *Plans of the Flat course (top), and the National Hunt course (bottom).*

How to get there:
From North: M1
From South: M1
From East: A612
From West: A609
By Rail: Nottingham
By Air: East Tollerton Airport; Helicopter facilities

Properly organized horse racing has taken place on the Nottingham site where it is currently staged since August 1892. Unlike its predecessor, which was owned by the local corporation, the present racecourse is administered and leased by a private concern, the Racecourse Holdings Trust. It is to be found less than two miles east of Nottingham's railway station (accessible from St Pancras) at Colwick Park. This can be reached by M1 travellers from junction 26 from which access can eventually be gained to the course via the B686 Colwick road. Motorists arriving from the north should leave the M1 at junction 25 and proceed to the course via the A52. Those flying in by helicopter can be accommodated on course, while fixed-winged aircraft can land at Tollerton two miles away.

As for the track itself, it is a left-handed, mainly level affair of approximately twelve furlongs in extent; its negotiation presents good horses with little difficulty as the only undulations it features are minor ones.

Such animals can quite often be seen in action at Nottingham since potentially top-class two-year-olds from the yards of leading Newmarket handlers often make their debut here in what are very fair and relatively undemanding circumstances. What is more, sprinters that have previously been considered good enough to take their chances in Goodwood's Stewards' Cup sometimes contest Nottingham's far from humble equivalent, a 6 furlong 15 yard handicap run at Colwick Park in early August.

The circuit is appreciated by powerful, galloping types for its long straights and fairly gentle left-hand bends. Furthermore if jockeys are instructed to come with a late run they will find the 4 1/2-furlong run-in ideal for such tactics.

A spur projecting from the final bend on the round course allows races to be run over 5 furlongs 13 yards and 6 furlongs 15 yards along a section of track that can be taken at speed since it is straight and mainly flat.

Experts maintain that runners allotted high numbers enjoy an advantage in these races, especially when the stalls are placed on the stands rails and the going is soft. If the stalls are on the far side and the going good to firm, lowly-drawn horses are favoured.

Marathons take place at Colwick Park; over 2 miles 9 yards and 2 miles 2 furlongs and 18 yards. After leaving the stalls that are positioned around four and a half furlongs from the post, the stayers involved race over virtually the full length of the run-in. Subsequently, they run round the rather semi-circular far turn, pass the 9 furlong 213 yard start and then enter Nottingham's flat and fairly lengthy mild dog leg of a back straight whose kink involves the point from which races over 1 mile 54 yards start. Thereafter, the round course involves a second, gentler left-hand bend, before it joins the straight course 4 1/2 furlongs out. As a left-handed course, it gives a slight advantage to runners drawn low.

By setting aside a special, rather scenic parking area on the rails and charging up to four occupants of a car a single reduced rate to enter it, the Nottingham executive have enticed many members of the public to take a picnic and go racing in Colwick Park.

NOVICES

Hurdlers or steeplechasers that are in the learning stage of their jumping careers. Many serious backers look on proven and speedy novice hurdlers as National Hunt's racing equivalent of two-year-old maidens and as thus providing, on occasion, some excellent betting opportunities.

NUMBER CLOTH

Officially known as a 'numbered saddle cloth'. It is the responsibility of the clerk of the course to see that a clean number cloth is provided for every horse for which a rider presents himself to be weighed out.

On entering the weighing room, a jockey takes a folded number cloth from a racecourse official. Shortly afterwards, this, the saddle, and a weight cloth, if any, are taken by the trainer or head lad to the racecourse stable to put on the horse.

NURSERIES

Handicap races for two-year-olds. Since the form of such animals is difficult to assess early in the season, such events only take place after midsummer.

Some backers associate nurseries with chicanery and sharp practice. Admittedly, there is more than one trainer who specializes in preparing runners to register surprise wins in such events, but this tactic usually involves such a legitimate 'finesse' as previously running the horse in question on going or over distances that are quite unsuitable. Stoutly-bred youngsters who have to wait until the end of the season for a chance to capitalize on their stamina may win 7- and 8-furlong nurseries and in doing so surprise many whose previously dismissive estimation of their racing ability has been based purely on their poor performances in sprints.

With this in mind, some backers search for runners in nurseries that have staying blood and previous form which, although undistinguished, suggests that a test of stamina may well be appreciated. Nurseries, of course, are run over 5 and 6 furlongs as well as over 7 and 8 and are not won by previously disappointing runners as often as is popularly believed.

Indeed, as Methodmaker, the systems expert of the *Raceform Handicap Book* once revealed, 'various checks across the years always show the same trend – more than 60 per cent of nursery winners had been placed last time out, with past first and seconds prevailing'.

Methodmaker has also pointed out that a nursery is more often than not won by a 'well-exposed youngster with acceptable recent form whose position in the weights lies in the top half of the handicap' and that two-year-olds are as capable of carrying penalties to victory as older horses. The services of a good claiming apprentice, particularly one claimed from his retaining stable, can often prove invaluable in a nursery handicap.

Sometimes a trainer, prevented from entering a two-year-old in 'plating' class (having won two selling races), may enter it in a nursery, where a lenient handicap may give it a far better chance than in a higher class conditions race for juveniles.

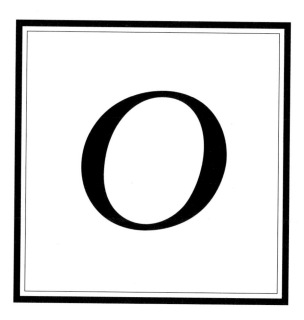

OBJECTIONS

These can be lodged against horses on several grounds such as crossing, jostling and not having run over the proper course.

Amongst the objections that can be made against jockeys, some are automatic; for example, if they do not present themselves at the weigh-in.

Objections are designed to give aggrieved parties (these can include the stewards) an opportunity to seek redress against alleged infringements of the rules of racing, either during a race or before the subsequent weigh-in. However, the fact that an objector may be fined if the stewards find his objection is frivolous or vexatious, ensures that the red flag with its 'E' for enquiry is none too frequently hoisted.

The raising of the blue flag signifies that the jockeys of the placed horses have all weighed in and that no objection has been lodged. If an objection (which must be made in writing) is overruled and the placings remain unaltered, a white flag is hoisted.

OBLIGE

Said of a racehorse that (co-operatively) wins its race.

OBVIOUS CLAIMS

Expression used to describe a horse whose chances of winning are readily apparent.

OFF-COURSE BETTING

Although this activity was carried on in betting shops in the West End of London in the 1860s and 1870s, thereafter it went underground until 1961 when a Betting and Gaming Act finally made the making of off-course bets in cash perfectly legal.

Prior to 1961 those wanting to place off-course wagers could resort to postal betting or open credit accounts with bookmakers and then bet by telephone. The former arrangement is almost defunct as a means of present-day off-course betting (the possibilities for which are currently vast and even include wagering via personal computers). As for patrons of modern betting shops, they are positively spoilt for choice; apart from being able to bet at board rates displayed in pre-race betting shows, they can wager at tote odds or starting prices and choose the type of wager they prefer from an ever-growing list of possibilities.

The principal disadvantage of off-course betting is that tax deductions are made which is not now the case on-course. Just as irritatingly, the pre-race betting shows relayed to licensed betting offices can, on occasion, be so incomplete or outdated that when some starting prices are eventually announced they can cause general consternation. Fortunately there is hope that this will be less of an annoyance in future.

OFFICE SUPPORT

If bookmaking multiples such as Ladbrokes find that some horses are heavily supported in their many betting offices, they will channel large sums back to the racecourse which are duly invested on these particular runners and so reduce their prices.

Such a practice can so radically affect the course market that some racegoers and the makers of a television documentary have suggested that the prices quoted against some runners do not accurately reflect their chances.

OFFICIAL GOING REPORT

Report on the state of the going on a particular racecourse. Sometimes form assessment services dispute the accuracy of this, as do some disgruntled trainers.

OFFICIAL HANDICAP RATINGS

All jumpers with good enough form to be rated are given numerical equivalents of the weights they would carry were they to contest a massive, complete handicap. Thus, a steeplechaser given an official rating of 100 would in effect be handicapped at 12st 7lbs. On the flat the scale of handicap ratings is 0-140, i.e. to a maximum weight of 10 stones.

Monitoring changes in the official handicap ratings is potentially profitable and is a process that the *Sporting Life* feature 'Ahead of the Handicapper' and the *Racing Post's* equivalent 'Weighting in Front' both greatly facilitate.

OFFICIALS

The principal officials present at a race meeting are the stewards (usually four in number), their secretary, the handicapper, the starter, the judge, the clerk of the scales and the clerk of the course.

ON-COURSE

The place where the backer is offered the greatest value. Here tax deductions are not made as they are on off-course wagers and priceless opportunities for taking generous opening prices (that are often denied denizens of betting shops) are available.

The advantages of going racing and thus being able to bet with bookmakers on a tax-free basis have been frequently extolled by Channel 4's colourful betting expert, John McCririck.

ON-COURSE STRATEGIES

Going racing provides access to information denied to stay-at-home backers. Indeed, careful scrutiny of 'runners and riders' boards can reveal the fact that highly profitable, if 'breakneck' dashes from one track to another have been undertaken by jockeys.

Apart, of course, from also being able to spot possibly significant switches of jockeys made at the last minute by the connections of some horses, racegoers can profit from being 'amongst the action' in other ways. Some swear by their belief that well-fancied runners are often the last to enter the paddock and, of course, if one is leaning over its rails, one can detect those contestants which look really fit and well.

Another on-course strategy is to compare the opening odds quoted against the runners with those featuring in newspaper betting forecasts. Many backers are wary of horses which are quoted at rates that are significantly higher than those at which they were quoted in the reliable forecast of a racing daily. Conversely, some racegoers look closely at contestants that, by being quoted at shorter odds than were expertly forecast, 'corner' a bigger share of the market than was anticipated. As for possibly significant contractions in the prices quoted against one's fancies (which at least offer some hope that these may be significant) these will invariably be first seen in Tattersalls. Thus the shrewd backer will position himself so that he can see precisely where is still to be found the 'value' price, which he must lose no time in taking before it is wiped away by a particular bookmaker who probably, because he is not paying for the services of a tic-tac, is one price, or even more, adrift of his colleagues.

OPEN DAYS

Trainers such as Luca Cumani and David Nicholson regularly throw open their flat and National Hunt stables on one particular summer Saturday or Sunday each year.

Such open days give ordinary members of the public a fascinating opportunity to see life behind the normally closed doors of racing stables and swell the funds of several charities.

Parades of horses and tours of yards, exercise gallops and stable premises are all part of what are invariably highly enjoyable days out. Some trainers even take the trouble to print souvenir programmes and to pass on some potentially valuable inside information about how they plan to place their runners and what each horse requires by way of ideal racing conditions.

Details of open days are announced in specialist racing dailies and some are advertised and signposted on roads close to the stables concerned.

ORIGIN OF THE THOROUGHBRED

(See Arab Influence, The)

As Daphne Machin Goodall once put it, 'the creation of a new strain of racehorses, later called the Thoroughbred ... from imported Eastern and North African sires and native and royal mares was a masterpiece of generation'. It was a gradual process that took several hundred years to mature and crucial to it were early importations into England of the Oriental horses mentioned above, since only when such animals were mated with native English 'running' mares did racehorses result that were far superior to anything previously seen.

In actual fact as early as the reign of Henry VIII a Barbary and two Turks – noted for their beauty and stamina, if not for their speed as such – stood at the royal stand at Eltham. By 1599, Markham, a leading authority on breeding, was recommending the courser of Arabia, particularly the Arab, as the ideal stallion to breed from for the turf and James I certainly took this advice by having several Arabians, including the Markham Arabian, stand at his own royal stud.

From 1721 to 1759, some 176 Oriental stallions were registered in Volume II of the *General Stud Book* and, of these, three – the Darley Arabian, the Godolphin Arabian and the Byerley Turk _ were destined to have such a potent influence on the foundation, consolidation and subsequent development of the thoroughbred that several contemporary authorities refer to them as the 'founding fathers', a description that best suits the Darley Arabian since his has proved the most influential gene contribution.

There were, of course, other Oriental stallions who exerted a major, though less crucial, influence on the breeding of racehorses. The Leedes Arabian must have been blessed with potency since his name appears in more racehorse pedigrees than any other, while every grey thoroughbred (such as Mahmoud or Desert Orchid) that has ever raced can trace its ancestry and distinctive coat back to another Arabian sire, Alcock's Arabian. Interestingly, these influential stallions seldom raced and were sent to stud, not because they were speedy but because of their sheer quality and ability to breed to type. The result of their original matings with English mares has been stock which, while less hardy than native Middle Eastern breeds and less capable of sustained effort, can run fastest of all over modern racing distances.

The most crucial female Arab influence on the early thoroughbred has turned out to be the mare, Old Bald Peg. Indeed, in the pedigree of the 1942 2000 Guineas winner, Big Game, repeat crosses of this particular dam appear 367,162 times!

'Thoroughbred' as a term was not applied to the racehorse until 1821, when it appeared in Volume II of the *General Stud Book*. Later still, Arabian outcrosses ceased and the English thoroughbred was established as a breed in its own right that was incapable of being improved through its crossing with other breeds.

OUT OF THE HANDICAP (See Long Handicap)

Said of a horse that, because it has its weight raised from what it was accorded by the handicapper to a higher but still minimum one in a handicap, has to hump much more than originally intended.

Some runners run well in these adverse circumstances and so advertise their claims for future consideration, if also for a rise in the handicap.

OUTSIDE

Adjective applied to all on-course betting that takes place away from Tattersalls and the rails that separate this main betting enclosure from that of the members.' As Charles Sidney has indicated, the betting done 'outside' (which includes the silver ring, as well as cheaper course enclosures) is minuscule compared with that done in Tattersalls.'

OUTSIDE RIDE

Many backers believe that when accomplished jockeys or leading apprentices are engaged by trainers who do not retain their services, or when these individuals are released from their contractual obligations, this can represent a significant development.

In order to spot 'outside rides', it is necessary to consult lists of those retaining the services of jockeys and apprentices. Very comprehensive ones are published in racing annuals.

OUT WITH THE WASHING

Said of a horse quoted at extremely long odds in the betting market.

OVERNIGHT DECLARATIONS

In racing annuals of the 1950s pleas were repeatedly made for declarations to be made the night before runners were due to go to post, since at the time there was no guarantee that an entry not listed as a 'probable' would not turn up at the course and win a race.

Fortunately the days when such runners were fairly frequent are long gone and evening newspapers now carry complete and reliable lists of the following day's runners. This is because overnight declarations have now to be made by noon on the day before a race is run.

OVER-ROUND

State of affairs achieved when the totality of prices displayed by a boards bookmaker makes it impossible for a backer to support all the runners in a race and still make a profit. Serious backers should always take account of the extent to which a particular set of prices is 'over-round'.

OVER THE TOP

Said of a horse that actually, or allegedly, has left its best form behind it.

OVERWEIGHT

Extra burden carried by a racehorse if its jockey cannot weigh out at the weight it was allotted by the handicapper or according to the conditions of a non-handicap. This particular imposition does not always annul a victory, but it can be responsible for a defeat. Colin Magnier having to put up 1lb overweight on Greasepaint in the 1983 Grand National perhaps explains why this Irish raider went down to Corbiere by three quarters of a length!

OWNERS AND OWNERSHIP

(See Championship, Owners')
Owners, some of racing's main paymasters, represent a very mixed lot. Whether sole or part, individual or corporate, home-based or foreign, small scale or massively involved, owners are necessarily optimistic since they seldom receive a financial return worthy of their cash injections into racing.

What most owners invest in is hope, that most valuable emotional commodity around which so much of the sport of horse racing revolves. Moreover, the kudos and privileges of being a racehorse owner often figure in the fantasies of would-be pools winners.

Fortunately, many businessmen, particularly those engaged in building and construction, are prepared to meet the high costs of purchasing, keeping and running a racehorse.

Many businessmen race for relaxation, perhaps because as Dennis Brosnan has observed, 'business and racing for pleasure are two absolute and complete opposites'; in the former risk is reduced, control exercised and no excuses accepted, while in the latter risk is high, caution can be counter-productive and excuses for failure abound.

As for tips from owners, these are often suspect since the blinkers of hope and optimism often blind them to the assets and qualities of rival horses.

Frequently what the backer will find is that bookmakers (who work to marked cards that indicate by means of a cross, a dot and a capital C, the likely first and second favourites and a third runner about which they are warned to be careful) recognize their initial vulnerability and so start to trade at rates that are distinctly ungenerous. Frequently, the opening show will, in fact, feature prices that unenticingly prove to be 'over-round' by well over 20 per cent, in which case, the backer should patiently note the opening prices, record the possibly significant percentages by which some may be higher or lower than the forecast rates, and hope for some overall improvement in the trading position.

Bookmakers, of course, can only exercise total control over their opening prices. These rates which have been 'floated' in a speculative fashion, will either contract or lengthen as soon as actual betting commences, according to the racing public's demand.

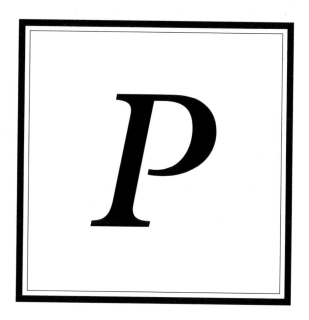

PACE

Some authorities argue that the ability to quicken the pace at any necessary stage of a race is the hallmark of a top-class racehorse. What is indisputable is that the pace at which a race is run has a crucial effect on its outcome. For this reason the specialist racing publication *Superform* states the relative pace at which each of the races they assess was run, out of the wise belief that if the pace of a race was slow, 'form might be suspect', particularly with regard to placed horses. Conversely, if a race was run at a fast pace it is likely the form of the horses involved can be relied on and that of 'close up placed horses should work out well'.

In general, it does seem sensible to suppose that easy winners of races run at a fast pace can be followed with some confidence.

PACEMAKER

Runner whose function is to ensure that the early parts of a race are run sufficiently fast to stretch the rivals of a stable companion so that its stamina and finishing speed can be capitalized upon.

Unlike in athletics, the rules do not allow pacemakers to drop out of contention once their selfless job is done. Like all runners, they have to strive for the best possible placing they can finally achieve.

On one occasion, in the 1989 Eclipse Stakes, the pacemaker Opening Verse actually beat Indian Skimmer (the horse to whom he was supposed 'to give the baton') into third place!

PACEMAKER PUBLICATIONS

Pacemaker Update International appears weekly and gives illustrated retrospective coverage to recently run races.

The most extensive Pacemaker publication has been its annual *Directory of the Turf* which, under the editorship of Martin Pickering, has made an indispensable addition to the library of those professionally involved in racing or who take an avid interest in it. *Pacemaker Update International* is produced by Haymarket Publishing Ltd of 22 Lancaster Gate, London W2 3LP.

PADDOCK

Racecourse area that is inaccessible to all save horses and their connections. As a term it either designates the parade ring alone or this area plus the weighing room and unsaddling enclosure. Those who stand in a paddock (whatever its shape and character) are frequently envied for their opportunity to make close observations of horses which can often provide useful pointers to future prospects.

PADDOCK POINTERS (See Conformation)
Horses whose hoof beats are virtually inaudible as they walk round the tarmac of a parade ring or who 'bounce' along as they trot round provide propitious signs that are just some of the paddock pointers that shrewd judges of racehorses look out for as they peer over the rails of the parade ring.

Well-muscled behinds in jumpers, gleaming coats, bright eyes, alert ears, undisturbed calm demeanour and lean racefit condition are other 'paddock pointers' of which to make particular note.

PARADE RING (See Paddock)
Area in which horses are paraded prior to being mounted. Often the latter proceeding follows the ringing of a warning bell. No racegoer worthy of the name is ever absent from this most colourful racecourse area since within it many indications of the likely prospects of runners are provided.

Some parade ring regulars make a note of runners that are late in entering it in the belief that much care may have been previously lavished on them or that a strongly fancied horse's connections want their runner to be as undisturbed by a race's preliminaries as possible.

The 'animated connections' plan involves supporting the horses around which the largest group of excited supporters has clustered. The problem here is that they may be members of a racehorse-owning syndicate!

PARI-MUTUEL BETTING
English bookmakers will pay *pari-mutuel* (totalizator) returns on major foreign events (such as the Prix de l'Arc de Triomphe run at Longchamp in October) even though they will also frame and advertise their own prices.

The French dividend declared in newspapers will be to a 1 franc unit inclusive of stake, with the returns involved being in both francs and tenths of francs. American dividends are to two dollars and are returned as dollars and cents. In France and America horses in the same ownership running in the same race are coupled together. This applies only to win bets. In France, *pari-mutuel* tickets are available in units of 10, 50, 100 and 500 francs from booths bearing the word *cassie*. A win bet is announced with the word *gagnant*, a place bet necessitates a Gallic pronunciation of the word 'place', whereas, logically, each-way requires *gagnant et place* to be spoken. Place wagers on races with five to seven runners pay a dividend on the first two finishers only.

As for straight forecasts, these involve the words *jumele avec ordre* and can be placed in races which involve five to eight runners. Dual forecasts are known as *jumele sans ordre*, while the self-explanatory term 'trio' will produce a pay out if three horses previously stipulated do finish first, second and third in any order.

Betting in France on the *pari-mutuel* has steadily increased in recent years thanks to some ever more exotic and ambitious wagers — the *tierce*, the *quarte et plus* and the *quinte et plus*.

These are 'big pool bets' in which backers have to predict the first three or four or five in correct order in handicaps. With these bets consolation dividends are paid for near misses.

Advocates of a tote monopoly on betting to mirror that of the *pari-mutuel* in France argue that this allows so much to be ploughed back into racing that prize money can cover 40 per cent of owners' costs (compared to 20 per cent in Britain, in which revenue from tote betting is only a minute fraction of that from bookmakers).

PASSPORT (See Identification of Racehorses)
This document, issued to ensure that a racehorse can be identified at all times, has to be produced and validated before a runner is allowed to enter a racecourse. Designed to preclude the running of ringers, it thoroughly documents horses' distinctive markings and coat colours and changes in the latter have to be recorded on it. A vaccination section of the passport furnishes proof that a racehorse has received certain required vaccinations.

PATENT (Seven Ways or Twist)
This is a wager on three selections permed in such a way as to produce a single or each-way on each one plus three doubles and a treble.

PATTERN RACE (See Group Race)
Prestigious non-handicap event that forms part of a carefully co-ordinated programme of top-class European racing.

In recent years the various racing authorities of Britain, France, Italy, Ireland and Germany – those European countries in fact in which flat racing reaches the highest standards – have together taken steps to ensure that each season the most prestigious races they individually stage receive international attention and, just as importantly, are co-ordinated in such a way as to form a distinct 'pattern'. The result is the formation of a series of races that is sufficiently comprehensive to test the respective abilities of top-class horses of various ages over distances ranging from sprints to 'marathons'.

All this recent international co-operation has also led to the publication under the combined auspices of the Irish Turf Club, La Societe d'Encouragement and the English Jockey Club of the official *Pattern Race Book* (a bi-lingual edition of which is published for the Jockey Club by Weatherbys of Wellingborough). This highly informative publication lists, describes and analyses the British contribution to what is a well-balanced international programme of prestigious racing. Of the 300 or so pattern races currently staged in Europe, the hundred or so that are run in Britain are divided into three categories, Groups One, Two and Three, in descending order of importance.

In addition to the pattern races that are contested on the British turf each season, many other well-known and traditional constituents of the English racing calendar, many of them top-class and often historic handicaps, are also officially 'listed' as important. This practice, which dates from a policy decision made at a meeting of American, French, Irish and British breeders in 1975, in effect means that the winners of these races are entitled to a preferential mention in bold black type when they appear in sales catalogues.

PEDIGREES

These seem to provide particularly useful pointers to the prospects of racehorses that run over extremely short or very long distances. This is why certain sires, Sharpo and Thatching for example, are expected to produce many winning two-year-olds and why in National Hunt and flat races run over 2 miles, special attention should be paid to any of the progeny of Deep Run and Strong Gale. Scrutiny of racehorse pedigrees can thus provide useful indications of the suitability or otherwise of runners to the distances of races in which they are due to compete.

Similarly, progeny may inherit from one or both parents a relish for racing on certain going.

However, the stud book should never take second place to the form book since full brothers and full sisters may perform to very different standards.

Since pure chance is still a major factor in breeding, racegoers should avoid getting too immersed in the chancy business of drawing conclusions from a runner's pedigree. However the stud sook will often help backers who find it difficult to decide between two contenders.

PENALTIES

Additional burdens which, for having won after being allotted certain weights in forthcoming races, horses are required to shoulder in these. They are designed, as the former annual publication *Winning Ways* once put it, 'to stop a rapidly improving horse from turning a potentially competitive race into a procession'.

Backers can take advantage of the fact that these penalties vary and are allotted quite arbitrarily. They should be wary of supporting horses whose recent narrow victories in hard run races last time out necessitate their having to shoulder heavy burdens over longish distances. By contradistinction, horses that are lightly penalized for winning comfortably over short distances should be given serious consideration.

When assessing the effect of penalties, it should be borne in mind that it has been estimated that, while a 3lb penalty will only cost a sprinter about a length, it will leave horses racing over 12 or more furlongs at least three lengths adrift.

A special note should be made of a winner last time out whose disqualification debars it from having to carry a penalty.

PENALTY VALUE

This particular prize money figure relates to the profit made by the winner's connections, i.e. it represents the winner's portion of the total prize money less entry and (for bigger races) forfeit and confirmation stakes. Whatever sum of money constitutes the 'penalty value' of a race, it is this that is used to determine the size of penalties to be carried in future races.

A race's penalty value is the best figure to use when one is trying to assess the class of a horse according to the prize money it has previously won.

PENCILLERS

Early bookmakers were known as 'pencillers' because of their habit of pencilling in details of the wagers they accepted as they walked amongst the betting public.

PERMIT HOLDERS

Those many sporting handlers who train racehorses merely for themselves and members of their families may be granted a permit to do this rather than a full trainer's licence. One of the most successful in recent seasons has been farmer Frank Gilman from Morcott in Leicestershire. His hunter 'chaser Grittar won the Grand National by 15 lengths in 1982.

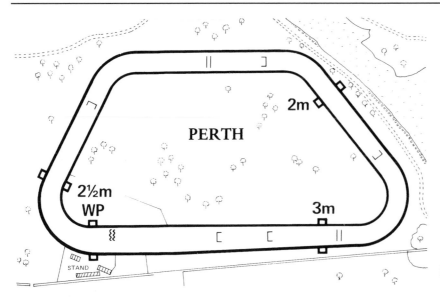

PERTH: Plan of the course.

PERTH

Perth Racecourse
Scone Palace Park
Perth PH2 6BB
Tel. (0738) 51597

How to get there:
From North: A93
From South: M90
From East: A8
From West: A8
By Rail: Perth
By Air: Helicopter facilities

There is no more northerly track in Britain than Perth racecourse which is most picturesque in being set in the wooded parkland that makes up the grounds of Scone Palace.

The fact that it is alternatively known as 'Perth Hunt' provides a hint of the Corinthian and very sporting flavour of the action that takes place here, mainly in autumn and spring, before and after the ravages of a Scottish winter.

The track lies 3 miles north of Perth just off the A93 and can be reached by those travelling from the Scottish capital via the M90. Perth station is accessible by rail from London's King's Cross some 450 miles away. Sassenachs who wish to fly should land at Perth aerodrome some three miles away, but only after phoning (0738) 52311 and booking a taxi to be on hand at their estimated time of arrival. This number also provides details of a car hire service.

As for the course, it is a mainly flat, rather oblong-shaped right-hander of 10 furlongs in extent. Its eight fences are easy affairs and the water jump is omitted in steeplechases on the final circuit. A run on this track is relished by nippy, adaptable horses who can handle its sharp bends and get into a longish lead by the time the 300 yard run-in has to be negotiated.

As much as the excellent view from the stands, most racegoers appreciate Perth's rustic charm that is epitomized by its old-fashioned grandstand, in which good crowds of friendly local hunt members are joined by visitors, many of whom take advantage of the fact that many meetings here are two-day affairs.

PHOTO FINISH

Finish involving horses that are so difficult for the judge to separate at the end of their race that he has to call for a photograph taken on the line by Racecourse Technical Services.

Not too long ago when camera techniques were less sophisticated it was possible for professionals like the legendary Alex Bird, to make a handsome living betting on the results of photo finishes. Bird's secret was that in a photo finish you get an optical illusion that the far horse is fractionally in front, so he always backed the horse nearest him, never the one farthest away and enjoyed an astonishing winning run of 500-600 photo-finish winners, making more than £1 million. Others just covered losses on their original selection. After 1975, when a revolutionary photo-finish camera was put into use, betting on close finishes no longer provided such vast profits.

As was once revealed in the *Raceform Handicap Book,* the camera introduced in 1975 was the result of a long association between Racecourse Technical Services and the Omega Company of Switzerland.

Today even more modern photo-finish equipment, using continuously moving film, makes a permanent record of events which take place on the finishing line in the order in which they occur. Two cameras are used; the first views the whole width of the track and the second is used in conjunction with a reflecting mirror on the winning post covering the far side of the track. An enlarged view of the photo-finish negative can be quickly produced if necessary. Such prints are invaluable to perplexed judges.

If there is a close finish for second, third or fourth place (if this happens to be significant), a further photograph can be made available to assist the judge.

Thus today, the backer has been left with little opportunity to profit from betting on photo finishes. Any odds offered on the results of these feature the expert view of the Tattersalls' tic-tac floorman. On receipt of his signal, bookmakers will often give a price against the horse which is believed to be the runner-up. It is almost a racing certainty that the close finisher that fails to find a quotation in photo-finish betting will prove to be the eventual winner. In such a case backers who have supported the wrong finisher, should not discard their tickets since

PHOTO FINISH: Today, thanks to modern photographic recorders, it is possible to separate the finishing order of horses even in a closely run race, like the one shown above at Newbury.

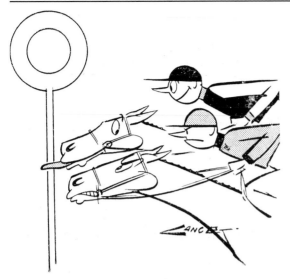

PHOTO FINISH: The taste of victory.

a subsequent objection to the actual winner may be announced and then sustained.

Sometimes, of course, the bookmakers' representative on the finishing line may make a mistake, perhaps by viewing this from a slight angle.

Betting on a photo finish is beset with further problems, some of which the racecourse commentator can quite inadvertently cause by confusing a horse's colours with those of another close finisher. The judgement of a racecourse commentator should never be preferred to that of Tattersalls' bookmakers.

PHOTOGRAPHY, RACING

So picturesque, colourful and action-packed is the racing scene that it makes quite as much appeal to photographers as to artists. Professional racing photographers like Gerry Cranham, whose work figures so distinctively in coffee-table studies of racing, have done much to celebrate the aesthetic side of racing and its sheer drama and excitement.

PIGEON CATCHER

Hyperbolic reference to a horse whose speed on the gallops suggests it is something of a flier.

PLACEPOT

A most sporting and popular tote wager whereby the investor is required to pick a horse to be placed in each race. If there are fewer than five runners in the race, the winner has to be named if a selection turns out to be a non-runner, the SP favourite is substituted and if there is more than one such market leader, the placepot backer's selection

becomes the horse with the lowest racecard number.

Placepot dividends are declared to a £1 unit stake. These can be large; one paid out at Sandown on the 29 November 1985 amounted to £1116 for 50p, whereas an SP place accumulator on the same horses only paid £36!

PLACING BETS (See Pari-Mutuel)

Now that computers are fairly commonplace, this can proceed by some sophisticated and high-speed means. Tote credit customers can, for example, via a recently introduced Tote Express service, take advantage of the very latest in computer technology, which allows personal computers to function as private tote betting offices, giving backers the opportunity to scan the racing pages of the *Daily Express* anywhere in the world as soon as this is published at around 11 p.m. London time – that is up to fifteen hours before the start of the next day's racing!

The Tote Express service turns a computer screen into a betting slip on which any of the popular tote bets can be made at the touch of a button and transmitted to the tote's own credit computer.

Customers of France's *pari-mutuel* can also bet from their homes on Minitel home computers and will soon be able to use telephones to dial bets direct into this sophisticated betting network.

Naturally, the placing of bets still largely involves the verbal citing of the numbers of horses at tote 'sell' windows, or the name of a horse and the amount of money wagered on it to racecourse bookmakers.

Off-course backers can also telephone their instructions to the staff who man the credit offices of the tote or leading bookmaking concerns or write these down on blank slips or the special forms that some complicated multiple forms of wagering involve.

The only time instructions relating to tax deductions need to be given by the backer is when credit bets are made by telephone or when writing on slips or forms in betting shops. Generally, the backer should pay off-course betting tax at the time a bet is struck; otherwise it is payable on a winning return. The tax percentage this ploy involves will not cause the return to be so substantially reduced. Clearly, it is far better to make a £10 off-course bet on a 10-1 chance, pay an extra £1 to cover a tax liability of 10 per cent and then expect £110 back as winnings plus stake, than to pay just £10 initially and find the £110 return is taxed at the same percentage so that one is

RACING PHOTOGRAPHY: This series of photographs by the Victorian photographer Edward Muybridge were the first to record the exact movements of the galloping horse, since it showed the order in which each leg hits the ground.

only handed back £99! If the act of placing bets is based on optimism (and some psychologists would dispute this) it should surely involve strategies designed to produce optimal outcomes.

PLATE

A race in which those managing the racecourse have put up a guaranteed sum of prize money and taken entry fees paid by the owners. This entrance money is limited to a small percentage of the value of the plate. Should the aggregate of this entrance money exceed the value of the plate, half the surplus is divided between two racing charities and the other half (in the ratio of two to one) between the owners of the second and third horses.

PLATES, RACING

Racegoers alongside the paddock should note whether horses are wearing dull, worn shoes or new looking, rather shinier racing plates. The latter weigh

a mere six to eight ounces and suggest that their wearer is better fancied than a runner in ten to twenty-four ounce working plates. Non-racing plates are burdensome in long races on heavy ground.

PLENTY TO DO

Said of a runner that appears to have a difficult task in view of the weight it is due to carry or the opposition it faces. Sometimes this expression is used of a runner that is well behind in its race.

PLOUGHING A LONE FURROW

Course of action taken by a runner that races alone on a different side of the course from its rivals. A horse that puts up a good performance in such circumstances may make further improvement next time out since the proximity of other contestants may spur it to make even greater effort. Horses tend to race alone either with, or sometimes without, their jockeys' approval.

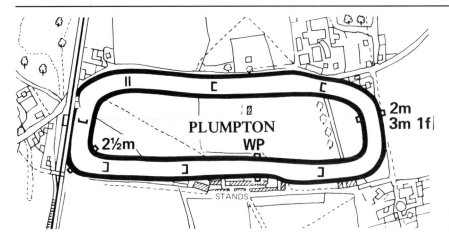

PLUMPTON: Plan of the course.

PLUMPTON

Plumpton Racecourse
Plumpton
Sussex
Tel. (0273) 890383

How to get there:
From North: A23, A275
From South: A23
From East: A27
From West: A272
By Rail: Brighton
By Air: Helicopter facilities

So tricky do some jockeys consider Plumpton that they are reluctant to race on it. However this extreme view is not generally held, which is fortunate since the sport staged on this Sussex track is very popular, particularly among bank holiday picnickers.

The course, which has a definite country feel to it, lies north-east of Brighton whence motorists should take the A27 to Lewes, join the A275 north of this town and then the B2116. Londoners should take the M23, the A23 and then the A272 until they see the racecourse signposted.

Rail travellers can journey from London Bridge or Victoria to Plumpton station which is a short walk away from the course. Helicopters can land on the course, after first obtaining permission.

As a racecourse, Plumpton is a left-hand, tight, undulating rectangular track of only 9 furlongs. Thus, understandably, there are only seven fences, two of which, on the far side, can cause several runners to come to grief. The run-in is short at only 200 yards — a further reason why this is a course which favours horses that are nimble enough and possess

sufficient stamina and adaptability to cope with its sharp bends and occasional quite sharp gradients.

In being so idiosyncratic, Plumpton is a track at which previous course winners should always receive close consideration.

POINT-TO-POINTS (See Mallow)
The first of such contests took place when in 1752 a resident of Buttevant in Ireland challenged a neighbour to a race from the church of this village to another at St Leger four-and-a half-miles away.

Such racing over walls, hedges, ditches and even ploughed land is now rare, since modern point-to-pointing takes place on properly laid-out courses. Modern 'pointing', as it is popularly known, involves steeplechases confined to horses which have been 'regularly and fairly hunted' with any recognized pack of hounds. A certificate attesting to this fact has to be obtained from a hunt's master.

Almost every hunt stages its own point-to-point meeting on its own course or one it shares with another hunt. Typically the races staged at such a meeting involve a members' race, one for adjacent hunts, open races and a ladies' contest.

The longest distance a point-to-point involves in Britain is 4 miles at the Exmoor point-to-point that takes place in Devonshire.

The pointing season lasts from February to the beginning of June and involves many varied fixtures. Invariably these are extremely enjoyable and most sporting. Being strictly amateur, a Corinthian spirit (hard to detect in some branches of professional racing) still abounds, despite the recent practice of running former steeplechasing 'cracks' in humble hunters' races.

Siegfried Sassoon, poet and foxhunter, once described a point-to-point crowd as 'made up of cheerful country folk intent on having as good a time as possible'. These words remain as apt today as when they were written earlier this century. The meetings certainly bring together a motley and fascinating collection of characters. Here and there can be seen rather studious-looking form students, all of whom carry voluminous home-made form books. These reference works are crammed with cuttings from the *Racing Post* or *Sporting Life* results services that supplement the less up-to-date, since annually published, 'bible' – MacKenzie and Selby's indispensable and wittily penned *Point-to-Pointers and Hunters' Chasers*.

Whether one finds a winner or not, a point-to-point is guaranteed to provide much fine sport and fuel for the imagination.

PONTEFRACT

Pontefract Racecourse
The Park
Pontefract
West Yorkshire
Tel. (0977) 703224

How to get there:
From North: A1(M)
From South: A1(M)
From East: M62
From West: M62
By Rail: Pontefract (Baghill)
By Air: Helicopter facilities

Once, such industrial landmarks as slag heaps, collieries, a coking plant and a power station's chimneys could be seen at various times from the grandstand at Pontefract. However, the vista looks less industrial and more attractive now and the proximity of this Yorkshire course to the major population centres of Bradford, Leeds and Sheffield (none of which is more than 25 miles away) ensures that it is well attended, as does its accessibility via motorways. If motorists leave the M62 at junction 32 they will soon find themselves on the track itself, while racegoers from the south will find the M1 and M18 are part of a route that joins the M62.

Rail travellers will find that Pontefract (Baghill) station can be reached via Sheffield which itself lies on the main line from St Pancras. Thereafter, they will need to take a short bus ride to the course.

Helicopters can land on the track by prior arrangement. Fixed-wing aircraft can be accommodated at Doncaster or Sherburn-in-Elmet, or alternatively at Yeadon.

Racing has long taken place at Pontefract which was one of only five courses on which racing was allowed to continue in 1942 – a year when many felt it might well be discontinued, such were the difficulties being faced by the Allies at the time.

More recently Pontefract has again been imperilled. One particularly serious threat not only jeopardized the stability of the racecourse site, but also brought the water table so close to its subsoil that even a heavy shower made soft going something of a certainty. Fortunately, rubble obtained on the demolition of a local Methodist chapel greatly fortified the original shale sand subsoil of the 10-furlong course. To counteract ground that is too hard, the executive installed a modern watering system in 1980.

Pontefract, a pear-shaped oval that in extending for well over 2 miles, is the second longest flat racecourse in Great Britain. Its circuit reminds some racegoers of Brighton or Epsom. Pontefract, in fact, resembles both these higher grade courses in one further respect: it is an undulating affair that features a sharp turn or two.

The longest distance on which races are staged round Pontefract's switchback of a track is 2 miles 5 furlongs and 125 yards and the shortest 5 furlongs. In 6-furlong sprint events the runners initially encounter ground that falls slightly before it begins to rise around the 5-furlong start. Soon, however, this rising ground gives way to a downhill stretch which leads to an ascent that continues around a gently sweeping bend into the ascending 2-furlong run-in.

Since runners in every race at Pontefract are finally confronted by three punishing furlongs or so of rising ground, limitations in their stamina, courage and resolution will be ruthlessly exposed on this testing track.

In fact, Pontefract's sprint courses are generally regarded as some of the most severe in the country; thus the credentials of two-year-olds tackling them should be thoroughly scrutinized and their claims disregarded if they do not appear to be likely to stay or to relish a struggle. If you find a fast starter and a front runner with stamina that can grind down the opposition, then so much the better.

Horses tackling longer races of 2 miles 1 furlong 22 yards, 2 miles 1 furlong 216 yards and 2 miles 5 furlongs and 122 yards have, once past the stands in the finishing straight, to race round a left-hand, fairly sharp bend that runs downhill into a long back stretch that descends once the 12-furlong gate has

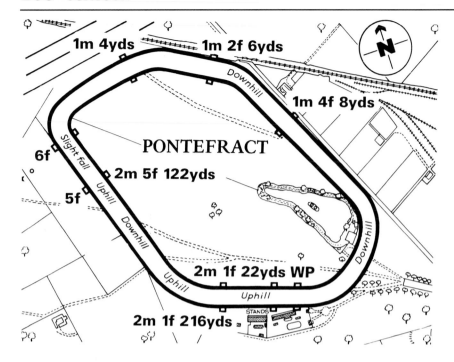

1m 4yds 1m 2f 6yds

1m 4f 8yds

Downhill

PONTEFRACT

6f

Slight fall

2m 5f 122yds

5f

Uphill

Downhill

Downhill

2m 1f 22yds WP

Uphill

Uphill

STANDS

2m 1f 216yds

PONTEFRACT: Plan of the course.

been passed. Then come two left-handed dog leg turns (both fairly gradual) that lead to the shortest straight section of track on the course, which extends from the starting point for 1-mile races.

Next comes Pontefract's sharpest turn of all (almost 90 degrees), the penultimate one, which leads to the sprint course.

This wide testing track features terrain that is so undulating it is not really suitable for big, ungainly types that may find they are thrown out of their long strides.

At Pontefract lowlydrawn horses are favoured, above all in sprint races when the stalls are positioned on the far side. On soft going this advantage increases even further. In races over 8 furlongs and 10 furlongs 6 yards, which involve two left-hand bends, low-drawn contenders also have an edge.

Understandably too, both horses and jockeys who have demonstrated mastery of this singular track enjoy an advantage.

Good viewing and much improved facilities make this well-run track definitely worth a visit. It stages popular evening meetings at which some racegoers patronize Pontefract's intriguingly-named 'third' ring (in which there is a children's playground) rather than the members', Tattersalls or the silver ring.

PONTOON
Six selection wager producing in rotation 6 singles, 5 doubles, 4 trebles, 3 fourfolds, 2 fivefolds and 1 sixfold accumulator.

❗ PONY
Bookmakers' slang for £25.

❗ PORK BUTCHER
Colourful slang for an amateur rider.

POST, THE
Structure around which the 'legs', or early racecourse bookmakers, would congregate. The expression 'ante-post' owes its origin to this activity which once formed a colourful part of the racecourse scene.

PREVIOUS WINNERS
Whether these scored over course and distance or last time out (and so demonstrated their fitness and well-being) or qualified for this designation by winning in the last seven days, or in the corresponding race when it was staged twelve months previously, they are contenders to which many backers pay particular attention.

This process is facilitated by the indexes to such performers that form part of *Raceform* and *Chaseform Notebooks* and a *Directory of Winning Horses* (which gives brief details of the distances and going over which such runners registered victories in the previous two years of their racing careers) which appears in the *Ladbroke Companions to Flat and Jump Racing* that are published each year. Many believe that what a horse has previously done it may well do again, so set great store by previous winners.

PRICE

Bookmaker-quoted ratio of a horse's chance of failure to its chance of success.

PRICEWISE

Value is the watchword of the professional backer and with this vital factor in mind, Mark Coton first produced this regular *Racing Post* feature.

Its aim is to monitor the morning ante-post prices available for runners in principal races in a bid to spot where a chink in the armour of any of the large firms of bookmakers has been made apparent by a price that is generously unreflective of the horse's actual chances. 'Pricewise' presents charts which compare the ante-post odds on big race runners quoted by such major bookmakers as Ashley, Bloxhams, Coomes, Corals, Denny, Dennis, Hills, Ladbrokes, Stanley, Surrey and the Tote.

This innovative and very useful feature even includes advice on staking.

PRIVATE BOX

So desirable is such a facility, especially at meetings like Aintree, Goodwood, Cheltenham and Royal Ascot, that sometimes the temporary use of it is advertised at prices that approach those asked for seats at Wimbledon.

Much needed revenue has been raised in recent years by making even more boxes for private parties available on racecourses. Even though their proliferation has led to the sometimes unwelcome sight of private security men to keep out racegoers unentitled to enter them, these facilities do allow racing to be savoured in luxury and comfort. The best known private boxes remain royal ones occupied so happily by many members of the Royal Family.

PRIZE MONEY

This, despite being so often bewailed in England and Ireland as pitifully inadequate, provides the backer with a useful indication of the class of a race or a runner. Many backers, in line with some computerized methods of winner finding, divide the total prize money previously won by a runner by the number of racecourse victories this involved so as to get a rough numerical indication of class.

Prize money figures also allow inferences to be drawn about the class of racecourses, although these need to be treated cautiously, as some tracks like Epsom stage both extremely valuable races and others with poor prize money. John Whitley of Racing Research has produced figures which give the averages of prizes available at Britain's racecourses.

PROFILING WINNERS

Now that data on the previous winners of many races is printed in several weekly newspapers and in Peter Braddock's book *Big Race Winners*, it is possible for 'profiles' to be drawn up of possible equine heroes.

THE POST: This print by Thomas Rowlandson shows early bookmakers congregating round the 'betting post'.

Most usefully, 'Ten Year Tell Tale', in the *Sporting Life Weekender* provides statistics for all flat and jumps races run on Fridays and Saturdays; these indicate the average odds and weights of the horses that have won these events during the preceding decade. The consequences of placing a level pound on the ten favourites and ten second favourites in these races are also revealed, as is the average number of days the winners of these races had been away from the racecourse and the percentage of winners that had been previously placed first, second or third.

PROSCRIBED SUBSTANCES

When Cantassium, not long ago, won a race, one of her owners revealed that its trainer, Jenny Pitman, takes the drug-free pure vitamin tablets of the same name as this spectacular 14-1 winner!

However, in the annals of the turf one comes across some instances of far less beneficial substances being administered to racehorses.

In 1811, for example, Daniel Dawson of Newmarket poisoned a water trough from which Spaniard, Pirouette and The Dandy took a draught that caused them agonizing deaths. Dawson, who was in the pay of bookmakers who had laid heavily against these and other horses trained at Newmarket by Richard Prince, had only intended to incapacitate them temporarily, but poured too much arsenic into their water trough. He was found guilty of poisoning and was duly hanged in front of a crowd of 15,000, despite the efforts of Lord Foley, one of the leading patrons of Prince's stable, to have him reprieved.

Another major racing scandal involved the alleged, if not the actual, poisoning of Orme. This, the son of the mighty Ormonde, had in his first season in 1891 shown great promise by winning five races, and his trainer, John Porter, naturally entertained high hopes for this colt in the following season's 2000 Guineas.

However, on the Friday before this Classic was due to be staged, Porter found that Orme's mouth was swollen and tender and that there were blisters under his tongue.

Hopes were high that Orme might eclipse the achievements of his mighty sire and so the suggestion that he had been the victim of poisoning by a ball of cloth saturated with mercury was truly newsworthy. Modern theories discount the allegation; whatever the case, Orme went on to enjoy a successful career.

Fears more recently expressed by the jumping trainer, John Webber, that air (polluted as a result of coffee-making at Banbury, not far from his stables,

and then inhaled by his Leicester winner Proud Pilgrim) may have caused theobromine to contaminate his urine and thus necessitate his disqualification, do rather suggest that the Jockey

RF SCENES. No. 70.—THE NOBBLER.

PROSCRIBED SUBSTANCES: *Police apprehending Daniel Dawson, who in 1811 had poured too much arsenic into the trough from which Spaniard, Pirouette and The Dandy drank, and instead of leaving them drowzy, as was the intention, suceeded in killing them in the most agonizing manner – he was duly hanged for this offence in front of a crowd of 15,000.*

Club is now faced with a situation that is almost the opposite of that which it had to deal with at the beginning of this century.

Then, as Wray Vamplew has revealed, American trainers had taken around £2 million from British betting rings largely by administering doses of cocaine to jaded horses!

In 1900 a leading trainer, the Hon. George Lambton, decided to demonstrate just how seriously this activity was threatening the integrity of English racing. He doped five of his own horses who, having previously shown no form at all, duly gained four wins and a second! Eventually in 1904, the Jockey Club heeded George Lambton's message and made doping a racing crime.

Such is the sophistication of modern methods of detecting proscribed substances that (as in the case of Proud Pilgrim) minute amounts of these can be easily detected in racehorses with the result that their often innocent connections have to forfeit large sums of prize money.

For this reason, some have argued that the Jockey Club should seriously reconsider its rules on doping since its desire to keep racing clean has been made redundant by the march of time, which has brought with it extremely sophisticated techniques of drug detection. Apparently too, the National Trainers' Federation would like a small level of contamination to be permitted. This would create fresh problems of deciding acceptable levels for each individual drug; such difficulties are at least precluded by current Jockey Club rules which simply ban the presence, in any quantity, of proscribed substances in racehorses.

Meanwhile, there will doubtless be further circumstances that will produce headlines such as 'Mars barred' which related to the horse No Bombs, whose snatching of this particular chocolate treat from an employee at his stable caused his disqualification as the winner of a £4000 race in 1979!

Since it has been discovered by Jockey Club scientists that feeds have been the source of the theobromine found in urine samples taken from several disqualified winners, the current official policy on doping means that, on occasion, thoroughly well-intentioned trainers are having to pay a high price to preserve the reputation for integrity that British horseracing has long enjoyed.

Interestingly, under a Jockey Club rule modification, jockeys will be liable to tests for such drugs as heroin, cocaine and cannabis, but not for substances such as that provided by the coffee that may have proved the undoing of Proud Pilgrim!

PSYCHOLOGICAL SELECTIONS

In *The Encyclopaedia of Gambling*, Peter Arnold makes the telling point that the backer can obtain in excess of the 'true odds' against a horse's chance of winning by applying a little psychology.

What Arnold's cunning approach actually involves is deciding which runners, rated as having good chances on form, are likely, by having a far from famous handler or being entrusted to an unfashionable jockey, to be passed over by so many punters that bookmakers will extend their odds.

Arnold even argues that the off-putting names of some horses – Mark's Methane, for example – result in them being ignored and thus guarantee that they go off at really good odds!

A further point of Arnold's is that xenophobia and jingoism on the part of British racegoers often guarantees that classy French or Irish raiders line up for (and sometimes win) English races at generous odds which belie their actual chances on form.

The fact that some little known-names have featured in the lists of riders with the highest winners to runners ratios at some tracks confirms the wisdom of not discounting horses that are unfashionably ridden. Some apprentices too are, to say the very least, unlikely to lessen the prospects of their mounts.

PUBLICATIONS, RACING

There is a vast range of these that are of particular interest to the racegoer. Amongst form guides, the best known are *Superform* published by Furlong Press, 116 High Street, Shoreham, Sussex BN4 5BD (Tel. 0273 452441); *Raceform* of Compton, Newbury, Berkshire RG6 0NL, and the pioneering *Timeform*, of Timeform House, Halifax, West Yorkshire.

Computer-aided, highly-sophisticated form evaluation is offered by *Computer Racing Form* published by Racing Research of 21 Upper Green Lane, Hove Edge, Brighouse, West Yorkshire HD6 2NZ (Tel. 0484 710971), while monitoring of possibly significant trainers' entries is carried out by *Futureform*, 82 Girton Road, Cambridge CB3 0LN (Tel. 0223 276243).

As for annual guides, there are several including the *Ladbrokes Pocket Companions* to both flat and jump racing, published by Aesculus Press, PO Box 10, Oswestry, Shropshire SY10 7QR and *Sun Guides to the Flat and to the Jumps*, published by Invincible Press Limited of 77-85 Fulham Palace Road, London W6 8JB, while *Racing and Football Outlook* of

63/67 Tabernacle Street, London EC2A 4AH, publish a budget-priced flat and jumping annual, as does the *Sporting Life* published by M.G.N., 33 Holborn, London EC1 PDQ.

Raceform publish the official form book, a recast version of which, in racehorse-by-racehorse format, is published by Aesculus Press, as are separate directories of racehorses and of 'chasers and hurdlers.

Details of racing's authorities and officials, owners, trainers and permit holders and of racecourses, studs, the racing press, ancillary companies and organizations, as well as results of prestigious races staged worldwide appear in the *Directory of the Turf,* an annual publication with which the *Racing Post* is now associated.

Horses in Training is an annual publication detailing the strings of both English and Irish trainers and usefully indicates the breeding of the horses these comprise. *Travelling the Turf* facilitates this actual activity and is published by Kensington West Productions, 4 Comeragh Road, London W14 9HP.

The main racing weeklies are two tabloid-style publications, the *Sporting Life Weekender* and Raceform's *Update* (its former handicap book now recast and transformed into four different sections that include a separate pull-out results analysis).

A glossier weekly offering is another publication from the Pacemaker stable, *Update International* which purports to offer the most complete weekly coverage from around the racing world.

The enthusiast is also served by several analyses of the behaviour of trainers. Typical examples are *Trainer Form* from Aesculus Press and *Trainers' Review* put out by the *Sporting Life.*

Course Form from Aesculus Press analyses past trends on a racecourse-by-racecourse basis, as does *Trackwise* published by Raceform.

The *Racing Post* of Cannon House, 120 Coombe Lane, Raynes Park, London SW20 OBA and the *Sporting Life* (as above) are the two racing dailies.

PULL

Said of a runner that wants to race harder than is to the liking of its jockey or which is so keen to run quickly that it proves hard to restrain when going down to post or competing in a race.

PULL HARD

Said of a runner which, because of a weight advantage it did not enjoy when it last took on a rival, seems to have an edge over it.

PUNCHESTOWN

Punchestown Racecourse
Naas
Co. Kildare
Ireland
Tel. (045) 97704

How to get there:
From North: R407, R411
From South: N18
From East: N7
From West: N7
By Rail: Newbridge
By Air: Dublin airport

Found in a most picturesque location, 3 miles south-east of Naas and accessible from Newbridge railway station, Punchestown is one of Ireland's most distinctive, historic, and prestigious racecourses. It is one of the places where Irish racing supporters love to congregate and at the same time enjoy getting dressed up for.

The prestigious late April festival meeting held here when the gorse is in bloom is unforgettable partly because this course is closer to open country than any other non-point-to-point track in England or Ireland.

Steeplechases at Punchestown take place on a right-handed undulating, rather rectangular-looking track that extends for two miles. With its sharp, almost 90-degree bend that horses negotiate on the first circuit after passing the stands, its mixture of plain fences and open ditches, its downhill run and uphill climbs, its distinctive bank fence (a double affair) and its tricky final turn into a long run-in, it is no wonder that Punchestown is regarded as a taxing, but fair test of a 'lepper'. Indeed, when the going is heavy here it often pays to support a lightly-weighted runner especially in a longish race.

The hurdle track runs inside the 'chasing course for almost 1 $^3/_4$ miles, while flat races can also be staged over 6, 7 $^1/_2$, 9 and 14 furlongs, on what is yet another testing track. On this high numbers have a slight advantage.

Of late, Punchestown's most prestigious races have been the Champion Novices Hurdle and Chase, the EBF Tattersalls' Gold Cup, the Champion Hurdle, the Irish Field Chase of 2 miles 4 furlongs (sponsored by Ireland's famous racing weekly) The Diners' Club Chase, an important

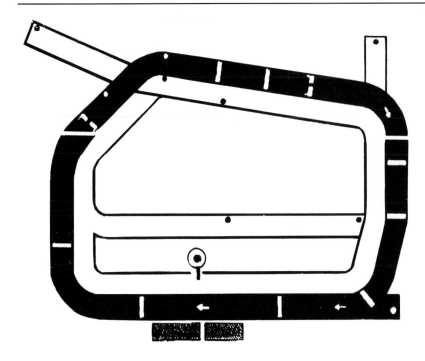

PUNCHESTOWN:
Plan of the course.

Grand National Trial of 3 miles 2 furlongs, the 3-mile Conygnhan Cup for Amateur Riders and the Durkan Brothers Chase of 2 ¹/₂ miles, sponsored by the racing-mad owners of an Irish construction company and run as a pre-Christmas appetizer.

Another top-class festival race run here over a daunting double-back fence is the morathon Le Touche cup.Such is the ambience at 'peerless' Punchestown, and so excellent the view and competitive the sport that it is popular both with true enthusiasts and on the social calendar. Punchestown is one racecourse on which few care if it rains or not.

In fact only cancellation (as in 1950 when the April meeting was snowed off in apparent rebuke of the administrators who were erroneously celebrating the course's centenary) can keep the crowds away

PUNTER

Unattractive term for a backer of racehorses. A 'mug punter' is an unintelligent, unthinking, deluded or gullible specimen of the breed whose extinction constitutes one of the aims of this encylopedia.

PUSHED OUT

Said of a finisher that has to be strenuously ridden out in the closing stages to attain its position at the post. Lazy horses, some of them champions, have to be so ridden and 'encouraged'!

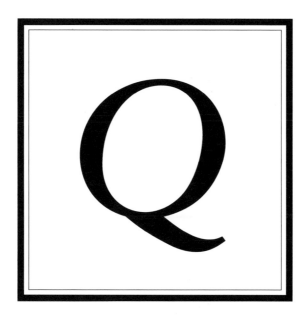

QUARTER HORSE

Breed of horse, so named for its alleged ability to run the quarter-mile faster than any other. Settlers in Virginia often raced horses over short quarter-mile stretches of laboriously cleared forest land.

QUEEN'S HOTEL, THE

The Promenade
Cheltenham
Gloucestershire GKL50 1NN
Tel. (0242) 514724

As a temple at which racing folk celebrate the major rite of spring that is the Cheltenham National Hunt festival, the Queen's Hotel deserves more than a passing mention.

Standing majestically at the head of a tree-lined promenade, this now Trusthouse Forte-controlled Regency hotel was opened in 1838 and suitably, given its status as a home for jumping enthusiasts, is styled after the Temple of Jupiter in Rome. In suitably imperious style, the Queen's 'reigns' over the beautiful Imperial Gardens.

During the Cheltenham festival so jovial is the junketing at the Queen's, so general the *joie de vivre*, so heavy the gambling in private rooms and so prodigious the spending of its very generous (largely Irish) guests that for a week in March Cheltenham comes to resemble Las Vegas.

The fact that this hotel has its own Gold Cup room provides yet further evidence of its long association with National Hunt racing. In addition to this and other areas for luncheons and dinner parties, its lounges and cocktail bars and its Regency restaurant overlooking the Imperial Gardens, the hotel has 96 rooms and a magnificent Queen Elizabeth suite, all decorated in the beautiful Regency style that is all-pervasive.

The Queen's is very centrally located in Cheltenham and is only 2 1/2 miles from the motorway network.

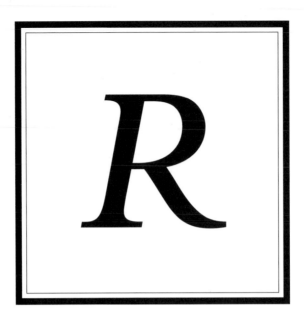

RACECARDS

Besides giving essential information about the runners, all racecards explain the conditions governing the races in which they are due to compete. One main advantage is that they provide information on the colours of jockeys' silks that newspapers (apart from specialist racing dailies) give only for really prestigious races or selected meetings.

Racecards also provide information (on such subjects as binocular hire, course layout, race club membership, record times for the course, commentary arrangements, facilities for tote betting and details of forthcoming fixtures) that may be omitted or merely outlined in specialist racing dailies. Racecards make attractive souvenirs and some associated with past runnings of big races like the Grand National or Derby are both very collectable and quite valuable.

RACECHECK

Feature introduced into the form coverage of the *Sporting Life* in the spring of 1990. This indicates how many winners, placed horses and unplaced runners have come out of a particular race since it was run. Such a precise statistical indication of the worth and 'productivity' of a race provides the backer with a most useful measure of the value of the form it features.

RACECOURSE ASSOCIATION, THE

Winkfield Road
Ascot
Berkshire SL5 7HX
Tel. (0344) 25912

As its name implies, this organization represents the interests of the fifty-nine racecourses that operate under Jockey Club rules. Indeed, many well-known clerks of the course and directors of racecourse-owning companies make up its board.

The association, which is a company limited by guarantee that does not have a share capital, has as its primary aim the welfare of all racecourse owners. With this in mind its board negotiates with the Jockey Club on all matters affecting the profitability and conduct of its member courses. It is represented on the Horseracing Advisory Council and on the board of Racecourse Security Services.

The association is constituted in three areas (Northern, Midland and Southern) and its board has been made up of those owning racecourses as diverse as Bangor and Newmarket.

RACECOURSE TECHNICAL SERVICES

88 Bushey Road
London SW20 0JH
Tel. (081) 947 3333

This subsidiary of the Horserace Betting Levy Board provides racing with such vital services as photo-finish arrangements, electronic race-timing, camera patrol, public address and race commentaries, starting stalls, on-course closed circuit television facilities, timing displays and video surveillance services.

Its familiar green vans and camera patrol gantries are familiar to regular racegoers, and of further interest to them may well be the fact that video recordings, photo-finish prints and commentaries of individual races are available for sale.

RACEFORM

Raceform Limited
Compton
Newbury
Berkshire RG16 0NL
Tel. (0635) 578080

This specialist publisher of various aids to winner-finding is best known for its long-established private handicaps and notebooks which cover both flat and National Hunt racing. It also publishes the official form books covering both these branches of the sport.

A telephone service, as well as *Trackwise* and the invaluable *Horses in Training* – guides to racecourses and to the horses that make up the strings of English, Irish and leading French trainers – also form part of the Raceform 'stable', as do various studies of winner-finding and the detection of value.

One particularly useful Raceform feature forms part of its Flat and National Hunt notebooks. This is an *Index to Winners* which documents the circumstances under which all previously successful horses gained their victories. Raceform also publishes an annual magazine that previews the flat racing season. This is available in March and is suitably titled *Racing Ahead*.

RACEGOERS CLUB

Flagstaff House
High Street
Twyford
Berks RG10 9AE
Tel. (0734) 341666

Founded in 1968 to promote racing, the main aim of this pioneering organization is both to encourage racegoing among the general public by securing cheaper admission to racecourses and to provide an insight into 'secrets' of the sport. Concessions on the cost of membership (by annual subscription) are available to members at many racecourses, who will receive a bi-monthly magazine the *Racegoer*.

RACEHORSE OF THE YEAR

Horse so nominated each year by racing journalists.

RACEHORSES

Annually published retrospective review of each and every horse that has run on the flat in a racing season. So comprehensive, well-informed, thoroughly researched, well written, lavishly illustrated and authoritative is this hardback *Timeform* publication that its appearance prior to a flat-racing season is eagerly awaited and accompanied by plaudits from well-known racing personalities.

A companion study of 'chasers and hurdlers is also published before National Hunt racing gets fully into its stride.

Past copies of *Racehorses* are so collectable that they are the *Wisdens* of horse racing. Complete sets dating back to the 1940s always attract keen bidding when they appear in auctions.

RACEHORSE OWNERS ASSOCIATION

42 Portman Square
London W1H 9FF
Tel. (071) 486 6977

This long-established organization has around 4000 members. As the only body whose remit is the representation and protection of both owners of flat racehorses and jumpers, it negotiates with the Jockey Club, the Horserace Betting Levy Board and other concerns. Its members receive such benefits as car parking labels for display when attending race meetings and advice on all aspects of racehorse ownership.

The association makes awards at its annual dinner and dance in December.

RACE MEETINGS, RULES FOR

These have evolved as the sport of horseracing has, over the centuries, gradually become more organized. Those of the Jockey Club are so comprehensive and thoroughly clear and concise that they have influenced the administration of racing in many countries.

This is not to say that the Jockey Club's rules are always seen as fair and just. However, the rules of racing and instructions by the stewards of the Jockey Club remain widely respected and do much to ensure that, despite its inadequate prize money, British racing remains remarkably straight and well-organized.

Rules for race meetings cover matters and contingencies as diverse as equine swimming pools, blinding hoods, flag starts and jockeys not placing their whips on the scale when weighing in or out!

RACE-READING

This difficult art aims to pinpoint horses which, even though they may fail to win or run into a place, run in a way that can be regarded as promising.

As Jack Leach has remarked, 'race-reading like everything else needs constant practice and experience'. So as to be able to readily identify several different runners in a race, Leach did not try to memorize many different and complicated sets of racing colours, but learnt instead to recognize the riding styles of the jockeys wearing them.

Leach's advice to inexperienced racegoers could be summarized as follows: watch the jockeys prior to the race and memorize the colour and design of the colours you have backed, plus, if possible, those of the favourite and one or two other well-backed horses; don't try to remember too many, especially to start with; you will forget the lot!

One of the secrets is to ignore the leading horse close to home and to concentrate, not so much on the main contenders, but on those horses that finish on their heels.

One possible source of future profit is the sight of a horse in the mid-division making good headway without being hard pressed in the final furlong.

Subscribers to the official form book and specialist racing dailies can capitalize on the race-reading skills of experts. The former publication, the bible of the racegoer, features comments provided by the team of professional race-readers employed by the Raceform organization.

RACE RIDING

This most difficult art (on which so much critical comment is passed on by 'riders in the stand' who criticize jockeys for losing on horses they have backed) is extremely hard to teach.

The Princess Royal took lessons in it from David, the son of 'Frenchie' Nicholson who ran a jockeys' academy that produced such masters as Pat Eddery. John Hislop's *From Flat to Finish* contains much that should interest racegoers and refine their appreciation of the art that is jockeyship.

RACING AND THE POCKET

CALCULATOR (See Computers and Racing) Since the evaluation of the form of horses frequently features numerical assessments of their prospects, it is not surprising that the pocket calculator has been used to synthesize such quantifications so as to indicate a top-rated selection. A paperback by J. White has covered this process in detail.

One concern has even made the Startrack advertised in mail-order catalogues advertising high-tech gizmos and labour-saving devices and features five pre-programmed functions that twice feature addition, as well as subtraction, a ratio and a square root calculation that allow numerical ratings of five variables considered crucial to a horse's chance to be combined so as to give a final rating for each runner in a race.

Recently, true pocket computers like the Psion Organiser have appeared which can be programmed to feature the user's preferred selection criteria.

RACING BY SATELLITE

This has been provided by:
Satellite Information Services
Satellite House
17 Corsham Street
London N1 6DR
Tel. (071) 253 2232
This organization has provided a service for thousands of betting shops as well as the homes of some racing professionals and enthusiasts.

Racing enthusiasts are also kept well-informed by live televised coverage.

RACING BY THE STARS

Some tipsters believe cosmic influences affect the performances of particular jockeys, trainers or owners. *The Directory of the Turf* lists the birthdays of these key participants in racing and many a would-be Russell Grant has backed one of them if his or her horoscope suggests a birthday winner is possible.

RACING CALENDAR, THE

Official Jockey Club publication that is produced by Messrs Weatherby. Its contents include lists of jockeys and trainers who have been granted licences, weights for handicaps, entries for future events, details of conditions of races at future meetings, racing colours, records of past races and many other items. Once the weights for a handicap have been published in the *Calendar*, they cannot be changed, even if there has been an error.

RACING MUSEUMS (See Memorabilia, Racing)

Thanks to displays at Aintree and at the National Horseracing Museum at 99 High Street, Newmarket, Suffolk CB8 8JL, the English racing enthusiast can be reminded of the rich history of one of the most popular of the nation's sports.

The commendable aim of the museum is to

'promote public interest in the preservation of all articles of historical or scientific interest in connection with racehorses and persons or places connected with them'.

Given its status as the headquarters of English flat racing, Newmarket was the obvious venue for a national racing museum. Opened by the Queen in 1983, it aims to tell the story of the sport of kings since Charles II's winning ride across Newmarket Heath.

In a most unstuffy and enlightened manner, exhibits are arranged around such interesting themes as scandals, famous events and horses and their jockeys. There is a faithfully reconstructed stable and weighing room that forms part of a nineteenth century jockeys' gallery.

A video featuring some famous races of the past even includes the disastrous 1913 Derby in which the winner was disqualified and Emily Davison died by throwing herself in front of King George V's runner.

If one becomes a 'friend' of this fascinating museum, one gains a year's free admission and two complimentary tickets. Invitations are also extended to a social function and to private previews of all temporary exhibitions, as well as free admissions to lectures.

The museum opens just before the start of the flat racing season and closes in early December.

RACING ON A BUDGET

Such an experience is perfectly feasible especially if one joins the Racegoers' Club. Course enclosures often offer good vantage points for spectators and within them many children can play quite happily. Several courses offer concessions to large groups of racegoers and admit under-16s free of charge.

RACING-RELATED GIFTS AND PRESENTS

These range from jewellery, car mascots, racing-related garden statuary, hats, coats, scarves and tea-towels to binoculars. Then there are racing videos, books, pocket calculators, computer programmes, board games, as well as a vast array of maps, photographs, posters and other artwork. For the racegoer, hip flasks, shooting sticks and even leather racecard holders can all be purchased. Umbrellas are also available bearing racing-related wording and logos, while bedspreads, sweaters and T-shirts can be provided in particular owners' colours. Displays made up of cigarette card studies of racing themes can be purchased from specialist dealers. Diaries,

playing cards, plates, mugs, trophies, greeting cards, as well as bronzes and ornaments, are also available.

One supplier specializes in the supply of racing-related presents. This is Sports Pages (Newmarket) Limited, The Paddock, 58 Bury Road, Newmarket, Suffolk CB8 8LB. Tel. (0638) 668350.

Perhaps the most appropriate racing present of all is a year's annual members' badge that will give its recipient admission to the best enclosures of a racecourse.

RACING RHYMES

Such is the visual splendour, human drama and appeal of racing's equine participants, it has often formed the subject of poetry.

Racing Rhymes is, in fact, the title of a small, but delightfully illustrated anthology of these that has been published by Michael Joseph. It contains racing-related poems (and a few prose extracts) by such well-known writers as Hilaire Belloc, John Masefeld, John Betjeman, 'Banjo' Paterson, Charles Kingsley and Philip Larkin.

RACING SCRIBES (See Horserace Writers' Association)

These, more commonly known as racing journalists, have always represented a very mixed lot. They range from the intense and sober to the raffish and flamboyant. All, however, have turned what is a hobby to many and an obsession with a few into a way of earning a living.In Britain, their professional association is the Horserace Writers' Association, while the Irish equivalent is the Irish Racing Writers' Association.

Some racing scribes like Jeffrey Bernard and Damon Runyon have spawned plays and acquired the status of folk heroes. The best of them, like the late George Lambton, Jack Leach and, currently, Brough Scott, Simon Barnes, Paul Hayward, John Oaksey Sue Montgomery, and the Irish writers, John B. Keene and Louis Gunning, have made the microcosm that is the world of horseracing seem not only comprehensible, but also alive and necessary.

RACING SHOES (See Plates, Racing)

RACING SPIRITS

A medium, one Doris Bulwark, was once reported to be passing on tips 'from beyond the grave by courtesy of Fred Archer, the celebrated Victorian jockey who went to the great unsaddling enclosure in the sky after committing suicide just over 100 years ago'.

This rather distasteful slur on the memory of a jockey revered in his day was doubtless inspired by stories that his ghost has frequently been seen riding around his home in Newmarket. One of his principal owners, the mercurial Captain Machell, shortly after Britain's best-known jockey (prior to Lester Piggott) had shot himself when depressed and delirious in the throes of typhoid fever, claimed Archer's ghost stood by him and touched him.

Apparently the Captain, only days before Archer's demise, had ignored him after choosing to believe allegations that this peerless horseman had not tried to win on Queen Bee.

Lady jockey Julie Bowker has very good reason to be even more superstitious than most of her colleagues, since on Friday the thirteenth, 1986, on her thirteenth outing and in a field of thirteen horses, she found her mount had been drawn thirteen and was carrying this number on its weight cloth.

At the start the horse in question then tried to duck under the starting stalls leaving Julie shaken, but fortunately uninjured.

RACING SWINDLES (See Corruption, Bizarre Moments)

These have been numerous enough for author Brian Radford to be able to collate details of the most audacious and intriguing and so produce his suitably named study *Taken for a Ride*. Radford categorizes racing swindles as variously involving owning, breeding, nobbling, malpractice by trainers and jockeys, betting irregularities and the running of ringers.

Another author, John Welcome, most entertainingly chronicles racing swindles both past and present in his *Great Racing Disasters*.

Horatio Bottomley once made the wrong sort of killing on the track when the one horse that, by bribing three jockeys, he had arranged to win a seller actually dropped down dead in running!

RACING TOURS

These can involve visits to racecourses, racing towns like Newmarket, museums, studs, stables and, on a more extensive basis can feature tourists' itineraries that are arranged around principal races staged all over the world. Many tours are organized by racing clubs for their members.

RADIO COVERAGE

Such is the detail of radio commentaries, some armchair viewers of racing combine these with the pictures their 'silenced' television sets provide.

Radio 5 currently provides the most comprehensive sports coverage of all non-local radio stations. Its 6.30 a.m. sports report is commendably early and is followed by many others, particularly on a Saturday.

RAIDERS

Horses that have travelled a long way from their home yards or home countries to run at race meetings are known as 'raiders'.

Those from Ireland always present a formidable challenge to the home contingent at Cheltenham's National Hunt festival in March. Many subscribe to the belief that since the bringing of certain runners to a race meeting has involved expensive transport arrangements this must be an encouraging pointer. But not all horses travel long distances to race meetings because they are strongly fancied by their connections. Some are sent to accompany their more fancied stable mates, and others complete long journeys because of generous travel allowances that some racecourses very occasionally provide.

Again many a genuinely fancied 'raider' has been robbed of its chance by the ordeal of its long journey to a racecourse.

Backers wishing to identify horses that are long-distance travellers will find the locations of their training quarters in racecards. Even more conveniently, in a feature called 'Travellers Check', the *Racing Post* reveals the precise length of the journeys such raiders have undertaken.

RAILS

These are essential to ensure that the runners keep to the prescribed course and distance over which they are required to race.

Now increasingly safer, and made from hollow plastic, they can be demolished fairly painlessly by wayward or frightened horses or by jockeys who are forced from the saddle.

On parts of some Irish courses runnings rails are replaced by poles that are driven into the ground in regular vertical positions.

Jockeys often hug the rails, especially if such a practice gives them an advantage on certain flat racecourses. One or two jockeys have been put over the rails – this was once almost the fate of Lorna Vincent at the hands of some sexist flat-race rivals – and one or two have been cool and dashing enough to come between the 'paint and the rails' and win in a close finish. Some jockeys make it clear that they regard the ground near the rails as their territory.

RAN OUT

Said of a horse that during running leaves the prescribed course. Such, sadly, was the fate of Davy Jones, on whom Lord Mildmay led the 1936 Grand National field over the penultimate fence. However, on landing the buckle of the reins came apart in his hands, and Mildmay was unable to prevent his 100-1 outsider from running out in front of the final fence.

READY RECKONER

Showing returns before tax.

READY RECKONERS (see following page)

These are useful features of racing annuals and diaries. Many allow winnings to be calculated and some indicate what procedures should be adopted by way of staking to produce a desired return.
The examples overleaf of both these types of ready reckoner (by pre-tax return on stake and by percentage) should prove particularly useful.

RECOGNIZED MEETINGS

Those at which proceedings are regulated by Jockey Club or Irish Turf Club rules and which are thus recognized as officially sanctioned fixtures.

RECORD TIMES

A glance in the *Guinness Book of Records* at the fastest times taken for horses to cover various distances will not reveal the presence of very many top-class performers. This is because freak conditions often conspire to produce record times; thus meaningful conclusions can rarely be drawn from them.

REDCAR

Redcar Racecourse
Redcar
Cleveland TS10 2BY
Tel. (0642) 484254

How to get there:
From North: A1(M), A19
From South: A1(M), A19
From East: A1085
From West: A1085
By Rail: Redcar
By Air: Teesside Airport Middlesbrough

Like Andy Capp, the cartoon character in the *Daily Mirror* who gave his name to a race once staged on its left-handed surface, Redcar racecourse is unpretentiously distinctive. Its excellent facilities rival many more fashionable courses, and are available at very competitive prices.

What is so refreshing about Redcar, apart from its bracing location near Middlesbrough on the Yorkshire coast, to the north-east of some scenic moorland, is the fact that such impressive facilities as private viewing and dining boxes are available to racegoers on a 'first come, first served' basis at very reasonable rates. There has been a great atmosphere at Redcar under the managing directorship of the Earl of Ronaldshay.

Well-equipped stands which afford an excellent view, many generously sponsored races, a picturesque floral paddock and a children's playground help to make racing at Redcar (where the Princess Royal once triumphed) a rather special experience. It is also likely to be a rather happy, carefree affair: the racecourse executive offers free admission to those under 16 and special discounts to parties that book in advance, and many meetings take place during the holiday season.

Nor is there anything about this very fair Yorkshire track, (apart from two sharp, semi-circular, left-hand bends that have to be negotiated in races of more than 1 mile) that is likely to bring any unhappiness to the horses that have to race over it.

The course is long, narrow, practically flat and

(continued bottom of page 183)

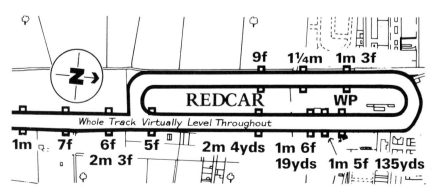

REDCAR: *Plan of the course.*

STAKE

S.P.	10p	20p	25p	50p	£1.00	£5.00
1/3	.13	.27	.33	.67	1.33	6.67
2/5	.14	.28	.35	.70	1.40	7.00
4/9	.14	.29	.36	.72	1.44	7.22
1/2	.15	.30	.38	.75	1.50	7.50
4/7	.16	.31	.39	.79	1.57	7.86
8/13	.16	.32	.40	.81	1.62	8.08
4/6	.17	.33	.42	.83	1.67	8.33
8/11	.17	.35	.43	.86	1.73	8.64
4/5	.18	.36	.45	.90	1.80	9.00
5/6	.18	.37	.46	.92	1.83	9.17
10/11	.19	.38	.48	.95	1.91	9.55
Evens	.20	.40	.50	1.00	2.00	10.00
11/10	.21	.42	.53	1.05	2.10	10.50
6/5	.22	.44	.55	1.10	2.20	11.00
5/4	.23	.45	.56	1.13	2.25	11.25
11/8	.24	.48	.59	1.19	2.38	11.88
6/4	.25	.50	.63	1.25	2.50	12.50
13/8	.26	.53	.66	1.31	2.63	13.13
7/4	.28	.55	.69	1.38	2.75	13.75
15/8	.29	.58	.72	1.44	2.88	14.38
2/1	.30	.60	.75	1.50	3.00	15.00
9/4	.33	.65	.81	1.63	3.25	16.25
5/2	.35	.70	.88	1.75	3.50	17.50
11/4	.38	.75	.94	1.88	3.75	18.75
3/1	.40	.80	1.00	2.00	4.00	20.00
10/3	.43	.87	1.08	2.17	4.33	21.67
7/2	.45	.90	1.13	2.25	4.50	22.50
4/1	.50	1.00	1.25	2.50	5.00	25.00
9/2	.55	1.10	1.38	2.75	5.50	27.50
5/1	.60	1.20	1.50	3.00	6.00	30.00
11/2	.65	1.30	1.63	3.25	6.50	32.50
6/1	.70	1.40	1.75	3.50	7.00	35.00
13/2	.75	1.50	1.88	3.75	7.50	37.50
7/1	.80	1.60	2.00	4.00	8.00	40.00
15/2	.85	1.70	2.13	4.25	8.50	42.50
8/1	.90	1.80	2.25	4.50	9.00	45.00
17/2	.95	1.90	2.38	4.75	9.50	47.50
9/1	1.00	2.00	2.50	5.00	10.00	50.00
10/1	1.10	2.20	2.75	5.50	11.00	55.00
11/1	1.20	2.40	3.00	6.00	12.00	60.00
12/1	1.30	2.60	3.25	6.50	13.00	65.00
14/1	1.50	3.00	3.75	7.50	15.00	75.00
16/1	1.70	3.40	4.25	8.50	17.00	85.00
20/1	2.10	4.20	5.25	10.50	21.00	105.00
25/1	2.60	5.20	6.50	13.00	26.00	130.00
33/1	3.40	6.80	8.50	17.00	34.00	170.00

READY RECKONERS: For details of how to use the tables see the details on the preceding page.

TABLE SHOWING ODDS EXPRESSED AS PERCENTAGES/AMOUNTS TO BE STAKED TO WIN 100 POINTS

Odds available	Percentage equivalent
100/1	0.99
66/1	1.49
50/1	1.96
40/1	2.44
33/1	2.94
25/1	3.05
22/1	4.35
20/1	4.76
19/1	5.00
18/1	5.26
17/1	5.56
16/1	5.88
15/1	6.25
14/1	6.67
13/1	7.14
12/1	7.67
11/1	8.33
14/1	6.67
13/1	7.14
12/1	7.67
11/1	8.33
12/1	7.67
11/1	8.33
10/1	9.09
9/1	10.00
8/1	11.11
15/2	11.76
7/1	12.50
13/2	13.50
6/1	14.29
11/2	15.38
5/1	16.67
9/2	18.18
4/1	20.00
7/2	22.22
100/30	23.08
3/1	25.00
11/4	26.67
5/2	28.57
95/40	29.63
9/4	30.77
2/1	33.33
15/8	34.78
7/4	36.36
13/8	38.10
6/4	40.00
11/8	42.11
5/4	44.44
6/5	45.45
11/10	47.62
Evens	50.00
10/11	52.38
5/6	54.55
4/5	55.56
8/11	57.89
4/6	60.00
8/13	61.90
4/7	63.64
8/15	65.71
1/2	66.67
4/9	69.23
40/95	70.37
2/5	71.43
4/11	73.33
1/3	75.00
30/100	76.92
2/7	77.78
1/4	80.00
2/9	81.82
1/5	83.33
2/11	84.62
1/6	85.71
2/13	86.67
1/7	87.50
2/15	88.24
1/8	88.89

(continued from page 181) oval with a circumference of approaching two miles.

Redcar's longest races are staged over 1 mile 6 furlongs 19 yards and 2 miles and several yards, and thus are started some way short of the winning post.

After racing over a straight section of track, those involved have to negotiate a tight left-hand bend around which an inexperienced jockey may cause his mount to lose ground. Thereafter Redcar's long back straight allows powerful galloping types to lengthen their strides and increase the pace. Then, after rounding a second 90 degree left-hand bend, those running in longer races enter a final straight run-in of 5 furlongs along which jockeys can ride a late finish as they tack over to the stands side. Making such a move as the straight course is joined seems very wise, as surveys have shown that of those contesting races of 8, 7 , 6 or 5 furlongs, horses drawn high nearest the stands have an advantage, especially when the stalls are positioned on the stands side or in the centre of the track.

The course requires a jockey who has mastered Redcar's tight bends, and a horse with stamina, especially if there is some give in the ground. In such conditions the virtually level run-in rides far more slowly than the rest of the straight course.

Racing used to take place on the sands but is now staged on grassland on which the going is, in fact, frequently good.

The course itself lies on the south-eastern edge of Redcar and is a seven minute walk away (via West Dyke Road) from the local railway station, which is around 250 miles from King's Cross (via Darlington). It is a quarter of an hour's drive from the junction of the A19 and the A66. Those arriving from the west should take the A66 which Londoners take after leaving the A1 when it becomes the A1(M).

Redcar racecourse is too narrow for landings of any sort to be made but two miles south, at Turners Arms Farm at nearby Yearby (Tel. (0642) 484340), a 600-yard east/west grass runway is available. Thoughtfully, the racecourse authorities provide transport for those who land there.

Redcar's enlightened management and the fact that its racing, through generous sponsorship, has recently become far more prestigious, augur well for its future.

At present, the race that generally attracts the largest numbers of paying customers is the Zetland Gold Cup – a 10-furlong event run in May – while in June, the 7-furlong Ronaldshay Handicap honours the course's managing director.

At Redcar's important two-day August meeting, the Pat Phoenix Handicap, a 27-furlong race for three-year-olds, continues the populist trend first established by the now defunct Andy Capp Handicap, while the magic is provided by the Paul Daniels Nursery Handicap of 5 furlongs.

Finally, a race run in October, the Provideo Handicap, commemorates this record-breaking two-year-old of 1984.

REFUSE

Action of a horse that declines to jump a hurdle or a fence during a race.

Despite the pile up in the 1967 Grand National (caused when, on the second circuit, a leading horse ran right across Becher's Brook), during this race only three of the forty-four runners actually refused.

Interestingly, earlier this century, the American jockey Todd Sloane once lay on his back in the paddock and refused to ride until the remonstrations of connections caused him to change his mind.

RELIGION AND RACING

Despite the fact that still today in some minds the mere mention of horse racing conjures up scenes of near Hogarthian degeneracy, it is a sport that, its venality notwithstanding, has long had many close connections with men of the cloth.

Former Archbishop Runcie once confessed to being more knowledgeable about the sport of kings than his flock might have imagined, and older Midlands racegoers may well remember Hully Gully, a racecourse tipster of the 1960s, whose monastic robes suggested that he had the ear of the Almighty.

Those with a 'religious' passion for racing may also be intrigued to know that not long ago the incumbent of the parish of Exning near Newmarket ran his horse, St Wendred, even though this runner did seem conspicuously lacking in divine assistance.

And the Reverend Emilius Bailey owed his christian name to Emilius, the 1823 Derby winner. As soon as the winner of the big race was known, his parents had their son secularly christened in a punch bowl of wine, prior to his proper Christian baptism.

Finally, it is a regrettable fact that some racegoers rather blasphemously call for divine aid to help along their fancies.

RESULTS SERVICES

Whether these services take the form of stop press newspaper reports, SIS, Ceefax or Oracle transmissions, transmissions available to subscribers to premium rate telephone information services, displays, transmissions on the racepager's electronic messenger or fully detailed returns in racing dailies, the results they offer are keenly awaited and are the cause of both delight and disappointment.

RETAINERS

Arrangements, sometimes involving large financial inducements, by which jockeys agree that certain trainers or owners can claim their services.

Top-flight jockeys may have two, three or even more retainers. Lists of jockeys' retainers are printed in many annual guides, and the study of jockeys' mounts occasionally reveals that a retainer has magnanimously relinquished a claim to accommodate a non-retaining owner or trainer. Backers sometimes feel that 'outside' mounts featuring release from contractual arrangements provide winning pointers.

Every jockey at the termination of his apprentice riding agreement is free to seek a retainer. Half of a retainer is usually paid in advance and the balance on termination of the agreement involved.

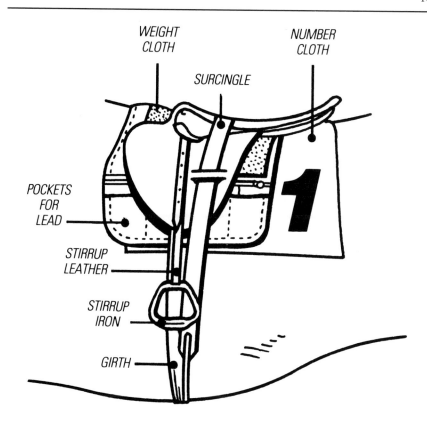

WEIGHT CLOTH

NUMBER CLOTH

SURCINGLE

POCKETS FOR LEAD

STIRRUP LEATHER

STIRRUP IRON

GIRTH

RIDING WEIGHTS:
This diagram shows where
the lead weights are carried
in the saddle.

RIDING OFFENCES

These include stopping a horse from achieving the best possible placing, whipping a rival jockey, or taking the ground of another runner.

Generally, jockeys who ride in any manner considered dangerous, reckless, careless or improper fall foul of the stewards, as they do if they are seen to inflict pain and suffering to a horse by whipping it in an unauthorized or excessive manner. Jockeys are not allowed to school horses in public or prevent another runner from achieving the best possible placing. They must not cross the paths of rival horses or bump, bore or baulk them. Failure to keep a straight course and so cross a rival has cost many a jockey a race in the stewards' room.

RIDING PLANS

Careful study of the impending rides of jockeys may well reveal indications of the plans they have hatched with owners and trainers.

If jockeys fly from one meeting to another, particularly in one afternoon, as well as to an evening fixture from a earlier one, it may be possible to divine precisely why this has been expensively and stressfully arranged.

There may be some significance in jockeys undertaking marathon journeys to go from one meeting to another held on the next racing day. For example, if a jockey rushes from a night meeting at Hamilton to take a ride in an early race at Goodwood on the following day, some might feel there is a compelling reason for this, especially if he or she is not contracted to such an arrangement.

RIDING WEIGHTS

These are published in racing annuals and specialist racing dailies and are of interest to backers averse to supporting any runners obliged to carry a good deal of dead weight. Some backers believe the total absence of any extra leaden weight on a horse's back may well give it an edge, while other backers set great store by a jockey wasting down to ride below his usual riding weight.

RING INSPECTOR

Invariably well-respected, tactful and courteous, this official is empowered to arbitrate in any on-course dispute between a backer and a bookmaker, and can often resolve such disputes satisfactorily, as the editor of this work was once happy to discover.

THE RING: *This photograph shows the large number of small traders dealing in the betting ring enclosure at a Newmarket race meeting.*

The ring inspector returns to a designated racecourse location at regular intervals throughout a race meeting and then takes the complaining backer to his own version of the stewards' room where the circumstances of the complaint are discussed and, if possible, action is taken to settle it.

RING, THE

Assemblage of bookmakers betting in Tattersalls. Sometimes these traders make up what is called the 'big ring'. To them this ring is often known as 'inside' to distinguish it from other smaller affairs in enclosures other than Tattersalls which are classified as 'outside'.

At some racecourses all the bookmakers congregate in Tattersalls since there is no other place for them to go. The ring itself has dwindled in recent years as a consequence, so some claim, of legislation and the tax man.

RIPON

Ripon Racecourse
Boroughbridge Road
Ripon
North Yorkshire
Tel. (0765) 603696

How to get there:
From North: A1
From South: A1
From East: A61, A170
From West: B6265
By Rail: York
By Air: Helicopter facilities

Ripon, the 'garden racecourse', is to be found on meadowland between the River Ure and Ripon Canal in the Yorkshire Dales. It is not so sharp nor as narrow as Redcar and also differs from it in being right-handed.

The track itself, which is under two miles south-east of Ripon off the B6265 Boroughbridge Road, is some four miles from the Great North Road from the south (the A1). The 200-mile train journey from King's Cross terminates at Harrogate, some 11 miles away. Helicopters can land on-course and fixed-wing aircraft can be accommodated at Leeds/Bradford airport.

The course is a fairly tight oval of almost 14 furlongs. It presents thoroughbreds with a really fair test since its long wide straights are conducive to a good gallop.

A spur projecting from the round course provides a sprint track of 6 furlongs that has two distinguishing features whose extent or even existence have not always been acknowledged: a dip about a furlong out and relatively minor surface undulations throughout.

The best known sprint staged at Ripon is the great St Wilfrid Handicap which is run over 6 furlongs in late August. Named after the patron saint of this cathedral city, it serves as a reminder of Ripon's ecclesiastical importance. A splendid silver trophy of St Wilfrid on horseback is presented to the winner.

The most prestigious race run on this course and the only one that qualifies for 'listed' status is also over 6 furlongs. The Champion Two-Year-Old Trophy (which High Top, the 1972 2000 Guineas winner captured prior to his triumph at Newmarket) is one of the main attractions of the holiday meeting that is held on the last Monday in August.

In general, Ripon's sprint track favours fast starters and front-running types that can steal a march over their rivals on its wide straight.

A glance at the Ordnance Survey map suggests that the bends on this round course are tight and likely to be appreciated by handy, well-balanced animals. However, the map does not reveal the banking that has made their negotiation a little easier in recent seasons. Despite this, some long-striding types lose their balance round the last bend.

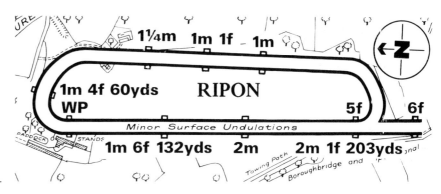

RIPON: Plan of the course.

The 12 furlong and 60 yard start lies mid-way round the first tight turn that is taken by those racing in long-distance events. Then comes the long back stretch along which races run over 10, 9 and 8 furlongs are started. A second tight turn joins the sprint course just over five furlongs out and so jockeys have every chance to come with a late run.

Races of 8 to12 furlongs at Ripon tend to confer an advantage on the highlydrawn. The best-known of such events, The Ripon Rowels Handicap, formerly run on a Monday in late August, took its name from the pointed wheels of spurs for whose manufacture Ripon was famous. James II was presented with a pair when he visited this ancient city, continuing the royal connection established when the royal studs of Henry VIII stood here.

There are several reasons why the present course provides a first-class racing surface. Firstly, its proximity to both the Ripon Canal and the River Ure ensures that the ground is unlikely to be hard. Fortunately too there is gravel as well as clay in the subsoil so the course drains well and is not plagued by really heavy ground, nor likely to remain water-logged for long. Moreover, the grass at Ripon is a tough strain of rye grass which is ideal for racing purposes.

ROARER

Horse that makes a deep roar, which can alarm its jockey, when galloping during its race because of an affliction of the larynx. Fortunately a cure can be effected by hobdaying or tubing.

ROSCOMMON

Lenabane Racecourse Road
Roscommon
Co. Roscommon
Ireland
Tel. (0903) 26231

How to get there:
From North: N61
From South: N61, N63
From East: N60
From West: N63
By Rail: Roscommon
By Air: Dublin Airport

This 10-furlong, right-handed, oblong-looking track can be reached from Dublin via the N4 to Longford and then by taking the N63. Racegoers from Sligo can also journey south on the N4 and N61, while

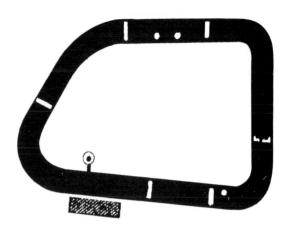

ROSCOMMON: *Plan of the course, where the annual National Hunt Novice Hurdle is staged.*

those from Galway take the N17, then the N63. The track is close to Roscommon's railway station.

The course is set in an area of rich pastural land on which a fair amount of soft rain often falls, so it tends to get soft around its bottom bend. However, Roscommon's summer fixtures and evening meetings in June and August can be superbly warm. Roscommon is a very fair, well-managed track on which many trainers like to introduce their novices to jumping fences. Its tightness tends to suit front runners. However, its uphill finish and the heavy ground that it sometimes presents to runners at its September, October and April fixtures mean that it often pays to support a horse of proven stamina.

The annually contested National Hunt Novice Hurdle is the principal race run at Roscommon, while Dr Michael Smurfit, Chairman of the Irish Racing Board, has also sponsored a steeplechase here.

ROUNDABOUT

Three selections in three bets. It consists of a single, any-to-come (a-t-c) and a double-stakes double on the other two, three times. So a £1 win Roundabout ABC is £1 win A a-t-c, £2 win double BC; £1 win B a-t-c, £2 win double AC; £1 win C a-t-c, £2 win double AB. Total stake £3.

ROUNDER

Three selections in three bets: a single on each a-t-c, a single stakes double on the other two, three times. So £1 win Rounder ABC is £1 win A a-t-c, £1 win double BC; £1 win B a-t-c, £1 win double AC; £1 win C a-t-c, £1 win double AB. Total stake £3. Also called 'Roly Poly', 'ABC' or 'Box Up'.

ROUND ROBIN

Three selections combined to make ten bets consisting of three doubles and a treble, plus the three selections in 'Single Stakes About' (S-S-A) bets in pairs; a £1 win Round Robin ABC (total stake £10) is:

£1 win doubles AB, AC, BC

£11 win treble ABC

£1 win A, £1 win B S-S-A

£1 win A, £1 win C S-S-A

£1 win B, £1 win C S-S-A

A 10p Round Robin costs £1.

ROUND THE CLOCK (r-t-c)

Three or more horses combined in any-to-come bets. The number of bets corresponds to the number of selections. The bets consist of a single on each,

any-to-come (a-t-c), and a single on the other selections rotating. A £1 win Round the Clock ABCD (total stake £4) is:

£1 win A a-t-c, £1 win B a-t-c

£1 win C a-t-c, £1 win D

£1 win B a-t-c, £1 win C a-t-c

£1 win D a-t-c, £1 win A

£1 win C a-t-c, £1 win D a-t-c

£1 win A a-t-c, £1 win B

£1 win D a-t-c, £1 win A a-t-c

£1 win B a-t-c, £1 win C

ROYALTY IN RACING

Whether involving the past race-riding successes of the Princess Royal (which belied the nickname of RSJ – Royal Stopping Jockey – initially given to her by trainer David Nicholson's sceptical stable lads),

ROYALTY IN RACING: Her Majesty the Queen and the Prince and Princess Michael of Kent who are keen followers of racing, cheer on the winning horse at Epsom.

the racehorse-owning achievements of her mother and grandmother, the passion for the turf of Edward VII (the only monarch to have won both the Grand National and the Derby), the establishment by Queen Anne of Ascot as a fashionable race meeting, or the crucial early patronage of Newmarket by Charles II who even held court there, the influence of royal individuals on racing has been extensive. They have done much to increase the kudos, glamour and social acceptability of a truly royal sport.

Currently the Jockey Club's only two patrons are Her Majesty the Queen and Her Majesty the Queen Mother.

RULES OF BETTING

Bookmakers' rules vary and should always be studied. the *Sporting Life* offers an arbitrational service that consists of written judgements on betting disputes described by some of its readers.

Tattersalls' Committee produce regularly revised rules on betting that have weight behind them in that this body has the authority to settle all questions relating to bets, commissions for bets and any matters arising either directly or indirectly out of wagers or gaming transactions on horse racing, to adjudicate on all cases of default and, at their discretion, to report defaulters to the Jockey Club.

Tattersalls' rules on betting always form a part of the *Ladbrokes Companion to Flat Racing* published by Aesculus Press.

RULES OF RACING

These, the sport's standing orders, are a study in precision and clarity. They represent a comprehensive response to all foreseeable situations and contingencies associated with a race meeting. A copy of them can be purchased from Messrs Weatherby, Sanders Road, Wellingborough, Northants NN8 4BX. The copyright of the rules of British racing resides with the trustees of the Jockey Club. A particularly fascinating constituent of the rules of racing consists of a list of precise definitions. These spell out the exact meanings of such terms as 'scratching' and 'maiden'.

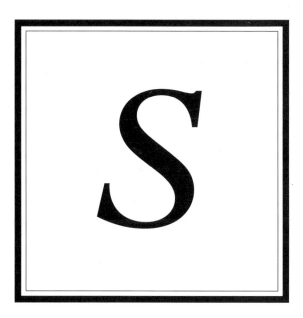

SADDLE-CLOTH (See Number Cloth)
A rectangular cotton cloth that bears a runner's racecard number. On the flat, saddle-cloths were first used in 1922.

SALISBURY

The Racecourse
Netherhampton
Salisbury
Wilts 5P2 8PN
Tel. (0722) 326461

How to get there:
From North: A345
From South: A338
From East: A30, A303
From West: A30, A303
By Rail: Salisbury
By Air: Helicopter facilities

Salisbury's downland course is held in high regard, with not just local handlers operating from several training centres in the area (Marlborough and Devizes to name but two) but also by trainers from much further afield. This is because, in being so testing and yet quite fairly so, Salisbury allows trainers to introduce promising newcomers to racing and to assess their potential.

This particular ploy was demonstrated to perfection as long ago as 1912 when Aboyeur, the eventual 100-1 winner of the Derby of the following year, made a winning debut in an important two-year-old race, the 6-furlong Champagne Stakes. Fifty-eight years later, Mill Reef, after making an impressive winning debut at Salisbury, went on in his second season to capture the Derby in 1971, and so \underline the lesson.

Historically then, Salisbury has attracted horses of the highest class. One of these was the legendary Eclipse, winner of all the 26 races and matches in which he took part before his death in 1789. Interestingly, one of these victories was in the City Bowl Handicap Stakes, a race for four-year-olds and over that is now run over 8 furlongs in early May.

Another historical and prestigious Salisbury race is the Bibury Cup, a 12-furlong contest for three-year-olds that is staged in late June. A two-day fixture in June, is still known as the 'Bibury Meeting'; it includes the 6-furlong Champagne Stakes, Salisbury's best-known race, which always features some classy two-year-olds.

Another race over the Derby distance, a 6-furlong handicap run in early July, recalls Fred Darling's

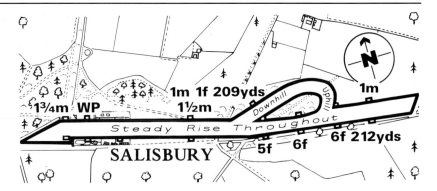

SALISBURY: Plan of the course.

Owen Tudor. Other famous horses commemorated by Salisbury races are the speedy Myrobella, by a 5-furlong sprint for two-year-olds in early July, and Fair Trial, remembered by a mile handicap for three-year-olds run at the same fixture.

Developing types running at Salisbury will often reveal whether they have sufficient courage, stamina and resolution to compete successfully in the highest class. Moreover, if horses that can hold their own on top-class courses have a run at Salisbury while still not fully fit, they are likely to do themselves full justice when they subsequently step up in class.

Large numbers of horses compete at Salisbury's fairly frequent meetings. Indeed, on Thursday, 11 September 1980 the Marlborough Stakes for two-year-old maidens attracted no less than 62 runners and thus had to be divided into four divisions!

The course proves popular thanks to its conformation which makes considerable, but not Draconian, demands on racehorses in every race in which rising ground is encountered.

Runners over 1 3/4 miles, the longest distance on this rather punishing track, start with their backs to the winning post that is not far behind them. Then it's downhill past the 12-furlong start and soon afterwards they swing left to enter a sharp right-hand loop which initially involves the 9-furlong 209 yard start and a straight stretch of still descending ground. Then comes an extremely tight, semi-circular, right-handed bend that rises as, about six and a half furlongs from home, the loop runs into the so-called 'straight' course which, in fact, features a right-handed elbow. Thanks to a spur, the straight course extends for a mile of which most of the first two furlongs is uphill. Then a fairly flat section of track extends for a furlong or so until, thereafter, the ground rises steadily for the final four furlongs so that by the post the runners are 76 feet higher than at the start of the course. Salisbury's largely uphill straight course calls for resolution in those who tackle it.

Apart from possessing stamina and courage, horses running on the round course need to be sufficiently handy and adaptable to cope with its cambers and its very sharp and semi-circular, top right-hand bend. Jockeys need the skill both to tack over gradually to the inside running rail on entering the loop and go the shortest way round the final turn and also help their mounts keep something in reserve for the rather punishing closing stages of their races.

Racing over 5 and 6 furlongs, 6 furlongs 212 yards and 1 mile is, if anything, an even more taxing experience than running in longer races because for those concerned the ground, especially in the closing stages, rises relentlessly to the line.

As for the draw at Salisbury, in races up to a mile, this favours the lowly drawn if the stalls are on the stands side or in the centre, but high-drawn horses have the edge if the stalls are on the far side.

Soft or even heavy ground is sometimes found at Salisbury whose subsoil is downland chalk. This, however, supports a deep layer of luxuriant and resilient spring turf which makes for an unrivalled racing surface.

Salisbury is one of England's oldest racecourses (a meeting was held here in 1584) and is a most civilized racecourse that is strictly managed, picturesquely situated, and offers a scenic view of Salisbury Cathedral.

Buses are on hand at Salisbury station (which is just over 80 miles from Waterloo), to take rail travellers a further three and a half miles westwards to the course. Motorists will find this lies off the A3094 road to Netherhampton which can be reached via the A354, A338 and A30. The track is, in fact, situated 23 miles from Southampton and 30 from Bournemouth and offers free car parking facilities. Those who wish to travel in style can make use of a helicopter landing pad, unlike Queen Elizabeth I who apparently took in a Salisbury meeting before seeing off Drake's task force against the Armada.

SANDOWN PARK

Sandown Park Racecourse
Esher
Surrey KT10 9AJ
Tel. (0372) 463072

How to get there:
From North: M1, M25
From South: A3
From East: M25
From West: M3, A3
By Rail: Esher
By Air: Helicopter facilities

Those who regularly patronize this attractive track enjoy a veritable feast of first-class sport. Indeed, the racing fare they are offered in the course of a season is extremely varied and is made up of some rather exotic ingredients.

One has a distinctive Chinese flavour in featuring the Royal Hong Kong Jockey Club Handicap, while a colourful Sloane Ranger fixture includes a Green Welly Claiming Stakes when it is staged in mid-July.

It should not, however, be concluded that racing at Sandown is bizarre. This, after all, is the course on which the Eclipse Stakes (England's first £10,000 race whose inaugural running took place in 1886) is staged in honour of the Darley Arabian's great-great-grandson who established himself as the greatest racehorse of the eigtheenth century.

Sandown's spring meeting on the last Saturday in April, boasts the 10 furlong 7 yards Classic Trial which can provide useful pointers to the Classic chances of the top-class three-year-old colts and geldings that contest it as part of their Derby preparation. The winner of this race will often be in a high position in the ante-post betting lists for the colts' Classic. Run over the same course and distance is the Gordon Richards Stakes which is limited to more mature horses. Another top race run at the late April meeting is the Trusthouse Forte Mile.

A later Sandown fixture (towards the end of May) includes the 5 furlong 6 yard Temple Stakes, in which three-year-olds have often defeated their older rivals. Also run at this meeting are the historic 2 mile 78 yard Henry II Stakes that is suited to four-year-olds and often won by one and the Brigadier Gerard Stakes which commemorates John Hislop's celebrated winner of the Eclipse Stakes over course and distance. This generally falls to a four-year-old.

As for the Eclipse Stakes, which brings together the very best middle-distance three-year-olds and their seniors in intriguing rivalry over 10 furlongs 7 yards, it is run on the first Saturday in July so that Classic contenders at Epsom have time to prepare for it. Past victories have been divided equally between three-and four-year-olds. Quite regularly the Eclipse is won by a Classic winner – recently by Nashwan, the earlier winner of the 1989 Derby.

The Solario Stakes is an important 7-furlong 16-yard contest for two-year-olds that takes place at Sandown in late August. It commemorates a colt whose victories during 1925 and 1926 in the St Leger, Coronation Cup and Ascot Gold Cup were over rather longer distances.

Sandown nestles in a natural amphitheatre and offers an excellent view of the racing, which seems particularly spectacular largely because its oval circuit extends away from the stands and so is clearly and completely visible from them.

The flat course is an oval affair that extends for about 13 furlongs on which the longest races (like the Henry II Stakes) are staged over 2 miles 78 yards. Those involved in such contests start in the finishing straight three furlongs or so from the post, and thus have to initially contend with the majority of the course's rather stiff, four-furlong run-in that only levels out about fifty yards from the finish. Horses tackling not only 2 miles, but also 14 furlongs, at Sandown, encounter some undulating terrain after the winning post has been passed and they negotiate a reasonably sweeping right-hand bend. This leads to a downhill straight section of track which precedes a sharper right-hand bend that falls as it turns to join Sandown's largely level back straight. This course section (which has two spurs projecting from it to allow races over 10 furlongs 7 yards and 1 mile 14 yards to be staged) is fairly flat.

It is when they have negotiated the track's final, fairly sharp and semi-circular, right-hand bend that for around four and a half furlongs all Sandown finishers are confronted with rising ground.

As is to be expected of those running on this right-handed round course, the highlydrawn are favoured.

Sandown also has a separate straight course on which, unusually, no 6-furlong races are contested since it only extends for a little over five furlongs. However, to compensate for lack of length it rises steadily throughout its five furlongs. Thus, it is worth checking to see if one's selection, particularly if it is a two-year-old, has some stamina on its side.

SANDOWN PARK: HRH The Queen Mother's Special Cargo, ridden by G. Oxley, taking the last fence to win the Horse and Hound Grand Military Gold Cup at Sandown.

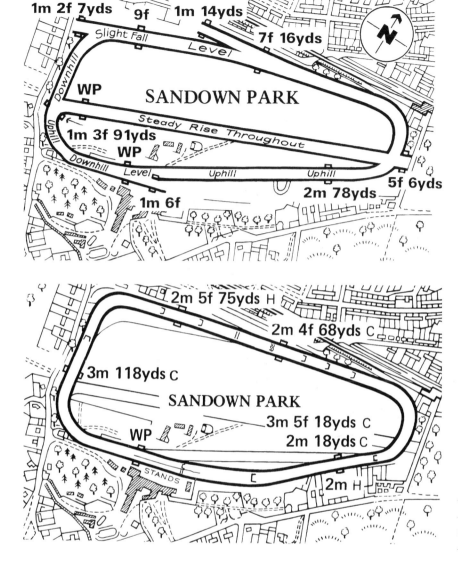

1m 2f 7yds · 9f · 1m 14yds

7f 16yds

Slight Fall · Level

N

Downhill

WP

SANDOWN PARK

Steady Rise Throughout

1m 3f 91yds

WP

Uphill

Downhill · Level · Uphill · Uphill

5f 6yds

2m 78yds

1m 6f

2m 5f 75yds H

2m 4f 68yds C

3m 118yds C

SANDOWN PARK

3m 5f 18yds C

2m 18yds C

WP

STANDS

2m H

SANDOWN PARK:
Plans of the Flat course
(top), and the National
Hunt course (bottom).

As for the draw, it has been estimated that at Sandown if a sprint is run on soft going and the stalls are placed on the far side, high-drawn horses have as much as a 1lb advantage per stall, which is significant since 10lbs can be considered as equivalent to an 'edge' of over three lengths.

Jockeys must appreciate the danger of prematurely easing their mounts on both the hilly section of the run-in and its final flat fifty yards and shouldn't leave them too much ground to make up in the taxing final stages of their races.

Generally, Sandown favours dour long-striding galloping types whose strong suit is stamina, while it tends to expose the limitations of irresolute animals that are unlikely to stay. It does not really suit front runners, yet is not too severe a test for the stout-hearted.

Since it stands on soil that drains well, the going during the flat season is seldom heavy.

As for steeplechasing, Sandown is, in the view of many, the pre-eminent park racecourse. Indeed, for many the jumping year only really starts with the running of the Mildmay Cazalet Memorial Handicap Chase which recalls the Queen Mother's former trainer, Peter Cazalet and the late Lord Mildmay. This 29-furlong race provides a Grand National pointer and is frequently won by an eight-year-old.

The Imperial Cup is a handicap hurdle that is a 'curtain raiser' to the Cheltenham festival when it is staged on the first or second Saturday in March. This often open contest has frequently fallen to a five-year-old outsider and has in its time been captured by many a small stable.

Sandwiched into Sandown's 'mixed' late April meeting is the Whitbread Gold Cup which is run over 3 miles 5 furlongs 18 yards and often produces some thrilling finishes as when Special Cargo narrowly prevailed in 1984. Some high-class horses have won this splendid spectacle including Pas Seul, Arkle, Mill House, The Dikler, Diamond Edge and Desert Orchid. Nine-year-olds often go well on the firmer ground that this race often involves.

Such conditions rarely feature in the William Hill Handicap Hurdle in early December. This race is always a fairly competitive affair and can involve some heavy betting.

Sandown's compact jumping track is a right-handed oval of around 13 furlongs which finally involves a taxing uphill run after the last bend has been rounded. Its eleven fences, especially the three so-called 'railway' fences that come in such quick succession in the back straight, represent a severe a test of a horse's jumping ability. The first fence that three milers take is downhill; then in the back stretch come two plain fences that are followed by an open ditch. Next comes the water jump and then three plain 'railway' fences. The plain 'pond' fence is part of the bend into the straight in which there are two final obstacles. The first is a plain fence, while the second is 'split', in that on the first circuit an open ditch is involved, but on the final lap the runners take a plain fence which is followed by an uphill run to the line of 300 yards. All hurdle races are run on the flat course.

Few today would regard a day out at Sandown as dauntingly expensive. While a few might see its splendid facilities (which include banqueting suites) as the trappings of privilege, refreshingly all the facilities on-course are available on a 'first come, first served' basis, and lady racegoers are made to feel particularly welcome.

This attractive, meticulously managed, course lies off the A307, five miles from Kingston and 14 miles from Guildford. It is adjacent to Esher station which can be reached rapidly and conveniently from Waterloo some 15 miles away. Motorists coming from the capital tend to take the A3.

A playground in the park enclosure caters for children and, for adults, generous reduced rates of admission are offered to parties of more than 100 racegoers, a concession quite frequently granted.

If there is a slight shortcoming at Sandown it is the course's failure to present thoroughbreds with an opportunity to race over the full Derby distance. However this is a minor deficiency.

SATELLITE INFORMATION SERVICES
(See Racing by Satellite)

SCALE OF COMMISSION
The rates of commission paid by bookmakers to their agents depend on the type of race on which these individuals have taken bets. The fact that they are most generously rewarded for passing on multiple bets and do almost as well by bringing in business on handicaps with more than five runners, would seem to suggest that such events give bookmakers an edge.

SCHOOLING
Allowing inexperienced racehorses to learn more about racing as opposed to winning races. As racecourse behaviour this represents malpractice and trainers resorting to it fall foul of the stewards. Sometimes horses will be seen being 'schooled' with the permission of racecourse executives once a race meeting has ended.

SCOPE (Of a horse)
Potential to improve and do well.

! SCORE
Slang for £20 or 20-1.

SCRATCHED
Said of a horse that has to be withdrawn as an entry for a future race for which there is a declaration or forfeit. Such a proceeding is often unavoidable because of ill-health, lameness, lack of fitness, injuries or death. The *Racing Calendar* carries details of 'scratchings', as do specialist racing dailies.

SCRUBBED ALONG
Said of a runner a jockey has tried to galvanize by moving his or her legs backwards and forwards in time with its stride and by wielding, but not using, the whip. Useful with an unwilling runner, this is unlikely to do much to boost a tiring one's efforts.

SECTIONAL TIMING
The timing of races to feature separate figures for parts of them. This practice is common in Australia and North America, but in England and Ireland only a few private individuals (like journalist Michael Tanner, for example) resort to it on a regular basis. Sectional timing can tell trainers a good deal about the well-being or otherwise of their charges. Michael Tanner's sectional timings are sometimes presented in Pacemaker publications.

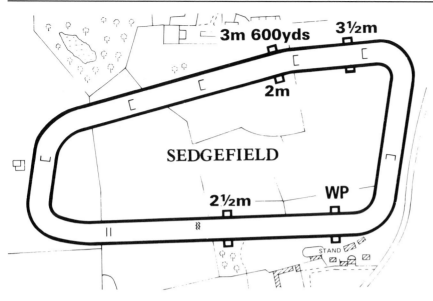

SEDGEFIELD: Plan of the course.

SEDGEFIELD

Sedgefield Steeplechase Co Ltd.
23a The Green
Billingham
Cleveland TS23 1ES
Tel. (0642) 557081 or 559050

How to get there:
From North: A1(M)
From South: A1(M)
From East: A689
From West: A68
By Rail: Stockton-on-Tees
By Air: Tees-side Airport, Middlesbrough

On this left-handed, undulating track there are eight fairly easy, well-made obstacles. Despite the fact that Sedgefield means 'Cedd's open land', its racecourse only extends for 10 furlongs and is a sharp affair. Its fences are quite closely positioned; thus a run on this track calls for both jumping ability and adaptability.

It also puts the stamina of those (especially steeplechasers) who run on it fully on trial, since from the second last there is a steep downhill run that is followed by a punishing final uphill stretch which extends for over 500 yards, the water jump being omitted on the final circuit. Thus, when the going is heavy here one needs to side with a dour stayer.

On the hurdle course the run-in from the last obstacle is only 200 yards.

The viewing at Sedgefield is excellent and often horses can be seen in spectacular action and silhouette against the winter skyline.

The fact that so many days racing are staged at Sedgefield – most of them on Tuesdays - testifies to its popularity. This is partly due to its proximity to the towns of Middlesbrough, Darlington and Durham. The track itself, which offers splendid viewing, is to be found in a peaceful rural location. Indeed, its remoteness deters some rail travellers who have to take an eight-mile or so taxi ride to the course, from either Stockton or Darlington station.

The course is just off the A1(M) and is best reached via the A689. Those travelling north-west from Middlesbrough should take the A177, join the A689 and look for signs directing them to the course which is to the south-west of Sedgefield itself. Those coming westwards from Bishop Auckland can remain on the A689.

Helicopters cannot be accommodated on-course. These and fixed-wing aircraft can, however, land at Teesside airport from which taxis can be taken.

The McEwans National is an often thrilling, long-distance handicap steeplechase that is staged at Sedgefield in early March. Confined to five-year-olds and above, this is a three and a half mile contest.

SELLING RACES
The conditions of these events stipulate that each losing horse running in them may be claimed and the winner must be offered for sale by auction. The money to be paid to the owner for the sale of the horse is specified in the conditions of the race and whatever the price realized at auction, the owner only receives this specified sum. Any surplus is

divided between the owner of the second horse and the racecourse executive or a charitable fund.

Those assessing selling race form might usefully consider:

1. Whether a horse comes from the yard of a selling race specialist; check in *Trainers Record* or *Trainers Review*.

2. Whether a horse that has run disappointingly in sellers over a particular distance is tackling a different trip for the first time. It is a legitimate 'finesse' within racing for a trainer to run a horse over an unsuitable distance in order that its potential (when conditions are in its favour) cannot emerge.

3. Whether particular trainers send out 'dark horses' – those with no previous public form – to make winning debuts in sellers. *Trainers Record* will reveal whose first time out runners in sellers should be noted.

4. Whether a horse has been running in non-selling races and is being dropped down to plating class for the first time. It is also worth noting if it has previously run fast enough to be rated by a time expert; this may suggest it could 'run the legs off' opponents, as might private handicap ratings that indicate it is well clear of its rivals on form.

5. Whether some runners in auction events carry weights (illogically determined by their purchase prices as yearlings) that would be far higher were they to be assessed on their past form as two-year-olds.

6. Whether horses are being sent long distances to run in sellers (particularly those carrying poor prize money). Given the price of petrol, such 'raiders', especially those from 'struggling' yards, may be gambled on successfully. To check on this factor, *Horses in Training* and a good map will prove useful.

7. Whether a top-flight 'job' jockey or leading apprentice (whose ability hardly entitles him to the weight allowance he usefully receives) has been engaged to ride or replaces a less impressive looking pilot who was previously listed as the likely rider.

If a jockey or apprentice has been released from his commitment to his retaining stable and is being allowed to take an 'outside' ride, this hint is worth taking.

8. Whether a springer's closing odds in the betting market have shortened by a greater percentage than the odds of other runners have shortened. A selling race favourite whose odds have been only marginally trimmed may, in fact, not be the 'best-backed' runner.

9. Whether a runner has been unsuccessfully gambled on in past sellers. If so, it may be out to retrieve previous heavy losses. If it is due to encounter different conditions it may well atone!

10. Whether the ages of the runners or the time of year when the seller is being run, may have a bearing on the task of winner-finding. Plating form (as in non-selling races) often tends to work out better from May to mid-September, whereas, because platers are still developing in their second season and run over many varying distances, sellers confined to three-year-olds are often 'trappy' affairs that are difficult to assess. On the other hand, four-year-old platers tend to run rather more consistently.

SETTLE

To pay, either a backer his winnings (as a bookmaker) or a bookmaker, if one is a losing backer. Those who have 'bilked' their bookmakers have far outnumbered 'welshing' bookmakers.

Bets are settled on the basis of what a bookmaker's clerk has recorded in his betting book or 'captain', which takes its name from two cockney rhyming slang expressions: captain kettle-settle and captain Hook-book.

SEX-ALLOWANCE

Intriguingly-named, rather sexist weight allowance (often of 5lbs) that race conditions sometimes make to a filly or mare that takes on male rivals.

SHADES (See Blinkers)

SHARPS

Approbative term, sparingly bestowed, for particularly astute backers whose expertise, intelligence and shrewdness bookmakers have learned to respect or even fear.

SHARP TRACK

Racecourse with a small circumference whose bends are tight. Chester's 'Roodeye' and many Irish racecourses provide good examples of such a configuration.

SHOOTING STICKS

Traditional, portable seats of racegoers, as well as sometimes disparaged (since none too sophisticated) devices with which local stewards may gauge the going. Some shooting sticks double as umbrellas, but many racegoers have abandoned these traditional items in favour of portable seats that resemble large versions of collapsible baby buggies.

SHOW (See Over-round)

Term used to designate a set of prices quoted by bookmakers against a field of runners. It is always worth calculating from an opening show just how ungenerously or otherwise bookmakers are trading and then making subsequent calculations from later shows to see if the trading position has changed in one's favour as a backer.

SINGLE LAP (Waterfall)

This involves any number of selections. The bet consists of a single on each selection any-to-come (a-t-c) and a single-stakes win bet on the next selection. It is the same as a 'Round the Clock' bet, except that the any-to-come element only involves the next selection. So a £1 win Single Lap ABC would work out as:

£1 win A a-t-c, £1 win B
£1 win B a-t-c, £1 win C
£1 win C a-t-c, £1 win A
The total stake would be £3.

SINGLE STAKES ABOUT (Up and Down)

This is similar to an any-to-come (a-t-c) bet but it operates in both directions – up as well as down on two selections – so making two bets. These consist of a single a-t-c and a single stakes single reversed. Example:

£1 win A, £1 win B Single Stakes About gives:
£1 win A a-t-c, £1 win B
£1 win B a-t-c, £1 win A
The total stake would be £2.

This bet can be indicated on a betting slip as S-S-A or shown by placing one or more crosses between the selections it constitutes.

SIRES

Male parents of racehorses. Backers should note that the race distances that may well suit the progeny of particular sires are given (by kind permission of the *Statistical Record*) in *Ladbrokes' Pocket Companion to Flat Racing*, and that *Horse and Hound* gives extensive coverage to National Hunt sires.

Sires (as well as dams, of course) may pass on particular preferences for certain types of going.

SKIN

Winner that obliges bookmakers to pay out nothing, or virtually nothing, from their satchels.

SKULL CAP

'Crash helmet' now mandatory for jockeys to wear.

SLEEPER

Uncollected winnings that remain in a racecourse bookmaker's satchel by the end of a meeting. Sometimes, like shoes long ago left for repair, a sleeper is eventually collected.

SLIGO (Cleveragh)

Sligo Racecourse
Cleveragh
Co. Sligo
Ireland
Tel. (071) 62484

How to get there:
From North: N15
From South: N4
From East: N16
From West: R242
By Rail: Sligo
By Air: Sligo Airport

Sligo races are held in April and at two-day fixtures that include evening meetings in late June and late August.

The course, in a most picturesque setting inside Doorly Park by the River Garavogue, is a somewhat egg-shaped, very tight, mile round right-hander on which the going can be soft at its April meeting.

The track is used for steeplechases, hurdles and flat racing. Since its bends are fairly sweeping it tends to suit some long-striding gallopers that can handle its right-handed configuration. Many trainers feel its well-built fences present jumpers with a very fair test; indeed they are also used for point-to-points. Prestigious races staged on this all-purpose track include the Union Foods Distribution Chase and the Heineken Sligo Chase.

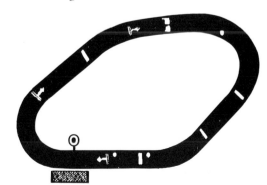

SLIGO: Plan of the course, which is used for steeplechases, hurdles and flat racing.

Sligo, which can be reached by rail, is the principal town of north-west Ireland. The racecourse is only a mile from the centre of Sligo city which Dubliners can reach if they take the N3 to Enniskillen and then the A4 and N16. Enthusiasts from Derry can journey to the course by heading south-west to join the N15 coastal route, while the N17 northwards is the route for Galway residents.

SLOWLY AWAY

Said of a runner that by whipping round, dwelling at the start or just getting off slowly, is left behind its rivals in the early stages of a race.

SMART

Approbative term used to designate a racehorse of considerable ability.

SMUDGE BOX

Colloquial term for the photo-finish camera, dating from the days when the prints were none too distinct.

SNATCHED UP

Said of a runner that in the critical closing stages of a race has to be reined in to prevent it colliding with a runner in its path, so spoiling its chances of a placing.

SOUTHWELL

Southwell Racecourse
Rolleston
Newark
Notts
Tel. (0636) 814481

How to get there:
From North: A1(M), A614
From South: A1(M), A614
From East: A617
From West: A617
By Rail: Nottingham
By Air: Newton Aerodrome

Formerly operating merely as a National Hunt course, Southwell has come into further prominence of late as a venue for all-weather racing.

A racetrack has long been sited at Rolleston, north-east of Nottingham, some three miles from Southwell just off the A614. Southwell's jumping circuit is a 10-furlong, triangular, left-hander with tight bends and seven reasonably easy fences. However, since these are unevenly spaced – two in the long back stretch are close together just before

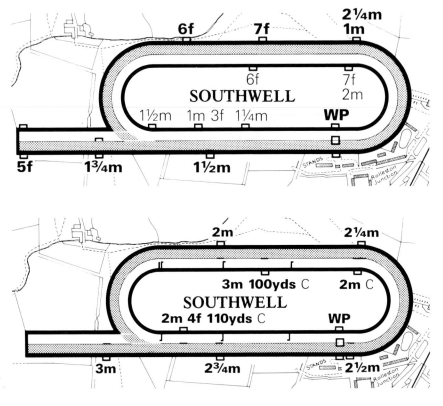

SOUTHWELL: Plans of the Flat (turf and all-weather-course), and the National Hunt (turf and all-weather-course).

the sharp final turn into the short 250 yard run-in – they can present difficulties to long-striding gallopers.

Speedy, adaptable runners do well on this sharp course on which the viewing is perfectly adequate.

Nottingham can be reached from St Pancras by rail and a bus service connects the city to Rolleston. This scenic course is four miles west of Newark and can be conveniently reached on the A617. Junction 29 is the one to make for if travelling on the M1.

The all-weather Fibresand course is 10 furlongs in extent and features a 3-furlong run-in. Flat and hurdle races are run on the same course. A 5-furlong course is provided by a spur while the 6-furlong track takes in two semi-circular bends.

Fibresand, now a well-tried, all-weather racing surface, tends to be fairly taxing to race over so it is worth checking to see whether one's selection at Soouthwell has stamina on its side.

SPECIAL PLACE BETTING

In certain races, usually those in which normal place betting is uneconomical, special place betting odds may be offered by a bookmaker.

SPECIAL PLACE BETTING

When there is an odds-on favourite many bookmakers have special (restrictive) rules on place betting.

SPEED AND TIME RATINGS

These, since they are non-subjective, would seem to offer the backer a precise means of assessing the performance of racehorses.

Although rateable form remains a fundamental factor for consideration, it may often be fallible since slowly run races often give highly misleading indications of the relative abilities of those taking part. The strengths and weaknesses of racehorses are revealed most clearly in rapidly, that is truly run, races, so the backer should concentrate on the claims of horses which have run races in times which are below standard or 'par' for previously recorded performances over set distances on particular courses in certain conditions. He should suspect the credentials of contestants whose impressive-looking runs or even facile victories were achieved in times that proved to be well over par.

To discount most of the runners in a race the backer must put the claims of the particular horses that private handicap ratings urge him to take seriously to the 'time test'. He will look for ratings based on previous races and their times that indicate an animal which has the stamina, and also the speed

to 'run the legs off' its opponents. Moreover, if the race is actually run at a crawl in its early stages, it is comforting to know that, when jockeys have to start 'scrubbing' their horses along, to accelerate and sprint to the finish, one's chosen animal will not be found wanting. By confining their attention to valuable non-handicaps, backers will consider only horses of the highest class – those which possess the ability to quicken the pace at any stage in a race.

Successful professional punters set profitable store by time ratings whose positive indications are corroborated by encouragement from the form book. Indeed, the brand name of Timeform, chosen by the late Phil Bull for the most comprehensive and most highly-respected set of racehorse assessment services, should serve as a constant reminder to backers of how important it is to 'keep time on their side'!

However, there are further considerations to winner-finding based on the clock.

All the variables, such as the going, track topography, fitness, class of race and time of year should as nearly as possible be those which applied when the horse earned its speed figure.

Several respected authorities believe that high weights can cause horses to slow down.

Conversely, lower weights than previously carried may not cause a horse to run appreciably faster than before; natural speed and class are more important.

It is also very possible that many penalized horses which are top-rated on time (especially for gaining facile, as well as fast, victories over short distances) can shrug off their burdens and win again if they rapidly re-encounter ideal conditions.

Moreover, few horses due to run in low-class novice, maiden or selling company will have recorded speed figures of any consequence.

The *Sporting Life's Annual Guide to the Flat* lists the previous season's fastest time performances; those achieved by horses which are four or more years old can then be used as 'bench-marks' by which to gauge when an old campaigner may be approaching its seasonal peak – perhaps in the same month as when the horse ran into form during previous seasons.

Sprints come nearest to providing homogeneous enough conditions to make race timing a profitable activity and yet these are influenced by the draw.

SPEEDY TWO-YEAR-OLDS

Many professional backers look to two-year-olds for sound betting opportunities, believing that horses, which are seldom given too hard a time during their first season, are not likely to have become soured by

YOU PROBABLY KNOW THE COLOURS, BUT CAN YOU NAME THE STABLE?

You don't have to be a racing buff to recognise the famous brands above.

Some of them have a history almost as ancient as the National itself.

But without a close study of the form book, you may not have realised that they're all from the Seagram stable.

You know us best as sponsors of the world's greatest steeplechase.

We just thought you might like to know what we do the rest of the year.

SEAGRAM. THE SPIRIT BEHIND THE NATIONAL.

SPONSORSHIP: The sponsorship of racing is now very big business and it allows for large prizes to be offered to the winners. Even some of the Classic races now have within their title the name of a sponsor.

racing, and therefore tend to run with a degree of consistency. Indeed, for most of their campaign such runners repeatedly take part in truly run sprints, over only a handful of distances, on similar straight sections of racecourses.

The stopwatch often proves useful in assessing the chances of two-year-olds because of their tendency to take part in races that are so truly run: this is less true in the early part of the season. This is also the time when some two-year-olds tend to run far less impressively on racecourses than on their home gallops.

Fortunately, there is one sound way of assessing, right from the start of the flat-racing season, whether certain two-year-olds may merit support. This involves examining its time figures in the *Sporting Life Weekender*. If they show a horse has previously run a race in a time which is below standard or 'par' for older and more mature sprinters running on the same course, then the backer should take note; he should also take the going into account.

A two-year-old with a fast time on its previous outing is worth backing, particularly if the time is faster than an older animal's over the same distance.

❗ SPLONK, THE
Bookmakers' slang for the favourite.

SPONSORSHIP
Increasingly common way by which prize money is increased and publicity gained for the sponsor concerned. One 'psychological' plan involves supporting the runners of race sponsors in the belief that the latter will be most anxious to win back their own money.

Sponsorship has given rise to such bizarre race names as The Plumb Centre Grundfos Pump Selling Handicap or the Ladbrokes' No One Gives You More Handicap!

SPORTING SILK
Old-fashioned term for riding a racehorse.

SPREAD A PLATE
Said of a runner on which a horseshoe has become loose in its seating. The re-shoeing of such a runner can delay the start of its race.

SPRING DOUBLE, THE
Sporting wager involving the Grand National and the Lincoln Handicap.

Few trainers in modern times have ever trained the winners of both races in their careers, let alone in the same year. Dermot Weld did manage to win the 1984 Lincoln with Saving Mercy at 14-1 and to send out Greasepaint to finish second in that year's National at 9-1. One trainer who did win both races, but not in the same year, was Ivor Anthony, with Royal Mail in the 1937 National and Quartier Maitre in the 1940 Lincoln.

SPRINGERS
Horses whose opening prices contract by very large proportions. There are problems over their identification in that fairly small weekday stakes at minor meetings may cause the odds to be slashed, whereas at major meetings such bets are unlikely to affect the market.

Thus, if horses running at top-class meetings have their odds reduced by large proportions, one is fully entitled to regard them as true 'springers' and to scrutinize their claims.

STABLE LADS' ASSOCIATION
4 Dunsmore Way
Midway
Burton-on-Trent
Staffs DE11 7LA
Tel. (0283) 211522

This body watches over some of racing's most vital functionaries. One of its main aims is to improve the economic and social well-being of its members and to represent their interests in any dealings with other organizations.

STABLES IN FORM
Specialist features, such as 'Trainerform' in the *Sporting Life*, indicate which stables are in form or running into or out of form. This is vital information since a trainer producing a winner after a lean spell may well go on to produce several others.

STAKEHOLDERS
Person or body holding the total money allotted and contributed for a race, out of which the owners of the winner and placed horses will be paid.

STAKING
That this is a widely neglected aspect of horserace betting is regrettable since the serious backer should have enough capital never to have to risk too great a proportion of it on any one speculative undertaking.

The best staking plans allow backers to stand the onslaught of an initial losing run, make a rapid recovery and stand sizeable stakes for further bets.

THE START: Here the horses are being led into the starting stalls at Newmarket. By using stalls it is possible for all the horses to have an equal advantage at the begining of the race (although the draw can still play a vitally important role).

STAMINA OF SIRES' PROGENY

An invaluable table showing the average distance in furlongs of races won at three years and upwards by the progeny of all leading stallions over an extensive period is reproduced in such useful publications as *Raceform Notebook* and *Ladbrokes' Companion to Flat Racing*.

This table is especially useful when one is trying to assess whether unrated horses (especially two-year-olds) will be suited by particular distances.

STANDARD TIMES

Once sufficient races have been run over particular distances on racecourses, it is possible for average 'standard' times for these to be calculated. Such figures form useful yardsticks with which to measure the abilities of horses. Times that are well below standard, especially those achieved by juveniles, often augur well for the horse. Sometimes the letter (b) is used to denote such times, while (a) is employed to indicate those slower than standard.

Many time ratings are based on standard times and lists of these appear in *Courseform* published annually by Aesculus Press.

START, THE

Place where a surprising number of races are lost and won. It used to be the scene of much chicanery when horses were merely lined up. Today, even with the widespread use of starting stalls, untoward occurrences can happen.

Fortunately today however, false starts, which characterized and seriously delayed races as prestigious as the Derby in earlier centuries, are extremely rare.

When all is ready for the race to be started, a white flag is hoisted and the field is then said to be 'under starter's orders'. From that moment any horse backed becomes a liability to a bookmaker or backer. Thus, if a horse is withdrawn or fails to start after the white flag has been raised, it cannot be regarded as a non-runner.

STARTING GATE

Featuring elasticated webbing stretched across the course, this was first used in Newmarket in 1897. The fact that it hinged on manual operation led many jockeys to anticipate the actions of starters.

This method (which in its earlier days could catapult jockeys out of the saddle) is still used to start jumping races.

On the flat stalls, introduced at Newmarket on 8 July 1965, are always used.

STARTING STALLS

Method of starting imported from America in the mid-1960s. Interestingly, the actual positioning of the stalls on racetracks can influence the results of certain races. As an aid to starting, they are now taken for granted, such is their efficiency. However, entering them daunts some horses and a few have been so traumatized within them that they have ducked in their desperation to leave them and so have injured their jockeys.

STAYERS

Horses best suited to races of 12 or more furlongs on the flat and to those of 24 to 32 or more over jumps. Sadly, pressure has been applied to reduce the marathon distances over which such races as the Ascot Gold Cup, Goodwood Cup and Doncaster Cup have by tradition been staged.

The Grand National and the Ascot Gold Cup are testimonies to the popularity of stayers' races.

STAYERS' RACES

Events especially designed to put stamina on trial. Over jumps, one thinks of the English, Scottish, Welsh and Irish Grand Nationals. On the flat, the cup races at the Ascot, Goodwood and Doncaster festivals in June, July and September are the best-known marathon contests.

! STEAMER

Bookmaker's slang for a mug punter (i.e. steam-tug-mug) or for a horse whose price considerably contracts in pre-race betting to sugget it is fancied.

STARTER, THE

This official (often an ex-officer) is supplied by the clerk of the scales with a list of the runners and riders and the numbers they have drawn. He ensures the field line up in order of these numbers, with the lowest number on the left.

If the tapes are broken by a National Hunt jockey or his mount or if the starter considers that through a fault in the starting gate a fair start has not taken place, this official can order the jockey to return to the post by signalling to his assistant who stands about 100 yards from the post and who then waves a red flag.

STARTER'S ORDERS

Expression to denote the fact that the runners are under the control and direction of the starter.

The horses having gone to the start, the roll is called as are the numbers allotted to jockeys' mounts in the draw (if appropriate).

STEEPLECHASING (See Mallow)

This to many racegoers is the finest racing spectacle. While no longer actually staged cross-country from steeple to steeple, on such courses as Punchestown it still resembles this. Its blue riband is the Cheltenham Gold Cup.

On racecourses, a steeplechase might be defined as a race over fences of a stipulated length as well as open ditches and (according to Jockey Club rules) a water jump.

The first steeplechase took place at Buttevant in Ireland in 1772; the first organized steeplechase meeting was held in 1830 at St Albans.

STEWARDS

Four stewards are appointed to oversee a race meeting's organization. They have power in exceptional circumstances to abandon a meeting, to abandon a race or to postpone any races to a more appropriate time. The stewards have control over all stands, rooms, enclosures and other places used for the purpose of the meeting and have the power to exclude any person from these areas. Some racegoers support runners owned by officiating stewards.

STEWARDS' ENQUIRY

This is arranged should the stewards of a race meeting wish to enquire into the circumstances of an objection made to them or into a matter which may appear to them to constitute a breach of the rules of racing. Such enquiries are not as rare as some novice racegoers might believe so one should never immediately throw away one's losing tote or bookmaker's ticket.

STICK

Colloquial term for a jockey's whip.

STOP AT A WINNER

Instruction to a bookmaker from a backer. It is a conditional bet since the making of subsequent wagers is contingent on the loss of previous ones. As this instruction suggests the betting stops with a winning selection.

STRAIGHT

Said of a horse whose appearance in the paddock suggests it is fully fit and well and likely to do itself full justice on the racecourse.

STEWARDS: The four stewards who are appointed to oversee every race meeting's organization have total control over the running of every race. This print of 1847 shows the runners parading prior to the race in front of the steward's stand at Ascot.

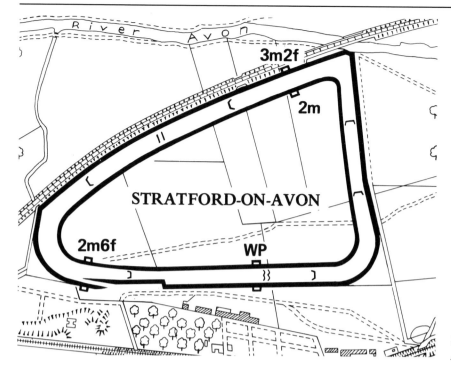

STRATFORD-ON-AVON: Plan of the course.

STRATFORD-ON-AVON

Stratford Racecourse
Luddington Road
Stratford-on-Avon
Warks CV37 9SE
Tel. (0789) 267949

How to get there:
From North: A3400
From South: M40, A3400
From East: A46
From West: A46
By Rail: Stratford-on-Avon
By Air: Helicopter facilities

With its view of the bard's resting place at Holy Trinity and of some pleasant countryside, Stratford-on-Avon's racecourse is a pleasant place to spend a Thursday or a Saturday afternoon.

It is well-managed, especially by its ground staff, and is popular with racing professionals and parties of racegoers, a great number of whom seem to speak with Welsh accents.

The track itself is a fairly triangular, tight left-hander that extends for 1 1/4 miles. It is largely flat except in parts of its back straight. The eight fences, which include a water jump, well-positioned in front of the stands, are not terribly testing.

Unusually, there is only one fence in the home straight and since the run-in is only 200 yards, horses need to be handily placed as they round the final well-banked, rather sweeping, turn which is far less tight than the top bend. The latter is close to the 2-and 3-miles starts in a spot quite remote from the stands.

The course lies a mile outside Stratford off the A439 Evesham road. The A46 is an ideal route from north or south: motorists from the latter direction will now find this connects with a recently completed stretch of the M40. The A422 is a useful route for those arriving in Stratford from the west who, after Alcester, should proceed along the A46.

The opposite bookend to Stratford's significant Saturday meeting in October is the final Saturday in June when the Horse and Hound Champion Hunters' Chase, staged in front of a large crowd, effectively closes the jumping season.

Another important hunter 'chase is staged at a Friday evening meeting prior to 'Horse and Hound' day in June (which actually features a parade by huntsmen and the Warwickshire pack of foxhounds); this is the John Corbet Cup. Other Stratford races recall Garrick, the Shakespearean actor, and the course's close involvement with racecourses as diverse as Warrnambool in Australia and Oslo in Norway.

Stratford is memorable for its competitive racing, sporting atmosphere and an excellent view of the action, even from the cheapest enclosure.

STRETCH

Length of track, as on back stretch (straight), or term used to describe a horse that takes long strides in 'stretching out' really well.

STRIKE RATE

Ratio of successes to failures. Trainers' and jockeys' strike rates (ratio of winners to runners at certain tracks during certain periods and in relation to certain types of horses) often appear in the *Racing Post, Sporting Life* and in annually published guides to racing.

STYLE OF RUNNING

Several publications – for example *Timeform* and *Superform* – reveal how a horse has run to advantage in the past. Knowing when and how a horse runs best can help the backer decide whether the course on which it is due to run will favour its style of running.

SUNDAY RACING

Common in France and increasingly popular in Ireland, this is yet to be a regular feature of the British racing scene. It is a subject over which arguments still tend to become rather heated and an issue on which the racing industry in Britain is very divided.

SUPER HEINZ

Seven selections giving 120 bets. It is, in essence, a seven-horse Yankee with 21 doubles, 35 trebles, 35 fourfolds, 21 fivefolds, 7 sixfolds and 1 sevenfold.

SUSPENSION

Fate meted out to participants in racing adjudged to have broken the rules of the sport. Most frequently it is suffered by jockeys, but trainers can have their licences suspended and owners can be 'warned off' the turf for a stipulated period.

SWALLOWING THE TONGUE

Breathing problem which causes horses to fail to run up to their form. Like many tipsters the author has wished he could perform this feat, having once tipped a dead horse to win the Grand National.

SWEEPSTAKES

A sweepstake is a race in which the entrance fees, forfeits, subscriptions or other contributions of three or more owners go to the winner or placed horses. Any such race is a sweepstake when money or another prize is added.

Other unofficial sweepstakes are organized on races like the Derby by racing enthusiasts at workplaces.

In former years there was a major nationwide sweepstake for the Irish Derby and proceeds from it did much to improve health care in the Republic.

SYNDICATES

Racehorse-owning syndicates usually involve far from wealthy individuals and have been the financial salvation of many a small trainer.

SYNDICATION OF STALLIONS

A former racehorse's 'capitalization' into forty shares, this number being taken to represent the mares a stallion may well cover in a season. Such is their value, many champion sires are syndicated.

SYSTEMS

Fred Astaire is said to have tried many different systems; all showed a profit – for about two weeks. After years of systematic assaults on the bookmakers, Fred finally came up with the ultimate system – to back the first two winners and then go home!

The many systems which feature the inappropriate application of crude generalization about past events to unique coming ones naturally find favour with bookmakers. Many systems involve the support of a market leader, a designation, as R.W. Griffiths has reminded us 'which only operates within the context of one race, outside which it has no valid existence'.

Apart from backing favourites, most of the more plausible systems (which enrich not just bookmakers, but also those who sell them to the gullible in genuine or pirated editions) involve various interpretations of form, the weights horses carry, the selections of newspaper corespondents, betting forecast quotations or the time factor.

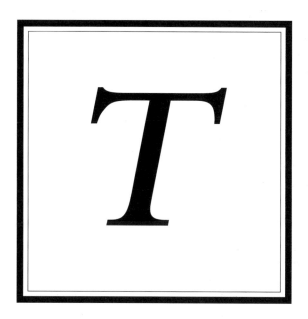

TATTERSALLS

Terrace House
Newmarket
Suffolk CB8 9BT
Tel. (0638) 665931

This firm, founded at the end of the eighteenth century when the development of the English thoroughbred was in some crucial early stages, is now world famous for its bloodstock sales. Tattersalls' British sales are now confined to Newmarket where they take place during specific periods throughout the year. In October the sales are devoted exclusively to yearlings.

Tattersalls' Irish operation is based at Fairyhouse, Co. Meath, (Tel. (3531) 256777) and sales take place in February and for three days in September (for yearlings). There is a 'Derby' sale in June, and in December a Breeding Stock sale. National Hunt sales take place in August and November.

Tattersalls is also the name of a racecourse enclosure which is separated from the members' by some rails over which leading bookmakers ply their trade, and it gives its name to a stylish check shirt sported by many racegoers.

Tattersalls are also generous race sponsors, of for example York Musidora Stake and the Cleveley Park Stakes run at Newmarket.

TATTERSALLS' RULES ON BETTING

Betting rules compiled by Tattersalls Committee, the only body with the authority to settle all questions relating to bets and any matters arising directly or indirectly out of wagers or gaming transactions on horse racing, to adjudicate on all cases of default and, at their discretion, to report defaulters to the Jockey Club.

Enquiries should be addressed to Mr Peter Guard, PO Box 13719 Hatherley Road, Reading, Berks RG1 5QD. Tel. (0734) 65402.

TAUNTON

Taunton Racecourse
Orchard Portman
Taunton
Somerset TA3 7BL
Tel. (0823) 337172

How to get there:
From North: M5
From South: M5, B3170
From East: A358, A378
From West: A38, A358
By Rail: Taunton
By Air: Helicopter facilities

TATTERSALLS: This print by 'Lib' from an 1887 issue of Vanity Fair *shows the Tattersalls sale at Newmarket, an annual event since the late eighteenth century.*

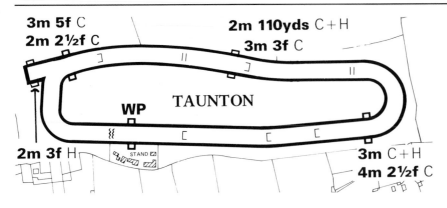

TAUNTON: *Plan of the course.*

Taunton is very much a country racecourse which affords fine views of the Blackdown Hills to the south and the Quantocks to the north. It lies more than two miles south of the town from which it takes its name.

It is a long, oval-shaped, right-handed course of 10 furlongs in extent which, in essence, consists of two long straights and two rather tight, but still reasonably easy, semi-circular bends. There are eight unformidable fences on what is rather misleadingly called Taunton's 'circuit' whose most taxing feature is a final 3-furlong stretch of rising ground.

The short 150-yard run-in is encountered once the final three fences in the finishing straight (which are visible from the stands) have been negotiated.

Past course winners should be supported on this rather singular racecourse.

Of the principal races staged at Taunton, two are memorable affairs commemorating Gay Sheppard and John Thorne while, interestingly, a Hangover Selling Hurdle has also been contested.

This informal, friendly racecourse (on which pleasant picnics can be taken in its central enclosure) is readily accessible since it is close to junction 25 of the M5. Those arriving by road will find that the track is quietly, even sleepily, situated south of Taunton off the B3170.

Rail travellers need to depart from Paddington for Taunton station and thence take a taxi-ride of approximately three and a half miles to Orchard Portman itself, or rather the estate of this name on which, in 1927, the track was laid out by the fifth Viscount Portman.

Air travellers should note that, with prior permission, helicopters can land on Taunton's runway.

However they arrive racegoers will find themselves in a picturesque setting among some genial jumping enthusiasts.

TAX ON

Since serious backers seek to profit from the racing game, they are more likely to attend race meetings where tax is not imposed. If betting off-course, again for sound financial reasons, they will usually elect to pay tax when making their wagers.

The alternative is to have the appropriate proportion deducted from one's winnings, which will be a much larger sum. The backer who sees betting as a serious business venture should always pay 'tax on' when making off-course wagers.

TELEPHONE INFORMATION SERVICES

At premium rates of 36p per minute off-peak and 48p at peak times, these provide racing tips, commentaries and results, as well as details of which horses have been top-rated for impending races by well-known form assessment services. All these services use recorded messages that are regularly updated. Strict regulations govern the operation and advertising of telephone information services for horse racing.

TELEVISION COVERAGE (See Racing by Satellite)

Thanks to the advent of satellite television, this is now extensive in thousands of licensed betting offices. Indeed, live fixtures have been beamed into these of races being staged as far away as Hong Kong, to the great delight, no doubt, of Chinese customers.

Races televised by both ITV and BBC are also screened in betting shops, and there are two handbooks, *The Channel Four Book of Horse Racing* and *The Racing Year* – the latter a month by month guide to the events covered by Channel 4. Two other books, *My Most Memorable Races* and *Calling the Horses*, recount the reminiscences of Peter Bromley and Peter O'Sullevan of the BBC who recall the many broadcast races they have commentated upon.

TESTING

Term used to describe a demanding configurational feature of a racecourse. It can also refer to steeplechase fences or to going that is so soft or heavy as to constitute a severe test of stamina, courage, jumping skill or ability to cope with sodden ground.

❢ THICK 'UN

Slang for a large bet.

THIRSK

Thirsk Racecourse
Station Road
Thirsk
North Yorkshire YO7 1QL
Tel. (0845) 522276

How to get there:
From North: A1, A19
From South: A1, A19
From East: A170
From West: A61
By Rail: Thirsk
By Air: Helicopter facilities

Thirsk's extremely scenic racecourse once had a link with top-class racing through a Classic trial, a Guineas rehearsal, that was once staged on the fine old grassland of this extremely pleasant track.

The demise of this particular race was most unfortunate. From its inception in 1948, it attracted high-class horses and was won in its time by Alycidon, Nimbus (the 1949 2000 Guineas and Derby winner), Sweet Solera (victorious in both the 1000 Guineas and the Oaks), and more recently, by High Top (winner of the first of the colts' Classics of the 1972 season).

Fortunately an even more historic race has survived: the Hambleton Cup Handicap, a 12-furlong affair that is contested in early September.

This event, which was staged before racing commenced on its present site in 1855 and was formerly a 2-mile Cesarewitch trial, is a reminder to racegoers that Northern racing folk used to hold meetings at what was once their 'headquarters' at Hambleton. Noteworthy too is the perhaps better known Thirsk Hunt Cup, a fairly valuable mile handicap contested in early May.

In fact, racing does not take place all that frequently on this fairly flat, quite sharp, left-handed oval track which has rather a small circumference of ten furlongs or so. The bends at Thirsk are not as difficult to negotiate as a glance at the Ordnance Survey map might suggest; nonetheless, speedy, adaptable types relish a run on this track on which long-striding animals or awkward runners can sometimes fail to settle.

Thirsk is a very fair track, popular with both trainers and jockeys, with some of its races contested by sizeable fields which often also include one or two 'raiders' from southern stables.

The turf at Thirsk provides a good racing surface on which the going is seldom extreme. An irrigation system ensures that firm ground, which once caused fields to cut up fairly appreciably during dry spells, is now more rare.

As for the course, it is a straightforward affair that in appearance is rather reminiscent of a paper clip. Basically, the straight sprint course of 6 furlongs and 216 yards, which also allows races to be staged over the minimum distance, is rather more undulating than the final straight of the round course into which it runs just under four furlongs out.

In the large fields that frequently line up for sprint races, those drawn high seem to have an edge when the stalls are on the stands side (where the runners tend to converge), an advantage increased on soft ground, as a better surface only involves a narrow strip near the stands rail.

Horses tackling 2 miles at Thirsk also travel along the straight spur that allows sprints to be staged. On joining the round course after just over two furlongs, they encounter ground which features undulations that are even more gradual than any they have

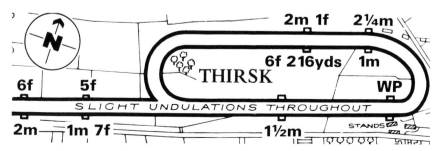

THIRSK : Plan of the course.

already negotiated on the spur. Just before the final stages of the run-in, prior to passing the finishing post for the first time, the runners pass the point from which races over 12 furlongs are started. The rest of the round course is virtually flat. It takes them round the first of Thirsk's bends which is more gradual and less sharp and semi-circular than its successor.

Thirsk's back straight, along which races over 8 furlongs and 6 furlongs 216 yards are started, extends for approximately three furlongs. Finally, once a fairly tight final bend has been rounded, all that remains is the run-in of just under four furlongs which undulates along its complete length.

The railway station, a half a mile walk away from the track, lies on the mainline from King's Cross. Station Road is 1 mile to the west of Thirsk and can be reached via the A61 from Ripon or the A170 from Pickering and Scarborough. Those arriving from the south will find that Thirsk lies 6 miles east of the A1. From York the A19 should be taken.

Despite the fact that it is not particularly close to large population centres, Thirsk is well attended and often patronized by southern professionals, even though it is over 210 miles from the capital. Some of these individuals arrive in helicopters that can land on the course's hockey pitch, while those in fixed-wing aircraft can land at Allanbrooke Barracks at Topcliffe, close to Thirsk (Tel. (0845) 577371).

Much has been spent on course improvements, including new stands in the enclosures.

THREE AND A BIT

Bookmakers' reference to 4-1.

THURLES

Thurles Racecourse
Thurles
Co. Tipperary
Ireland
Tel. (0504) 22253

How to get there:
From North: N62
From South: N8, N62
From East: N8
From West: R503
By Rail: Thurles
By Air: Light Aircraft facilities

As the town of Thurles and its racecourse are bounded by the Silvermines and Devil's Bit

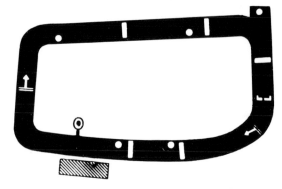

THURLES: Plan of the course, an undulating, oblong, sharpish affair of 10 furlongs.

mountains, there is some splendid scenery to be enjoyed. Those travelling to the course (which lies to the west of the town off the R498) from Limerick to the west should take the R503, whilst Dubliners should head south-westwards on the N7 to Port Laoise and then southwards to Thurles on the N8. Rail travellers should alight at Thurles station. Aircraft landing facilities are also available on-course.

As for the track itself, this is yet another Irish right-hander, an undulating, oblong, sharpish affair of 10 furlongs in extent whose new, slightly smaller fences are rated a 'great addition' by racing professionals. Two of these are positioned in the finishing straight (well in view of the stands).

The 2 1/2-mile PZ Mower Chase for six-year-olds and above is probably the best-known race staged at Thurles; this is contested on a Wednesday in mid-February and such is its class (it has listed status), that it provides pointers to Irish prospects at both Cheltenham and Liverpool. Another well-known Thurles race is the 2 miles 6 furlong Seskin Chase, also run in mid-February, while a race that accompanies it, the Devil's Bit Handicap Hurdle, recalls an ancient local myth.

TICKETS, BETTING (See Ring Inspector) These are issued as a receipt by bookmakers or tote employees and have to be shown if payment of any winnings is required. If a backer loses a winning ticket issued on-course, he should inform the clerk who, along with the number of this 'receipt', will have recorded the details of the transaction in question. If these details are accurately reported and, if after a decent time interval, the sum involved has 'slept' in the bookmaker's satchel, i.e. significantly failed to be collected, payment may be made to the backer, despite his failure to provide documentary evidence. Disputes involving missing betting tickets can sometimes be settled by a ring inspector.

Regular racegoers often inscribe details of the wagers they have made with bookmakers on betting tickets they receive once their transactions have been entered in bookmakers' field books.

TIME (See Speed and Time Ratings)

TIMEFORM (See Speed and Time Ratings) Pioneering form assessment service which currently serves the backer via several specialist offerings.

The most comprehensive and expensive are its separate annual directories of flat racehorses and National Hunt campaigners. Each week an updated 'black book' combines ratings and commentaries on racehorses. Racecards covering particular meetings are also available.

A recent addition to the Timeform stable has

been *Perspective*, an interpretative weekly form book that is despatched to subscribers every Wednesday.

What Timeform's expert staff consider to be the day's best wagers are passed on to subscribers by a phone service and the information this provides includes advice on staking..This world-famous publisher of information on horseracing was created by the late Phil Bull, a coalminer's son born near Pontefract, who first based his conclusions on the ability of racehorses solely on his timings of their performances. Copies of his *Mathematics of Betting* are widely sought by collectors of racing's most collectable racing books along with wartime editions of Timeform's *Annual Guides to Racehorses,* which are extremely scarce and valuable.

Timeform has also been active in race sponsorship, notably through its charity day at York which raised well in excess of a million pounds in the first twenty years of its staging.

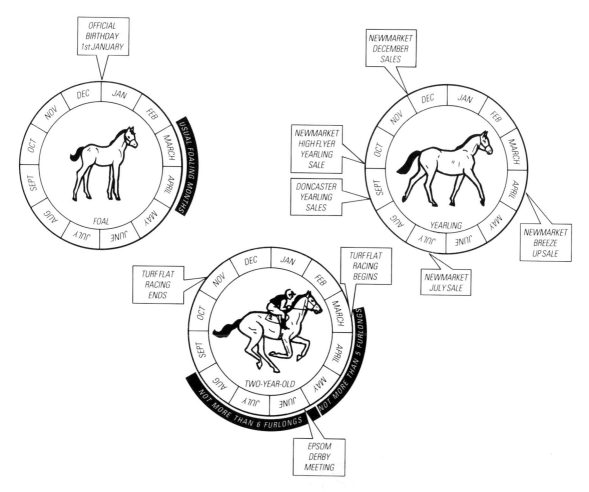

TIME OF FOALING (see over page): This diagram shows the times of foaling and birthdays. It shows that the official birthday for all horses is 1 January even though they might have been born much later than that.

Senior Timeform race reader Jim McGrath who combines his duties with television presentation for Channel Four, and also pens a regular newspaper column as Hotspur of the *Daily Telegraph*.

A visionary who first envisaged many developments in racing (such as camera patrol of runners) which are now well-established, Phil Bull has made more impression on thoroughbred racing than anyone else this century. Through Timeform he certainly made the art of winner-finding into something approaching a precise science.

TIMEFORM RATINGS

These are so widely respected they are featured in sales catalogues and used to allow comparisons to be made between recent winners of prestigious races and horses formerly successful in these.

Timeform ratings, which aim to give accurate information as to the merit of every horse racing under Jockey Club rules, appear in pounds; the number of these accorded a runner is equivalent to the weight its performance would entitle it to receive in an average Free Handicap; thus a horse Timeform rates at 119 is one regarded as worthy of carrying 8st 7lbs.

TIME OF FOALING

In the Northern Hemisphere the age of a thoroughbred is taken to be 1 January of the year in which it was foaled (see diagram on previous page).

As the usual foaling months in the major breeding centres are March and April, most of the two-year-olds that run when the British flat-racing season opens early in the spring are, in fact, officially two years old, even though some may be two months older than that. Understandably, such animals should be better able to acquit themselves early in the season than their rivals which, since born in the summer or the autumn following the customary foaling period, will only have had twenty-one months or even a year and a half in which to have grown and matured.

Winners-to-runners percentages by foaling dates for two-year-olds, covering a recent whole season, read as follows:

January foaling	12.3%
February foaling	9.4%
March foaling	9.6%
April foaling	8.3%
May foaling	7.7%
June foaling	6.9%

Clearly these statistics indicate that it is essential to look for that little extra age and experience when it comes to supporting two-year-olds.

Foaling dates also provide a useful key to the enigma of later, under-exposed two-year-olds. Interestingly, another 'key' to unlocking such performers' prospects can be found in the average distances of races won by their sires' progeny. Such data can be found in *Ladbrokes' Pocket Companion*.

TIMES, RECORD (See Best Times)

TIPPERARY

Tipperary Racecourse
Limerick Junction
Co. Tipperary
Southern Ireland
Tel. (062) 51357

How to get there:
From North: N8, R497
From South: N8, N662
From East: N74

TIPPERARY: Plan of the course.

From West: N24
By Rail: Limerick Junction
By Air: Helicopter facilities

Tipperary's racecourse is scenic and rural, yet managed by a forward-looking executive. Indeed, it was the first Irish course to introduce a new style of steeplechase fence with the result that the number of fallers that used to mar its meetings was drastically reduced. Backers thus now stand far more of a chance on this flat, round course that extends left-handed for 10 furlongs and presents jumpers with six obstacles.

The circuit is a good galloping one on which, especially at fixtures held in late February, the going can be very soft. However, it is a very different story at the track's midsummer meetings.

Horses wishing to foot it well round the Tipperary circuit are at an advantage if they are drawn near the inside of the track, while on the straight, flat sprint course those allocated middle numbers enjoy the edge.

The track itself, in being situated near Limerick Junction, is accessible via the railway station of this name. It is some 112 miles from Dublin from where it can be reached by following the N7 to Port Laoise, proceeding west to Cashel, taking the N74 to Tipperary and then continuing further westwards along the N24 road to Limerick. Racegoers from Cork should head northwards to Mitchelstown and then follow signposts to Galbally and Tipperary via the R662. Those arriving by helicopter can land on-course, while fixed-wing aircraft can be accommodated at Limerick/Shannon airport, some forty miles away.

The major races run at Tipperary are the listed Dawn Milk Stakes and the Coolmore Kilfrush Sprint.

TIPS (See Inside Information; At the Flip)
Advice given regarding possible winners. This term also relates to the tic-tac signal for 5-4 which involves touching one's right-hand wrist with the tips of the fingers of one's left hand; the term is also used by bookmakers.

TISHY

A betting forecast for each race that an expert supplies to racecourse bookmakers to help them frame their opening prices.

❢ TOM MIX

Slang for six or 6-1.

TOOLS

Pieces of equipment used by a racecourse bookmaker. These consist of a tripod which supports a 'silver' tray for small change and a board (bearing his trading name at the top) with clips on its sides to hold the list of runners for each race, a leather satchel, known as a 'hod' and a large umbrella.

TOP MAN

Premier tic-tac and often independent operator who positions himself at the end of the stand nearest the Silver Ring, from where he acts as a liaison officer for course bookmakers, passing on prices sent up to him from the floorman in Tattersalls to the cheaper enclosures and placing wagers for all those who wish to use his services. A joy to watch, this key figure is a colourful, highly-skilled and indispensable part of racecourse bookmaking operations.

❢ TOP OF THE CRUST

Bookmaker's term for 5-2.

TOP TRAINERS

Expression used for racehorse handlers who achieve pre-eminence by virtue of prize money won in a season, number of wins registered in a particular season or over a specified period at a particular racecourse. Most usefully, such pre-eminence takes the form of a winners to runners ratio.

TOP WEIGHTS

Horses carrying more weight than their rivals. In handicaps this will have resulted from a previously noteworthy performance.

Horses allotted top weights are likely to be less inconvenienced if these have to be humped over short distances of solid ground. Thus, in-form and racefit sprinters can often defy top weights if they have to carry these on firm going.

Backers should always search for the reason why the handicapper has accorded a particular runner its top weight.

TOTE BETTING

This has recently been extended to include the tote 'Trio' which, as its name suggests, involves forecasting the first three horses to finish in certain races. Unlike a Tricast offered by a bookmaker, this wager allows the nominated horses to finish in any order.

A video, *Lady in Red* (red being the colour of the uniform worn by its employees), has been produced by the tote to provide a 'window' on its operations.

You can bet Win, Each Way or Place only

We pay Place dividends on:
1,2,3 and 4 in handicaps of 16 runners or more;
1,2,3 in all races of 8 runners or more;
1,2 in races of 5,6 and 7 runners.

Look for the WIN, PLACE and DUAL FORECAST odds displayed on closed circuit Tote television.

TOTE DUAL FORECASTS

... on all races with three or more runners. Just pick two horses to finish first or second - it does not matter in which order they finish - first and second, second and first - *YOU STILL WIN.*

You get your money back in the Win Place and Forecast pools if you bet on a horse which subsequently is withdrawn without coming under starter's orders.

The minimum unit stake on the Win, Place, and Dual Forecast pools is £2, but £1 Each Way is accepted in all enclosures EXCEPT the Members, and £1 Dual Forecast combination bets in all enclosures.

TOTE JACKPOT

Pick the winner of races 1 to 6 at the Jackpot meeting.If there are no outright winners the balance of the pool is carried forward.

TOTE PLACEPOT

Pick a horse to be placed in races 1 to 6. If there are fewer than 5 runners you name the winner, otherwise, any horse on which a place dividend is declared qualifies. The Placepot operates at ALL meetings.

- Jackpot and Placepot dividends are declared to a £1 unit stake. The minimum investment per line is £1
- Permutations of 10p and upwards are accepted for total stakes of not less than £1.
- In the Jackpot and Placepot, non-runners are put on the S.P. favourite. If there is more than one favourite, you are on the one with the lowest racecard number.

If you are unable to cash a winning ticket, post it to:

Horserace Totalisator Board (Dept. T), Tote House, 74 Upper Richmond Road, London SW15 2SU.

We regret late pay tickets cannot be cashed in person.

TOTE BETTING: *As can be seen by this advert, the tote offers a variety of ways to win a possible fortune.*

The tote channelled £23 million back into racing between 1986 and 1991, mainly out of takings from the 'standard' offerings (shown above) that the tote has, for many seasons, made available to racegoers.

In 1991, a course-to-course service was further introduced to allow racegoers to bet into the win, place, dual forecast, jackpot and placepot pools at the meetings this arrangement involves.

TOUT

Gallops-watcher who passes on information for money. *Chambers Dictionary* also intriguingly defines such an individual as 'a low fellow who hangs about racing stables to pick up profitable information'.

Such information can be 'touted' or used as an obtrusive sales pitch by racecourse tipsters or hustlers (like the Lemon Drop Kid in a Damon Runyon story) who persuade gullible strangers to entrust him with cash to make their bets for them.

TOWCESTER

Towcester Racecourse
Easton Neston
Towcester
Northants NN12 7HS
Tel. (0327) 50969

How to get there:
From North: M1, A5
From South: M1, M40
From East: A428
From West: A45(M)
By Rail: Northampton
By Air: Helicopter facilities

The truly rural and Corinthian flavour of racing at Towcester is certainly suggested by the fact that one of its principal races has been the Empress of Austria Hunters' Chase, the highlight of a May meeting.

The racecourse was originally laid out on a picturesque Northamptonshire country estate.

The course is square and extends for approaching a mile and three-quarters. Even though its back stretch is downhill, the circuit ends in an uphill 6-furlong slog which is understandably very punishing to race over when rain makes the clay racing surface extremely sticky. Thus many front runners tire and are overhauled on the 200-yard or so run-in.

In the summer firm ground can prevail and this is one further reason for checking that one's selection is a stayer and a good enough jumper not to be unsettled by two tricky fences in the downhill back stretch.

One of the charms of this track is the fine aerial view one can obtain from its lofty stand of horses running over the stamina-sapping ten-fence circuit that, for good measure, is a right-hander.

The track is nine miles south-west of Northampton and lies one mile south-east of the town from which it takes its name. It can be conveniently approached via the A43 which can be reached from the M40. The M1 runs nearby; leave at junction 13 if coming from the south, or junction 16 if travelling from the north.

Taxis run from Milton Keynes, which is eleven miles away, and Northampton, nine miles away – whose stations can be reached from King's Cross. Helicopters can be accommodated on-course.

Lying only sixty miles from London, Towcester attracts good crowds. Many of its fixtures coincide with public holidays, including a two-day Easter meeting featuring the Schilizzi series of races.

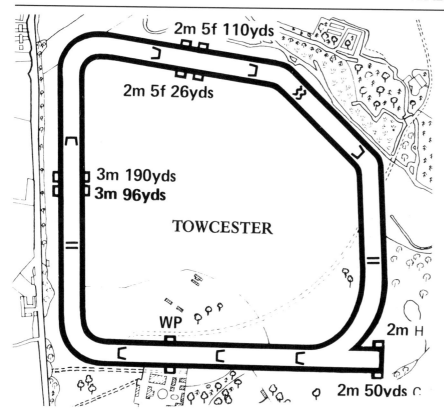

2m 5f 110yds

2m 5f 26yds

3m 190yds
3m 96yds

TOWCESTER

WP

2m H

2m 50yds

TOWCESTER: Plan of the course.

TRADE BETS

In the trade of racecourse bookmaking, it is usual to give and take the 'bits' or to 'pinch the oddments'. Backers can ask for this concession and may be obliged by being given odds like 100-8, rather than the less generous 12-1.

A list of prices quoted to the public together with their more generous 'trade' equivalents is given below:

Public	Trade		
11–2:	100–18	50–9	25–41/2
6–1:	100–16	50–8	25–4
7–1:	100–14	50–7	25–31/2
8–1:	100–12	50–6	25–3
9–1:	100–11	50–51/2	
11–1:	100–9	50–41/2	
12–1	100–8	50–4	
14–1:	100–7	50–31/2	
16–1:	100–6	50–3	
33–1:	100–3	50–11/2	

TRADE BETS: This table shows the difference between the prices quoted to the public, and those that are quoted to the 'trade'.

TRAGEDIES OF THE TURF

Whether involving the deaths of much-loved champions like Dawn Run or of lady jockeys like the gallant Jane Thompson, the suicide of such household names as Fred Archer, the disablement of horses and riders, or cruel blows which, for example, have prevented the Grand National being won by horses like Crisp, owners like the Queen Mother or jockeys like Lord Mildmay (who twice had certain victory denied him), these tragedies are part and parcel of a sport in which mere participation involves an element of risk.

Fortunately, the annals of the turf feature quite as many triumphs over tragedy as tragedies themselves. Equine cast-offs and former cripples have not only raced again, but triumphed, as have jockeys written off by doctors or doubters who felt they would never regain their nerve or conquer such problems as alcoholism. Moreover some trainers have distinguished themselves despite being wheelchair-bound.

Dick Francis often features both tragedy and triumph over tragedy in his racing bestsellers, and perhaps a racegoer having the courage to return to the racecourse after a losing day is in a small way victorious over tragedy.

TRAGEDIES OF THE TURF: Bob Champion on Aldaniti, seen here winning the 1981 Grand National after cancer threatened to cut short his life.

Probably the most celebrated defeat of tragedy was the victory of Bob Champion on Aldaniti in the Grand National after cancer looked likely to cut short his life.

TRAINERFORM

Most useful *Sporting Life* feature that indicates precisely those stables in form or which are running into, or out of, this.

TRAINERS AS BUSINESSPEOPLE OF HABIT

This conception of racehorse handlers has led the authors of several specialist publications, for example, *Trainers' Review* or *Dark Secrets of the Turf* (published by Rosters) to analyse the habitual ploys of these highly important members of the racing industry.

There is no question that some racehorse trainers seek to farm certain races, and like to win at particular tracks for certain owners, at particular times of year, and with certain types of racehorses.

Trainers' winners to runners ratios at particular tracks, as well as details of horses successful in races staged on them in previous years, are often well worth scrutinizing, as trainers do often proceed in methodical and sometimes very predictable ways.

TRAINERS, STRATEGIES (See Trainers As Businesspeople of habit)

Many racehorse handlers are very methodical businesspeople who adopt a seasonal strategy that varies little from year to year. Knowing exactly what this involves can be a great boon to the backer.

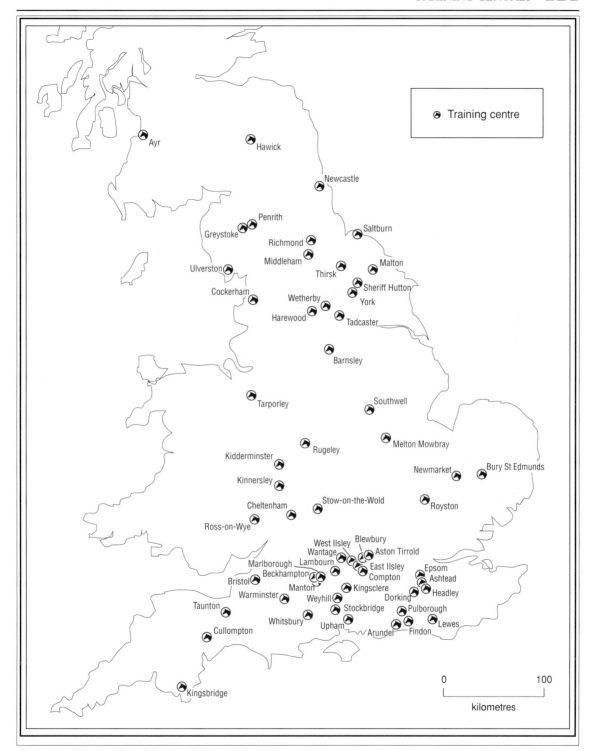

TRAINING CENTRES: This map show the distribution of training centres arouind the country.

TRAINING CENTRES

These are scattered throughout the British Isles, so a knowledge of them enables the backer to spot horses lining up at their local tracks or travelling possibly significant long distances to courses. A runner's training centre is indicated on the racecard.

Especially at the start of a season, racehorses from certain training centres can be particularly forward.

Great Western Railway.

EPSOM RACES

ON MONDAY, MAY 25TH, 1868.

Lewis's Excursion Train Will Run from Shrewsbury at 10.55 a.m. to

LONDON

FARES FOR THE DOUBLE JOURNEY

COV. CARRIAGE 12/-

FIRST CLASS 24s.

Returning on the following Thursday, May 28th, from the Paddington
Station, London at 10-30 a.m.

Excursion Office, 7, Pride Hill, Shrewsbury

J. Edmunds Printer, Blists Hill, Madeley, Salop

*TRAINS TO THE
RACES: Even as early as
1868, racegoers were able
to travel to the races by rail,
as this early poster shows.*

TRAIN ON

Said of a three-year-old that has continued to thrive,
grow and mature into an even more capable racehorse.
Many two-year-olds fail to do this and thus do not
live up to the promise of their first season's form.

TRAINS TO THE RACES

These, including British Rail's racing-orientated rail
travel promotions, are detailed in the racing dailies.

TRALEE

Tralee Racecourse
Ballybeggan Park
Tralee
Co. Kerry
Ireland
Tel. (066) 26188

How to get there:
From North: N69
From South: N70
From East: N21
From West: R558, R560
By Rail: Tralee
By Air: Light Aircraft facilities; Farranfore Airport

Tralee dominates Irish horseracing for a whole week during late August/early September, which coincides with the International Rose of Tralee contest.

The Rose of Tralee, winner of the beauty contest, is, of course, required to attend Tralee races that their organizers see as the centre-piece of the Rose of Tralee festival!

Whatever its focus, the festival of Kerry has become synonymous with Tralee races which, until the former's development, were but a pale shadow of their present splendour.

The festival action now begins on a Sunday amidst colourful floral displays. Major races which have been run during the six-day fixture include the Denny Havasnack Plate which, over the years, has thrown up some exciting jumping prospects, the Tralee Handicap Chase, the Rose of Tralee Ladies'

Race (which has had Indian, American and French, as well as Irish and English winners), the Denny Gold Medal Chase, the Tralee Gold Cup, the Kerry Petroleum Cup and the Shell Handicap.

The 9-furlong track is sharpish, undulating and essentially circular with six obstacles. The steeplechase course runs inside the flat and hurdle course and its final feature is a taxing steep uphill climb to the finish. Tralee is a course which makes considerable demands on the stamina of those who run on it, especially when the ground is soft, as it can be during the odd rainy August.

There is usually plenty of drama and entertainment at the five-day race meeting to add to that provided by the resident Folk Theatre company, the firework displays, carnivals, processions and street dancing.

The racecourse is only half a mile from Tralee station, while air travellers can be accommodated, if appropriate, on a 200-metre on-course airstrip if they are previously granted permission (Tel. (066) 36148). Farranfore regional airport is 16 miles away.

Motorists coming from Cork should take the N22 north-westwards, from Dublin the N7 westwards towards Limerick, and from there the N21 or the N69 coastal route via Tarbert.

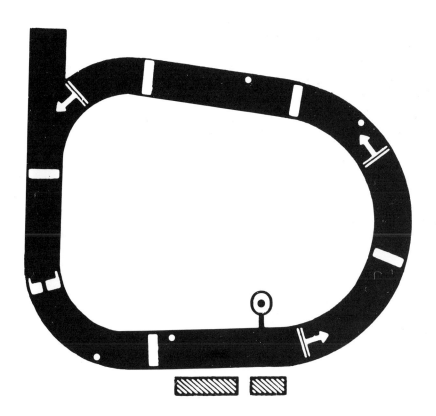

TRALEE: Plan of the course.

TRANSPORTATION, RACEHORSE

Once this merely involved walking racehorses to meetings. A runner was first transported in a padded bullock cart in 1816 and increasingly racehorses were despatched on long journeys to run at distant meetings, after Elis won the 1836 St Leger by being transported to Doncaster from his Sussex stable.

Today, racehorse transport via custom-built horsebox has replaced the railway wagon in which many runners were transported to racecourse halts up until, and even shortly after, the Second World War.

Now the consignment of racehorses also involves air travel and arrangements that are highly sophisticated and comfortable.

TRAVELLING THE TURF

Travelling the turf is not just the name of a well-known annual guide to Britain's racecourses, it is also an activity that can provide a profitable pointer by highlighting racehorses which are making marathon journeys to race tracks.

If the 'leading trainers' table for a particular racecourse contains the name of a handler who hails far from it, it is worth scrutinizing any runners he or she has sent there.

Those who wish to capitalize on the belief that horses, especially those from small yards, are unlikely to undertake marathon journeys to racecourses for nothing, should arm themselves with a good map and Raceform's *Horses in Training*.

On racecards the location of each runner's stable is usually given. Moreover, the *Racing Post* will show which horses have travelled long distances to line up on racecourses.

TRAVELLING TIPS

These are sometimes provided when horses, jockeys and trainers put in appearances at racecourses remote from where they are based.

TRIO

Forecast bet on the first three horses home in any order. In contrast the Tricast, available on handicap races of eight or more runners, requires the backer to select the first three in correct order. Some leading bookmakers no longer offer a bonus on Tricasts for sprint races since on certain courses, well-drawn horses are very likely to finish in the frame.

Triton Research, 204 Imperial Centre, Grange Road, Darlington, Co. Durham, has pinpointed five courses on which it is claimed Tricasts can often prove successful if certain principles are applied.

TRIP

Expression used to denote a race distance. An ideal trip is thus one of a length adjudged as highly suitable for a racehorse.

TRIPLE CROWN

Impressive threefold achievement of a champion three-year-old in winning the English or Irish 2000 (or 1000) Guineas, the Derby or Oaks and the St Leger. Only top-class thoroughbreds are capable of this achievement and one, Sceptre, won both the 2000 and 1000 Guineas, the Oaks and the St Leger in 1902! Before that, in 1868, another filly, Formosa, won the 1000 Guineas, deadheated for the 2000 and won the Oaks and the St Leger.

TRIPLE YANKEE

Six selections involving three Yankees. This bet has the guarantee of a full Yankee if there are five winners. Example:

£1 win Triple Yankee ABCDEF is:

£1 Yankee ABCD;

£1 Yankee ABEF;

£1 Yankee CDEF;

Total stake £33.

TROPHIES, RACING

These, sometimes so splendid as to turn up on 'Antiques Roadshow' programmes and astonish their owners as to their value, take many, often very aesthetic, forms.

Many are ornate, some vast and all feature the work of creative artists and craftsmen. So age-old and protracted is the history of the turf that many ancient racing trophies of the past turn up in salerooms.

Some past and present day racing trophies are truly exquisite. One example is the Chester Gold Cup of 1766 which, before it was sold at Christies in 1965 for £6,800, had been bought only 15 years earlier for a mere £720.

It should not be imagined that the biggest and best racing trophies are presented to owners capturing the biggest and best races. Refreshingly, in fact, the victor in one Stratford-on-Avon race for fairly humble, if champion, novice hunters' steeplechases – the John Corbet Cup – is presented with a massive cup by Paul Storr that was originally presented to Corbet (the virtual founder of foxhunting in Warwickshire) on his retirement in 1811. It stands over a foot high and weighs 160 ounces.

Interestingly, Jean Walwyn (a relative of the late

royal trainer) and Philip Blacker, the ex-steeplechase jockey, are just two individuals who have been involved in racing both as participants and as sculptors of racing trophies.In modern times trophies have featured new materials, designs and concepts.

TROUBLE ON THE RACECOURSE

Racecourse rowdyism was commonplace in earlier times and attempts to explain or eliminate it have also received wide coverage in the annals of the turf. In one of the best of these, *A Social and Economic History of Horse Racing*, Wray Vamplew recalls how earlier this century such disturbances began to involve gangs of organized criminals, wholly different to the old thimblemen and card sharps who had long taken part in overtly criminal activities on racecourses. The boom in racing that followed the end of the First World War brought a good deal of money into the sport with the result that violent criminals began to rob bookmakers, demand protection money and to settle their differences with razors.

Fortunately, such incidents were short-lived as a result of swift action by the authorities and the success of the Bookmakers' Protection Association which was originally founded to guarantee the physical welfare of its members.

As it happened, the razors proved far less of a nuisance than the ruffianism and hooliganism that were formerly accepted features of British racecourses. It was not until 1875, when enclosed racecourses were introduced, that racing became more select and respectable.

Of the factors that in former years gave racing the bad name that, rather unfairly, it still suffers from in some quarters, only one, the ready availability of alcohol, still characterizes the modern racing scene.

However, the turf remains, as John Hislop once expressed it, a searching test of a man's character, and a handful of spectators fail this.

TUBING

Inserting a tube into a racehorse's wind-pipe by means of a tracheotomy to prevent it roaring.

TURF ACCOUNTANT

Euphemism for off-course bookmaker.

TURN OF FOOT

Speed in a racehorse.

TWIST/TWIST CARD

Racecard bearing numbers that do not correspond with those on the official racecard. It permits bookmakers to pass information and business to each other in complete confidence.

On a twist card the runners are listed in the same alphabetical way in which they appear on bookmakers' boards.

UNDER STARTER'S ORDERS (See Starter's Orders)

UNDULATING

Term used of a racecourse whose racing surface, instead of being flat, features falling and rising ground. If a course is severely undulating it can sap the stamina of some contestants, especially if the going is heavy.

Course and distance winners proven in such going are often worth following on undulating racecourses.

UNEXPOSED

Description applied to a runner whose ability is known only to its connections since it has yet to be seen by racecourse observers.

Such 'dark horses' can be detected if one subscribes to *Future Form* which identifies them by assessing the value of future races in which they have been (often expensively) entered.

UNION JACK

Nine selections giving eight trebles, as indicated in the diagram opposite.

The selections are numbered 1 to 9 and the trebles are 123, 456, 789, 147, 258, 369, 159 and 357. The outlay is small compared with the potential returns. Whatever is regarded as one's 'banker' is placed in the middle of the flag (number 5) and this appears in four of the trebles. Numbers 1, 3, 7 and 9 are in thee trebles, while 2,4, 6 and 8 appear in two. Backers should simply number their selections and mark their bets 'Union Jack'.

UNSADDLING ENCLOSURE

Self-explanatory term for the racecourse area adjoining the weighing room in which winners and placed horses are unsaddled.

Since the sheer delight a winner's connections show in this racecourse area is almost infectious, racegoers should make a point of visiting it after a race has been contested.

The unsaddling enclosure is also the scene of disappointment, tragedy, and even some sham acting, as in attempts once made to lower the bidding for a selling plate winner by muzzling it.

UP AND DOWN (See Single Stakes About)
A bookmaker's term for even money that takes its name from the tic-tac signal that is given for those odds.

UPSIDES

Said of a contender that is running its race alongside or abreast of the leaders.

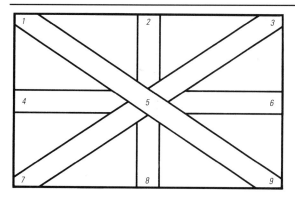

UNION JACK: This diagram shows the nine selections giving eight trebles.

❗ UP THE PICTURES

Colourful expression used to describe an unplaced finisher.

UTTOXETER

Uttoxeter Racecourse
Wood Lane
Uttoxeter
Staffs ST14 8BD
Tel. (0889) 562561

How to get there:
From North: M6
From South: M6
From East: A50
From West: A50
By Rail: Uttoxeter
By Air: Helicopter facilities

Staffordshire contains some good hunting country and it is appropriate that the Ansells National, formerly the Midlands' Grand National, takes place at Uttoxeter, which is to be found in the middle of this county close to the Peak District.

The track will be found in a pleasantly rural location and adjoins Uttoxeter railway station, itself accessible by train from St Pancras if one completes a 135-mile journey by changing at Derby.

Given its central location in being only 16 miles from Burton-on-Trent, Uttoxeter draws crowds from all points of the compass.

Many motorists take the M6, leave at junction 14 and then continue on the ring road. The track will be found east of Stafford from which it is best approached via the A518. Those taking the M1 should leave the motorway at junction 24 and then, after making for Derby, head further westwards on the A516 and A50. Helicopters can be accommodated on the course.

The track, a spectator's delight, is an essentially oval left-hander of around 11 furlongs with a flat home straight and a short run-in of around 170 yards from the last fence.

The Ansells National is run over 4 miles on some undulating terrain (there is a 1 furlong uphill stretch in the back straight and a short slight fall round the final bend); Uttoxeter's fairly easy bends and fences (the three most demanding of which are all in the home stretch) mean that front runners are favoured, as are speedy gallopers.

As well as its often thrilling Aintree rehearsal, the March fixture also features another prestigious race, the Bet with the Tote Novices' Handicap Chase.

Another prestigious race staged at Uttoxeter is the Staffordshire Hurdle that is sufficiently important to be included in diary lists of principal races contested each season. This is staged early in May.

Uttoxeter is deservedly popular both with racegoers who appreciate such amenities as the Jimmy Nipps' champagne and seafood bar and by their children who can find fun fairs on hand to entertain them.

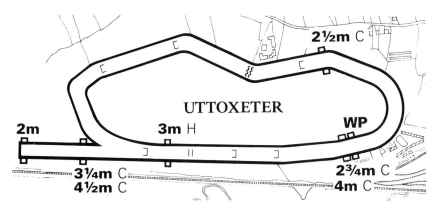

UTTOXETER: Plan of the course.

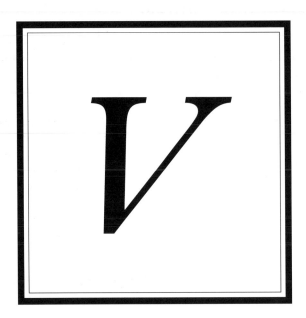

VALETS

Often forgotten but indispensable racecourse functionaries whose demanding and gruelling task involves supplying jockeys with whatever clothing, boots and equipment they require during a race meeting.

These are some of racing's true 'insiders' and revelations of their dealings with some of the most cheerful and humorous sportsmen to be found anywhere are often fascinating. This is why *Tales from the Weighing Room*, the reminiscences of valet John Buckingham, who himself rode Foinavon to a sensational 100-1 Grand National victory in 1967, was so well received when it was recently published.

VALUE

This is the watchword of the professional.

Just as one should, within one's means, purchase something of quality if its price is appealing, so one should invest what one can afford to lose if the odds and detached objective assessment make a selection an attractive proposition.

Indeed, betting should be thought of as rather analogous to shopping and, as such, involves timing the 'taking' of prices, either promptly before a bargain disappears, or eventually when prices represent good value.

The best method of determining value is to calculate the odds against a horse winning on the basis of the form and time ratings it has been accorded. If such calculations indicate that a horse should start at 2-1 and it is offered at 4-1, the latter price obviously represents good value.

At race meetings good value can often be obtained from bookmakers who lay odds against horses winning or coming second to a named horse (usually the favourite). One has two chances of winning, yet some of the odds offered by bookmakers trading in this particular way can prove remarkably generous.

In general, better value can be obtained on the back lines of bookmakers in Tattersalls and at the bottom end of the front line of layers. Such traders often offer marginally better terms to attract business away from premier front line pitches. It is better to bet in the Silver Ring on weekdays, especially on winter ones, but in Tattersalls at major meetings on Saturdays or at well-attended summer meetings.

Recently, accountant Malcolm Howard published his *How to Find Value when Betting* under the Raceform imprint. This most usefully includes a table indicating just which prices quoted in 'against the favourite' betting shows represent good value. Betting at poor odds is a surprisingly common act.

VALUE TO WINNER (See Penalty Value, Prize Money)

This indication of the prize money actually won by a racehorse can provide a useful indication of its class. Divide a previous winner's career prize money (or that registered in the current season) by the number of victories to get an approximate indication of its class.

VETERINARY OFFICER

Racecourse official whose attendance at race meetings is vital. He or she is seldom seen by the racegoing public, but represents its safeguard that everything possible will be done to minimize any suffering by racehorses. Every racecard will show the name of the officiating 'veterinary'.

VICTORIA CLUB

A London Sporting Club which used to be the scene of call overs at which ante-post odds for big races were formerly determined.

VIDEOS, RACING

These cover human and equine champions, past and recent races, and reviews of racing years and regular events. Video Vision (PO Box 120, Harrogate HG1 4TP) even offers a beginner's guide to tic-tac so that the racegoer can learn the secret signals relating to runners and odds. The videoing of races has recently been used in official attempts to eliminate non-triers.

VIRUS, THE

A reason why horses can inexplicably disappoint. The virus is, in fact, 'a multitude of viruses' all producing similar symptoms. Coughs, temperatures, runny noses and dull coats are some of the most common.

It is difficult to identify the equine equivalents of human coughs, colds and other viral complaints before horses are due to compete. It is only when these animals fade rapidly under pressure or pant for long periods after their races that there is firm evidence. Unfortunately, by this late stage they may have caused large sums to remain in the ring, confounded their connections and made a mockery of the form book!

When several fancied horses from the same stable fail to make the frame, it is probably 'the virus' that is responsible. They may well regain fitness at about the same time. It is worth studying reports in specialized racing dailies in case these contain speculations or warnings about the virus.

Fortunately, bids to combat the effect of the virus are ongoing at the Equine Research Station and the Animal Virus Disease Institute at Pirbright.

VISOR (See Blinkers, Shades)

Special pair of blinkers with a slit cut in each of its eyeshields. Unlike 'complete' blinkers, visors allow horses some lateral vision so that their view of horses racing upsides them is not completely blocked.

WALK OVER

If there is only one runner in a race, all his jockey must do, having weighed out as usual, is to 'walk' his mount over the finishing line past the judges' box. For understandable reasons such a race is usually staged at the end of programmes.

WARN OFF

Action taken by the stewards of the Jockey Club towards anyone found in serious breach of their rules regarding the conduct of racing.

Originally this punishment involved being warned off or banned from Newmarket Heath to which the Jockey Club's authority was formerly confined, but it now covers banishment usually for a specified period, from all racecourses the Club administers in Britain.

Gatemen on these have instructions to refuse entry to anyone known to have been 'exiled' from racecourses.

WARWICK

Warwick Racecourse
Hampton Street
Warwick
Tel. (0926) 491553

How to get there:
From North: A46
From South: M40, A429
From East: A425
From West: M40, M42
By Rail: Warwick
By Air: Birmingham Airport

One of the oldest racecourses in the country is to be found at Warwick, close to the centre of this attractive county town.

By the early nineteenth century racing was well established here and was certainly more prestigious then than is the case today. However, despite the fact that the sporting fare on offer here is hardly top-class, it is pleasantly palatable which seems appropriate in that so many of its ingredients like the Brooke Bond Oxo Man Appeal Stakes have had connections with food.

The track itself, often misleadingly described as almost circular, is a broad, round edged quadrilateral-like affair which extends for over 1 mile and 5 furlongs. The longest races at Warwick are not staged over this distance but over 2 miles 2 furlongs and 214 yards. Those concerned start from the five-furlong start on the spur that allows sprints to be staged and, after negotiating a left-handed dog leg past the winning

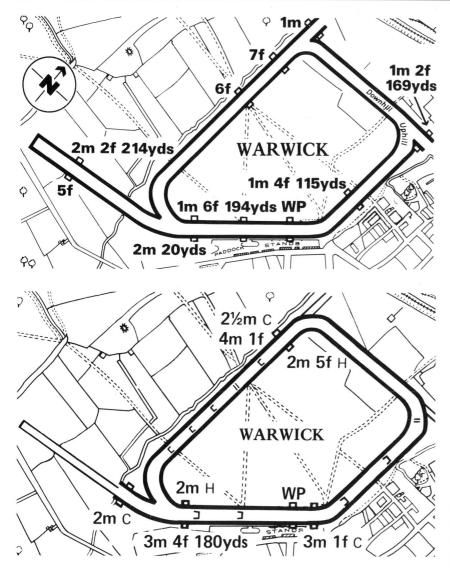

WARWICK: Plans of the Flat course (top), and the National Hunt course (bottom).

post, then negotiate the least sharp of Warwick's four turns. Passing the 1 mile 4 furlongs and 115 yard start, they encounter steeply rising ground into the next straight track section as they round a fairly tight bend (from which a spur projects to provide an opportunity for horses to run over 1 mile 2 furlongs and 169 yards).

Thus, those involved in such events initially race up an incline before descending ground is encountered. The turn into the far straight is tight and from it a second spur projects to allow races to be held over 1 mile. Also started from points along this back stretch (which is the longest straight section of the course) are events over 7 and 6 furlongs.

Warwick's short run-in extends for not much more than two furlongs. It also forms the final stage

of a 5-furlong sprint course that is initially provided by a longish spur which projects at a fairly sharp, around thirty-degree, angle from the final bend. The most pronounced feature of the sprint track is the elbow it begins to describe just before it joins the circuit.

If anything, advantage in the draw for races over 5 furlongs lies with those allotted high numbers. For races over 10 furlongs and 169 yards and 12 furlongs 115 yards, low-drawn runners enjoy a slight edge.

Since much of the course has a clay subsoil there is occasionally some give in its ground.

The Warwick Oaks run over 1 mile 4 furlongs and 115 yards in mid-or late-June is typical of races here in not being particularly prestigious. Some, like the Kingmaker Handicap and the Anne Hathaway

Stakes, have served as reminders of Warwick's historical importance and Shakespearean connections.

Horses can win over distances at Warwick that they would fail to get on rather more testing courses. In general, this track is appreciated by handy types that are able to cope with its sharp turns and by fast, front runners who relish its short run-in. It is ill-suited to horses that are one-paced or which need time to settle. Warwick also takes some riding, as jockeys who have failed to keep in touch in the early stages of sprints have found to their cost.

The course, 21 miles from Birmingham and 17 from Rugby, lies close to the A46 Stratford to Coventry road, more accessible now the M40 joins this. It is less than three miles to the course by bus or taxi from Leamington station served by Paddington.

National Hunt racing is also staged at Warwick, most spectacularly via the Racephone National and the Crudwell Cup (which commemorates a prolific steeplechase winner of the 1950s). The former is the better known contest and is often fiercely contested, while the latter is a handicap 'chase, staged over 3 miles and almost 5 furlongs in early March.

The water jump is taken after the winning post has been passed. This is but one of ten fairly stiff fences (five of which have to be jumped in quick succession in the back stretch) that make up the 'chasing circuit whose fairly sharp bends and occasionally undulating terrain can unsettle some jumpers. In general, adaptable, speedy National Hunt runners are favoured at Warwick, as are front runners since the run-in is short at 240 yards. Warwick has boxes for hire at reasonable rates.

WATERFORD AND TRAMORE

Waterford and Tramore Racecourse
Tramore
Co. Waterford
Ireland
Tel. (051) 81425

How to get there:
From North: N9
From South: N25
From East: N25
From West: N24
By Rail: Waterford
By Air: Waterford

Situated eight miles from Waterford and its railway station, this racecourse stages races such as a 2 mile 6 furlong 'chase, that are sponsored by former Cheltenham benefactor, the Waterford Crystal Company.

The nine or so days of racing that take place here mainly in the summer are on an ultra-tight, 7-furlong, right-handed, bullet-shaped course which is extremely undulating. Most unusually, the track's five fences are made of gorse rather than birch and of these, the two in the downhill stretch that is encountered once the winning post has been passed, are so closely spaced as sometimes to catch out novices or older jumpers that aren't concentrating. Flat races, as well as hurdles and steeplechases, are staged on the course.

Strand races used to be staged at Tramore (as they

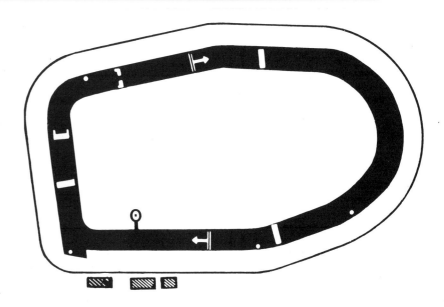

WATERFORD AND TRAMORE: Plan of the course.

WEIGHED IN: This early print shows horses being weighed in and rubbed down.

still are at Laytown) until, early this century, this became impossible; the town has many other attractions as a lively seaside resort.

In August Tramore hosts its own four-day mini-festival of racing that is either preceded or followed by an even more maritime day's racing at Laytown.

Tramore is just eight miles south of Waterford from which it is best reached on the R675. Racegoers from Limerick should journey east on the N24 to Waterford then follow signs to Tramore. Many Dubliners make their way here via the N11 to Enniscorthy before continuing on to Waterford on the N79, while some fly in to Waterford airport. However they arrive all racegoers appreciate the atmosphere and the ozone!

WEATHERBYS

Since 1773 members of this family firm have compiled the *General Stud Book*, the authoritive register of all British and Irish thoroughbreds, and acted as keepers of the Match Book to the Jockey Club. Its London office is in the Jockey Club's HQ at Portman Square.

Currently, from its Wellingborough office, Weatherbys acts as the Jockey Club's secretariat. As this organization's agents they publish the *Racing Calendar*, act as stake-holders, distribute prize money, draw up registers of horses' names, racing colours, trainers' licences and permits and partnerships between owners, issue passports for racehorses, update horses' records and register entries and declarations.

The firm opened a *General Stud Book* subsidiary in Dublin in 1963 to facilitate its four-yearly updating of this register of every British and Irish thoroughbred horse and mare.

WEIGHED IN

Announcement that the jockey of a winning racehorse has weighed in (a process which also concerns riders of the second, third and fourth horses) to the satisfaction of the clerk of the scales. Not until this fact is announced or signalled, should bookmakers pay out or a backer expect them to, so bookmakers' or tote tickets should not be discarded prematurely.

WEIGHING OUT

Process whereby jockeys are weighed by the clerk of the scales at least a quarter of an hour before a specified race.

No whip, bridle, martingale, rings, plate or anything worn on a horse's legs is allowed on the scales, but a hood, visor, blinkers, martingale, breastplate or clothing must be included in the jockey's weight.

WEIGHING ROOM

Carrying their saddles, which may be weighed down by lead, jockeys enter this inner sanctum from their dressing rooms where they'll have changed. Folded number cloths will be handed out and identifying cards handed to the clerk of the scales before riding weights are checked. This involves jockeys sitting in the scales along with their equipment.

Then the saddle number cloth and weight cloth (if any) are left on a rail in the weighing room for the trainer or his head lad to collect and take to the racecourse stable.

Once the race is over, the weighing room is a cheerful place in which the jockeys of the first four finishers, each carrying a saddle, a number cloth and a weight cloth are weighed to ensure that they can still make the required weight.

WEIGHT FOR AGE

Principle whereby differences in the abilities of racehorses caused by maturative factors are allowed for. This recognizes that, as the flat season progresses, the edge enjoyed by a four-year-old over a three-year-old is likely to be greater over longer, stamina-sapping distances than over sprint ones, but that this edge will diminish as the season moves from March to September.

A similar principle is applied in jump races so that older horses are often required to concede weight to younger rivals, but again this concession is reduced as the latter mature during the course of the August to June season. Thus, in January over three miles, a five-year-old is adjudged to be a stone superior to a four-year-old, but by the following December, the latter would be considered sufficiently mature to compete with the former on equal terms.

WEIGHT FOR AGE SCALE

Table indicating allowances older horses need to make to younger ones to allow for the fact that they have had longer to grow, develop and mature. The following are the scales currently in use for Flat and National Hunt racing:

SCALE OF AGE WEIGHT AND DISTANCE (Flat Racing)

See p. 252

SCALE OF AGE WEIGHT AND DISTANCE (National Hunt Racing)

See p. 252

WEIGHTS

These are individually allotted in handicaps and in non-handicap 'conditions' races according to general criteria that involve past performances, prizes previously won, the sex of runners or their original purchase prices.

Some horses are better at carrying high weights than others and it is seldom wise to expect one's selection to make light of a burden which is far heavier than it has previously carried to victory.

Any disparities between a jockey's natural weight and that allotted to his mount are made up in lead, whose inanimate, unmovable nature makes it awkward to carry.

This is why some backers look closely at any runner given a weight that equates with its jockey's 'dynamic' racing weight.

When the weights are published for such important spring handicaps as the Grand National and the Lincoln and for the Cambridgeshire and the Cesarewitch (that comprise the later 'Autumn Double'), they tend to occasion rather more comment than criticism.

WETHERBY

Wetherby Racecourse
York Road
Wetherby
West Yorkshire LS22 5EJ
Tel. (0937) 582035

How to get there:
From North: A1
From South: A1
From East: B1224
From West: A659, A661
By Rail: Leeds
By Air: Helicopter facilities

This left-handed, oval-shaped jumping course is occasionally undulating; it features a rise to the winning post that continues after it has been passed and ground that descends into the long finishing

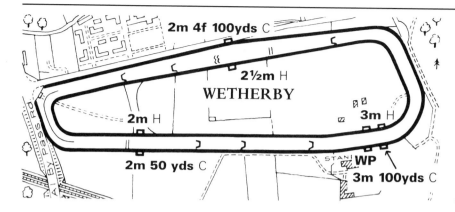

WETHERBY: Plan of the course.

straight with its short run-in of around 200 yards from the final obstacle.

The course is 12 furlongs in extent and is widely regarded as a testing one, thanks in part to the uphill finish and to its nine formidable fences which are, after those at Aintree on the Grand National circuit, regarded as the stiffest in Britain. There are five fences in the back stretch and four in the home straight. The first fence in the straight and the second along the far straight are open ditches, while the water jump is in the middle of the five 'out in the country'.

Wetherby tends to be appreciated by fearless, bold jumping, resolute, long-striding gallopers who can stretch out over its long straights. Such animals need to be able to cope with the track's two very abrupt and tight bends. The first of these is a very tight left-hander of 90 degrees or so that follows a long back straight on which five obstacles are positioned so they can be readily viewed from the stands. The second last fence is particularly formidable.

The hurdle course here is a sharp, 10-furlong affair and a horse well rated on time often runs well on this if its jockey has a chance to put his foot down on the long straight.

Wetherby is popular with the racing fraternity partly because of the very fair, but searching, test it imposes on jumpers (which is why so many established and promising stars are sent here) and partly because it is so well-appointed, comfortable and friendly. Another reason for the popularity of this picturesque course is the quality of its fixtures.

Perhaps the most widely known Wetherby steeplechase is the Rowland Meyrick Handicap Chase, an often thrilling 3-miler staged on Boxing Day. Such well seasoned performers as Cheltenham Gold Cup winners The Thinker and Forgive 'n Forget have prevailed in past runnings of this classy 'chase.

Another prestigious 'chase is the Charlie Hall Memorial Chase, also a 3-miler, which is contested at the end of October. Past winners of this once again include Forgive 'n Forget, as well as Burrough Hill Lad and Wayward Lad (who won it twice).

Racegoers will find that Wetherby lies 12 miles north-east of Leeds, just south-east of the delightful Yorkshire town of Harrogate, some nine miles away. The track benefits from its proximity to the Yorkshire training centre of Malton and also to the A1 which is the logical choice of route for those arriving from the north or south.

Motorists travelling from York should take the B1224, while those leaving Leeds are advised to arrive via the A58. There is a rear exit from the course car park which gives access to the A1.

Rail travellers, many of whom leave from King's Cross, will find that fairly long taxi-rides will need to be taken from either Leeds, York or Harrogate, while air travellers can be accommodated on-course if arriving by helicopter.

The course's excellent facilities allow spectators to view the paddock area without having to venture out into the cold. One of the charms of this course is that, since the grandstands are at an angle, spectators can enjoy virtually a head-on view of the last four fences.

WEXFORD

22 North Main Street
Wexford
Ireland
Tel. (053) 42307 or 23102

How to get there:
From North: N11
From South: N25
From West: N25

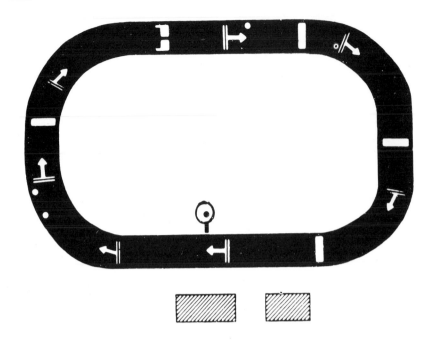

WEXFORD: *Plan of the course.*

By Rail: Waterford
By Air: Waterford
Approximately 80 miles from Dublin

Another tight Irish course, Wexford extends for just under nine furlongs. Understandably, then, horses running in the shorter flat races (which, as well as steeplechases and hurdles, are staged on this right-hander) have an advantage if they are drawn nearest the inside of the track. This is a rather oblong, lozenge-shaped affair with only five fences, all fairly evenly spaced around it.

There is a downhill run into a short finishing straight and this and the track's tight nature means that it tends to suit front runners.

High-drawn runners and front-running types tend to set the pace here. The fact that Wexford racecourse (which lies about a mile from the town) stands on recently claimed so-called 'slobland' should not in any way suggest that this is a down-market meeting. Indeed, the town and its track are extremely atmospheric and the former, especially, steeped in history. The course was established fairly late in the nineteenth century.

Two of the principal races staged at Wexford each season are the Cummins Campus Oil Hurdle and the Talbot Hotel Novices' Chase named after Lord Forte's local hostelry.

Wexford racecourse is accessible from Dublin via the southbound N11, a fine coastal route, while Limerick-based racegoers should travel on the N24 and N25. The course is too small to take aircraft which can, however, be accommodated at Waterford, 36 miles to the west.

WHIP, USE OF

As a steering aid and as a means of galvanizing lazy or tired horses into more energetic action, the whip has long been wielded, but in modern times far greater restrictions on its use have been imposed and cases even made for its total prohibition.

Some experts, like former jockey Lord Oaksey, see this as a possibility worth experimenting with in flat racing. While others might disagree, it is certain that, of late, increased sensitivity to animal rights has led jockeys wielding whips to fall foul of more vigilant stewards and to adopt techniques that fall within guidelines designed to make whipping racehorses a far more humane proceeding.

WHISTLING (See Roaring)

Deep roaring sound made when cantering or galloping by a racehorse with an affliction of the larynx. This can be cured by hobdaying or tubing.

WILD CARD TRAINER

Expression used to denote a racehorse handler who could well send out a surprise, long-priced winner on a particular racecourse. As this term suggests, such a trainer is likely to be a gambler.

USE OF WHIP: Gordon Richards wins his 100th race of the 1945 season – the Castle Hill Plate – on Sez You.

WINCANTON

Wincanton Racecourse
Wincanton,
Somerset BA9 8BJ
Tel. (0963) 32344

How to get there:
From North: A319, A3081
From South: A357

From East: A303
From West: A303
By Rail: Gillingham
By Air: Helicopter facilities

This right-handed racecourse situated mid-way between the Somerset towns of Yeovil and Frome in a picturesque part of the West Country is easily accessible both to Lambourn yards and many local handlers. Thus it continues to be popular. It is 11

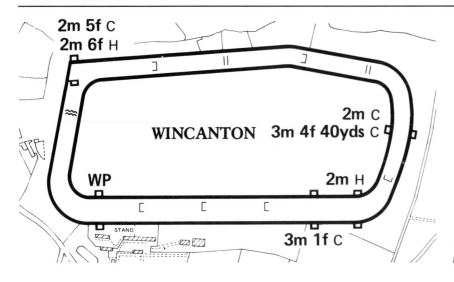

2m 5f C
2m 6f H

WINCANTON **3m 4f 40yds** C

2m C

WP

2m H

STAND

3m 1f C

WINCANTON: Plan of the course.

furlongs round and rather like a cross between an oval and a quadrilateral and its nine fences have been stiffened in recent years.

There is a short run-in of around 200 yards and spectators get an excellent view, particularly of the last three obstacles in the finishing straight. Given its two long straights, Wincanton is quite a galloping course undulating mildly with rising ground once the winning post has been passed and a last turn downhill into the long finishing straight. Horses need to be able to race right-handed and also cope with the testing fences; front runners often poach leads that are unassailable on the short run-in from the last.

Rail travellers can reach the course from Waterloo by travelling to Gillingham and then taking a taxi for a further seven miles. Once in the town of Wincanton, motorists should proceed northwards beyond it for a mile or so on the B3081.

The major races staged on this east Somerset track are the Kingwell Hurdle, Coral Golden Hurdle and the 2 mile 5 furlong Terry Biddlecombe Challenge Trophy Chase run in honour of the former distinguished and colourful National Hunt jockey. The Badger Beer Chase is run over the same distance, with a Hangover Handicap Chase on Boxing Day the inevitable result.

WINDSOR

The Racecourse
Windsor
Berkshire
Tel. (0753) 865234

How to get there:
From North: M25
From South: M25
From East: M4
From West: M4
By Rail: Windsor & Eton/Riverside/Central
By Air: Helicopter facilities

Although many of the races staged at Windsor, such as the Royal Borough Handicap and the Star and Garter Nursery, have names that capitalize on this course's proximity to a royal castle and its historic connections with members of England's foremost family, they are in the main rather modest contests.

Many Windsor races are twilight affairs, since around 70 per cent of flat-race meetings that take place here each season are staged in the evening. The majority of these are held on Monday nights; indeed, four successive ones take place in July, Windsor's busiest month during which minor miracles of restoration have to be carried out by the groundstaff in order to maintain a good surface for racing.

Clearly the Windsor executive has great faith in evening racing since, not only does it provide more of this than any other British racecourse, but does so just as soon (in late April) and as long (until the very end of August) as it is possible to do so.

Windsor is very popular with both layers and their customers. Its often fine-sounding races tend to attract large fields of moderate sprinters and performers over 'intermediate' distances. This is because in 1966 the second right-handed loop was shortened and made over half as tight as it had been since its opening in Rays Meadows in 1865. Thus after the former date races could no longer be staged over 12 furlongs and 2 1/2 miles 110 yards.

Windsor's short distances attract large fields of

immature and non-staying animals. This is what makes racing here so competitive. It also explains why the course betting market has often been so strong. Some notable, even spectacular, 'coups' have been staged here.

The popularity of Windsor with the betting public can also be explained by its accessibility. In fact it is one of the few racecourses that can be reached by air, land and water, since (by prior arrangement) helicopters can land here, trains run regularly from Paddington and Waterloo to the nearby stations of either Windsor and Eton Central or Windsor Riverside, while a river bus from Windsor promenade takes racegoers to a racecourse jetty which is close to the paddock.

Moreover, the course is only 22 miles from Central London. The M3's third interchange is not far away and from here motorists should take the A332 Windsor road. Those eventually arriving via the M4 should leave at junction 6 and will find that the track is just off the A308.

The racecourse itself is one of only two in Britain (the other is Fontwell) that describes a figure of eight. In doing so it obviously features right-and left-hand bends. Interestingly, the latter are only negotiated by horses running in Windsor's longest races – those staged over 1 mile 3 furlongs 135 yards

and 10 furlongs 7 yards.

Those tackling the former distance initially race over straight track that soon 'elbows' to the left. Next they encounter another straight stretch of track and then run round a slight and rather gradual left-hand bend that takes them into the longest straight section on the loop nearest the stands. Those tackling 1 mile 67 yards at Windsor initially negotiate a spur that forms a short extension to its second loop.

On this the runners encounter a sharp, semi-circular, right-hand bend that runs into the sprint track, used for races over 5 furlongs 10 yards and 5 furlongs 217 yards.

The ground hereafter continues to run the straight course it has followed since the longer sprint start until it 'elbows' to the right at the point where Windsor's two loops intersect, but not to such an extent that effectively foreshortens the run-in.

Thus, this can to all intents and purposes be regarded as a five-furlong affair. Also, along with the track's many other shorter straight sections, it makes Windsor's frequent classification as a very sharp track rather inappropriate.

Jockeys have an opportunity to come with a long late run on long-striding, galloping types which are not as unsuited to Windsor as is popularly believed.

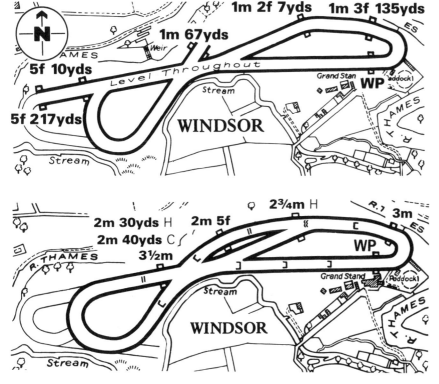

WINDSOR: Plans of the Flat course (top), and the National Hunt course (bottom).

Indeed the flat course is not really quite so sharp as many people imagine.

The sprint track, which is all that remains of the 'old course', tends to suit fast-starting animals that can soon reach a challenging position. In races run over 1 mile 67 yards high-drawn runners enjoy a slight edge.

Since Windsor is bordered on three sides by the River Thames, it is scarcely surprising that soft or heavy ground can be found on the track if racing takes place on it during a wet spell. Fortunately, however, the course is no longer subject to serious flooding of the type that, in 1947, brought three feet of water into the grandstand!

The Thames is now under effective control and seldom encroaches onto the course. It should be pointed out, in all fairness, that the course is quite quick-draining when the water table beneath the subsoil is fairly low.

In conditions of the other extreme, a modern watering system comes into play once the ground starts to harden.

Windsor's riverside location, its picturesque features and its historical associations perhaps explain why there is often a long waiting list for club membership.

Horses seem to be able to run well under heavy weights on this very fair track on which form generally works out quite well. It is also odds-on that each and every runner will be fairly treated by the Windsor stewards.

This apparently was not always the case; a certain Captain Wiggie Weyland once officiated here and, on one occasion, 'delayed the hearing of an objection because he was down on the rails with the bookmakers betting away happily on the result of it'!

Jump races are held on an almost totally flat racing surface that extends for a mile and three-quarters and takes in fairly sharp bends and long sections of straight track. Thus, the handy, speedy jumper is at home at Windsor whose nine fences (seven of which are on the large upper loop) make no great demands on those who have to face them.

New Year's Day at Windsor is notable in that it features a hurdle race of that name, a valuable 2 mile 30 yard affair that always precedes the Freddie Starr Handicap Chase of 3 miles. The 3 mile Fairlawne Chase for five-year-olds and over is the highlight of a mid-February fixture.

WINNERS ON LOOKS (See Conformation and Paddock Pointers)

WINNER WITHOUT A PENALTY
Such a well-treated runner, while hardly favoured by its earlier disqualification, may well atone as a 'blot on the handicap'.

WINNING AND LOSING (See Scribes, Racing)
All those involved in racing have their disastrous days. Backers should thus operate according to a staking plan that has some built-in protection against the prolonged desertion by lady luck which is bound to be their fate in the fullness of time.

To some racegoers, God may seem to be a member of the Bookmakers' Protection Association and all of life, as Damon Runyon put it, appear 'to be 6-4 against and a whole lot longer on the horse player'.

WINNINGS' CALCULATOR (See Ready Reckoner)
Such a useful table is often a feature of racing diaries and annual guides to horse racing.

WINNING SEQUENCES
These are likely to be shorter than losing ones as a glance at tables showing the fates of the newspaper naps of racing correspondents will almost invariably confirm. However, the winning sequences of such selections can approach and, on rare occasions, even exceed double figures.

Following a previously unbeaten runner is often a sound ploy, especially if such a contestant is not racing in a far higher class of race.

In racing, as in so many spheres, nothing quite succeeds like success. When 'on song' trainers and jockeys can also run up impressively long winning sequences.

WITH THE FIELD
An instruction given to a bookmaker to couple a backer's stipulated selection in a race with all the other runners this features. For example, a 'with the field' instruction could involve one's 'banker' being doubled with all the horses running in a later four-horse race.

WITH THE THUMB
The 'thumbs up' tic-tac sign is given after a rate of odds to indicate that this is likely to contract. Thus, the expression 'with the thumb' is bookmakers' parlance for being well-backed. The fact that only about 15 per cent of horses whose prices contract actually win suggests to some backers that the 'thumbs up' is an inappropriate sign for bookmakers to use.

WOLVERHAMPTON

Wolverhampton Racecourse
Gorsebrook Road
Wolverhampton WV6 0PE
Tel. (0902) 24481 or 772038

How to get there:
From North: M6, A449
From South: M5, A449
From East: A5
From West: M54
By Rail: Wolverhampton
By Air: Birmingham Airport

Those who might be tempted to look down upon
Wolverhampton's serviceable track ought to
remember that in 1974 a horse that was beaten in a
spring handicap restricted to apprentices and run over
its largely flat and fair surface went on to win the
Eclipse Stakes at Sandown Park!

This Midlands track is set in over 100 acres of
Dunstall Park, a mile north-west of Wolverhampton's
city centre and about the same distance from a railway
station known as Wolverhampton High Level.

It is popular both with professional racing people
and with local patrons who seem to appreciate the
contrast it provides to much of the industrial area in
which it is located; it provided Britain's first Saturday
evening fixture in July 1962. One respondent to a
recent survey of favoured lovemaking venues actually
named the Wolverhampton course's water jump as
first choice!

While there is nothing really impressive about the
racing on this very fair course, it is pleasant enough.
Moreover, several Mondays in the summer months
would not quite be the same were the Wolverhampton
meetings to disappear from the calendar.

It is perhaps rather misleading to describe this
track as pear-shaped, since it is a rather triangular,
left-handed affair that extends for over 12 furlongs.

Some unusually named races have recently been
run at Wolverhampton. Examples are the Swan Lake
Handicap over 1 mile and 134 yards, the Raspberry
Nursery Handicap run at a mid-August fixture and a
Gooseberry Maiden Stakes.

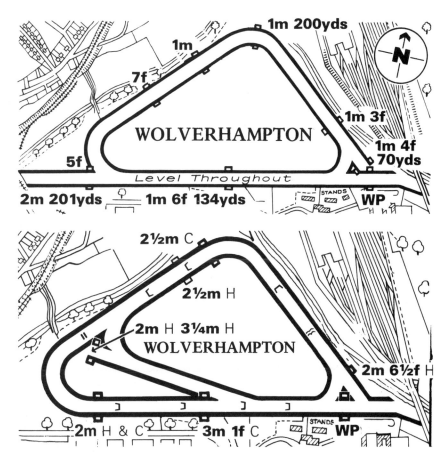

WOLVERHAMPTON:
Plans of the Flat course
(top), and the National
Hunt course (bottom).

Those tackling the Derby distance at Dunstall Park race along practically the whole of the round course. They start from a spur off the far straight which extends for around three furlongs. The runners in middle-distance events of 11 furlongs, 9 furlongs and 1 mile 200 yards, also tackle Wolverhampton's top left-hand bend that is soon followed by a rather sharper, semi-circular successor that has to be negotiated by runners in races over 8 and 7 furlongs.

After they have negotiated the track's final fairly tight bend, the runners enter a long finishing straight from which a short spur projects to allow sprints over 5 furlongs and races over 2 miles 201 yards to be run on the course.

In general, long-striding, galloping types tend to appreciate a run on Wolverhampton's long straights, which together with its fairly gentle bends and its long, nearly five-furlong run-in represent the main reasons why form tends to work out well here.

As for the draw, it would seem that, if anything, low numbers seem to be marginally favoured in sprints, but only when the stalls are placed on the stands side and the ground is soft, while on the round course in 7 furlongs and 1 mile 200 yard races, as one would expect on a left-handed course, the lowly drawn enjoy a slight advantage.

The Dunstall track makes no great demands on jockeyship and provides a racing surface that the groundstaff take pains to preserve. A watering system prevents the ground from getting too hard.

The course can be reached on the A449 from, if necessary, junction 12 of the M6, or from junction 2 of the M5. The M6 also runs close to the course.

Wolverhampton's nearby railway station can be reached from Euston, while helicopters can land on-course if prior permission is obtained. Those arriving in fixed-wing aircraft need to make for Halfpenny Green, eight miles to the west of Wolverhampton.

National Hunt racing is also staged on a triangular track that presents jumpers with eight obstacles, of which the stiffest is the first in the straight of about four furlongs which features a short 180-yard run-in from the last.

Hurdle races are run round a tighter circuit but, in general, this is a course which best suits long-striding, galloping types.

The best-known jump races staged each season are the Wolverhampton Trial Hurdle and the Reynoldstown Cup, a novices' hurdle in November that commemorates the 1935 and 1936 Grand National winner, as this champion 'chaser was trained not far away in Leicestershire.

WORCESTER

Worcester Racecourse
Pitchcroft
Worcester
Tel. (0905) 25364

How to get there:
From North: M5, A449
From South: M5, A38
From East: A422
From West: A44
By Rail: Worcester
By Air: Light Aircraft and Helicopter facilities

Worcester's course, rated by authorities like Peter Scudamore as a fine steeplechasing circuit, is a flat, oval-shaped, left-hander of 13 furlongs which skirts the old flat-racing course. There are easy, fairly sweeping turns and nine fences (five in the back stretch and four in the home straight) of a fairly average degree of difficulty, although some runners come to grief at the open ditch in the back straight. The finishing straight at Worcester, a long one of around four furlongs, contains four fences and ends in a 1 furlong run-in. Races over 3 miles start in an extension to the far straight. All in all then, Worcester is a good, galloping, very fair track that allows a novice to gain experience of jumping.

The track is close to the city centre and attractively situated in picturesque Pitchcroft Park (ideal for picnicking) close to the River Severn which can present it with water-logging problems. However, when racing is frequently possible at Worcester, it proves highly popular with trainers from many parts of Britain. One measure of the course's popularity is the fact that it attracted a record entry for a National Hunt track – 229 runners on 13 January 1965.

Several races at a mid-August early season fixture recall Edward Elgar's close association with Worcester; these include the Pomp and Circumstance Novices' Chase and the Enigma Handicap Hurdle.

The action tends to hot up a little when the prestigious Rayburn Supreme Handicap Chase is contested over 3 miles in mid-November, while the Harry Brown Handicap Chase over 2 miles 4 furlongs that is run on Boxing Day recalls the last amateur to head the list of National Hunt riders.

The course can be reached by rail via the nearby station of Worcester Foregate Street which lies on the Paddington line.

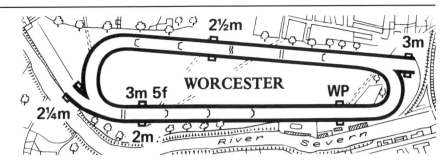

WORCESTER: Plan of the course.

The fact that Worcester is prone to waterlogging in wet winters perhaps explains why a wooden building in the course's central enclosure has served as the social club for local anglers lured by the nearby River Severn. A race run at Worcester even recalls this prominent local feature.

WORKMANLIKE

Description applied to a capable, businesslike performer who looks so well suited to the task of racing that it may well add to its tally of past victories or open its account.

WORK RIDER

Occasionally a trainer will allow a highly-experienced horseman who has partnered a particular horse during its home gallops to ride it on the racecourse. Such a booking of a jockey can provide a most propitious pointer.

❗ WRIST

Bookmaker's slang for 6-4. This is derived in part from the tic-tac sign which features this particular part of the anatomy and it is extensively used in racecourse signalling.

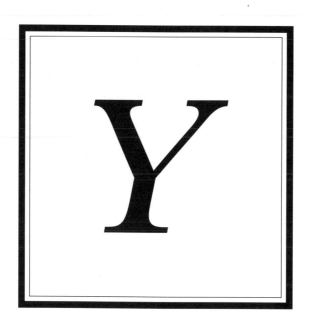

YANKEE

Wager involving four selections, fully permed to provide 6 doubles, 4 trebles and 1 four-fold accumulator, i.e. a total of 11 bets. Thus, a £1 Yankee on four horses costs £11.

YAP

Four selections with full cover i.e. a Yankee plus a single wager on each of the four selections this involves. This gives a total of 15 wagers.

YARMOUTH

Yarmouth Racecourse
North Denes
Great Yarmouth
Tel. (0493) 842527 or 856100

How to get there:
From North: A149
From South: A12
From West: A47
By Rail: Yarmouth
By Air: North Denes

After Light Cavalry had triumphed in the 1980 St Leger, it emerged that his trainer, Henry Cecil, had given him a gallop on Yarmouth racecourse as part of his preparation for the final Classic.

The striking similarities between Yarmouth's 1 3/4 mile course (as it was then) and Doncaster's 14 furlongs 132 yards were also appreciated and exploited by Joe Lawson who brought the 1954 Derby winner, Never Say Die, back to full fitness for the Doncaster Classic by running him at Yarmouth.

The Norfolk course is more of an oval than Doncaster and lacks the pear-like shape of this more prestigious course, but, far more crucially, both these largely flat tracks present long-distance performers with lengthy straights and a sharp final left-handed bend leading into a run-in of approximately five furlongs. It is often utilized by trainers as a course on which to test newcomers or progressive types.

Yarmouth's popularity with southern professionals is largely due to its proximity to Newmarket. Indeed, 18 out of the 19 races contested at a three-day meeting held here in September 1980 were won by horses from 'Headquarters' – many of them trained by some of the country's leading handlers; and the horses that run at Yarmouth are often of far better class than those seen on other rather lowly racecourses. Those trained by Henry Cecil, for example, often run in rather humble maiden contests which, on their way to far better things, they generally win quite easily, if at fairly prohibitive odds.

There is a good deal about Yarmouth that explains why the races staged upon it are so extensively farmed by Newmarket handlers. It provides a surface for racing that can almost be guaranteed to be in good condition since it drains rapidly because there is so much sand in its subsoil. A run here imposes a far more revealing test than is obtainable on some rather easier racecourses, yet involves nothing that is harsh enough to sour an inexperienced runner.

The longest races staged on the round course, which extends for around one and a half miles, take place over 2 miles 2 furlongs and 51 yards. They are started from the same point as events over 5 furlongs 43 yards. The horses thus initially race over the entire length of Yarmouth's shortest sprint course.

Immediately after the winning post has been passed for the first time, long distance performers at Yarmouth run round the first of the track's two semi-circular, tightish, left-hand bends. Next they pass the 11 furlong 100 yard start on the long back straight of 5 furlongs that runs almost parallel to the run-in.

After a final turn that is just as sharp as its predecessor, the round course joins the run-in that represents the last five-eighths of Yarmouth's straight 1 mile 3 yard course. This is a flat affair which apparently confers a slight advantage on the highly-drawn if the stalls are positioned in the centre but, if they are placed on the far side, the lowlydrawn enjoy a slight edge. The straight course is provided by a long spur which allows races over 1 mile 3 yards, 7 furlongs 2 yards, and 6 furlongs 3 yards to be staged. One of these, the Jack Leader Nursery Handicap, run over 7 furlongs 2 yards in mid-September, recalls a genial and well-known member of a famous Newmarket training family.

Since Yarmouth's meetings do not start until June its location on the coast is an added attraction. Londoners have only 126 miles to travel. There is one slight drawback about being a spectator at 'Newmarket-by-the-Sea', a raised section of the golf course within the oval track (which is municipally-owned and controlled) obscures one's view from the grandstand of some of the running on the back straight. However, this is a minor problem and no threat to the takings at the turnstiles.

One further reason why Yarmouth provides the local corporation with so much revenue is because, as a racecourse, it is so accessible. It lies on a bus route, is only a mile to the north of Yarmouth's town centre and its Vauxhall railway station can be reached fairly rapidly from Liverpool Street.

Motorists should arrive via the M11, A11 and A47 via Norwich or approach via the A12. Those coming from the north should progress beyond the M1 on the A47.

If racegoers are in a hurry they can always take a light aircraft or helicopter and make, not for the course, but for North Denes airfield which is only about 300 yards away.

YEARLING
Filly or colt that has celebrated its first, but not its second birthday.

YEARLING SALES (See Tattersalls)
Study of the prices of the horses these feature is made possible by regular reports that appear in racing dailies. Many yearling sales are held in September and October.

YEAR, THE RACING
This features a richly varied fare made up of both flat and National Hunt racing staged at a large number of English and Irish courses, each with its own distinctive character. From spring to autumn and from autumn until early the following summer, respectively flat racing and jumping enthusiasts are extremely well-catered for, whether this be at race meetings that are key constituents of the racing calendar or at local 'gaffs' of country race meetings.

Each racing year is guaranteed to provide so much drama, disappointment, excitement and euphoria, despair and heartache, as well as heart-warming sights and triumphs over tragedy that, understandably, it forms the subject of several annual reviews.

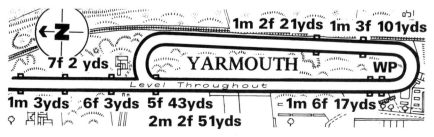

YARMOUTH: Plan of the course.

YORK: This print by Thomas Rowlandson shows the famous upset when Dr Syntax lost all of his money on Voltigeur, the clear favourite, who had won the previous seasons' Derby and St Leger.

YORK

York Racecourse
York YO2 1EX
Tel. (0904) 620911

How to get there:
From North: A1, A19
From South: M1, M18, A19
From East: A64, A1079
From West: A59, A64
By Rail: York
By Air: Helicopter facilities

Although York is referred to by southerners as the 'Ascot of the North', most northern sportsmen and many professionals consider this a somewhat odious comparison, since, in some respects, York's three-day August festival is possibly a superior occasion.

Since market leaders tend to perform quite well at the main August meeting, it is popular with professionals, many of whom either take an early summer holiday during Ascot week or journey to the Berkshire course merely to join in the junketing and make notes on the running for future reference.

Despite its popularity with professionals, the Knavesmire is not a place where form always

on what is reputedly Lester Piggott's favourite British racecourse. Of several other Group races staged here, one, a highly regarded rehearsal for the Epsom Oaks, is the Musidora Stakes for three-year-old fillies which is run over 10 furlongs and 85 yards at the May meeting. This commemorates one of the late Captain Charles Elsey's very best horses, the filly that captured both the 1000 Guineas and the Oaks in 1949.

Also run over the same distance in mid-May is the Dante Stakes, an important trial for the Derby. In 1978, Shirley Heights won it and triumphed at Epsom some three weeks later, as did Shahrastani in 1986 and Reference Point a year later.

Another well-known race run at the May meeting (when the late maturing grass on the Knavesmire is not always at its best) is the Yorkshire Cup over 13 furlongs 194 yards, a high-class event confined to horses of at least four years of age. One other Group race, the Duke of York Stakes, a sprint over 6 furlongs for three-year-olds and upwards, also takes place at the first meeting.

Apart from the Great Voltigeur Stakes, several other important races are staged at the August meeting. The most valuable of these is the International Stakes for three-year-olds and upwards which in its time, apart from featuring some dramatic upsets, has been won by Derby winners Roberto and Troy, 2000 Guineas winner Wollow, and St Leger hero Commanche Run.

The Yorkshire Oaks, like the International, has caused the undoing of several previously undefeated horses or acknowledged champions. In fact, several Epsom heroines have failed to prevail on the Knavesmire, possibly because by mid-August they had begun to 'train off'.

Noteworthy too on the festival programme are several races for two-year-olds. One of the most prestigious is the Lowther Stakes, a Group Two 6-furlong affair for two-year-old fillies.

The Gimcrack Stakes is another race for first-season performers staged over 6 furlongs during the August fixture. This contest commemorates a famous grey that won 26 of his 36 races. Although in recent seasons it has lost some of its kudos, the Gimcrack still attracts some of the best two-year-olds in training and on occasion is won by a horse that goes on to capture a Classic in its second season. This feat was achieved by Mill Reef in 1970, who trounced his rivals at York some 10 months before his triumph in the 1971 Derby, and by the Irish colt Nebbiolo who, after his Gimcrack win, prevailed at 20-1 in the 1977 running of the 2000 Guineas.

works out well. Indeed over the years some short-priced favourites have been sensationally beaten.

One particularly well-documented form upset was the defeat in 1851 of Voltigeur (the previous season's Derby and St Leger winner) by the Flying Dutchman, a colt that had triumphed in these two particular Classics in 1849; an event witnessed by 100,000 mainly local spectators.

In calling an 11 furlong 195 yard St Leger trial that is one of the highlights of the main August festival the 'Great Voltigeur Stakes', the York executive has, thus, acted most appropriately – especially since this particular colt also won the season's final Classic twice.

Naturally, many other top-class contests are staged

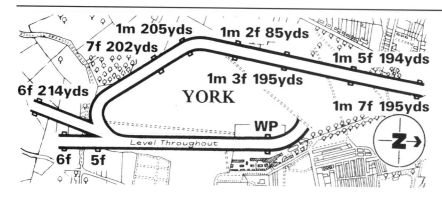

YORK: *Plan of the course.*

The Ebor Handicap, when it was first run over 1 3/4 miles in the middle of the nineteenth century, established a precedent at York, since races there had previously been staged over a gruelling 4 miles.

It is usually the chief betting race of the three-day August meeting, the highlight of its second day and a reminder of York's history since Ebor is a shortened version of Eboracum, the name the Romans gave to York (archaeological research suggests that they also held race meetings in this city).

Rather sadly, the 'Ebor' is now only 'listed' as important. However, it is still a competitive and rather spectacular contest. On the rare occasion when it is won by a runner with more than 8st 7lbs on its back, then one can be sure that victory has gone to a really good horse. This was the case when Sea Pigeon at the age of nine triumphed in the 1979 running under the welter-weight of 10st. Four-year-olds often go well in this stayers' handicap.

Meetings are also held at York in mid-June and mid-July and early in September and October and these all feature good class sport. Many feature a famous race. One well-known one is the 6-furlong William Hill Golden Spurs Handicap Trophy which takes place just before Royal Ascot, while perhaps an even better known event is the John Smith Magnet Cup, run over the International Stakes distance and the highlight of a Saturday card in July.

The York course takes some getting; indeed its negotiation involves a fairly gruelling test of stamina, especially if there is some give in the ground. It is for resolute, courageous types who relish a struggle.

As its very name of 'Knavesmire' suggests, York is not one of the fastest draining racecourses, especially since its subsoil contains sufficient clay to make sticky going something of a certainty if it has rained fairly heavily prior to, or even during, a race meeting. By way of compensation, the moisture-retaining turf is seldom made hard by the heat of an average British summer.

While the track is sometimes likened to the letter 'U' or described as 'horseshoe-shaped', it is perhaps rather more reminiscent of a fish hook. It is wide and extends for 2 miles and in general it tends to suit long-striding, galloping types who can stretch out well and come with a late run on its extensive, near five-furlong run-in.

Those taking part in 15 furlong 195 yard contests initially race along the far straight that extends for over three-quarters of a mile alongside the Tadcaster road. Then, having passed the points from which races of 13 furlongs 194 yards, 11 furlongs 195 yards and 10 furlongs 85 yards are started, they begin to sweep round the more gradual of York's two well-banked left-handed bends. Then, after passing the 1 mile 205 yard starting point, they continue to race along the shorter back straight, passing the 7 furlong 202 yard start and Knavesmire woods as they do so. Next they round York's second and rather sharper turn into its long finishing straight.

York's separate sprint course, which is initially provided by a spur of just over a furlong, allows races to be staged over 6 furlongs and the minimum distance. It is perfectly straight and tends to confer an advantage on the lowly-drawn when the stalls are placed on the stands side or in the centre of the track.

The runners in 6 furlong 214 yard races initially negotiate a longish, tangential spur of two furlongs which runs into the middle of the final, almost semi-circular, but not excessively tight, final left-hand turn on the round course. This effectively means that this track forms something of a dog leg that is completed by York's long run-in of approximately four and a half furlongs.

As is to be expected of a course on which races are so often run at a fast pace, York takes some riding. Indeed, many shrewd judges have attributed Roberto's shock and fast time defeat of Brigadier Gerard in the 1972 running of the Benson and Hedges Gold Cup (now the International Stakes) in large part to his jockey Braulio Baeza, whose superb artistry and judgement of pace had already gained him a reputation.

It is also often to a jockey's advantage if he can place his mount in a handy position rounding the final turn.

The amenities at York match the splendour of the races. No wonder then that this impressive course often achieves the highest daily average attendance in the country. It also attracts the highest daily level of support from sponsors.

As for York's superb amenities, these are perhaps unrivalled on any British racecourse. A museum devoted exclusively to the sport of kings is housed in the grandstand, from which the racegoer can obtain such an excellent view of the proceedings. So attractive and luxuriously appointed are York's facilities that many of them are hired for varying functions on non-race days.

The layout of the public areas also betokens much careful forethought by a commendable and open-handed executive. For example, terraces that overlook the parade ring. In many ways the social calendar for August would never be quite the same were York races ever to disappear from it.

Racegoers should note that since the Knavesmire is virtually flat it can be taken at great speed. Thus, if one-paced animals take on top-class performers here, their limitations are likely to be ruthlessly exposed. Indeed, York is a track that tends to unsettle horses that cannot go the pace with powerful galloping types that like to make the running.

York is readily accessible. The city's railway station is not much more than a mile from the course and can be reached from King's Cross. The A1 is an obvious and direct, if congested, route that brings many racegoers close to the city on race days and the A64 will bring them to within sight of signposts to the course.

Those travelling from further northwards should try to arrive via the A19. The considerate York management have arranged for light aircraft to land at Rufforth Aerodrome, telephone (0904) 704922, some four nautical miles west of York. A landing fee is charged and transport can be arranged to the Knavesmire.

YOURS AND MINE
Bookmakers' term for even money: the winner of the bet receives 'your money and mine'.

YORK: This print from 1861 shows the grandstand which today houses among other things a museum dedicated to the sport of kings.

RACECOURSES IN ENGLAND

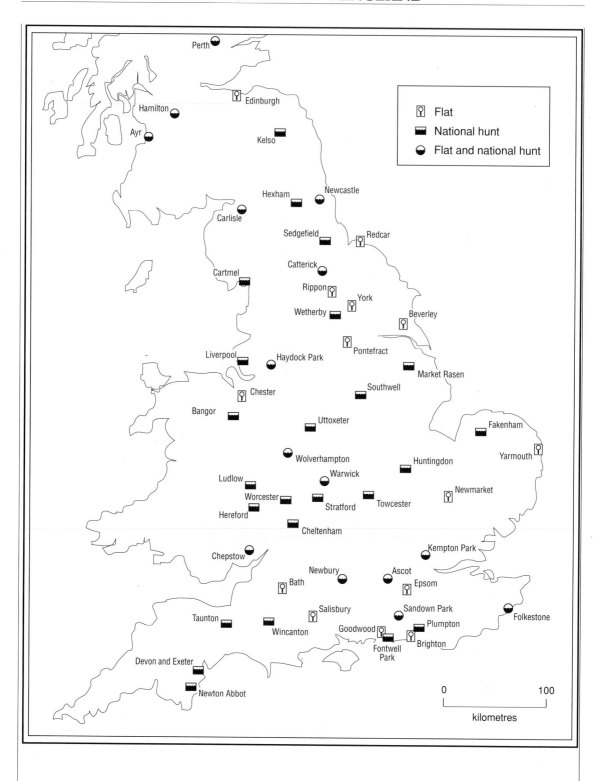

RACECOURSES IN IRELAND

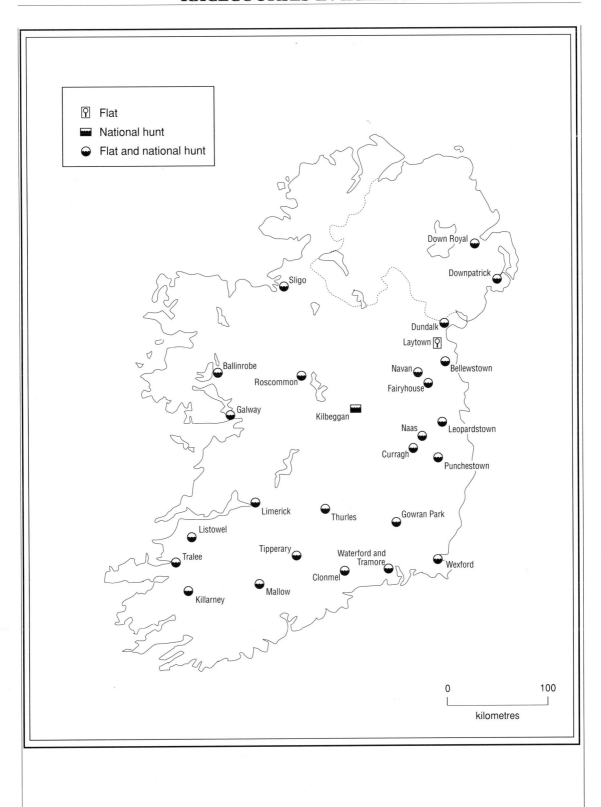

Flat

National hunt

Flat and national hunt

Down Royal

Downpatrick

Sligo

Dundalk

Laytown

Ballinrobe

Navan

Bellewstown

Roscommon

Fairyhouse

Galway

Kilbeggan

Naas

Leopardstown

Curragh

Punchestown

Limerick

Thurles

Gowran Park

Listowel

Tralee

Tipperary

Waterford and
Tramore

Wexford

Clonmel

Killarney

Mallow

0   100
kilometres

SCALES OF AGE, WEIGHT AND DISTANCE

SCALE OF AGE, WEIGHT AND DISTANCE; FLAT *(see page 234)*

Distance / Age	5 Furlongs 2	3	6 Furlongs 2	3	7 Furlongs 2	3	8-9 Furlongs 2	3	10 Furlongs 3	11-12 Furlongs 3	13-14 Furlongs 3	15-16 Furlongs 3	2 1/4 Mile 3	2 1/2 Miles 3
Apr 1-15	6.11	9.1	-	8.13	-	8.12	-	8.10	8.9	8.8	8.7	8.6	8.5	8.3
16-30	6.13	9.2	-	9.0	-	8.13	-	8.11	8.10	8.9	8.8	8.7	8.6	8.4
May 1-15	7.2	9.3	6.13	9.1	-	9.0	-	8.12	8.11	8.10	8.9	8.8	8.7	8.5
16-31	7.5	9.4	7.1	9.2	-	9.1	-	8.13	8.12	8.11	8.10	8.9	8.8	8.6
Jun 1-15	7.7	9.5	7.2	9.3	-	9.2	-	9.0	8.13	8.12	8.11	8.10	8.9	8.7
16-30	7.9	9.6	7.4	9.4	-	9.3	-	9.1	9.0	8.13	8.12	8.11	8.10	8.8
Jul 1-15	7.10	9.7	7.6	9.5	-	9.4	-	9.2	9.1	9.0	8.13	8.12	8.11	8.9
16-31	7.1	9.8	7.8	9.6	-	9.5	-	9.3	9.2	9.1	9.0	8.13	8.12	8.10
Aug 1-15	8.2	9.9	7.9	9.7	-	9.6	-	9.4	9.3	9.2	9.1	9.0	8.13	8.11
16-30	8.4	9.10	7.12	9.8	-	9.7	-	9.5	9.4	9.3	9.2	9.1	9.0	8.12
Sep 1-15	8.6	9.11	8.1	9.9	7.12	9.8	7.7	9.6	9.5	9.4	9.3	9.2	9.1	8.13
16-30	8.8	9.12	8.3	9.10	8.0	9.9	7.8	9.7	9.6	9.5	9.4	9.3	9.2	9.0
Oct 1-1	8.1	9.13	8.4	9.11	8.1	9.10	7.10	9.8	9.7	9.6	9.5	9.4	9.3	9.1
16-31	8.12	10.0	8.6	9.12	8.3	9.1	7.12	9.9	9.8	9.7	9.6	9.5	9.4	9.2
Nov	8.13	10.0	8.9	9.13	8.5	9.12	8.0	9.10	9.9	9.8	9.7	9.6	9.5	9.3

For horses aged 4 years and upwards, use 10.0 in all cases.

SCALE OF AGE, WEIGHT AND DISTANCE; NATIONAL HUNT *(see page 234)*
HURDLE RACES

Distance / Age	2 Miles 5	4	3	2 1/2 Miles 5	4	3	3 Miles 5	4	3
Jan	12.7	11.9	-	12.7	11.8	-	12.7	11.7	-
Feb	12.7	11.11	-	12.7	11.10	-	12.7	11.9	-
Mar	12.7	11.13	-	12.7	11.12	-	12.7	11.11	-
Apr	12.7	12.1	-	12.7	12.0	-	12.7	11.13	-
May	12.7	12.2	-	12.7	12.1	-	12.7	12.0	-
Aug	12.7	12.4	11.1	12.7	12.4	11.1	12.7	12.3	10.12
Sep	12.7	12.5	11.3	12.7	12.5	11.2	12.7	12.4	11.0
Oct	12.7	12.6	11.4	12.7	12.6	11.3	12.7	12.5	11.2
Nov	12.7	12.7	11.5	12.7	12.7	11.4	12.7	12.6	11.3
Dec	12.7	12.7	11.7	12.7	12.7	11.6	12.7	12.7	11.5

For horses aged 6 years and upwards, use 12.7 in all cases.

SCALE OF AGE, WEIGHT AND DISTANCE; NATIONAL HUNT *(see page 234)*
STEEPLECHASES

Distance / Age	2 Miles 5	4	2 1/2 Miles 5	4	3 Miles 5	4
Jan	11.11	-	11.10	-	11.9	-
Feb	11.12	-	11.11	-	11.10	-
Mar	11.13	-	11.12	-	11.11	-
Apr	12.0	-	11.13	-	11.12	-
May	12.1	-	12.0	-	11.13	-
Aug	12.4	11.6	12.3	11.5	12.2	11.0
Sep	12.5	11.7	12.4	11.6	12.3	11.1
Oct	12.6	11.8	12.5	11.7	12.4	11.2
Nov	12.7	11.9	12.6	11.8	12.5	11.3
Dec	12.7	11.10	12.7	11.9	12.6	11.4

For horses aged 6 years and upwards, use 12.7 in all cases.

PICTURE CREDITS

SELECTED BIBLIOGRAPHY

Armfield H. (ed.), *150 Years of the Aintree Legend*, Kingsclere Publications, 1988

Ayres M. & Newbon G., *Under Starter's Orders*, David & Charles, 1975

Barnes S., *Horsesweat and Tears*, Heinemann Kingswood, 1988

Bland E. (ed.), *Flat Racing Since 1900*, Andrew Dakers, 1950

Campbell B., *Horse Racing in Britain*, Michael Joseph, 1977

Churchill P., *Horse Racing*, Blandford Press, 1981

Clark T., *The Sun Guide to the Flat*, various annual editions, Ring Publications

Cope A., *A racegoers Encyclopaedia*, various annual editions, Cope's Publications

Craig D., *Horse Racing*, Penguin, 1953

Day C., *Around Ireland*, Gentry Books, 1982

Druid, The, *Post and Paddock*, Vinton, 1856

Educational Publications, *Know the Game* - Racing, 1956

Ennor G. (ed.), *Winning Ways*, various annual editions, New English Library

Flint J. & North F., *How to Win More at Racing*, Sphere, 1980

Flint J. & North F., *How to Pick Winners*, Norfli & Beaverbrook Newspapers, 1971

Gill J., *Racecourses of Great Britain*, Barrie & Jenkins, 1975

Green R., *A Race Apart*, Hodder & Stoughton, 1988

Hislop J., *From Start to Finish*, Hutchinson, 1959

Hislop J. & Swannell D. (eds.), *The Faber Book of the Turf*, Faber, 1989

Holland A., *Grand National*, Queen Anne Press, 1988

Howard M., *How To Find Value When Betting*, Raceform, 1989

Hunn D., *Epsom Racecourse*, Davis Poynter, 1973

Ikerrin D. (ed.), *Ladbroke Pocket Companions*, various annual editions, Aesculus Press

Lehane B., *The Companion Guide to Ireland*, Collins, 1985

Mortimer R., *The Flat - Flat Racing in Britain Since 1939*, G. Allen & Unwin, 1979

Murray W., *Horse Fever*, Dodd, Mead, 1976

MacGinty T. (ed.), *Irish Racing Annual*, various annual editions, Aherlow Publishers

Onslow R., *Headquarters*, Great Ouse Press, 1983.

Pickering M. (ed.), *Directory of the Turf 1990*, Pacemaker Communications, 1990

P.J.M. (ed.), *Racing Rhymes*, Michael Joseph, 1986

Plumptree G., *The Fast Set*, André Deutsch, 1985

Racing Review, various monthly editions, 1949-54

Radford B., *Taken for a Ride*, Arthur Barker, 198.

Ramsden C., *Ladies in Racing*, Stanley Paul, 1972

Rudd P. (ed.), *News Chronicle Racing Annual*, 1957 & 1958 editions, News Chronicle Book Departmen.

Runyon D., *Guys and Dolls*, Penguin, 1956

Seth-Smith M., *Knight of the Turf*, Hodder & Stoughton, 1980

Sidney C., *The Art of Legging*, Maxline International, 1976

Slattery F., *Horse Racing*, Killarney Races Committee, 1986

Stewart K., *A Background to Racing*, J.A. Allen, 1978

Summerhays R.S., *Summerhays' Encyclopaedia for Horsemen*, Threshold Books (revised edition) 1988

Welcome J., *Irish Horse Racing*, Macmillan, 1982

Welcome J., *The Cheltenham Gold Cup*, Pelham Books, 1973

West J., *Travelling the Turf*, various annual editions, Kensington West Productions,

White J., *Dark Secrets of the Turf*, Rosters, 1991

White J., *First Past the Post*, ACG Publications, 1989

Whitley J., *Computer Racing Form*, Racing Research (revised edition), 1989

Williams D. (ed.), *The Horsemans' Companion*, Eyre Methuen, 1978

Wright H., *The Encyclopaedia of Flat Racing*, Robert Hale, 1986

INDEX

NOTE: this selective index draws together dispersed references to main topics. Subjects mentioned only in their own alphabetical entry are not included. Main references are indicated by bold type.

Aintree **10-12**, 73, 83, 178; *see also* Grand National
Alexandra Park, London 63
Anne, HRH Princess Royal 13, 14, 123, 178, 181, 189
Archer, Fred 45, 67, 103, 118, 136, 179-80, 219
Ascot 12, **16-20**, 54, 83, 123, 141, 190; dress 20, 57, 84; Gold Cup 19, 68, 149, 193, 205; Royal Hunt Cup 16, 18, 21; royal meeting 16, 17-19, 20, 23, 31, 63, 76, 84, 92, 114, 246
Autumn Double 21, 23, 47
Ayr 12, **21-2**, 67, 84

Bath **25-6**, 63
Bentinck, Lord George 70, 93, 94, 95, 115
betting: accumulator 8, 59; across the card 8-9; advance in 9; against horses 28; ante-post 14, 21, 53, 75, 138, 169, 229; any to come 14; bar 25; betting without/bet bar one 27-8; blue bet 33; bluffing 30, 33; board rates 28, 33, 155; book, betting 28; Canadian 39; off the card 28, 158; carpet 41; on close finishes 162-4; by computer 155, 164, 178; computer forecast 60, 89, 106; Computote 128; contracting odds 61, 156; on corner horses 61; coupled 63; covering one's selections 64; disputes 68, 99, 185, 187, 190; domino 69; dual forecast, tote 106; each way 74-5; fivespot 87; flag 87; forecasts 29, 139; hedging 30, 32, 47; Heinz 104, (Super) 208; laying off 14; level stake 129; Magnificent Seven 135; market movements 137; odds-on 38; opening prices 98, 156, 158, 217; over-round 158; *pari-mutuel* 128, 160, 164; patent 160; placing bets 164-5; pontoon 168; ready reckoners 181, 182-3; roll-up 8; roundabout, rounder 188; round robin, round the clock 189; rules of 190, 209; single lap 199; single stakes about 199; slang 29-30; special place 201; Spring and Autumn Doubles 21, 23, 47, 203; staking 203; stop at a winner 206; systems 208; tax 155, 156, 164-5, 212; tickets 214-15; trade bets 219; trio 224; triple Yankee 224; Union Jack 226; up to 30; value 228; Yankee 244; yap 244; *see also*: bookmakers; Tote
betting shops 29, 106, 123, 129, 155
Beverley 12, **30-1**, 57
Bogside 63
bookmakers **34-5**; balancing a book 23; betting against horses 28; betting well 30; blower activity 32-3, 123; bluffing 30, 33; board prices 28, 33, 155; Bookmakers' Protection Association 35, 225; card prices 28, 158, (twist card) 225; commission agents 59; commission 196; credit accounts 64; dentists 66, 83; display of rates 28, 33, 225; disputes 68, 99, 185, 187; early 14, 34, 161, 168, 169; easing up 75; and false favourites 84; 'fiddlers' 47, 85; field books 39-40, 198; field money 85-6; floorman 87; fraud 63; going up early 98; hedging bets 30, 32, 47; joints 116; laying under the odds 126; laying, laying off 14, 125; office support 32-3, 156; opening prices 98, 156, 158, 217; outside 157; paying out 13, 214-15, 233; on rails 28, 77, 98; ring 90, 186, 187; Tattersall's 90, 186, 187, 209; tools 116, 217; top man 217; twist card 225; *see also*: betting; betting shops; tic-tac
breeding 36, 45; Arab steeds 15-16, 36, 157; *General Stud Book* 92, 157, 233; in-breeding 110; origin of thoroughbred 157; pedigrees 161; sires 199, 204
Bromford Bridge, Birmingham 63
Bunbury, Sir Charles 77, 115
Buttevant 136, 166, 206
Byerley Turk 15, 16, 36, 157

Cambridgeshire Handicap 21, 23, 47, 149
Cesarewitch 21, 149-50
Cheltenham 12, 31, **47-50**, 83, 92, 99; dress 57, 84; Gold Cup 48, 50, 98, 206, (winners) 47, 81, 125, 129-30, 145, 235; Irish at 98, 180; Queen's Hotel 175
Chepstow **50-2**, 57
Chester **52-4**, 84, 132, 224
coups 43, 63, 86
Curragh, The 27, 31, **64-5**

Darley Arabian 15-16, 36, 157
Darling, Fred 46, 144, 191-2
Davison, Emily 67, 68, 179
Derby, Earls of 46, 77, 106
Derby, Epsom **77-80**; death of Emily Davison 67, 68, 179; doping of Pinturischio 71; dress 84; Piggott and 34, 79, 80; prestige 33, 78; racecards 176; trials for 53, 131-2, 247; winners 16, 19, 20, 33, 36, 46-7, 70, 78, 80, 95, 132, 140, 144, 149, 184, 190, 191, 193, 213, 244, 247; *see also* Triple Crown
Derby racecourse, closed 63
disasters 67-8, 219
Doncaster 12, 66, **69-70**; *see also*: Lincoln Handicap; St Leger
doping 71, 170-2
draw 14; *see also under individual courses*

Eclipse 16, 149, 191, 193
Edinburgh *see* Musselburgh
Elizabeth II, HM Queen 20, 46, 115, 179, 190
Elizabeth, HM Queen, the Queen Mother 48, 50, 110, 115, 123, 190, 219
Epsom 12, 14, 57, 76, **77-80**, 84, 141; Classics 18, (*see also*: Derby; Oaks)

Fairyhouse **81-2**, 209
films and videos 39, 135, 229
Fontwell Park **89**, 112, 239
form: books 9, 77, 167, 172, 173, 177, (official) 9, 173; computers for 59-60; previous winners 168, 177; race-reading 178; speed and time ratings 90, 201, 203, 204; Timeform assessments 215-16; trainers' 173, 203, 208, 220; upsets 23
France: *pari-mutuel* betting 128, 160, 164; Prix de l'Arc de Triomphe 144, 160; runners in UK 88, 96, 120, 149, 172; Sunday racing 208

Gatwick; closed racecourse 63
gifts for racegoers 14, 179
Godolphin Arabian 16, 36, 157
Goodwood 12, 23, 84, **93-7**, 99
Gosforth Park *see* Newcastle
Grand National **10-12**; celebration of wins 9; disasters 36, 67, 83, 181, 184; fences 11, 12, 73, 235; jockeys 13, 36, 36, 181; pointers to winners 98, 129, 195; racecards 176; Spring Double 21, 23, 47, 203; winners 11, 24, 31, 47, 81, 89, 90, 108, 129, 142, 158, 161, 190, 220, 228, 242

Haldon (Devon and Exeter) 67
handicaps 101-2, 112-13, 133, 156, 157; publications 101-2, 177, 178
Haydock Park 12, 57, 73, 83, **102-3**, 141

horses' qualities: age, weight and distance tables 252; aged 9; class 55-6, 169, 229; colours 58; conformation 60-1, 78, 79, 160; favourites 84-5, (beaten) 26; and the going 92-3; hunter 'chasers 108-9; identification 160; length 127; maidens 135; maturity 138-9, 215, 216; novices 154; pace 159, 249; stamina 204; style of running 208; two-year-olds, speedy 201, 203; weight 217, 234, 252; *see also*: breeding; form
Hurst Park 63, 90

Ireland: races, (Derby) 36, 65, 208, (Grand National) 81-2, 140, (1000 Guineas) 224, (St Leger) 27, (2000 Guineas) 224; runners in England 18, 98, 149, 172, 180

Jockey Club **115-16**; course supervision 53, 56, 112; discipline 64, 71, 152, 172; and four furlong races 90; handicappers 101; and Newmarket 149; mission to Gulf 16; *Racing Calendar* 77, 178; royal patrons 115, 190; rules 177, 230
Jockeys: allowances 13; amateur 13-14, 38, 54, 166, 168; apprentice 13, 15, 23, 38, 45, 54, 102; Association 114; bookings 34, 116, 184; chalk 44; Championship 45; conditional 38, 54, 60; corruption 62-3; courageous 36, 219-20; drug tests 172; Injured Jockeys' Fund 110; jockeyship 116, 178; lady 13, 31, 123-4, 180, 219, 223; offences 185; retainers 54, 184; riding plans 185; strike rate 208; switches 156; as tipsters 111; weight 136, 158, 185, 198, 234; work riders 243; *see also* weighing in

Kempton Park 12, 20, **118-20**
Kemptown 35, 36-7
Kiplingcotes Derby 31

Lanark; closed course 63
Lansdown *see* Bath
Laytown 125-6, 233
Lewes 35, 63
Lincoln Handicap 14, 21, 47, 70, 103, 203
Lincoln; closed course 63
Lingfield Park 13, **130-2**

Manchester; closed course 63
Mildmay, Lord 36, 50, 67, 181, 219
Musselburgh 12, **75-6**

Newbury 12, 57, 83, **143-5**, 163
Newcastle 12, 83, **145-7**
Newmarket 12, **147-50**, 190; dress 57, 84; Free Handicap 90; Jockey Club and 115; museum 178-9; Tattersall's bloodstock sales 209, 210-11; *see also*: Cambridgeshire; Cesarewitch; 1000 Guineas; 2000 Guineas
Newton Abbot 67, 110, **150-1**

Oaks 72, 77-8, 80, 224, 274; winners 46, 47, 135, 150, 213, 247; *see also* Triple Crown
Ogden (first bookmaker) 34
1000 Guineas 18, 140, 148, 149, 150, 213, 247; *see also* Triple Crown
owners 45-6, 59, 158, 177, 208; Arab 16, 45, 46, 47, 126

Phoenix Park, Dublin 63
Piggott, Lester 45, 136, 138, 247; and Derby 34, 79, 80
Pontefract 12, 57, **167-8**
prize money 55, 169, 229

publications **35-6**, **172-3**; J.A. Allen & Co 12-13; on betting without 27; on bookmaking 112; on breeding 36; on Channel 4 racing coverage 212; *Directory of the Turf* 173; entries, analysis of 172; on form 9, 77, 167, 172, 173, 177; *General Stud Book* 92, 157, 233; on handicaps 101-2, 177, 178; on hunter 'chasers 109; Jockey Club *Racing Calendar* 178; on jockeys' successes 116; journalists 90, 135, 179, (forecasts) 21, 29, 150; literature 133, 179, 219, 228; on pace 159; *Pattern Race Book* 161; on point-to point racing 167; on prize money 55, 169; *Racehorses* 177; on racing inns 110; ready reckoners 181, 182-3; sectional timings 196; speed and time ratings 201, 203, 215-16; on trainers 126, 173, 203, 208, 220; on winners 110, 168, 169-70, 177; *see also*: *Racing Post; Sporting Life*

Racing Post 34, 36, 45, 55, 69, 133, 169, 173
Redcar 12, 123, **181**, **183-4**
royalty: past 45-6, 143, 147, 149, 188, 189-90, 192; present 115, 189-90, (*see also*: Anne; Elizabeth I; Elizabeth)

St Leger 18, 69, 70, 77, 95; winners 47, 70, 135, 193, 244, 247; *see also* Triple Crown
Sandown 12, 57, 76, 83, 84, **193-6**
selling races 23, 31, 90, 197-8
Southwell 13, **200-1**
Sporting Life 55, 77, 170, 173, 173; on breeding 36; dispute arbitration 68, 99, 190; handicap listings 133; Racecheck 176; Trainerform 220
Spring Double 21, 23, 47, 203
strand racing 125-6, 232-3
Stratford-on-Avon 12, 36, 57, 207, 224

Tattersalls: bloodstock sales 209, 210-11; Committee 68, 190, 209; enclosures 33, 77, 90, 186, 187, 209
tic-tac signals 123, 217, 226, 229, 240, 243
tips and tipsters 20, 111-12, 158, 184, 208, 217, 218; newspaper forecasts 21, 29, 150
tote 15, 57, 89, 106, 114, 123, 155, 160, 164, 217-18, 218-19
Towcester 57, 123, 141, **218-19**
Town Moor, Doncaster 70, 145
trainers: championship 46-7; and doping 172; form 173, 203, 208, 220; leading 126, 217; National Trainers' Federation 142; open days 156; permit holders 161; strategies 220
Tramore 26, **232-3**
travel to races 12, 173, 180, 222, (*see also under individual courses*)
Triple Crown **224**; winners 46, 53, 61, 65, 122, 149
2000 Guineas 18, 144, 149, 224; winners 150, 157, 187, 213; *see also* Triple Crown

United States of America: betting 160; identification of racehorses 110; Kentucky breeders 20; Man O'War 16; owners win UK Owners' Championship 46; racing holidays in 105; racing writers 107

weighing in 13, 56, 154, 233-4
Wetherby 12, 83, **234-5**
Windsor 12, 57, **238-40**
Worcester 12, 57, **242-3**
Wye, Kent 63

York 12, 57, 84, 123, 124, 215, **246-9**